Behavior Therapy with Children

The Editor

ANTHONY M. GRAZIANO is an associate professor of psychology at the State University of New York, Buffalo. He received his B.A. from Columbia College, his M.S. from Michigan State University, and his Ph.D. from Purdue University. In addition to his teaching, Dr. Graziano serves as a consultant to hospitals, clinics, schools, and correctional institutions and acts as special consultant to the County Commissioner of Mental Health. Among his publications are articles on teaching machine programs, behavior therapy with children, diagnostic testing, the history of psychology, and evaluations of the contemporary mental health professions, particularly with regard to the political realities of current mental health services. In 1963, Dr. Graziano established and directed the first behavior therapy program in Connecticut for severely psychotic children. In 1970, turning also to adult behavior modification, he constructed the first token economy system in a maximum security prison.

Behavior Therapy with Children

×–×–×–×–×–×–×–×–×–×–×–×–×–×–×–×–×–×–×–×

ANTHONY M. GRAZIANO

Editor

With the assistance of Michael M. Matthieu

ALDINE PUBLISHING COMPANY/Chicago

Address all inquiries to
Aldine Publishing Company
529 South Wabash Avenue
Chicago, Illinois 60605

ISBN 0-202-26046-1

Library of Congress Catalog Number 79-8096

Printed in the United States of America

Designed by Andrea Clark

Second printing,   1972

Third printing,   1972

Fourth printing,   1972

Fifth printing,   1973

Sixth printing,   1974

Acknowledgments

I wish to thank Drs. Leroy Ford, State University of New York at Buffalo, Cyril M. Franks, New Jersey Neuropsychiatric Institute, Donna M. Gelfand, University of Utah, and Leonard P. Ullmann, University of Illinois, who took time out from their own busy schedules to read and comment upon the introductory material. Their help was most valuable.

I wish to thank as well the authors and publishers of these writings, who gave me permission to reprint them in this volume.

Contents

III. MODIFICATION OF PSYCHOTIC BEHAVIOR

IV. MODIFICATION OF ANTISOCIAL BEHAVIOR

V. BEHAVIORAL APPROACHES TO
SCHOOL AND MILD CONDUCT PROBLEMS

VI. SOME IMPLICATIONS OF BEHAVIOR
MODIFICATION CONCEPTS: THE NEW THERAPISTS

Behavior Therapy with Children

Animism and Modern Psychotherapy

Anthony M. Graziano

In every culture and time some people have exhibited bizarre, distorted, and notably different behavior and, as a result, have been set apart and dealt with in some special manner. The explanations and treatment of the observed deviant behavior have varied throughout history, and often progress takes the form of old concepts re-emerging at later times. These explanations and treatments, ancient and modern, all seem to revolve around a similar observation: the individual is not "in control of himself" but is under the influence of powerful, disruptive, internal forces. Primitive man thought of these internal forces as independent and self-directing which, for their own diabolic reasons, impelled the unfortunate possessed person to disordered behavior. The major control primitive man thought he had over such forces was through magic, and he utilized magical rites in attempts to force the demons and spirits out of the afflicted person's body. Later in cultural development religion began to displace magic and man prayed to and beseeched supposedly higher powers than himself to intervene and drive out the demons.

Against this background of religious and magical animism, the classical Greeks and Romans developed naive but none the less naturalistic and humanitarian views of disordered behavior. They sought organic, physical causes and a few—such as the Roman physician Soranus—insisted upon humanitarian treatment for mental patients.

During the Middle Ages, however, the earlier beginnings of natu-

1

ralistic and humane treatment were submerged as religious animism was revived in the treatment of persons thought to be "possessed." The major approaches of the Christians were at times drastically inhumane as both secular and church people tried to drive out the devils through severe exorcisms.

In the sixteenth century the earlier mental illness concept was revived by St. Vincent de Paul, among others, who asserted that "mental disease is no different than bodily disease and Christianity demands of the humane and powerful to protect and the skillful to relieve the one as well as the other" (Coleman, 1963). This revived "illness" concept, while objecting on humanitarian grounds to the vicious treatment of disordered persons, retained the basic idea that the individual's behavior is caused by internal forces beyond his control. That people were then seen as possessed by mysterious internal forces of illness rather than by demons and devils does not alter the basically animistic nature of the concept. The major focus of treatment, as in demonology and exorcism, was on driving out, reducing, redirecting or otherwise weakening the pathological forces within the individual. This animistic focus, in some form of face-to-face contact between the "possessed" and the "healer," has remained the cornerstone of contemporary psychodynamic theory and practice.

In the eighteenth century an alternative concept, that of "moral treatment," developed. Its impetus came not from science but from a broad, world-wide revolution which introduced humanitarian social ideals and reforms. Moral treatment, the application of humanitarian ideals to the organized group living of mental patients (Bockoven, 1963) did not utilize the mental "illness" concept but, as Bockoven noted: "The moral therapist acted toward his patients as though they were mentally well. He believed that kindness and forebearance were essential in dealing with them. He also believed in firmness and persistence in impressing on patients the idea that a change to more acceptable behavior was expected" (p. 76).

Moral treatment was soon eclipsed by the subsequent strengthening of the "illness" model, through the assumption of dominance by the medical profession, which had taken over the role of the priests in the care and treatment of the mentally ill. As humanitarian reforms continued, the imposing fortress-like asylums of the nineteenth century evolved into mental hospitals which began to provide continual medical care, strengthening the concept of mental "illness" and clearly defining its treatment as a medical responsibility. This reassertion and subsequent full development of the medical model was a major factor in the demise of moral treatment. On this point Ullmann and Krasner (1965) wrote: "There was a complete shift from the procedure of treating the patient as well and expecting more acceptable behavior to the concept that the patient was, by definition, a danger to himself and others" (p. 5). As a result, little other than passive cooperation was expected of the patient while he was custodially contained in order to receive treatment. The earlier focus on meaningful group living, which included social stimulation and pleasant, comfortable surroundings, was soon considered an unessential luxury which might even interfere with the "real" task of treatment.

By the end of World War I, treatment of mental "illness" had clearly emerged as a medical responsibility and was beginning to be influenced by the developing concepts and techniques of psychoanalysis.

Psychoanalysis, as both a personality theory and a psychotherapeutic system, grew out of nineteenth-century biology, physics, and the medical model, employing its traditional "disease entity" view of internal pathology as the major condition reflected in the overt behavioral "symptoms." In this approach, to attempt symptomatic treatment alone, without arranging for internal, psychodynamic changes, presumably results in a substitution of symptoms which leaves the essential condition, internal pathology, basically unchanged or even worse, since the prior symptom was the most economical one intrapsychically.

Psychodynamic therapies have pursued complex systems of diagnosis and techniques of going "beneath" symptoms in order to ameliorate the underlying pathology. In the twenty years between the two world wars, anthropology, psychology, and sociology increasingly influenced psychiatry to define the underlying psychopathology of mental illness as a combination of organic, psychological, and sociological factors. Freud's hypotheses were modified and supplemented by a long line of theorists from several disciplines. Whatever the extent of these modifications, however, psychodynamic therapies continue to be based on the "disease entity" model, emphasizing the primary importance of the underlying basic pathology and de-emphasizing overt behavior, which is considered to be only symptomatic.

RECENT CHANGES IN APPLICATION OF THE MEDICAL MODEL

World War II, with its huge complex of military establishments, spurred new directions in health efforts, such as the active involvement of the federal government in large-scale mental health service for military personnel and veterans and in exploratory research. This federal activity led to an emphasis on mental illness as a public health problem and assigned considerable responsibility to public agencies. Because increasingly large numbers of persons demanded assistance, efforts to find newer, quicker, more efficient techniques were initiated. Better uses of trained personnel and an increasing involvement of nonmedical psychotherapists, primarily psychologists, evolved. After the war, the practice of psychotherapy became an interdisciplinary endeavor, utilizing the "team" approach, in which the psychiatrist is the team leader and psychologists, social workers, nurses, and others are admitted into the medical specialty as ancillary professionals. Psychotherapy became a set of skills common to several related professions. This process of widening the base of professional involvement in psychotherapy occasioned difficulty, often stirring interprofessional hostilities which persist today in the form of opposition to the use of medically-based techniques by persons without medical training. As long as they continued to espouse traditional medical approaches, the "ancillary" professions remained ancillary.

In addition to this widening professional base, there has also been a deepening of mental health personnel to include subprofessionals, people with less formal traditional training and experience. Much of what occurs as "psychotherapy" may be relatively routine, and long years of intensive study are not always required to help bring about desired changes. What is psychotherapeutic does not necessarily occur only in psychotherapy or under the direction of a trained psychotherapist. One of the recommendations of the Joint Commission on Mental Illness and Health (1963), for example, included this point: "Every effort must be made, then, to provide nonpsychiatrically trained personnel in many fields with as much knowledge of mental illness and principles of its treatment as possible. They are treating the mentally and emotionally disturbed and will continue to do so. They must be given additional skill" (p. 123).

Attempts to implement this suggestion have been reported by Holzberg (1963) and by Knapp and Holzberg (1964) who noted success with college student volunteers in "Companion" and "Aide" programs for state mental hospitals. Branch (1963) wrote of the need to develop new kinds of mental health personnel, and Rioch et al. (1963, 1965) reported on a successful program in training married women as psychotherapy "technicians." Goodman (1964) described attempts to create a training program for nurses to improve their understanding of mental illness and its treatment; Schurmans (1965) and Armstrong and Rouslin (1963) indicated that the nurse can be qualified to do intensive group psychotherapy. Haring and Phillips (1962) described a structured academic program designed as therapeutic, and they strongly endorsed the teacher as a potentially important psycho-therapeutic agent.

At present, mental health services are drastically limited. The most frequently stated reason is the paucity of highly trained mental health professionals. This lack of professional manpower affects our entire society but, as with so much in life, the poor are affected most. Although the lowest socioeconomic groups have the highest occurrence of severe personality disorganization, they also have the fewest available mental health services (Hollingshead and Redlich, 1958). To compound the inequity, those mental health services that are offered to the economically deprived are based on the customary mental health approaches and the customary professional training which reflect culture-bound middle-class modalities and may be ineffective when applied to those who live in the subculture of poverty. Thus, current mental health services are both least available and least appropriate to those who presumably need them most.

As noted, the evidence grows that a high degree of training and education in psychotherapy is not necessary for many psychotherapeutic functions. If nurses, teachers, housewives, and college students are trained as successful therapists, then every community may very well have the potential manpower to provide sufficient mental health services for all who need them. The implications are important, and it will be up to the professionals in each community to seek ways of identifying, training, and supervising such mental health personnel.

Thus two of the significant recent trends in psychotherapy based on the medical model are the widening professional base for therapists and the deepening subprofessional pool from which psychotherapists are drawn. Psychotherapy need not be a narrow, limited specialty so restricted that its practitioners are scarce and its services limited to a relative few. Rather, psychotherapeutic functions can be carried out by persons from many professions and even by nonprofessionals; recognizing this, our communities may move closer to a realistic solution to manpower problems.

⋈

THE LIMITED DELIVERY OF TRADITIONAL SERVICES FOR CHILDREN

Psychotherapy based on the medical or "disease entity" model has frequently been modified and has continued to develop, but it has always retained the basic assumption that internal psychodynamic conditions constitute mental illness and must be altered in order to bring about meaningful or lasting improvement. In recent years, particularly in the 1960s, approaches based on the "disease entity" model have been severely criticized for their continuing serious limitations and obvious failure to provide effective service to all persons. In 1963, for example, the Joint Commission on Mental Illness and Health, focusing on children's services, stated that "the present operation of clinics leaves much to be desired if we continue...to set adequate or sufficient therapeutic service as our goal." Providing such service for children obviously involves complex problems of finance, public education, identification, personnel, and physical facilities. Each of these and numerous other problems pose complex and difficult tasks cutting across conceptual, professional, political, and logistical areas. Together their collective challenge is staggering; millions of dollars and millions of professional and lay man-hours are being poured into the support of complex and costly clinical structures which are presumably justified on the basis of one, and only one, major assumption: psychotherapy works. If this assumption is questioned and found to be untenable, then so must the entire present clinical structure be questioned.

The efficacy of psychotherapy has, of course, been directly challenged by Eysenck (1952), Levitt (1957), Wolpe (1958), Astin (1961), and many others. These studies and reviews indicate, among other things, that "treated" and "untreated" persons seem to recover at the same rates. Even when evidence is presented for its effectiveness, there are so many methodological problems in measuring improvement in internal, inferred psychological states that the criteria of improvement used in most studies must be questioned. (See Berg, 1952; Edwards and Cronbach, 1952; Saslow, 1954; Pascal, 1959; Sargent, 1960; and Astin, 1961.) Thus the effectiveness of psychotherapy has yet to be clearly demonstrated and validated.

Several writers have discussed the obscurities and confusions existing in this field, which nevertheless relies so heavily on professional expertise. Silver (1963), reviewing progress in therapy with children, wrote, "It is clear that the essence of what is effective in therapy...is still obscure (p. 47). Colby (1964) noted that the "foremost impression" gained from his search of a year's literature in psychotherapy "is the sensing of chaos. Everyone seems to be going his own way...regardless of the ensuing disorder" (p. 347). Hersch (1968), commenting upon the many critiques of the effectiveness of psychotherapy, concludes that "what we know with certainty about the effects of therapy is not heartwarming to the conscientious practitioner" (p. 503). Thus it appears that what is most certain about the field is its exceeding uncertainty.

Not only has the effectiveness of the psychotherapeutic procedures been questioned but so, also, has the practical availability of mental health services, particularly for children. Smith and Hobbs (1966), writing about current planning for comprehensive mental health centers, note that mental health programs traditionally tend to neglect children, and that plans submitted by states for their mental health centers were "conspicuous in their failure to provide a range of services to children" (p. 16). Traditional psychotherapy with children is adult-oriented, proceeding through interpretive and highly verbal psychotherapy, which does not appear to be relevant to the problems of childhood. They term the child guidance clinic movement a "less than encouraging experience," and point out that, by and large, mental health professionals have still not yet come to grips in any relevant and significant manner with the problems of the "disturbed" child. Smith and Hobbs assert that new approaches and concepts are clearly needed: "Since current patterns of mental health service are intrinsically and logistically inadequate to the task, responsible programming for the comprehensive community mental health center must emphasize and reward innovation" (p. 15).

Hersch (1968) writes that innovations stimulated by discontent within the mental health field have reached critical levels where they are changing the field itself. Hersch's basic proposition is that "there have been striking changes in the mental health field over the past ten or fifteen years which have arisen not on the basis of a rational growth of knowledge but rather out of an explosion of discontent" (p. 497). This writer agrees with Hersch that rational science has had little to do with stimulating real changes in mental health practice but would also argue that mental health innovations over the past decade have been isolated as "research" and, despite their often high degree of conceptual innovation, have not significantly altered the everyday pattern of applied clinical services. Further, practical improvements in actual clinical services will depend upon basic changes presently unlikely in the entire mental health professional–political power structure. The essentially political nature of local mental health power structures nullifies, or at the least decelerates, innovation (Graziano, 1969). In the conceptually fertile sixties many innovative ideas have been conceived and put forth, such as the creative use of subprofessional manpower, the re-emergence of behavior therapy, and ambitious plans for comprehensive mental health centers. But whereas the conception of new ideas in mental health depends upon creative humanitarian and scientific forces, their implementation depends upon a broad spectrum of professional and social politics; and political power structures, by definition, resist change. A case in point is the development of comprehensive mental health centers. When a community commits itself to the vastly expensive reality of a mental health center, and then refers control of that center back to the existing power structure, it has created innovation without change, to enrich and reinforce the old power structure and to make it vastly more capable of further entrenching itself.

Thus, (1) conceiving innovations through science and humanitarianism on the one hand, and implementing new ideas through the existing sociopolitical structure on the other, are directly incompatible and mutually inhibiting factors, and (2) the existing structure tends to prevail over innovation, and the pursuit of professional–political power has replaced both humanitarianism and science in the mental health field. When Smith and Hobbs write of the need for innovation, and when Hersch notes that significant changes have occurred, they seem not to have considered the hard reality of the basically political nature of the mental health professions and the concomitant overriding push for political structures to maintain control by negating change and thus support the status quo. A good deal of conceptual innovation seems to have occurred in the 1960s, but there has been little change in the actual delivery of clinical services. Except for small-scale demonstrations of, for example, new behavioral approaches with children, most clinics, hospitals, and schools seem to operate in essentially the same way they did before World War II.

✖

THE RE-EMERGENCE OF BEHAVIOR MODIFICATION

One of the areas of recent conceptual innovation and small-scale demonstration is that of "behavior modification," a body of theory and practice which seems to be gaining new adherents daily. Behavior modification connotes to many psychologists a truly new departure from traditional psychotherapy. Its emphasis is on overt behavior, the detailed arrangement of stimulus control and reinforcement contingencies, careful planning of behavioral goals, and a de-emphasis on internal psychodynamic processes as focal points of intervention. It is a psychological learning approach aimed at altering readily observable behavior by applying the scientific rigor of experimental psychology to aid the troubled.

However new behavior modification approaches may appear to be, they are of course direct descendants of the basic work of Pavlov, Watson, Thorndike, Guthrie, and Hull, to name a few. Further, as Ullmann and Krasner (1965) point out, specific clinical applications of behavior theory were theoretically explored and actually carried out in the 1920s, before clinical psychology wandered into the psychodynamic miasma that has surrounded it for a quarter century and more. There is, for example, the work of Haberman (1917), Watson and Raynor (1920), Burnham (1924), Jones (1924), Kantorovich (1929), and Jersild and Holmes (1935). In 1932 J. Stanley Gray's article, "A Biological View of Behavior Modification," urged the educator to disavow, in good Watsonian tradition, the focus on subjective, internal, teleologic explanations and, instead, to focus on behavior itself. He wrote that science "has refuted those theories of learning which are based on non-scientific postulates. It has rescued the organism from the field of teleological phenomena and definitely established it as part of a physical universe.... Such terms as insight, experience, feelings, will power, consciousness, intuition, etc., unless they are interpreted to be forms of behavior, must not be used in the description of educational techniques and certainly not considered as educational goals. Educators must use scientific terminology if they are to be understood even by each other."

In 1932 Gray asserted that teachers should avoid teleological and subjective concepts; should clearly focus on behavior; should carefully determine, for each child, *what* behavior is to be modified and then, with careful attention to details, control and manipulate all relevant variables in the learning environment. Gray maintained that any failure in learning is due to the failure of the educator to manipulate the relevant learning variables effectively. Thus, nearly forty years ago behavior modification concepts had already been directed to the problems of maladaptive behavior, that is, to therapy, and also to the education of what are called normal children in schools. Psychology seems to have returned, on a more sophisticated level, to the behavioral focus of the twenties and thirties.

According to Ullmann and Krasner (1965) the re-emergence of a generation-old focus seems to have been occasioned largely by the increasing influence of psychology on psychiatry beginning in World War II. Clinical psychologists, at first used to supplement military medical staffs as part of the essentially medical specialty dealing with emotional components in military recruitment and service, accepted psychiatry and trained for and worked within the psychiatric periphery, utilizing the basic "illness" or medical model. After World War II the increasing number of clinical psychologists introduced greater research sophistication into the field of mental health and more questioning of the traditional methods generally accepted by psychiatrists, who lacked sophistication in research and evaluation.

Clinical psychology, however much it became a "peripheral psychiatry" in the fifties, was and still is an applied professional discipline which is based on the empirical study of behavior. Ullmann and Krasner note: "Psychologists who were identified as research workers, such as Azrin, Bachrach, Bijou, Ferster, Goldiamond, King, Lindsley, Patterson, and Staats, turned their attention to clinical populations and problems so that the distinction between experimentalist and clinician became blurred." By the early sixties clinical problems were being looked at from the combined clinical-experimental vantage point, and the work of Pavlov, Watson, Thorndike, Jones, Burnham, and Guthrie joined with the work of Hull, Mowrer, Dollard and Miller, and Skinner to become the basis for more systematic empirical and operational approaches to malfunctional behavior.

Perhaps the basic difficulty in contemporary clinical approaches based on the medical model is the focus on internal conditions, all of which are abstractions, inferences, and are not well-defined empirically. Clinical services, then, may constitute attempts to use nonvalidated methods to measure ill-defined constructs which have only incidental, haphazard, and casual relationships to facts. The re-emergence of the more objective learning concepts as applied to clinical problems occurred as psychologists sought to clarify the vagueness of traditional psychodynamic thinking and to develop operationally defined and objective concepts, goals, and techniques. Work by French (1933) and by Sears (1936) had already begun to bring together Freudian and Pavlovian concepts, and perhaps helped to stimulate the now classic work of Dollard and Miller, *Personality and Psychotherapy* (1950), who translated psychodynamic theory into contemporary Hullian learning theory. In this work, Dollard and Miller accepted much of psychoanalysis, including the basic interpersonal psychotherapy situation. They presented analyses which not only clarified existing psychodynamic theory, but served heuristically as a point of departure, influencing several generations of students in psychology and stimulating thought and research increasingly toward learning theory concepts and, perhaps ironically, away from the psychodynamic theory which they had intended to support.

Dollard and Miller clearly emphasized the necessity for more rigorous scientific approaches in psychotherapy and personality theory and the importance of systematic theory construction for organizing empirical data and making predictions for future research. They made the laboratory and the clinic mutually accessible. This increased the probabilities that research psychologists would look more closely at clinical problems and thus make possible the more recent developments in behavior therapy.

Dollard and Miller put major emphasis on the systematic analysis of the learning and unlearning of neuroses. They wrote: "If a neurosis is functional... it must be learned. If it is learned, it must be learned according to already known, experimentally verified laws of learning or according to new, as yet undiscovered, laws of learning" (p. 9).

They wrote further: "If neurotic behavior is learned, it should be unlearned by some combination of the same principles by which it was taught...psychotherapy establishes a set of conditions by which neurotic habits may be unlearned and non-neurotic habits learned. Therefore we view the therapist as a kind of teacher and the. patient as a learner" (p. 8).

Accepting the concept that internal conditions, including conflicting learned drives, motivate overt behavior, and that overt behavior is cued by the environment and reinforced by anxiety reduction, they saw neurotic behavior as symptomatic of central conflicts. Thus they retained the basic medical model, but greatly influenced clinical psychology to shift its focus to a systematic analysis of the learning and unlearning of neurotic behavior.

Grossberg (1964) contends that while modern restatements such as that by Dollard and Miller have reduced much of the vagueness in psychodynamic terminology and have provided a common behavioral language and groundwork for clinicians and experimenters, they have also "served to perpetuate psychodynamic therapies unchanged and have failed to provide new or more effective therapeutic procedures" (p. 74). It appears to this writer that Grossberg's verdict is not entirely correct, and that Dollard and Miller are, in fact, among the major influences in shifting contemporary investigations away from psychodynamics and into a more detailed focus on the central role of learning in the development and modification of human behavior.

Gelfand (personal communication) suggests that both Grossberg and this writer are correct. Gelfand notes that the *initial result* of Dollard and Miller's synthesis was to perpetuate traditional psychodynamic conceptions by making them scientifically respectable, while their long-term impact was to emphasize the applicability of learning theory to the understanding and control of human behavior.

Other investigators began to specify overt, learned behavior as the most objective focus for applied psychology. Chapple and Donald (1946), attempting to objectify the complex interaction involved in personnel selection interviews, concluded: "existing methods of appraising personality were inadequate.... What was needed was an objective yardstick. We began, therefore, by agreeing to limit ourselves to those aspects of a person's behavior which could be directly observed and recorded" (p. 199).

In the fifties the growing emphasis on objective evaluation and manipulation of learned behavior was carried through by many investigators who focused on verbal behavior in psychotherapy. Through the systematic control of learning variables, such as verbal reinforcement, therapists attempted to modify the client's verbal behavior and thus bring about changes in, for example, "self concept." The focus on behavior provided a means of intervening in central cognitive or psychodynamic factors. Grossberg (1964) points out that a basic assumption in such verbal-learning approaches is that systematic changes in verbal behavior are necessary to bring about improvements in other maladaptive behaviors, and that such verbal changes in therapy do generalize to other, that is, to "real life," situations. This assumption, as he notes, has been challenged by Greenspoon (1962), Kanfer (1961), Bandura (1961), and Hobbs (1962). Grossberg concludes that there seems to be little evidence that verbal and insight therapies, even when they use reinforcement theory, achieve much other than changes in verbal behavior during the therapy sessions.

The next major shift was to focus on the overt behavior itself rather than on internal conditions as the therapeutic target. In more recent work the modification of behavior is the over-all goal of therapy, whereas in Dollard and Miller and in psychotherapeutic verbal learning the emphasis on behavior seems to have been primarily the means to attain the goals of changes in a psychodynamically conceived core condition. Thus in the past two decades psychotherapy appears to have moved away from the idea of central internal conditions that give rise to overt behavior which is only symptomatic and only important indirectly. It has moved toward, first, a focus on learning theory and overt behavior, including verbal behavior, as more objective, scientific means for achieving changes in the central condition; and thence to the view that learned behaviors themselves constitute the condition to be modified, and that there is no "underlying" central psychodynamic condition to be dealt with.

Salter (1949), Eysenck (1952, 1960, 1961), Wolpe (1954, 1958, 1961), and Wolpe and Lazarus (1966) all propose similar views of neuroses as maladaptive habit patterns formed through conditioning which can be permanently and significantly modified through the systematic application of learning principles. Like Dollard and Miller (1950) these writers accept a reinforcement, drive-reduction theory, but they differ in the importance they place on overt behavior. To Dollard and Miller, neurotic behavior is symptomatic of the internal neurotic condition; for Eysenck, Wolpe, Lazarus, and Salter, neurotic behavior itself is the neurotic condition.

Skinner (1953, 1956) also rejects the notion of a central neurotic state existing somewhere within the person, and he considers the label "neurosis" an explanatory fiction. For Skinner, people behave as they do, not because of internal and perhaps "distorted" motivations, but because of environmental contingencies which are subject to observation, control, and manipulation. Thus, human behavior can be significantly and permanently modified. Skinner goes further than other writers in rejecting the importance of central conditions, making no assumptions about drive, motivation, anxiety, and inhibition which, consistent with both Pavlovian and Hullian formulations, are utilized by Eysenck, Wolpe, and Salter.

This growing shift from clinic to laboratory concepts and from psychodynamics to learning factors in the modification of behavior is also seen in statements by Pascal (1959) in his excellent volume *Behavioral Change in the Clinic*. Pascal wrote, "If one is to extrapolate and speculate, the least one can do is to begin with some fairly well-known facts. The human organism behaves, and his behavior changes. These are data" (p. 1). And, "In any case, the findings of the psychologic laboratory are the only source of systematic knowledge bearing on behavioral change in the intact organism" (p. 4).

By the early 1960s, the application of learning theory principles to psychological intervention was being actively investigated and a good deal of work had already been completed. One of the most important reviews was that by Bandura (1961), who wrote: "Psychotherapy rests on a very simple but fundamental assumption, i.e., human behavior is modifiable through psychological procedures. When skeptics raise the question, 'Does psychotherapy work?' they may be responding in part to the mysticism that has come to surround the term. Perhaps the more meaningful question, and one which avoids the surplus meanings associated with the term 'psychotherapy,' is as follows: Can human behavior be modified through psychological means and if so, what are the learning mechanisms that mediate behavior change?"

Bandura reviewed studies which ranged over a variety of problems and of therapeutic techniques translated from learning theories. Thus Wolpe (1954, 1958, 1961) and many others cited by Bandura have used *counterconditioning*, which Bandura describes briefly as a process of evoking "strong responses which are incompatible with anxiety responses...in the presence of anxiety-evoking cues, [thus attaching] the incompatible responses to these cues and thereby [serving to] weaken or eliminate the anxiety responses." Counterconditioning has been reported as successful in treating phobic reactions (Jones, 1924), anxiety responses (Wolpe, 1958; Shoben, 1949), fetishes (Raymond, 1956; Max, 1935), alcoholism (Thirman, 1949; Thompson and Bielinski, 1953; Voegtlen, 1940; Wallace, 1949), obsessions (Wolpe, 1958); enuresis (Mowrer, 1938; Davidson and Douglas, 1950; Morgan and Witmer, 1939).

Another learning principle discussed by Bandura (1961) is *extinction*, the successive weakening and eventual elimination of a response when that response is no longer reinforced or rewarded. Success has been reported in treating tics (Yates, 1958), speech disorders (Sheehan and Voss, 1957), and other conditions (Jones 1955; Williams, 1959).

Bandura also discusses *discrimination learning*, which in this context refers to learning to react appropriately to different stimuli, without overgeneralizing from one to the other. The use of this technique has been discussed by Dollard and Miller (1950), Fenichel (1941), Rogers (1951), Adams (1957), Erikson (1958), and many others. *Reward*, the application of positive consequences following a response, probably most useful in developing new adaptive responses, has been successfully used with schizophrenics (King and Armitage, 1957; Atkinson, 1957; Peters, 1953; Lindsley, 1956; Ayllon and Azrin, 1965; Atthowe and Krasner, 1968; and others). *Punishment*, the application of aversive stimuli, not usually considered to be of major usefulness, has been employed in mild forms by Liversedge and Sylvester (1955), and in several of the studies using counterconditioning cited above. The last technique discussed by Bandura is *social imitation*—learning not through direct training but through imitation of the behavior of others.

In the years since Bandura's article appeared, there has been a sharp increase in the number of investigators and the variety of problems studied and techniques used. Several important works have appeared which add to the earlier work of Dollard and Miller, Eysenck, Wolpe, Salter, and others. Notable are the volumes by Berg and Bass (1961), Biderman and Zimmer (1961), Bachrach (1962), Bandura (1969), Bandura and Walters (1963), Staats and Staats (1963), Staats (1964), Franks (1964), Lovibond (1964), Ullmann and Krasner (1965, 1969), Krasner and Ullmann (1965), Wolpe, Salter, and Reyna (1965), Goldstein, Heller, and Sechrest (1966), Paul (1966), Eysenck and Rachman (1965), Eysenck (1967), and Wolpe (1967). Behavioral learning theory approaches to psychological problems have caught the interest of practitioners and experimenters, and they have turned out a voluminous amount of work, as is indicated by the extensive bibliography of behavior therapy research prepared by Barnard and Orlando (1967). As noted earlier, however, it has yet to be demonstrated that all this activity has had any significant effect in altering the traditional delivery of clinical services. This volume is being presented with the hope that it will make this recent work in behavior modification with children available to more practitioners and students and that they will find some areas of possible application and experimentation in their own current and future work.

\~

THEORETICAL MODELS FOR BEHAVIOR THERAPY

Behavior therapy is a varied field loosely organized around a few core concepts about the nature of psychological "disturbance," which, in

TABLE 1. Differences between Psychotherapy and Behavior Therapy

Psychotherapy	*Behavior Therapy*
1. Based on inconsistent theory, never properly formulated in postulate form.	1. Based on consistent, properly formulated theory leading to testable deductions.
2. Derived from clinical observation and made without necessary control observations or experiments.	2. Derived from experimental studies specifically designed to test basic theory and deductions made therefrom.
3. Considers symptoms the visible upshot of unconscious causes ("complexes").	3. Considerers symptoms as unadaptive conditioned responses (C.R.s).
4. Regards symptoms as evidence of repression.	4. Regards symptoms as evidence of faulty learning.
5. Believes that symptomatology is determined by defense mechanisms.	5. Believes that symptomatology is determined by individual differences in conditionability and autonomic lability, as well as accidental environmental circumstances.
6. Believes that all treatment of neurotic disorders must be historically based.	6. Believes that all treatment of neurotic disorders is concerned with habits existing at present; historical development is largely irrelevant.
7. Believes cures are achieved by handling the underlying (unconscious) dynamics, not by treating the symptom itself.	7. Believes cures are achieved by treating the symptom itself, i.e., by extinguishing unadaptive C.R.s and establishing desirable C.R.s.
8. Considers interpretation of symptoms, dreams, acts, etc., an important element of treatment.	8. Considers interpretation, even if not completely subjective and erroneous, irrelevant.
9. Believes that symptomatic treatment leads to the elaboration of new symptoms.	9. Believes that symptomatic treatment leads to permanent recovery, provided autonomic as well as skeletal C.R.s are extinguished.
10. Considers transference relations essential for cures of neurotic disorders.	10. Considers personal relations not essential for cures of neurotic disorders, although useful in certain circumstances.

From *Psychiatry Digest*, 27:5 (May 1966), 47.

essence, rejects traditional psychodynamic views. The behavior therapist emphasizes the learned nature of maladaptive behavior, focuses on that behavior as the essential target, the basic problem to be solved, and brings to bear methods which are as objective and experimentally well-founded as possible, in order to alter directly the maladaptive behavior. A tabular summary by Eysenck (1966) of the main differences between psychodynamic and behavioral approaches is reproduced here. Eysenck's approach is clearly based on Pavlovian and Hullian conditioning and drive-reduction concepts; except for his specific references to those concepts, the statements of points of view in this table are valid for the entire field of behavior therapy.

The most frequent criticism of behavior therapy by psychodynamic practitioners involves the symptom-substitution hypothesis, which might be stated as follows: Granted that behavior can be modified, behavior is only symptomatic of the basic underlying pathology. Altering the behavioral symptoms leaves the basic condition unimproved and leads to the formation of new symptoms. Eysenck (1966), Wolpe, Salter, and Reyna (1965), Ullmann and Krasner (1965, 1969), Bandura (1967, 1969), and Hersch (1968), among many, have discussed symptom substitution as a discredited hypothesis, not founded in fact. They maintain that symptom substitution does not, in fact, occur, and that behavior modification can result in permanent changes provided that the environment is modified to sustain those changes. To paraphrase a comment by Skinner (1954) about education, if science is to be brought into the art of psychotherapy, practitioners must be more cognizant of factual data and less enthralled with higher-order inferences with only tenuous factual bases. In terms of human activity, overt behavior constitutes a set of facts, and these facts ought to be the practitioner's focus. In this view, "symptoms" are learned responses to various stimuli. They do not merely represent the "basic abnormal condition," they *are* the "basic abnormal condition." Therapy is thus a process of arranging learning contingencies so as to weaken and extinguish maladaptive behaviors and replace them with learned adaptive responses. If all maladaptive behaviors are completely replaced by adaptive behaviors, then therapy has not merely replaced symptomatic behavior, but has altered the basic condition. Thus a neurotic patient who no longer exhibits any neurotic "symptoms," but rather behaves completely in a "normal" and adaptive fashion, is not a neurotic-in-remission-of-symptoms, but rather a person with a new hierarchy of adaptive responses.

Certainly to suggest that behavioral therapy can reshape and replace all of the person's "neurotic" or "psychotic" maladaptive behavior is nearly as ludicrous a goal as recasting his inner dynamics. However, behavioral therapy can focus on overt, observable, specific maladaptive behaviors and can weaken some and replace others with adaptive behaviors. It may be that in the total complex of the individual "psychotic" or "neurotic" behavior only a few particularly prepotent responses need be altered to allow that person once more to function successfully in society. Here then is the crux of behavior therapy: the behavior therapist asks, "What behavior must be directly modified?" and "what are the observable, external factors which control that behavior?" Always maintaining his focus on the behavior itself, the behavior therapist attempts systematically to manipulate eliciting, discriminative, and reinforcing stimuli so as to bring about a new, more adaptive response hierarchy. He utilizes a wide variety of concepts and approaches, and if specifically needed therapeutic techniques are not already in existence he may generate and experimentally test approaches tailor-made for a particular client. All behavior therapies share a basic focus on the behavior itself as the target of intervention, but they do not constitute a single theory and standardized procedures; as Franks (1967) remarked, "There seem to be virtually as many definitions of behavior therapy and opinions as to what does or does not constitute behavior therapy as there are behavior therapists." Behavior therapy, of whatever theoretical identity, does however share a common core. Franks (1967) noted, "for any technique to be regarded as behavior therapy it must be practiced within a framework which conforms to three closely-related principles...(1) some associationistic learning theory framework; (2) the delineation of specific bonds, either of a conventional S-R nature or in the form of more general "situation and outcome" relationship; and (3) an emphasis upon the systematic, rigorous and controlled methodology which has become the hallmark of the good behavioral scientist."

The application of behavior therapy encompasses many variations of learning theories which hold that a response can be strengthened and brought under the control of various stimuli by virtue of the nature of the stimuli which immediately precede or are contiguous with the response (respondent conditioning), follow the response (operant conditioning), or are continuous with the behavior (contiguity theory). These models lead to the assumption by behavior therapists that a client's observed maladaptive behavior can be both understood and controlled through the manipulation of current external environmental contingencies. Although the behavior therapist takes into account previously learned or historical contingencies and many behaviorists also consider inferred internal physiological states such as anxiety, inferences about internal, unconscious, psychodynamic conditions are not used.

Respondent conditioning research has clearly demonstrated that an unconditioned response — such as leg flexion, salivation, or the complex, automatic mobilization of body resources to meet some emergency — is elicited as part of the given physiological structure and function of the organism, by "natural" or unconditioned stimuli. When a neutral stimulus is repeatedly paired with an immediately following unconditioned stimulus, the previously neutral stimulus acquires the power to elicit the unconditioned response or at least some significant part of it. Behavior therapists following this model thus assume that neurotic behavior is the result of conditioning: some previously neutral stimuli have acquired the power to elicit internal emotional reactions as well as overt, observable maladaptive behavior. Their task, then, is to identify clearly the controlling conditioned stimuli and then bring to bear a variety of methods based on respondent conditioning concepts in order to weaken the bond between the conditioned stimulus and the maladaptive behavior and strengthen that between the original conditioned stimulus and new, adaptive behavior.

The operant model specifies that behavior is strengthened or weakened because of the reinforcing contingencies which follow the response. "Therapeutic goals" or terminal behavior must be observable and clearly specified so that they can be analyzed into discreet, constituent parts. Then, through carefully planned systematic application of appropriate immediate reinforcement, successive response approximations are utilized to shape up the eventual terminal behavior. The reinforcers may be primary, secondary, or both; they may be already effective reinforcers for that client or carefully developed as part of the therapy. Ratio and interval reinforcement can be used and the specific schedules varied as needed. Differential reinforcement utilizing extinction trials as well as attempts to occasion responses incompatible with identified maladaptive behavior can be used to weaken the undesirable behavior. Negative reinforcement and punishment may be used; discriminative stimuli are developed and manipulated and the generalization of new, adaptive behavior may be sought. Control over the maladaptive behavior is brought about essentially through the planned and systematic manipulation or programming of relevant environmental factors, particularly discriminative stimuli which precede the behavior, and reinforcing stimuli, which follow the behavior.

These two models of learning theory, respondent and operant conditioning, may be combined to explain complex human behavior as, for example, in the two-factor learning theory of Mowrer (1956,

1965, 1968). With specific reference to children, Lazarus, Davison, and Polefka (1965) argue for the use of both respondent and operant conditioning. Graziano (1968) discusses the wild tantrums of autistic children as "respondent-occasioned operants" and suggests that both models must be used to bring that behavior under control.

Contiguity theory, such as that developed by Guthrie (1942, 1946), has some scientific advantages in that it employs a minimum of assumptions, and can be utilized by behavior therapists. Its basic postulate is that "whenever a stimulus is contiguous with a response it becomes maximally associated with that response" (Osgood, 1953, p. 364). In other words, stimulus–response contiguity, and not reinforcement, is necessary for learning.

One theoretical variation which stands between reinforcement and contiguity theories and is applicable to behavior therapy is Denny's elicitation theory (Denny and Adelman, 1955; Denny, 1966), which maintains that respondent and operant conditioning are aspects of the same basic learning process: the repeated and consistent *elicitation* of responses. Both stimulus–response contiguity and reinforcement are basic to Denny's formulation because they are consistent elicitors of the behavior. Denny has applied his analysis to the modification of behavior of mentally retarded and psychotic patients.

Any of these positions and their variations may serve as the theoretical basis and source of concepts for behavior therapists. Clearly, then, behavior therapy is practiced in a diversity of forms; its plural nature, its continued diversity will, hopefully, prevent the formation of conceptual rigidity (Graziano, 1967). And one hopes that the present diversity suggests a future thoroughness.

Whether the behavior therapist approaches his task from a basic respondent, operant, or contiguity model, or, most likely, a combination of all three, he maintains his focus on the client's overt behavior as it relates to identifiable controlling stimuli. That is, behavior is always viewed in the context of stimulus control. When attempting to alter some behavior, the therapist's methods must refer to appropriate stimuli. To cite an important point made by Homme et al. (1968) in their article which appears in Part I of this collection, behavior modification can be defined as the application of two technologies: (1) *contingency management*, which refers to the strengthening or weakening of responses through the manipulation of reinforcing conditions, and (2) *stimulus control*, which refers to the probability that a given response will occur in the presence of some specified stimulus. While we can utilize reinforcement procedures to establish, for example, the verbal response, "Fine, thank you," in a previously nonverbal autistic child, it is equally important to develop the appropriate stimulus control so the newly acquired behavior will occur appropriately, in the presence of another verbal stimulus such as, "Hello, how are you?" The new behavior, strengthened through the application of the technology of contingency management, must also be brought under appropriate stimulus control, in order for it to constitute an adaptive, S-R unit. The behavior therapist, then, focuses on both behavior and the controlling stimuli in order to weaken the bond between the conditioned and/or discriminative stimulus and maladaptive behavior, and strengthen that bond between those stimuli and weak or newly-acquired adaptive responses.

✂

THE APPLICATION OF BEHAVIOR THERAPY

This collection brings together recent investigations of the use of behavior modification approaches with children in a variety of problem areas. The articles have been arranged in five parts, the first one serving as an introduction to and survey of the field. The second and third parts deal respectively with children traditionally labeled "retarded" and "psychotic." While the specific behaviors of such children are often identical, and differential diagnoses are very often not useful, the fact remains that the labels are still used and children are segregated accordingly. There is a good deal of overlap in these two parts and much of the work reported can be applied equally well to psychotic and retarded children.

Part IV presents articles dealing with approaches to the modification of antisocial behavior which, because of its social nature, calls for more complex programming than is required by many of the more discreet and often single-problem behaviors of the retarded and the psychotic children.

The fifth section deals with generally less severe and disruptive behavior and it even moves into clearly "normal" limits. Here the modification of maladaptive behaviors commonly found in a variety of public and private school situations is discussed.

The final part explores one of the major implications of behavioral approaches — that is, recognition that behavior is affected primarily by contingencies controlled by "direct care" persons such as parents and ward or cottage staff, rather than by a psychotherapist in an hour's weekly meeting. Therefore these persons who have the closest contact with the child must become actively involved in the therapeutic task.

❤

BEHAVIORAL DEFICITS AND SURPLUS

As indicated in the following papers, the behavior therapist defines his task with each new case in terms of the client's observed behavior and the identifiable eliciting or discriminative stimuli. In identifying the behavior-to-be-changed, he uses a variety of observational methods to obtain baseline or pretreatment data. Once the maladaptive behavior has been identified, it can be grouped as (1) "surplus" maladaptive behavior such as tantrums, aggressive behavior, stereotyped and repetitive behavior, etc., which must be *decreased* in order to improve the child's functioning, or (2) as behavioral deficits or lack of appropriate behavior, such as lack of or a low functional level of speech, toilet training, positive social behavior, etc. — that is, behaviors which must be strengthened and *increased* in order to bring about improved functioning. Such grouping of deficit and surplus behaviors immediately helps to define significant behavioral dimensions and the direction in which the therapist must work; that is, toward acquisition of new behavior, decrement of existing behavior, or some combination of both (Graziano, 1967).

❤

OVERCOMING BEHAVIORAL DEFICITS

In this collection examples of behavior therapy primarily aimed at overcoming deficit behavior by directly bringing about the acquisition of adaptive behavior are Hundziak, et al. and DeLeon and Mandell, who focus on overcoming deficits in appropriate toilet behavior; Minge and Ball and Whitney and Barnard established self-help behavior such as dressing and eating with retarded children; Blackwood, et al., who established a response to a simple social direction in a retarded child. Several authors describe their work in overcoming deficits in verbal behavior, sometimes, as with autistic children, beginning with a near-zero baseline verbal level (Doubros, Lovaas et al., Hewett, Brison). In a different form of vocal behavior, Esposito describes his approach to making up deficits in singing behavior in nursery school children. In Part II, Esposito also focuses on overcoming motor deficits in retarded children.

The authors describe many approaches to overcoming a variety of behavior deficits in different children. Making up behavior deficits, then, entails the acquisition of new behavior, and in all but one of these articles (DeLeon and Mandell) the authors have utilized primarily

operant techniques. Of the eleven papers that focus primarily on
making up deficit behavior, ten utilize operant techniques in their
major approaches.

><

REDUCTION OF MALADAPTIVE BEHAVIORAL SURPLUS

In contrast, of the eleven articles dealing primarily with the reduction
of surplus maladaptive behavior, four (Blackwood, Graziano and Kean,
Tate and Baroff, and Browning) used respondent or classical conditioning concepts. One study, Lazarus, et al., used both respondent and
operant concepts in its major approaches, while Welsh used a concept
of stimulus satiation, common to both respondent and operant models.
Respondent approaches, then, are more frequent, at least in the studies
included here, when the therapeutic task is the reduction of surplus
maladaptive behavior than when the task involves making up behavioral
deficits by bringing about the acquisition of adaptive behavior.

The articles that discuss behavior therapy aimed at the decrement
of surplus maladaptive behavior include Blackwood, who deals with
the reduction of maladaptive eating behavior and with conditioned
avoidance behavior in mentally retarded children; Tate and Baroff,
who focus on the decrement of self-injurious behavior of a psychotic
boy; Browning, who reduced stuttering in a psychotic child; Patterson
et al. and Graziano and Kean deal with the reduction of hyperactive
and grossly "upset" behavior; Wetzel discusses the reduction of stealing,
and Welsh describes the elimination of fire-setting behavior; Hart
et al., reduced surplus crying in nursery school children; Allen et al.
and Gardner eliminated, respectively, severe, self-injurious scratching
and psychogenic seizures.

><

DIFFERENTIAL THERAPEUTIC TECHNIQUES

In dealing with discrete, single-problem behaviors, the therapeutic task
is often one of either decrement of maladaptive behavior or acquisition
of adaptive behavior, and the choice of respondent or operant models,
and positive reinforcement or aversive control, is often clearly
indicated. However, when the behavior therapist is faced with more
complex multiple-problem and higher social behaviors, the task becomes
more complicated and involves careful programming to bring about

both the decrement of some behavior and the acquisition and strengthening of other behavior. In such programming, both respondent and operant models are used, as well as both positive reinforcement and aversive control, often presented in a variety of reinforcement schedules. The therapist must then balance, without conflict, a large number of complex variables.

In this collection nine papers describe complex programming to modify multi-problem and higher social behavior: the papers by Davison, Graziano, and Ney deal with social group programming for psychotic children; the papers by Burchard, Fineman, and Robert Schwitzgebel focus on antisocial behavior; Patterson and Brodsky deal with a child who presented multiple-problem behavior; Walder et al. and Wahler et al. discuss the training of parents to modify the social behavior of their own children.

SOME TENTATIVE GENERALIZATIONS

This volume presents just a limited sample of behavior therapy with children, and the conclusions summarized below are only tentative.

1. When the therapeutic task is defined as that of overcoming behavioral deficits by focusing on the acquisition of age-appropriate and adaptive behaviors (e.g., teaching speech and simple socially cooperative behavior to retarded and psychotic children), the behavior therapist tends to approach the task primarily through application of an operant conditioning model and *positive* reinforcement to strengthen the behavior.

2. When the therapeutic task is defined as that of directly bringing about a decrement of maladaptive surplus behavior (e.g., head-banging and other self-injurious behavior; aggressive behavior toward others; bizarre mannerisms), the behavior therapist uses either or both respondent or operant models and aversive control to weaken that behavior.

3. When the task is defined as that of decellerating maladaptive surplus behavior through strengthening some adaptive and incompatible behavior (e.g., desensitization of phobias through successive approximations; decreasing head-punching by increasing the child's appropriate use of his hands; decreasing withdrawn episodes by shaping more active, socially-cooperative behavior), the behavior therapist tends to use either or both operant and respondent models, and *positive* reinforcement to strengthen the incompatible, adaptive behavior.

4. When the therapist is faced with multiple-problem behavior and the development of complex social behavior, the task is defined as including both the acquisition of adaptive behavior and the decrement of maladaptive surplus behavior. In this situation the therapist uses carefully-planned programs in which goals of acquisition and decrement of behavior, respondent and operant models, and positive and aversive control are all carefully balanced.

5. When working with children diagnosed as mentally retarded, behavior therapists tend to define their basic task as essentially that of making up deficits by accelerating the acquisition of adaptive, age-appropriate behavior, and they therefore tend to use primarily operant paradigms, shaping procedures, and high positive reinforcement.

6. When working with children diagnosed as grossly psychotic, behavior therapists tend to define the task not only as making up deficits, such as with retarded children, but also in terms of rapid reduction of grossly interfering maladaptive surplus behavior. Although both tasks apply to retarded children, too, surplus maladaptive behavior appears to be markedly more pronounced with psychotic than with retarded children, and this task assumes greater importance with them. With approaches to psychotic children, then, we find combinations of respondent and operant models and positive and aversive control.

7. Although we have used standard diagnostic terms such as "mentally retarded," "psychotic," and "neurotic," we use them not to denote specific conditions or disease entities, but only as descriptive labels for what are approximate, gross categories of characteristic behaviors. *These labels actually are irrelevant to the major therapeutic tasks discussed above.* In the behavior therapist's approaches, psychological evaluations are focused on observable behavior defined in terms of surplus, deficit, and age-appropriate behavior, and on identifiable, controlling stimuli defined as elicitors, discriminants, and reinforcers. Psychological evaluations are not focused on central or disease-entity conditions; therapeutic programs are planned around learning theory rather than psychodynamic models; and the evaluation of progress is carried out primarily by comparing discrete, observed, baseline behavior, with equally discrete, observed therapy (training) or posttherapy behavior, all related to identifiable stimulus conditions. The need for detail in manipulating complex stimulus and response variables is so great in behavior therapy that vague terms such as "neurosis" have no useful function.

8. Related to the above, but important enough to be discussed separately, is the fact that moving away from the vague, global diagnostic categories where a child may be seen as "psychotic," i.e., as one

of many supposedly highly similar members of one large class, and moving to more explicitly defined and detailed observable behavior, brings the clinician closer to examining the *detailed realities of each client as a truly distinct and uniquely functioning individual.*

I

FROM THE LABORATORY

TO THE CLINIC

FIVE ARTICLES WILL SERVE AS INTRODUCTIONS AND SURVEYS of behavior therapy with children. The first two articles are by C. B. Ferster, an experimental psychologist who has applied laboratory principles to the clinical and the educational problems of children. In the first paper he discusses the transition from the animal laboratory to the clinic, describing the laboratory psychologist becoming aware of and impressed with the detailed and varied or rich experience which, so far at least, seems to have come primarily from the clinicians' and the educators' immersion in coping directly with the problem behavior of children. This type of experience is often unverbalized and Ferster points out the value not only in expressing it in terms of modern behavioral psychology but also in actively utilizing experimental psychology in the clinic to gain new and even richer detail and greater effectiveness. Having made the transition to the clinic, in the second paper Ferster discusses the use of positive reinforcement and aversive control, clearly preferring the first. He draws a technical distinction between "natural" and "arbitrary" aversive control, and discusses the important implications of each for work with children.

Homme, de Baca, Cottingham, and Homme discuss behavioral engineering as the application of laws of behavior to practical problems such as those confronting the clinician, the educator, and others. Although we often seem intent upon the systematic use of reinforcers — that is, contingency management — these authors point out that behavioral engineering involves two technologies, contingency management and stimulus control, both of which are necessary for the successful modification of behavior. Note also that in this article (which stresses the technology of behavioral engineering) the authors suggest that behavior therapists have neglected the study and development of behaviors such as those associated with joy, love, and the strengthening of a favorable self-concept.

Schwitzgebel, Schwitzgebel, Pahnke, and Hurd discuss an important but still too-little considered aspect of behavioral engineering: the sophisticated employment of electronic equipment in the understanding, maintenance, and modification of human behavior. Some critics would reject such development, seeing in it an overly mechanistic and dangerously dehumanizing influence. However it would be as specious for us to reject the potential value of electronics as it would be for the missionary doctor to discard his microscope and centrifuge because they are too mechanistic and divert him from his essentially humanitarian concern. After discussing recent technological developments in electronics and some potential applications in psychology, the authors discuss some ethical considerations which should direct and not impede our growing utilization of electronic tools.

The article by Gelfand and Hartmann reviews the literature on behavior therapy with children. After providing an integrated and thorough review of work dating through 1966, the authors highlight some major deficiencies still existing. For example, although behavioral treatment has been convincingly demonstrated in a number of studies, most are "inadequately controlled and incompletely recorded case studies" which fall short of experimental objectivity and control.

Experimentation with behavior therapy is still on a small scale, accounting for but a small portion of the total of mental health activity. It is still at a point where case studies and exploratory and suggestive papers are useful and even necessary in generating ideas and methods. However, behavior therapists will have to provide better controlled studies and more secure and convincing data than are now available or they will find themselves justifiably criticized in much the same manner as they now criticize psychodynamic therapies. The past decade has generated many small-scale demonstrations of what might be accomplished clinically through behavioral approaches. Until behavior therapists clearly demonstrate socially significant accomplishments in large-scale applied services, behavior therapy, despite its claim to more sophisticated science, will have achieved nothing more than have the traditional psychodynamic therapies.

Behavior therapists have access to rich fields, including previous clinical experiences and laboratory-derived concepts of behavior and electronic instrumentation. It remains to be seen whether these elements will not only successfully grow but also eventually become integrated with social and medical advances so as to effect significant and meaningful improvements in the human condition.

⚔ 1 ⚔

Transition from Animal Laboratory to Clinic

C. B. Ferster

This paper describes my experiences at the Linwood Children's Center, a day care and residential treatment center for autistic and schizophrenic children. Since the expertise I bring to Linwood is mainly that of laboratory experiments with animals, my participation in the Linwood project (Ferster, 1966) illustrates one mode of using laboratory knowledge to find more effective treatments and better teaching methods.

The bridge between my general knowledge about behavior and practical knowledge about children began when I observed Linwood's clinical staff, particularly the director, Miss Simons, who is an especially gifted therapist. One incident was an interaction between Miss Simons and Karen, a four-year-old autistic girl. Karen had been in day care at Linwood for about two weeks, during which she spent most of her time clutching a plastic doll and crying.

⚔

NOTES ON AN INTERCHANGE

My original notes give the flavor of Miss Simons' style and the kind of events I saw and recorded.

> Jeanne Simons placed Karen on a rocking horse where she stayed without crying as long as Miss Simons rocked the horse and sang to her.

From *The Psychological Record*, 17:2 (1967), 145–150.

After a few minutes, Miss Simons stopped rocking the horse for brief periods but kept on singing. She carefully sensed how long she could stop rocking the horse without losing control of Karen. The return to rocking always followed some behavior other than crying. In general Miss Simons stopped rocking the horse whenever she judged that Karen's behavior was strongly maintained by some current factor, such as playing with the handles of the rocking horse. Next, Miss Simons took the plastic doll from Karen's hands, set it on a nearby table, and quickly moved the table next to Karen who promptly picked up the doll. One would guess that under other circumstances taking the doll away from Karen would lead to screaming. Although Karen was without the doll for a few seconds, this situation provided the basis for the reinforcement of a specific constructive piece of behavior —reaching for the doll. This was the first time that Miss Simons required some behavior of Karen. Now Karen moved the rocking horse slightly, and Miss Simons' singing usually occurred contingent on the rocking. When Karen sat quietly, Miss Simons simply watched, smiled, and hummed gently. When Karen rocked, Miss Simons sang in rhythm to the movements of the horse. Then the episode with the doll was repeated, but this time the movements were a little slower and Karen was without her doll for a few seconds longer. When Karen returned to rocking, Miss Simons sang in rhythm. Soon Karen placed the doll on the table herself. This probably occurred because the behavior controlled by the rocking horse was becoming prepotent over that controlled by the doll. Also, it was difficult for Karen both to clutch the doll and to hold the handles of the rocking horse. Karen continued rocking without the doll for over a minute, as Miss Simons sang along. The magnitude and rhythm of the rocking were quite vigorous. Next Miss Simons kept silent for brief periods while Karen rocked. Technically this was intermittent reinforcement of the rocking. At this point Karen turned to the doll, possibly because she was less inclined to rock the horse when Miss Simons did not sing. But in picking up the doll Karen dropped it to the floor, perhaps accidentally, and for the first time during the episode, she began to cry. Miss Simons asked, "Do you want to pick up your doll? I'll help you," and extended her hands to Karen. When Karen touched Miss Simons' hands, Miss Simons clasped Karen's hands and helped her from the rocking horse. When Karen did not lift her foot over the saddle, Miss Simons simply held her there until she made some movement. When Karen did not move, Miss Simons prompted the behavior by moving the foot partially over the saddle and allowed Karen to complete the final part of the action. Miss Simons then held Karen in the vicinity of the doll until Karen picked it up, and once more she offered her hands as she said, "Do you want to get up?" Karen lifted her hands in the gesture which many children characteristically use as a mand for being picked up, but Miss Simons simply continued to hold her hands out until Karen touched them. Back on the horse, Karen now rocked without Miss Simons' singing. Once again she dropped her doll and the same episode was repeated. This time Miss Simons supported the behavior slightly less than she had on the previous occasion. Next Miss Simons placed the doll on a couch about fifteen feet away. Karen stopped rocking for a few seconds while she looked at the doll, but then began to rock again, and after about a minute Miss Simons picked up the doll, attracted Karen's attention by tapping it, and sang in rhythm to the tapping. Karen made some sounds and began rocking the horse in the same rhythm, possibly in response to the tapping. At this point Miss Simons returned the doll. Karen had been away from it for over a minute without crying. However, the next time Miss Simons took the doll away and placed it on the couch, Karen began to cry even though she continued to rock. Miss Simons sang in rhythm to the rocking and the crying stopped. At this point Miss Simons herself took Karen off the horse, and they walked over to the sofa where Karen picked up the doll and sat on Miss Simons' lap. A minute later Karen indicated some disposition to get on the horse again by tugging on Miss Simons. Miss Simons did not take her to the horse, but instead picked her up and hummed to her as she carried her about. Several times Miss Simons picked up Karen, smiled, and sang to her, but she did not place her on the horse.

The whole interchange lasted about 30 minutes, during which several hundred reinforcements altered Karen's repertoire substantially. In contrast to the food reinforcement employed in the usual animal experiment, very simple features of the child's environment were manipulated skillfully and rapidly in a symphony of action. Even though the behavioral processes were identical to those I have observed in animal and human laboratory work, I discovered many new ways to control and influence the behavior of the children at Linwood as I observed this and similar episodes. Although I saw applications of every principle of behavior I knew, there was a content here that could not come solely from laboratory experiences. I could make a functional analysis of the interaction, but I could not have designed it.

Note the unusual way in which Miss Simons weakened the doll's compulsive control of Karen. Miss Simons waited until Karen's behavior was strongly controlled by other reinforcers so that she could remove the doll for brief periods. She very slowly lengthened the intervals during which Karen was without the doll by pacing them with the development of these other behaviors. At no point during the intervention was crying directly extinguished in the sense that extinction is carried out in an animal experiment. Because of my limited experience with children, I might have kept Karen on the horse until her crying stopped before I handed her the doll or lifted her off. When Karen dropped her doll and began to cry, Miss Simons reacted immediately and used the doll itself as the reinforcer for generating a small increment in the child's repertoire. Instead of simply extinguishing the crying Miss Simons identified the operant reinforcer maintaining it and began to apply this reinforcer differentially in favor of behaviors, other than crying, which she judged to be more useful for the child. The extinction of the control by the doll and the extinction of the crying were by-products of the reinforcement of other behaviors. In the meantime, the amount of crying and emotional states were kept small enough so they did not disrupt the new repertoire.

It was not practical to interact with Karen on the rocking horse all day, so Miss Simons anticipated the next step by extinguishing performances reinforced by the rocking horse at the same time that she supported Karen's behavior in another way. For example, when they were sitting on the couch, Miss Simons did not reinforce Karen's gesturing toward the rocking horse. Instead, she picked her up and interacted with her via body contact and singing. I don't know what Miss Simons would have done if Karen had struggled in her arms and continued gesturing toward the horse. I suspect that Miss Simons already had gauged the probability of this when she shifted the reinforcer. In many other instances it appeared at first glance that primitive behavior was being reinforced. But after more observation I discovered that extinction was being carried out in a new way.

Another example is the boy who teased Miss Simons by pulling her hair. When Miss Simons continued to give him her full attention, I wondered why she didn't simply withdraw, since it was so clear that the annoying behavior was reinforced by her attention. But when I looked more closely I saw that Miss Simons was holding both her hair and the boy's hands so that all the boy was pulling was her hands. Furthermore, she released her grip on him only when his performance shifted in a direction that she wished to reinforce. This was another example of extinguishing a performance by finding another that would be prepotent over the one that was annoying. In this case the reinforcement was negative, the removal of the restraint she applied.

Miss Simons was amazed at how closely she was able to see herself in the notes describing her interaction with Karen. "Charles," she said, "I don't see how you can understand therapy. It takes years of training to do this." But I did have clinical experience even though it was with infra-human organisms. In my animal experiments I dealt with each subject as an individual. During the course of the experiment the conditions were changed continuously in space with the subject's performance. I learned the fine grain of my organism's behavior, and as an experimenter I responded to the details of it. Rarely was an animal too deviant to work with. I always looked for the factor responsible for each animal's uniqueness and tried to take it into account. Each pigeon differed in how much grain was necessary for reinforcement to maintain an adequate amount of behavior. The height of the key or lever had to be adjusted for the size of the animal, and the transition from one schedule of reinforcement to another was always a unique affair, carefully adjusted to the animal's current performance, even though the general form of the final performance was common to all of the animals. Each animal was different in many ways and the goal of the experiment was to find a common factor beyond the individual characteristics of each subject.

The observations that I made were not solely for my own benefit. Miss Simons' amazement at my close description of her encounter with Karen came partly because of the difficulty she had in conveying her procedures to other people. Despite Miss Simons' consummate skill with the children, other staff members fell far short of the mark, and they did not learn simply by watching her. Nor was she able to instruct them verbally. Terms such as "keep your antennas out" or "watch for the health in the child," often eloquent descriptions for those of us who appreciated a fine-grained analysis of behavior, did not help the staff in actual procedures with the children.

Miss Simons has suggested the impact of a technical language about behavior on her work thus: "I think I can explain the details of step-by-step procedures now so that people don't just look blindly at me with awe. I'm not even sure intuition is so mysterious. I think it's having eyes all over the place and seeing the tiny little things that children are doing and then suddenly the child reacts to it. And I am able to see the tiny little steps and explain much better what I am doing with the children. So the magic is out of Linwood — which I think is wonderful." Now she has an objective language that is simple and concise enough for everyone to understand. To supplement Linwood's magic there is a training program in the experimental analysis of behavior. It is a key part of the project. The course was designed to make more effective and inventive therapists and we constantly experiment with ways to improve it. The main emphasis is on a detailed technical analysis of animal behavior, because we have found that facility and skill in the fine-grained technical description of animal behavior makes it possible for therapists to observe systematically the details of the complex natural environment.

The DRO, differential reinforcement of other behavior, is an example of animal data and procedures which influenced almost every therapist who took the training course at Linwood. In the context of DRO, they understood how Miss Simons weakens primitive behavior by positively reinforcing other performances.

The functional analysis of her interactions with the children also changed Miss Simons' practices. As she became more self-conscious about her own activities, she saw more clearly which parts of her complex interchange with the child were having particular effects and, accordingly, refined her activities and increased the frequency of effective contingencies. Small, hour-by-hour increments in the child's repertoire became reinforcers for her as she learned to observe the fine grain of the interaction with a child.

Yet another consequence that came from learning a systematic language about behavior was an increased ability to design new ways of activating the child's environment. Reinforcement theory and a technical analysis of verbal behavior have led to new procedures in the schoolroom never before used at Linwood. For example, children are now taking part in classroom educational activities who have never done so before. Part of the reason for this has been the use of chains or sequences of behavior so that a child goes on to the next activity such as writing when he demonstrates that he can read a short text perfectly.

To sum up how the clinical staff at Linwood and I have modified each other's behavior: In general, we have found less benefit in using the literal methods of the animal laboratory than we have in a systematic and objective description of behavior. A systematic language about behavior allows the clinic to use its own special knowledge and experience more effectively.

At first the Linwood clinicians feared conditioning because they thought of the usual laboratory situation, in which the experimenter determines the behavior to be developed. When they thought of applying operant conditioning to children, it appeared arbitrary, immoral, and at the expense of the child's development. They discovered, however, that they, with their intimate clinical knowledge of the child, still decided what behaviors were to be developed. Principles of conditioning simply aided them in working more effectively.

From my point of view as an experimental psychologist, the reverse lend-lease has provided grist for my mill. The phenomena I dealt with in the animal laboratory I now see as a design in an actual fabric and I find many theoretical challenges in frequent discussions and observations of the children with my colleagues.

~ 2 ~

Arbitrary and Natural Reinforcement

C. B. Ferster

It has been clear for some time that many of the ills of human behavior come from aversive control. Behavioral scientists have studied it in the laboratory in the hope that technical knowledge of its processes would teach how to ameliorate psychopathology. Psychologists have speculated about a society from which aversive control has been eliminated particularly under the influence of Skinner (1948). Some psychologists, experimental and otherwise, felt so strongly about aversive control that they raised their children as much as possible by positive reinforcement alone. More recently, mostly as a result of the urgency of controlling self-destructive behavior in autistic children and because of the technical difficulties in controlling these children with positive reinforcement, the cycle has gone a full turn. Investigators such as Lovaas et al. (1965) have turned to aversive control, using stimuli such as intense electric shock, slapping, shouting, and isolation in order to suppress self-destructive behavior, reinforce attention and weaken tantrums. Other investigators and therapists have been using electric shock with adults in what is called aversion therapy.

It's difficult not to be moral about aversive control. The word aversive has the connotations of reject, avoid, escape, and withdraw. Most people's feelings about aversive control are that "It's better to give than to receive," which suggests something of the moral dilemma. Aversive control is obviously widely used in the normal environment

From *The Psychological Record*, 17:3 (1967), 341–347.

because it achieves something. The reasons for its use are not hard to find. First it produces behavior immediately. Second, if it is made severe enough, the behavior it controls will override any other performance the person might engage in. Third, the aversive stimulus itself is the motive for the behavior that is required. It is not necessary to take into account the dispositions of the person who is controlled (Skinner, 1953). On the other hand, despite their immediate control aversive stimuli make us uneasy because they produce by-products such as anxiety and other general disruptions of the operant repertoire (Skinner, 1966). Aversive control leads to avoidance of the controller and general aggressiveness. Furthermore, it substitutes avoidance and escape for productive behavior. The problems that come from aversive control are not so much the behaviors that the controller intends to produce as the behaviors that occur unintentionally. The same aversive stimulus produces both.

In order to evaluate the consequences, the desirability and usefulness of various kinds of aversive control in human behavior I would like to discuss technically two kinds of aversive stimuli, natural and arbitrary. Negative reinforcement, escape from an aversive stimulus, is very common and necessary in the natural human environment because aversive stimuli occur so widely and frequently. Any time there is an aversive stimulus, there is potentially some performance which will terminate it. In bright sunlight we put on sunglasses, shade our eyes with our hands, turn away from the sun, or reduce the amount of light by squinting. Such aversive control obviously does not have drastic side effects, nor is it unproductive or undesirable. Youngsters quickly learn to put their fingers in their ears when there is a loud noise. Visual aversive stimuli commonly reinforce the behavior of turning the head away. Performances such as opening a window, taking off clothing or turning on an air conditioner occur because they reduce the temperature of the air around the body. A pebble rubbing the foot inside the shoe reinforces removing it. In the presence of extreme odors we pinch our nostrils or hold our breath momentarily. The examples can be repeated at great length (Ferster and Perrott, in press). A statement attributed to Thorndike points out that the zero point, the first level of intelligence and productive behavior, is spitting out a bitter substance that enters the mouth. These simple aversive stimuli are natural rather than arbitrary because they reinforce any behavior which works. A performance reinforced by escape operates physically and directly on the aversive stimulus. For example, turning the dial of the television set blots out the commercial or averting the gaze interrupts the light entering the eye. All of these behaviors have the same result on the aversive stimulus and they are equally effective in terminating it. The property of the aversive stimulus could be phrased theoretically by saying that it reinforces a class of behaviors. In most cases the aversive stimulus interacts with and shapes existing behavior. The particular performance that an aversive stimulus will reinforce will depend, of course, on the total repertoire the person brings to it. Bright sunlight will reinforce squinting or wearing sunglasses or a hat in the case of the person who needs to spend time outside. A person with little behavior under the control of reinforcers outdoors will simply stay out of the sun.

In contrast to the natural reinforcers there is the aversive stimulus which is applied arbitrarily by one person to control the behavior of another. Examples of this kind of arbitrary control are the child who picks up his toys because doing so terminates the parent's threat, a student who does an assignment because it avoids ridicule in class the next day, or an employee who does his job only when there is a threat of being fired.

Such arbitrary social reinforcement differs in two ways from the natural reinforcer that was just described. First, the performance that is reinforced is specified narrowly rather than broadly as the large class of behaviors that can get rid of the natural aversive stimulus. Thus, a parent who says "Come here this minute or I'll get angry," requires one particular performance. The child cannot, for example, escape the parent altogether by leaving the room. In that case the parent will adjust the aversive stimulus until the *only* way to terminate it is to come. The usual laboratory experiment with a rat, a lever, and an electric shock illustrates this same property of arbitrary reinforcement. The electric shock can potentially reinforce lying on the back, hanging from a projection on the wall or standing between the grids on the floor. Because the experimenter needs a performance that can be recorded automatically he arranges the apparatus and procedure so that only pressing the bar can terminate the shock. He shaves the fur from the rat's back, incarcerates him in a chamber, eliminates projections from the walls and uses closely spaced grids. From the rat's point of view all that is required is that the intolerable stimulus be terminated. It is the experimenter who has an investment in lever pressing. The parent who uses aversive control to get a child to pick up his toys is establishing the same arbitrary relationship to the aversive stimulus as the experimenter has done with the rat and the electric shock. The child cannot simply escape from the parent's anger as he could from a hot fire because there is no behavior in his repertoire which has any physical relation to the aversive stimulus. The parents require a particular performance and adjust the application of the aversive stimulus until they get it.

A second property of arbitrary reinforcement is that the individual's current repertoire does not influence the behavior it produces nearly as much as is the case with natural reinforcers. While we sometimes apply aversive stimuli for the individual's own good, the immediate reinforcers benefit only the controller. The controller gets the behavior he wants: The child temporarily terminates an aversive stimulus which a controller such as a parent can reapply any time he wants another performance. The reinforcement is arbitrary because there is no reinforcer currently maintaining the desired behavior or behavior similar to it in the child's repertoire. With an arbitrary stimulus, the controller can coerce a particular performance, whatever the child's current repertoire. A mute child under the control of a graduate student whose course grade depends on producing speech is in such a position. Speech which is arbitrarily reinforced without reference to the child's current repertoire may disappear as soon as the acute intervention ends unless there is planned transition to a natural reinforcer. Aversive control is often said to benefit the child because the behavior that is coerced will be useful to the child later. The child does not benefit, however, in the sense of achieving a durable reinforcer which will maintain behavior without the coercive control.

Another characteristic of control by an arbitrary reinforcer is that it is designed to pre-empt the rest of the individual's behavior. Thus the child facing a threatening parent cannot turn to other behaviors as he could in the face of an aversive stimulus which had a fixed physical relation to his behavior. The requirement that he emit a *particular* performance will pre-empt all other behaviors.

In contrast to the arbitrary reinforcers, the natural reinforcer has no motive. It doesn't care how it is terminated and will be satisfied with any performance that eliminates it. As a result it may seldom if ever occur if it is aversive enough to maintain the operant behavior that avoids it. A child may escape and avoid a hot stove for years without being burned. The hapless rat in an experiment or the socially controlled child, however, will be re-exposed to the aversive stimulus each time the experimenter or parent wants some more behavior.

The arbitrary control of behavior, for the benefit of the controller rather than the controllee can occur in positive as well as negative reinforcement. Let me develop the properties of natural positive reinforcement first. The aphorism, "You can lead a horse to water but you can't make him drink," illustrates a natural positive reinforcer. Water can reinforce a variety of behaviors in a water-deprived horse, such as pawing the ground, turning the faucet on the trough with its foot or searching the countryside for a stream, pond, or puddle. Each of these performances comes from the horse's existing operant repertoire.

Arbitrary reinforcement occurs when the horse isn't thirsty and a reinforcer is used to make him drink. One procedure would be to apply an electric shock which is terminated whenever he drinks. Such procedures have been carried out many times (Williams and Teitelbaum, 1956) and the arbitrariness of such reinforcement has already been discussed. But we could also reinforce drinking by giving the horse food every time he drinks. It is necessary in such a procedure to restrict or incarcerate the horse so that he can't roam the countryside looking for places to graze. From the point of view of the horse's repertoire, there are already many behaviors reinforced by food that have a higher probability than drinking water. Such restriction would have to be carried out by aversive control in order to prevent or suppress the positively-reinforced eating behavior already in the horse's repertoire. The crux of the matter is that the horse's drinking is reinforcing to the horse only because the experimenter has arbitrary control of him. One might properly ask why one would want to make a horse drink who isn't thirsty. It would be much simpler to wait a period of time, and the horse will surely drink one way or another since such behavior is always a durable part of any horse's repertoire.

This distinction between arbitrary and natural positive reinforcement becomes practically important when we consider building behavior in children in the natural environment and particularly therapeutically (Ferster, 1958, 1961, 1966). The following is an example of the arbitrary application reinforcement by a therapist: "If you put on your coat, I'll give you a cooky." Such an episode begins with a child who has no disposition to put on his coat and a disposition to eat cookies. The therapist is reinforced when the child puts on his coat but not necessarily when the child eats cookies. Such behavior benefits the therapist and will cease as soon as he stops giving the cookies. The child's natural environment has never reinforced putting on a coat with cookies and is not likely to do so in the future. The same performance could be reinforced naturally, however, if the coat served to prevent the child from being cold outside.

Even a small part of the repertoire may be reinforced naturally. The child may stand still and extend his arms when the therapist puts on his coat on a cold day before going to the playground. In this situation the child is already emitting a performance, extending his arms, which is negatively reinforced by avoiding cold air outside. Under these conditions the therapist may gradually assist the child less, paced with the child's ability to complete the task of dressing. For example, at one stage the therapist might hold the last sleeve in position until the child pushed his arm through. The completed repertoire will be natural in the sense that it will be durably maintained by its effect on the child's comfort long after the therapist has gone (Ferster and Simons, 1966).

There are many opportunities for the therapist to interact with performances which exist in the child's repertoire because they have a natural and stable effect on the child's environment. These situations are illustrated by phrases such as, "If you want to leave the room, you need to turn the knob," as opposed to "you can have the cooky if you put the puzzle together." In the first case, the child already has engaged in the behavior of leaving the room reinforced by the new location he goes to. The therapist can successively approximate new behaviors such as turning the knob, speaking to someone or getting a key, by minor prompts and supplementary supports which then can be faded away. Such behavior is for the child's benefit rather than the therapist's in the sense that the therapist has brought the child into better contact with a reinforcer that is already maintaining the child's behavior. The distinction is the same one that is suggested by Skinner's discussion of the mand and the fact (Skinner, 1957). New enlargements of the child's repertoire such as turning a door knob will, of course, make it possible for the child to come under the control of new reinforcers not currently maintaining his behavior. Opening doors is a repertoire which can lead to reinforcers other than those originally supporting the behavior.

Many clinicians implicitly understand the distinction between arbitrary and natural reinforcement. The following statement by Jeanne Simons, Director of Linwood Children's Center, expresses the connotations of natural reinforcement.

> And that's why we walk behind the child. He feels your protection when you walk behind. If you give him a chance to go in any direction, he may be wrong when he goes this way or that. Just follow him. If it's a dead end, pick him up gently and bring him to the main route. But never think that you know the answer, because you are dealing with an individual who may want to go very different routes which for him may be better. That's why I feel more comfortable behind the children so I can see where they are going.

Walking behind the child denotes a broad statement of the principle of operant reinforcement. The repertoire may be partially ineffective, however, and these parts will decrease by extinction as the therapist supports, prompts, and otherwise encourages those behaviors which are successful. By beginning with the initial behavior and reinforcers that the child brings to the therapeutic environment, we preserve the unique contribution of his own repertoire, and we avoid decisions about his life which are too arbitrary.

In summary the same problems arise with positive reinforcement as with aversive control in evaluating its properties and usefulness in the control of behavior in the normal environment. The undesirable by-products of aversive control are well known but equally serious are the results of its arbitrary application. Natural reinforcers, on the other hand, have the advantage that they persist without the intervention of the parent and therapist, and they do not require collateral aversive stimuli and incarceration to be effective.

~ 3 ~

What Behavioral Engineering Is

**Lloyd Homme, Polo C'de Baca, Lon Cottingham,
& Angela Homme**

The phrase "behavioral engineering" has been around a long time and all of us understand it. The only trouble is, we haven't told anyone, including ourselves, what it means. It probably is true that everyone would agree that behavioral engineering is "arranging the environment so that one gets the behavior one wants,"* or, more generally, that behavioral engineering is the application of laws of behavior to practical problems. Nevertheless, the topic of what behavioral engineering is could stand some elaboration. This becomes most apparent when one sets out to shape up a behavioral engineer. Then it quickly develops that behavioral engineering is a blend of two technologies: the technology of contingency management and the technology of stimulus control. Needless to say, no special degrees or certificates are required to put the technologies to use. The laws of nature do not care about such matters; they go on working in any case.

In analyzing a behavioral engineering task, the engineer must determine: (a) exactly what behavior he wants to occur, (b) what stimuli are to control it, and (c) what reinforcers are available.

The technology of contingency management deals with managing reinforcers (c), and the technology of stimulus control with arranging stimuli so that they come to control (b). Society at large generally decides on what behaviors should occur (a), but the time may have arrived when behavioral engineering itself may have something to say.

From *The Psychological Record*, 18 (1968), 425–434.

* R. E. Ulrich, personnal communication, 1967.

The relationships between the technology of contingency management and the technology of stimulus control and behavioral engineering may be summarized by relating them to the familiar three-term contingency (see Figure 1).

discriminative stimulus → performance → reinforcing event

technology of stimulus control   technology of contingency management

behavioral engineering

FIGURE 1.   Relationships between the three-term contingency and behavioral engineering.

Clearly it is possible to be a contingency manager and understand little about stimulus control, but the reverse certainly is not true. In order to bring a behavior under stimulus control, contingencies have to be properly managed.

THE TECHNOLOGY OF CONTINGENCY MANAGEMENT

Contingency management is the management of what events are contingent upon what behavior. It is clear that contingency management is merely the taking seriously (literally) that great law of life: When reinforcing events are contingent upon a given behavior, the behavior will increase in strength; when they are not, the behavior will decrease in strength. The power and generality of contingency management is by now becoming clearer and clearer (Ferster and Perrott, 1968; Homme, 1967; Krasner and Ullmann, 1965; Ullmann and Krasner, 1966).

The great law of life is simple, but this fact ought not be allowed to obscure another fact: The law is powerful.

Also, the simplicity of the overriding consideration of contingency management (that behavior depends on its consequences) should not lead one to believe it is always simple to teach; some trainees grasp the principle and are able to put it to work instantly; others, in our experience, never. The critical ingredient appears to be an emotional commitment or willingness to *pay off* for desirable behavior. With this commitment, things proceed apace; without it, nothing good happens.

One can make a pretty good case that, basically, there are only two things that a good contingency manager has to know and do: (a) to reinforce the behavior he wants, and (b) to recognize and reinforce approximations to this behavior.

✄

THE RELATIONSHIP BETWEEN OPERANT
CONDITIONING AND CONTINGENCY MANAGEMENT

Everybody strengthens, weakens, or suppresses operants, and everybody, in this sense, is an operant conditioner. And, since everybody, at some time or other, arranges consequences for behavior, everyone is a contingency manager. Assuming that we all agree that these usages are too broad to be useful, let us get on to narrowing them down.

Let us reserve the phrase "operant conditioning" to designate the basic laboratory science from which behavioral engineering is derived. This means, then, that an operant conditioner is an operant conditioner only as long as he remains in his laboratory. When he leaves the laboratory and systematically applies the principles of behavior to problems like getting his offspring to pass a progress check on his homework before he gets points which can be used to buy reinforcers, the operant conditioner becomes a behavioral engineer. We are calling him a behavioral engineer, rather than a contingency manager, because we are assuming he knows the rules underlying the technology of stimulus control as well as those underlying contingency management. From this standpoint, then, the nurses whom Ayllon and Michael (1959) called behavioral engineers should more properly be called contingency managers: Ayllon and Michael were the behavioral engineers. Similarly, in the Gelfand, Gelfand, and Dobson study (1967) of who reinforces what in a mental hospital, the patients, the nurses, and the nurses' assistants were contingency managers (albeit poor ones), not behavioral engineers. In the same view, when Ogden Lindsley (1960) did his pioneering work on psychotics pulling plungers in an experimental enclosure, he was an operant conditioner, but now that he is teaching teachers and parents to teach (Lindsley, 1966), he is engaged in behavioral engineering. Both Lindsley and Homme were once operant conditioners, but they quit.

It may be worthwhile to mention some differences between the operant conditioning laboratory model and contingency management, which employs the principles of operant conditioning but not the intact model of the operant conditioning laboratory. To elaborate: In the animal operant conditioning laboratory, one usually is working with a deprived organism; the deprivation operations serve to insure that one class of events will be a reinforcer — the presentation of the event of which the beast was deprived. The reinforcing event, for example presentation of food, is thus stable and highly effective as a reinforcer both within and between experimental sessions. With non-deprived humans, the model is often unsatisfactory; reinforcers often wear out and lose their reinforcing properties quickly. Because of this, Premack's differential probability hypothesis, which states that any response can reinforce any other response of lower probability, is of immense usefulness (Homme, 1966; Premack, 1959). The differential probability hypothesis combined with the use of a reinforcing event menu, on which many reinforcers are listed or pictured (Addison and Homme, 1966), is highly useful in generating tens or hundreds of reinforcers where only one or two were available before. By having *S* select his reinforcer from a menu, one determines precisely what is the most effective reinforcer here and now for this *S*.

➤

THE TECHNOLOGY OF STIMULUS CONTROL

A behavioral engineer's definition of stimulus control is a simple one: Stimulus control exists to the extent that the presence or absence of a stimulus controls the probability of a response. It is interesting to compare this with the basic researcher's definition: "Stimulus control refers to the extent to which the value of an antecedent stimulus determines the probability of occurrence of a conditioned response" (Terrace, 1966, p. 271). The key difference in these two definitions lies in the words *extent* and *values*. It is clear that the behavioral engineer is really interested in approximations to only two probability values, 1.0 and 0.0; the basic researcher, on the other hand, has to worry about values between these two values — the slope and shape of generalization gradient.

Faulty Stimulus Control

"He won't mind!" "He's stubborn!" "He knows how to do it, but he doesn't feel like it." "I meant to do it, but I forgot." In all these cases, one is speaking of faulty stimulus control. As a matter of fact, one could make an excellent case for the view that most behavioral engineering problems are problems of faulty stimulus control; that is, the *S* has the response in his repertoire, all right, but it is not made when the stimulus is presented.

Correcting Faulty Stimulus Control

The fundamental rule for correcting faulty stimulus control is the same as that for establishing stimulus control in the first place. Get the behavior (or some approximation to it) made while the *S* is attending to the stimulus which is to control it. This means, among other things, that the engineer must be able to reinstate the control stimulus whenever he wants to.

Using the Behavior of the Subject to Reinstate the Discriminative Stimulus

Over thirty years ago, Guthrie (1935, p. 18) published the following story about stimulus control. It may be time to take it seriously.

> The mother of a ten-year-old girl complained to a psychologist that for two years her daughter had annoyed her by a habit of tossing coat and hat on the floor as she entered the house. On a hundred occasions the mother had insisted that the girl pick up the clothing and hang it in its place. These wild ways were changed only after the mother, on advice, began to insist not that the girl pick up the fallen garments from the floor but that she put them on, return to the street, and reenter the house, this time removing the coat and hanging it properly.

With the usual perspicacity of mommies, the lady for two years had been getting the response out in the presence of the wrong stimuli. The stimuli which were supposed to control the response were those prevailing immediately after the child entered the house; instead, the response was repeatedly evoked in the presence of some stimulus such as, "Please pick up your coat."

To show that the laws of behavior do not change every thirty years or so, it is worth examining one more example. Evans relates that, during a visit, his four-year-old niece was exhibiting a minor, but irritating, behavior disorder.* The child, who was nicely toilet trained, never seemed able to remember to flush the toilet at the appropriate

* J. L. Evans, personnal communication, 1965.

time. Instead, she would leave the bathroom and have to be ordered back to do that job.

This problem, it turned out, had persisted for at least a couple of years until finally Uncle Jim intervened. Instead of ordering the child back to flush the toilet, he instructed her to make believe that she was just finishing going to the toilet; she was to make believe to the extent that she was to take down her pants, climb up on the toilet, imagine she was just finishing, get off the toilet, pull up her pants, then flush the toilet and rejoin the adults. This exercise worked; the child gives every sign that she will grow up to be a happily married lady who flushes the toilet a lot.

><

THE EFFECTIVENESS OF GUTHRIE'S TECHNIQUE

There are at least two considerations which account for the effectiveness of Guthrie's technique of getting the *S* to go back and run off some of the behavior chain which leads up to the point of difficulty. The first is that the effect of a stimulus persists for some time after the stimulus is terminated. The second is that an important portion of the stimuli which are going to control behavior is response-produced.

Both of these factors can be seen at work in the case of Guthrie's example. The effects of the "outdoor stimuli" obviously do not terminate the instant the child crosses the threshold. If it is a brisk day, for example, she may still be feeling the effects of the cold, she may be panting from running, and the little tyke may even be saying sentences to herself such as, "Christ, it's cold today."

It is worth noticing in the same example that all of the stimulus changes under discussion were produced by the behavior of the organism: The visual and other changes brought about when the *S* opened the door; the changes in stimulation caused by the removal of the coat and dropping it on the floor; the other changes in visual stimuli caused by the child's moving her head or her eyes. Note that a description of proprioceptive stimuli, as important as they may be, was not required in this discussion of response-produced stimuli. This is worth noting because sometimes proprioceptive stimuli and response-produced stimuli tend to get equated when, of course, they should not be.

In summary, then, the technique of requiring the *S* to run off the part of the behavioral chain just preceding the response which is giving difficulty is as successful as it is, because it is a way of ensuring that the stimulus which is to control the response is, in fact, reinstated. Notice that this is true whether or not the behavioral engineer can specify all of the portions of the stimulus complex which are likely to be present when the response is to be executed; running off the immediately preceding chain members automatically guarantees the presence of the control stimuli.

✕

AN EXAMPLE OF BEHAVIORAL ENGINEERING:
TEACHING PHONIC READING

There are children who cannot read, but whose parents or teachers insist that they "know phonics." It may be true that they know phonics in the sense that, shown any letter, they can give its sound. Thus, to the printed-word stimulus *cat* the student can respond, "cuh-aa-tuh." It is from here on that trouble arises. To the self-generated stimulus, "cuh-aa-tuh," he may respond "supersonic transport," or whatever else happens to be at high strength at the moment. Analysis of phonic reading, then, yields the kind of chain shown in Figure 2.

$$\text{visual stimulus} \rightarrow \text{vocal response} \rightarrow \text{auditory stimulus} \rightarrow \text{vocal response}$$

$$\text{CAT} \rightarrow \text{"cuh-aa-tuh"} \rightarrow \text{"cat"}$$

FIGURE 2. Stimulus-response analysis of a beginning phonic reading sequence.

It is obvious that the hypothetical S who responds "supersonic transport" simply has not learned the last member of the chain — the translation of "cuh-aa-tuh" to "cat." In the laboratory, the last member of the chain is the first one taught (Homme and Klaus, 1967); so we adopted the same strategy in teaching reading. The first thing taught to the child is the "sound-the-word game," which consists in making reinforcing events contingent upon the child's translating phoneticized words. For example, the contingency manager may say to the child, "Tell me what I'm saying: 'Chuh-air.'" The child who knows the game will answer, "Chair." The contingency manager then says, "Good. Choose what you'd like to play with from the menu." It has been our experience that very shortly the child begins to make up phoneticized words with which to puzzle the contingency manager.

Once the end of the chain (the translation skill) has been established, it is a simple matter to move up the chain, step by step.

With these kinds of procedures, it has been possible to keep preschool children responding eight hours a day and to teach phonic reading in a matter of days, rather than semesters or years.

✖

BEHAVIORAL ENGINEERING RESEARCH

The behavioral engineering field is at about the same stage of development as Goddard's rocket program was in 1935 (Lehman, 1963). At this time, those who know about such matters say that not only had the basic research been done, but plenty of technology was available to put an object into space. (Goddard had already blasted a rocket up a thousand feet.) What was required, and what took our society about twenty years to realize, was a real effort at implementation.

Just as space scientists and engineers did not have to wait until the "gravitational process" was better understood before the law of gravity could be exploited, so behavioral engineering need not wait until the "learning process" is better understood before it can get on with some important jobs. For openers, we in the field can develop a technology for routinely producing superior human beings. We may have sufficient technology — here and now (Homme, 1967) — to be able to guarantee that, given a physiologically normal human being, and given control of his reinforcement contingencies and stimulus conditions, we can shape him into a superior organism. He will be superior not only intellectually, but emotionally as well. He will be happier than most; he will have a better self concept; he will have a better repertoire in all the ways we can think of to make it better. Another way of saying this is that we have the technology for installing any behavior we want. The problem now is to decide what behaviors we want installed. Some leading candidates are a preschool academic repertoire, a favorable self concept, love, and joy.

The Intellectual Repertoire of the Preschool Child

No one knows how much a preschool child can learn, despite the thousands of developmental studies on how much children *usually* learn by a given age. There is no research which has, in a systematic manner, explored the limits of a child's capacity to learn when contingencies were intelligently managed, and stimulus control criteria were met.

Since behavioral engineering views reading as discriminative responding, the ridiculous problem of "When is the child ready to read?" never arises. From a behavioral engineering standpoint, a child is reading objects as soon as he can discriminatively respond to them (for example, name them). Once a child has begun to read, no one knows, really, how fast his education may proceed. With the opportunity to read coupled with unsystematic contingency management, one scholar who learned to read at age three read at the fifth-grade level by the time she was five.* (Her brother, the control group, learned to read exactly when educational researchers said he should — at 6.5 years of age.) Once having learned to read, even at a primitive level, the child can begin going through existing programmed instructional materials — say, in arithmetic. With contingency management, the excuse that existing programs are boring, dull, or no good, is not valid. One does not hear the rat in the Skinnerbox or the human at the slot machine complain about the dullness of his task. He eagerly does his job, although he may have done the same thing hundreds of times before. And programmed instruction, even when bad, does offer more variety than slot machines; the payoffs are what remain to be arranged.

And even if stimulus control in the program is faulty — as is often the case — the faults can be corrected by means of progress checks. Progress checks are short tests on material just covered in the program — criterion items which should have been, but were not, built into the program. The sequence of events shown in Figure 3 thus results.

N frames of program → progress check → reinforcer

FIGURE 3.   Sequence of events which maintains behavior and insures appropriate stimulus control.

With a schedule of events of this sort, no one knows how fast a child's intellectual development might proceed. We do have enough preliminary data to know that there is no danger in "pushing" a child too fast with such a system. Three-year-olds have been kept working eight hours a day with no signs of the "I don't want to do this any more" response. On the contrary, having found a place where someone was willing to pay off for desired behavior rather than punish for

* J. L. Evans, personal communication, 1967.

unwanted behavior, they wanted more of the same at the end of the day — to the despair of the worn-out contingency managers.

Joy

Psychologists have been assiduous in studying the unpleasant aspects of life. Pain, depression, and anxiety have received considerable attention, but the same cannot be said for joy and happiness. No "Manifest Joy Scale" exists. The point is, the serious study of joy is overdue.

Skinner (1953, p. 127) has observed that the emotion called joy involves the whole repertoire of the organism: "our [joyful] subject speaks to everyone, reacts in an exaggerated fashion, walks faster and seemingly more lightly, and so on. This is particularly obvious in the behavior of young children — for example, on the eve of a holiday or festival."

It may be that the overwhelming nature of this fact — that joy involves the whole repertoire — is what has impeded the study of joy. Behavioral engineering certainly has no tools for dealing directly with a whole repertoire at once. But if we behavioral engineers take seriously what Keller and Schoenfeld (1950) and Skinner (1953) have said about what joy is, we can reduce the joy problem to manageable size. They say that joy is the anticipation of reinforcing events. This simple, but profound, observation is clearly borne out by the amount of laughter and smiling which occurs when children's contingencies are planfully managed. Reinforcements are frequent, and there is little doubt that the child quickly learns to anticipate reinforcing events and to plan what he will next select from a reinforcing event menu.

In order for the behavioral engineer to strengthen the joy response, then, he calls for it immediately preceding a reinforcing event. To a child, for example, he says, "Tell me something good that's going to happen to you; then go to the menu and choose what you'd like to do." In less formal situations the same rules hold: Make the *S* pay for reinforcing events by verbalizing the anticipation of other reinforcing events. "Tell me something good that you're going to do, and then we'll go to the store."

Of course, since everyone is an organism, one can try this out on oneself. One can increase the frequency with which one coverants joy events (Homme, 1967) and observe the effect. (The word "coverants" is a contraction of covert operant, and is pronounced "kuhverant"; when used as a verb, it means "think about," "imagine.") A convenient property of self-management research is that one always has an *S* close at hand.

Love

Joy is difficult to define, but perhaps even more difficult is love. Many famous writers, for example, have written a great many words to persuade the reader that the love *he* is talking about is indescribable. That may be so, but the behavioral engineer, assuming that love in the repertoire is desirable, must get on with the job of trying to install it.

If one examines the behavior of a human who is said to exhibit love, one can quickly detect one very public behavior. This is verbal behavior with the verb "love" in it. Assuming that this is a genuine signal of love, or an approximation to it, it is a straightforward matter to install this kind of verbal behavior. For example, the following class of verbal behaviors can be easily and quickly installed in a *S*'s repertoire.

"Why do you love Becky [the contingency manager]?"

"I love Becky because..."

If one also accepts the proposition that love is manifested by a tendency to reinforce, then another approximation would be to evoke and strengthen reinforcing verbal behavior in the *S*. "Go whisper to Becky that you love her because..." Observations suggest that verbal behavior such as this from a preschool *S* can turn an adult on. This state of affairs makes it almost unnecessary to instruct the contingency manager to reinforce. We have the impression that she couldn't refrain if she tried.

A Favorable Self Concept

A favorable concept of the self is also a complex phenomenon, we are told. How can you teach someone to think favorably of himself? Put this way, the question may indeed seem formidable. However, analysis leads to the same conclusion as that to which Ellis (1958) has come. To speak of a self concept may simply be to talk about the aggregate of sentences the *S* says to himself (and to others) about himself. Viewed in this light, to install a favorable self concept one simply strengthens a class of verbal behavior. After a good performance, one says, "That was a fine job. Go whisper to your teacher, 'I am a fast learner.'" At this point, the teacher reinforces verbally and by making the menu available. It has been our experience that after a very few trials of this sort, the "I am a fast learner" conception of himself competes quite successfully with the child's "I sure am dumb" concept.

A similar technology can be brought to bear in psychotherapy. For example, the "poor, helpless me" self concept is replaced by the self-mastery statement, "I'm in charge of my own behavior," by having *S* program himself so that this coverant occurs with high frequency.

There are many, many fascinating engineering research areas which have not been touched upon, of course. For example, Bandura's modeling concepts (1964), if taken seriously, suggest that before a great child can become a great adult, he has to know a great adult. Behavioral engineers may have to face up to the fact that the Fred Skinners of the world are not spread thin enough.

~ 4 ~

A Program of Research
in Behavioral Electronics

**Ralph Schwitzgebel, Robert Schwitzgebel, Walter N. Pahnke,
& William Sprech Hurd**

The objective of behavioral electronics is the application of electronics to the understanding, maintenance, and modification of human behavior. Although this objective is becoming increasingly feasible in view of the rapid advances in instrumentation, telemetry, and molecular engineering, it has as yet received little attention from either experimental or clinical psychologists. Perhaps this lag exists because the content of behavioral electronics falls within that vast excluded area between the laboratory of the experimental psychologist and the clinic of the psychotherapist. And here, between the laboratory and the clinic, lies almost the entire natural environment of humanity, practically untouched and unexplored by direct scientific procedures.

Hefferline (1962, p. 100) has urged a greater use of newly available devices, techniques, and situations. He comments: "There is no intention [here] to applaud the psychologist turned gadgeteer. However, although instrumentation of itself cannot solve the problems of psychology, it may be remembered that astronomy found the telescope helpful and that the study of fine structure took a turn for the better with the invention of the microscope.... With artificial eyes, ears, and hands, recording impartially and without lapse of attention, the psychologist, as he deals with a complex situation, gets a fuller and more trustworthy answer to the question of what is going on."

From *Behavioral Science*, 9 (1964), 233–238.

The use of electronics as an aid to observation is only the first level of potential application. The next level would be the use of electronic instruments in therapy as interventional or prosthetic devices. An even more advanced level of application would be the direct control of behavior by restricting voluntary actions or by eliciting involuntary ones. Beyond this, there is the possible integration of electronic systems to permit one or more persons to function at various behavioral levels as an integrated unit.

It should be clear that the term "behavioral electronics" as used here is intended to imply not only a technological development but a conceptual one as well. Let us turn first, however, to an examination of some specific advances in technology.

➤

RECENT TECHNOLOGICAL DEVELOPMENTS

A person wearing electronic equipment is no longer entangled in a complicated series of wires. Some FM transmitters broadcasting within a range of several feet are small enough to be worn inside the body or even swallowed (Mackay, 1961). Nearby receivers may then pick up these signals and retransmit them. The respiration rate of a flying duck has been monitored (Lord, Bellrose, and Cochran, 1962) and the brain wave activity of freely wandering cats has been recorded (Sperry, Gadsden, Rodriguez, and Bach, 1961). The molecular engineering of electronic circuits opens even greater possibilities of miniaturization (von Hipple, 1959; Rosenblith, 1961). Pressure-sensitive paint or pressure cells called "microducers" are equally significant developments in the area of transducers (Hefferline, 1962).

A small, portable transmitter called a Behavior Transmitter-Reinforcer (BT-R) is now being designed. The BT-R weighs about 20 ounces and is small enough to be easily worn. With a transmitting range of approximately $\frac{1}{4}$ mile under adverse city conditions and a receiving range of about 2 miles, the BT-R may be integrated with a recording graph located at a laboratory base station or the wearer's home. Information about a particular behavior is transmitted to the graph either automatically or manually by the wearer. The BT-R system, now operating on the crowded citizens' band frequencies, is presently capable of handling four people. This number could be effectively increased to fifty or sixty through the use of scrambling mechanisms or by shifting to clearer frequencies. Since each BT-R unit may be designed to transmit and receive a unique pulse train on the same frequency as other BT-R units, the number of people who may be integrated into a BT-R system theoretically depends only upon the band width and clearness of the frequency being used.

One of the central functions of the BT-R, which operates as both a sending and a receiving unit, is the immediate and accurate recording of behavioral events as they occur in the wearer's natural environment. A cumulative record of relevant behaviors of a person or group may be obtained over a considerable period of time. Another feature of the BT-R is that the wearer can receive signals from the base station where the behavior is being recorded. These signals may be arranged into "behavioral feedback" systems which may have considerable therapeutic potential.

><

POTENTIAL APPLICATIONS

Obtaining Behavioral Data

It is increasingly accepted that the symptomatic behaviors of many patients are a result of disturbances in their life situations. Yet techniques for obtaining information about the daily life situations of people are markedly inadequate. Barker and Wright (1954, pp. 2–3) have noted: "Although we have daily records of the behavior of volcanoes, of the tides, of sun spots, and of rats and monkeys, there have been few scientific records of how a human mother cared for her young, how a particular teacher behaved in the classroom and how the children responded, what a family actually did and said during a mealtime, or how any boy lived his life from the time he awoke in the morning until he went to sleep at night. Because we lack such records we can only speculate on many important questions.... Moreover, the lack of field data limits the discovery of some of the laws of behavior. It is often impossible to create in the laboratory the frequency, duration, the scope, the complexity, and the magnitude of some conditions that it is important to investigate.... This should not be discouraging. Experiments in nature are occurring every day. We need only the techniques and facilities to take advantage of them."

Since the memory and report of the respondent is required, data about life situations obtained from interviews and questionnaires are essentially "second-hand." The McCords (1961) have compared 5-year *observation data* on certain behaviors of children with *interview data* on these same behaviors obtained from the mothers of these children. Statistical analyses revealed highly significant differences between these two sets of data (particularly as related to socioeconomic factors). Similar differences between observation and interview data have been reported in studies of morbidity (Gray, 1955; Cartwright, 1963).

In one case which illustrates a possible recording process, a delinquent subject carried a small, manually-operated pocket counter (a theoretical prototype of the BT-R) to record the number of thoughts he had about committing crime (usually breaking and entering and the number of thoughts he had about his girl friend. There were initial, wide fluctuations in the number of recorded thoughts which are characteristic of records in which subjects record subjective phenomena. (Subjects usually describe this initial fluctuation period of ten or twenty days as a time during which they attempt to define for themselves what they mean by a thought or a feeling. After they arrive at a usable concept, there is a relative stability of definition and use, although there are always subjective events which the subject is not sure how to classify — particularly as his subjective feelings change.) After this initial period of adjustment to the recording process, thoughts about his girl friend and thoughts about crime covaried at a statistically significant level. Once when he was frequently thinking about crime, the subject was actually involved in stealing money. In a different case, the frequency of smoking and the recorded impulses to smoke were measured and were simultaneously reduced through the administration of a nicotine derivative. The quantification of subjective events by this or related means may eventually facilitate our correlation and prediction of behaviors.

It is probable that the system of measurement used in these examples produces results different from those which would be obtained by observing a person who is unaware or is not participating as a subject in an experiment (Rosenthal and Fode, 1962; Orne, 1962). At least two types of error may result. The person may fail to record an event which actually did occur or the person may record an event which did not occur. Or the recording system itself may change the actual frequency (or other parameters) of an event. Subject error may be eliminated by using automatic recording equipment. The second type of error or bias, the influence of the recording equipment upon the event to the measured, is much more difficult, perhaps impossible, to eliminate. The usual procedure has been recording without the subject's awareness. For example, the use of electric-eye toll gates in stores probably does not strongly influence the number of people who enter a store. Another approach has been to obtain the subject's cooperation and evaluation in the measurement procedure. This does not eliminate the bias; rather, it attempts to make the effects of the bias clear enough so that the data can be interpreted accurately. The alteration of various parameters of a behavioral event by such an explicit measurement procedure does not invalidate the accuracy of the behavior record *under the specified measurement conditions*. Rather, it restricts the generalization of the data to situations involving similar measurement. The necessary conditions of reliability and inspection can still be met.

Assisting Behavioral Change

The objective recording of a behavior over an extended period of time can provide the therapist with a long-range perspective which would be useful in selecting and evaluating various treatment procedures. Daily or weekly inspection of behavior records could supplement long-term evaluation studies. Frequent inspection may reveal cyclical trends or periodic dysfunctions often obscured by usual sampling techniques or single-inspection follow-up studies. Treatment procedures then can be modified by the therapist on the basis of daily or weekly feedback when they are most appropriate.

Behavior records also contain another therapeutic possibility: the feedback of information from the record to the patient. The patient is provided with a long-range perspective on his behavior in much the same way as the therapist. For example, an overweight teenage subject who wanted to reduce his weight kept a graph of the amount of ice cream eaten each day. The categories ranged from one small ice cream cone to two sundaes. Near the top of the graph the boy drew a line labeled "fat" which suggested to him that if he ate an amount of ice cream recorded above this line he was getting fat. This provided him with a clear visual measure of his daily success or failure. Keeping the line down on the graph acted as a powerful positive reinforcer, while going above the "fat" line acted as a negative reinforcer. Even more significant to him was a trend line (computed by the therapist) indicating the average amount of ice cream eaten. This long-range perspective, combined with the immediate daily reinforcement from the graph, was effective in changing this boy's behavior. This long-range perspective permitted him occasionally to go on ice cream "binges" which he justified (correctly so) by commenting that this would not ruin his weekly or monthly averages; that is, it would not interfere with obtaining his eventual goal.

This flexibility of behavior may be a frequently crucial factor in ego-oriented therapy. Often patients attempt to change completely in a very short period of time, and failing, then resort to the previous behavior with a feeling of helplessness. Lacking a clear temporal perspective, they do not recognize (or cannot experience) their gradual improvement which occurs as a result of growth or learning. The possibilities of therapeutic feedback systems are only now beginning to be investigated (cf. Shpuntoff, 1959; Sidman, 1962).

Another unexplored possibility is the use of electronic equipment as a direct interventional aid. The wearer of the BT-R may receive signals as well as send them. As with a walkie-talkie, two or more people may remain in intermittent or constant contact. However, unlike a walkie-talkie, the units of transmission of the BT-R are not words but behavioral events, feelings, or thoughts translated into coded electronic signals. These signals may have a wide range of meaning to the therapist and patient. They may be supportive, protective, informational, reinforcing, etc., depending upon the specific therapeutic contract between the wearer and the therapist. A mental patient may stay in some kind of communication with the hospital on his first trip into town by himself. Or, a student who has been warned that continued misbehavior in a certain class will result in his dismissal from school may be more able to control his impulses if he can signal his success by a transmitter and receive an immediate response from someone, perhaps a counselor, who is concerned enough to wait for the result. Or a person with suicidal tendencies may send a signal to the therapist as a "cry for help" in a crisis situation.

A communication system which permits such a wide variation in the nature and duration of therapeutic contact contains many dangers as well as possible benefits. It could increase a schizophrenic patient's fear of mind-reading or thought waves. It may foster excessively strong dependency needs with subsequent hostile acting out. Or, it may place too great a burden upon the therapist's time and energy. In fact, the disadvantages of the system may eventually outweigh the advantages; but this is a matter for careful empirical investigation.

Electronic Parole

Society has moved away from the physical confinement of a person to control his behavior. The stockade or the ball and chain were replaced by the institutional courtyard; the courtyard is now being replaced by the farm and half-way house. When specific offending behaviors can be accurately predicted and/or controlled within the offender's own environment, incarceration will no longer be necessary as a means of controlling behavior and protecting society.

The BT-R, as now planned, will be able to transmit information regarding the wearer's geographic location as well as other behavioral data. The location recording will be automatic and accurate within approximately one block within a prescribed 4-square-mile area. Special equipment is available to insure the proximity of the transmitter to the parolee, who may be either a mental patient or a prisoner. The application of this system may be illustrated by a hypothetical case of a parolee who frequently gets into trouble when drinking. The base station could receive telemetry information that the parolee is drinking. If his drinking becomes excessive, the parolee can be geographically located and a person sent to intervene in the situation before an offense is committed.

The use of such a system actually extends the rights of parolees by allowing them to live with their families and keep their jobs when they would otherwise be incarcerated. Society is also more surely protected against additional offenses than if the parolee is released without extensive surveillance. Furthermore, the parolee may at any time refuse parole and return to the institution if he finds that the system is not to his advantage. Although electronic surveillance is much more accurate and complete than the present parolee-inspection techniques, its area of control is much more specific and is limited to the particular offending behavior. This is, in effect, more protective of parolee rights than the present system under which a parolee may be incarcerated on the basis of, or prediction of, an alleged offense. An actual offense would be required for the surrender of the parolee to the institution, and hopefully the system would be capable of preventing such an offense or at least capable of giving the parolee a clear warning and thus a better understanding of the consequences of his choice.

━

SOME ETHICAL CONSIDERATIONS

The application of behavioral electronics to the solution of human problems presents us with social dangers as well as possibilities. The warnings contained in Huxley's *Brave New World*, Orwell's *1984*, or Zamyatian's *We* are relevant here. Indeed, some people may view the suggestion to utilize electronics in their daily personal relationships (excluding perhaps the telephone) as the most drastic invasion of privacy and freedom yet proposed. On the other hand, some people may view the electronic equipment proposed here as simply a kind of "Buck Rogers" toy. It is, however, no longer possible to regard technological advances as neutral or insignificant to human welfare. Such advances have produced atomic energy which, in Rostand's words (1959, p. 63), now compel us "to live our lives in a laboratory of atomic research ... since our houses ... are situated on the same small globe as are the great atomic factories of the West and of the East." Under such circumstances our passivity commits us as completely as our acts of zeal.

Many of the dangers of destruction and control through the misapplication of electronics are apparent. But there is also a less apparent, possible danger which the Christian mystic Berdyaev (1960, p. 226) has observed: "The overwhelming technical achievements of the nineteenth and twentieth centuries produced the greatest revolution in human history, far more important than all political revolutions. They brought about a radical change in the whole rhythm of human life, a break with the natural, cosmic rhythm and the appearance of a new, mechanically determined rhythm. Machinery destroys the old wholeness and unity of human life, it tears away, as it were, the human spirit from organic flesh and mechanizes the material life of man." Berdyaev, however, goes on to point out that within the framework of creative ethics technological progress may stand for "dematerialization and disincarnation, opening up possibilities of greater freedom for the spirit" (p. 227).

At a large hospital in Boston, a husband and wife, both physicians, wear small transmitters to keep in contact. During a laborious and difficult surgical procedure, the husband may receive a brief tone signal from his wife which says, in any words they may use, "I am with you." Thus, the mutuality of their lives is enriched by overcoming the limitations of space. A new horizon opens before us as human relationships can now begin to develop beyond the historical barriers of space and form. "Thus technology will become a world open to Everyman, and Everyman will be able to use its magnifying glass to wonder at human greatness, just as passionately as Rousseau wondered at nature through the magnifying glass of botany" (Armand, 1962).

If, however, we thoughtlessly permit our inventions to design our lives, the future may be quite dim. Alternatively, we may purposefully use our inventions to deepen the quality and outreach of life. Electronics may soon help a young child learn to tie his shoe and at the same time help a diplomat reach decisions of major import. These are immediate possibilities, and having come this far, we can no longer plead neutrality or ignorance.

⤞ 5 ⤝

Behavior Therapy with Children:
A Review and Evaluation
of Research Methodology

Donna M. Gelfand & Donald P. Hartmann

Children have become an increasingly popular client population for behavioristically oriented therapists. Some reasons for the widespread use of learning-theory-based therapy for children's problems may be the comparative brevity of the treatment, the relative ease with which children's social environments can be controlled, and the types of maladaptive behaviors for which children are often referred for treatment. An important element of most behavioristic treatment interventions is the manipulation of the client's environment so that undesirable behavior patterns are eliminated and prosocial responses are positively reinforced (Ullmann and Krasner, 1965, Ch. 1). The requisite environmental control is often easier to achieve for children in their homes and schools than in the typically more complex and varied social interactions of noninstitutionalized adults. Since the young child spends the major part of his time either among his family or at school, the therapist can effectively manipulate the child's social experiences by instructing a fairly small group of people, the teacher and parents. Moreover, these people have considerable control over the child, and are specifically responsible for the child's welfare and for teaching him appropriate behavior patterns.

From *The Psychological Bulletin*, 69:3 (1968), 204–215.

In addition, children are often referred for professional help for maladaptive behaviors which have proved to be among the most amenable to behavior-therapy techniques. When parents or school personnel refer children for treatment, the presenting complaint is often a well-defined behavior, such as bedwetting, a phobia, or temper tantrums — the type of problem which, as Grossberg (1964) has pointed out, behavior therapy most successfully treats. It has also been suggested (Krasner and Ullmann, 1965, p. 57) that the type of specific and detailed instructions parents receive from behavior therapists more nearly meet the parents' initial treatment expectations than do the more general and vague directions, for example to be demonstrative and accepting, traditionally given by children's therapists.

As a consequence, parents may be more likely to aid than to interfere with the therapeutic effort. Parental sabotage is thought to occur notoriously often in the more traditional play-therapy interventions, and it is not uncommon to hear a therapist state his belief that the parents do not sincerely want their child's adjustment to improve. To date, the same charge has not been made with any frequency by behavioristically oriented therapists, who by and large report parents to be cooperative and interested in aiding in the treatment process.

As used here, the term behavior therapy refers to treatment techniques derived from theories of learning and aimed at the direct modification of one or more problem behaviors rather than at effecting more general and less observable personality or adjustment changes. Because behavior therapists assume that both desirable and deviant social responses are learned, their treatment interventions consist of laboratory-derived learning procedures, for example, modeling and operant and classical conditioning.

Results of behavior therapy with a variety of subject samples have previously been reviewed (Bandura, 1961, 1967; Grossberg, 1964; Rachman, 1962; Werry and Wollersheim, 1967) and critically evaluated (Breger and McGaugh, 1965; Weitzman, 1967). It is the purpose of this paper to survey the behavior-therapy literature for subjects between infancy and eighteen years of age, examine the range of problems treated and the methods used, and critically review the adequacy of the therapy-evaluation attempts. This literature review is limited to reports of the clinical application of behavior-modification techniques.

Behavior-therapy studies can conveniently be classified in terms of the desired effect on rates of children's emission of both undesirable and prosocial behaviors. (This classification scheme was suggested by O. R. Lindsley in a workshop presentation, University of Utah, November 30, 1965.) Some treatment interventions aim to decrease the production of problem behaviors, others attempt to enhance the variety and likelihood of occurrence of desirable responses such as adequate language and motor skills, while a third approach combines acceleration of rates of prosocial behaviors with elimination of problem behaviors. This classification schema may have an advantage in clarity over those more commonly employed (for example, Bandura, 1961; Rachman, 1962) in which learning mechanisms have often been confounded with treatment procedures,, for example, extinction and negative practice (Grossberg, 1964). Moreover, a confusing variety of terms has been used to describe essentially identical manipulations; for example, desensitization, reciprocal inhibition, counterconditioning, deconditioning, and unconditioning have all been used to describe a single technique for the treatment of phobias. And finally, the sheer number of categories required by the use of previously employed descriptive terms plus the addition of new terms required by the increased use of operant techniques would be unwieldy.

Some therapy reports reviewed here included more than one technique. A therapist who intended chiefly to use a deceleration technique may have also included some informal social reinforcement of his client's prosocial behaviors. In such cases, the study has been categorized according to the therapist's stated intentions. Any classification system is somewhat arbitrary, and the schema used is designed simply to allow adequate description of a wide range of problems and treatment techniques.

✲

DECELERATION OF MALADAPTIVE BEHAVIORS

A large group of therapeutic interventions have as their aim a deceleration or decrease in the magnitude and frequency of a variety of problem behaviors.

Phobias

The elegant and long-neglected treatment of a child's fear of animals by M. C. Jones (1924a, 1924b) is a deceleration treatment. The technique used by Jones and by others in the behavioristic treatment of phobias involves pairing incompatible experiences of relaxation and enjoyment with the presentation of anxiety-evoking stimuli so that the previously fear-provoking stimuli become associated with pleasurable feelings (Bandura, 1961). Modifications of techniques developed for use with adults by Wolpe and his colleagues (Wolpe, 1958; Wolpe and Lazarus, 1966) are most often used in the treatment of children's phobias. Briefly, the procedure involves the therapist's inducing feelings of relaxation in the child through suggestion, hypnosis, or drugs. An anxiety hierarchy is constructed with items ranging from least to most fear-provoking situations, and the child is helped to imagine progressively stronger fear items under uninterrupted relaxation. This treatment technique has been used to combat irrational fear of water (Bentler, 1962), fear of hospitals and ambulances (Lazarus and Rachman, 1957), school phobia (Garvey and Hegrenes, 1966; Lazarus and Abramovitz, 1962), and dog phobia (Lazarus, 1959). Patterson (1965b) has treated school phobia with a shaping procedure, direct praise and candy reinforcement given to a child for tolerating separation from his mother and for making statements about a boy doll's bravery in a structured doll-play situation. An interesting and methodologically sophisticated variation in the treatment of dog phobia has been described by Bandura, Grusec, and Menlove (1967) who demonstrated that exposure to a fearless peer model displaying approach responses produces stable and generalized reduction in children's avoidance behavior. This study is particularly impressive because the authors (*a*) precisely identified the active therapeutic ingredient through the inclusion of several matched treatment and control groups, (*b*) developed a specialized performance scale to measure the strength of avoidance responses, and (*c*) included pretests and posttests as well as follow-up measures.

Antisocial and Immature Behavior

Behavior therapists have reported considerable success in the treatment of aggressive, antisocial, and immature behaviors. In a relatively early study, Williams (1959) controlled temper tantrums in a twenty-one-month-old child through extinction. The customary reinforcement the parents had accorded the child for his refusal to sleep was abruptly discontinued, and his crying was effectively controlled at the tenth extinction trial. Periods of time out from positive reinforcement have been used to decrease rates of thumbsucking (Baer, 1962), vomiting (Wolf, Birnbrauer, Williams, and Lawler, 1965), and stealing (Wetzel, 1966). A combination of mild punishment and time-out techniques was successfully used to control the generalized negativism of a five-year-old child truly gifted as a troublemaker (Boardman, 1962); aggression in a nursery-school class was controlled by instructing the teachers not to attend to either physical or verbal aggression and instead to reward cooperative behavior (Brown and Elliott, 1965).

Hyperactivity

The hyperactivity often associated with neurological deficit has long been thought unamenable to psychological manipulation and has been treated chiefly by administration of a variety of tranquilizing drugs. Patterson (1965a) and Patterson, Jones, Whittier, and Wright (1965), however, have used positive reinforcement in a classroom setting to control hyperactivity in nine- and ten-year-old boys diagnosed as brain damaged. Observing that the boys' inappropriate activities frequently earned them the acclaim of their classmates, Patterson reinforced the entire class for the subjects' desirable responses, with a consequent increase in their attending behaviors. Doubros and Daniels (1966) also reported success in controlling children's overactive behavior through positively reinforcing low-magnitude responses in a playroom setting, while another group of investigators (Homme, deBaca, Devine, Steinhorst, and Rickert, 1963) imaginatively used the opportunity to engage in noisy play as a reinforcer for children's sitting quietly and attending to their nursery-school teacher. James (1963) reported dramatic changes in a group of five hyperactive children by programming the teacher's behavior so that social reinforcers were made contingent upon the occurrence of socially acceptable behavior.

Tics

A popular technique for the control of tics is massed practice of the problem behavior voluntarily engaged in by the tiqueur. Massed practice has been used successfully with adults (Jones, 1960; Yates, 1958), and Yates predicted that it would be even more effective with child subjects because in their briefer learning histories the tic would not be overlearned so that, according to Hullian learning theory, massed practice would contribute more to growth of reactive inhibition than to habit strength. This expectation has, by and large, not been confirmed in the child-therapy literature. Although Walton (1961) effectively controlled multiple facial, arm, leg, and vocalization tics in an eleven-year-old boy in only 36 treatment sessions and Ernest (1960) reported eliminating a girl's inspiratory tic, two recent studies have reported massed practice to be ineffective in controlling bizarre, repetitive rocking at night (Evans, 1961) and head-jerk and eye-blink tics (Feldman and Werry, 1966). In the latter study, both tics actually increased in frequency over base-line levels as a result of massed practice of the head jerk. A third tic which had previously disappeared also recurred concurrent with the treatment attempt. Feldman and Werry attributed their negative results in this instance to a probable buildup in the child's anxiety level which was thought to be responsible for the tics.

The conditions under which a massed-practice technique will be successful have not yet been well established, and consequently descriptions of therapeutic failures can provide valuable information regarding crucial controlling variables. Unsuccessful outcome may be related to difficulty in policing the massed-practice trials in that the experience is probably very fatiguing and aversive for the child, who will attempt to avoid the practice session whenever possible, thereby defeating the treatment attempt. The therapist must also be careful not to reinforce the tics inadvertently, for example by writing or marking a record sheet each time the tic occurs and thus increasing the rate.

Self-destructive Behavior

Lovaas and his colleagues (Lovaas, Berberich, Perloff, and Schaeffer, 1966; Lovaas, Freitag, Gold, and Kassorla, 1965; Lovaas, Freitag, Kinder, Rubenstein, Schaeffer, and Simons, 1964; Lovaas, Schaeffer, and Simons, 1965) have treated self-injurious behaviors in schizophrenic children through administration of punishment via electric shock, critical comments, and slapping. Once the children's attention was focused on relevant social stimuli, appropriate behaviors could be positively reinforced more effectively. Both time out from reinforcement and electric-shock punishment were used to control a variety of self-destructive responses in a nine-year-old psychotic boy (Tate and Baroff, 1966). Not surprisingly, the shock procedure was the more powerful modification technique. In the course of the avoidance conditioning, the buzzing sound produced by the stock-prod used to administer shock acquired secondary reinforcing properties and was used to promote the child's eating and to control his holding a lake of saliva in his mouth and his persistent clinging to people. Although the main techniques used by Tate and Baroff in this case were time out and punishment, praise was also given the child for his prosocial responses.

✂

ACCELERATION OF PROSOCIAL BEHAVIORS

In some instances, therapists are faced not with the prospect of minimizing undesirable responses, but with increasing the extent of the child's behavior repertoire, which may be inadequate and restricted for his age group (Quay, Werry, McQueen, and Sprague, 1966). For example, Johnston, Kelley, Harris, and Wolf (1966) enhanced the development of motor skills of a generally awkward and inhibited nursery-school boy by making his teachers' attention and approval contingent upon his using a play-yard climbing frame. The same group of investigators also eliminated regressed crawling in a three-year-old girl through differential social reinforcement of her walking rather than crawling (Harris, Johnston, Kelley, and Wolf, 1964) and increased the frequency of peer as opposed to teacher interaction in a socially isolated nursery-school girl (Allen, Hart, Buell, Harris, and Wolf, 1964). In an attempt to maximize the extratherapeutic maintenance of new behaviors, Ferster and Simons (1966) have emphasized the importance of capitalizing on natural reinforcers in dealing with behavioral deficits in disturbed children.

Toilet Training

Toilet training is another developmental task apparently facilitated through judicious use of positive reinforcement (Madsen, 1965; Pumroy and Pumroy, 1965). To increase training efficiency, Van Wagenen and Murdock (1966) have developed a transistorized device which is placed in training pants and automatically activates a tone signal when the child has urinated or defecated, thus allowing parents to shape appropriate toilet use through the method of successive approximations. On successive trials the infant is positively reinforced for elimination closer and closer to the proper location.

The Mowrer electric-alarm method (Mowrer and Mowrer, 1938) and later modifications have seen considerable recent use in the treatment of enuresis (Coote, 1965; Jones, 1960; Lovibond, 1963, 1964; Werry, 1966; Wickes, 1958). Well-controlled studies by De Leon and Mandell (1966) and Werry and Cohrssen (1965) have demonstrated the comparative superiority of the bed-buzzer method over unspecified psychotherapy-counseling techniques and no-treatment controls.

Making positive reinforcement contingent upon bowel movements has been reported to be an effective procedure in cases of encopresis in mental retardates (Dayan, 1964; Hundziak, Mauer, and Watson, 1965), psychotics (Keehn, 1965; Neale, 1963), and children with no other reported problems (Gelber and Meyer, 1965; Peterson and London, 1965). Peterson and London also used hypnotic-like suggestion and reasoning with the child to help promote behavior change.

Retardation

The instatement and acceleration of prosocial behavior have also been accomplished in children displaying severe retardation in the learning of necessary social and motor skills. As a dramatic example, Fuller (1949) trained a bedridden eighteen-year-old vegetative idiot to move his arm to earn a food reinforcer. Rice and McDaniel (1966) provided useful methodological suggestions for manipulating the motor behavior of profoundly retarded children. Psychotic and mentally retarded children have been successfully treated for poverty in generalized imitation tendencies (Metz, 1965), self-help behavior (Bensberg, Colwell, and Cassel, 1965), and speech deficiency (Commons, Paul, and Fargo, 1966; Cook and Adams, 1966; Kerr, Meyerson, and Michael, 1965; Salzinger, Feldman, Cowan, and Salzinger, 1965; Straughan, Potter, and Hamilton, 1965). The treatment techniques used in the latter group of studies were combinations of modeling procedures and positive reinforcement for imitation or correct responding.

◿

MULTIPLE TREATMENT TECHNIQUES

Some studies have combined manipulations designed to promote adaptive behaviors with attempts to decrease the occurrence of problematic behavior. The use of such technique combinations with individual clients appears to be growing in popularity among behavior therapists, possibly because the child who displays a particular maladaptive behavior is likely also to have learned relatively few socially desirable means of acquiring the reinforcement which his deviant responses were intended to secure. Under such circumstances, it is possible that apparent "symptom substitution" will occur, with another problem behavior emerging after a treated deviant response has been successfully eliminated, simply because the child's response hierarchies include few prosocial behavior patterns (Bandura and Walters, 1963, p. 32). Thus the therapist can help prevent the appearance of additional problems by teaching the child alternative desirable responses likely to be maintained through positive reinforcement available in the child's social situation.

Delinquents

Delinquents exhibit a number of undesirable response patterns (for example, stealing, fighting, lying) in combination with a deficiency in prosocial responses (non-cooperation with authorities, irregular work habits, insufficient self-control). Not surprisingly, behavior-therapy interventions with delinquents have frequently involved the use of combined acceleration-deceleration techniques. For example, Burchard and Tyler (1965) used time out in an isolation room to control an institutionalized delinquent boy's antisocial behaviors, and at the same time positively reinforced his adaptive behaviors. He was awarded tokens which could be turned in for a number of reinforcing events for each hour he managed to remain out of isolation. Tyler (1965) has also reported successful use of time out in an isolation room for delinquents' misbehavior while playing pool. In the same paper, Tyler described promising pilot-study data indicating that reinforcing an adolescent delinquent's approximations to satisfactory academic performance will produce improvement in his school grades. Schwitzgebel (1967) has also demonstrated a significant increase in adolescent delinquents' cooperative and constructive behaviors when this class of responses was followed by positive consequences such as verbal praise or a gift. In a matched delinquent group, attempted punishment of hostile, antisocial statements through the therapist's disagreement or inattention failed to produce a corresponding decrease in deviant responding. Since Schwitzgebel's subjects were not institutionalized and engaged in the interview sessions on a purely voluntary basis, the experimenters were reluctant to jeopardize the boys' willingness to participate by exposing them to powerful aversive stimuli. Consequently, it is probable that the aversive consequences for deviant responses were simply too mild to have any effect, as Schwitzgebel himself hypothesized. In an earlier study (Schwitzgebel and Kolb, 1964), prosocial behavior was increased in adolescent delinquents through administration of positive reinforcers (small change and cigarettes) on a variable-interval schedule. The boys received reinforcement for keeping appointments, appropriately discussing and analyzing their feelings, and performing job-training tasks. Three years after termination of treatment, these subjects showed a significant reduction in frequency and severity of criminal offenses as compared to a matched-pair control group.

Autistic Behaviors

Simultaneous use of acceleration and deceleration techniques has proved to be a powerful approach to the treatment of particularly maladaptive and resistant behavior patterns, such as those often observed in psychotic children (Lovaas, Freitag, Gold, and Kassorla, 1965). For example, working with a severely autistic three-year-old boy, Wolf, Risley, and Mees (1964) produced considerable positive behavior change through a combination of positive reinforcement (food) and the procedure, described as "mild punishment and extinction," of isolating the boy in his bedroom when he had a temper tantrum. Other investigators have described similar brief isolation sessions as time out from positive reinforcement (Hawkins, Peterson, Schweid, and Bijou, 1966). Similarly, Zimmerman and Zimmerman (1962) have combined extinction of bizarre and tantrum behaviors with social reinforcement for appropriate responses in a special classroom situation, and Marshall (1966) has successfully used food reinforcement and mild punishment (slaps on the buttocks, extinguishing room lights) to toilet train an eight-year-old autistic child. Davison (1964) reported extinction of fear and aggressive responses as well as increased responsiveness to adult requests in a nine-year-old autistic girl through contingent application of candy, attention, and opportunities to look into a mirror and withdrawal of social reinforcement for undesirable behavior. Treatment of nonpsychotic children's aggression (Gittelman, 1965; Sloane, Johnston, and Bijou, 1966), storm phobia and anorexia nervosa (Hallsten, 1965; White, 1959), school phobia (Lazarus, Davison, and Polefka, 1965), and operant crying (Hart, Allen, Buell, Harris, and Wolf, 1964) seems also to be facilitated through simultaneous use of acceleration and deceleration techniques.

Parental Training

A new treatment technique which seems to have considerable promise is the training of parents to become appropriate reinforcement dispensing agents. In some instances, parents are invited to observe reinforcement-treatment sessions, first, to see that the reinforcement contingency actually does control their child's problem behavior, and second, to learn how and when to dispense reinforcers, both tangible and social. Thus far, parents have been reported to have been successfully trained as behavior therapists for their children's antisocial behavior (Hawkins, 1966; Russo, 1964; Straughan, 1964; Wahler, Winkel, Peterson, and

Morrison, 1965; Zeilberger, Sampen, and Sloane, 1966), excessive scratching and self-mutilation (Allen and Harris, 1966), and psychotic temper tantrums (Wetzel, Baker, Roney, and Martin, 1966). Patterson and Brodsky (1966) have made an ambitious attempt to treat a child's multiple problem behaviors through the concurrent use of several conditioning programs, including training the parents. The child's temper tantrums were modified through the use of an extinction-counterconditioning procedure; his separation-anxiety reactions were treated through another extinction-counterconditioning program; positive reinforcement was used to increase his positive interactions with peers; and his parents were trained to extinguish his negativistic and immature behaviors and to reward any evidence of cooperation and independence. Since there is some evidence that the environmental reinforcement contingencies to which delinquents (Buehler, Patterson, and Furniss, 1966) and adult psychotics (Gelfand, Gelfand, and Dobson, 1967) are exposed probably maintain their deviant behaviors, it is likely that the best hope for permanent positive behavior change rests in modifying the client's social environment. In the case of children, it may well prove more efficacious to modify the parents' child-rearing practices than to bring the child to the laboratory or clinic for direct interaction with the therapist. Parental education of this type may well have important preventive aspects also in that parents who are aware of the nature of their control of their children's behavior may be better able to prevent the occurrence of future problems and to promote appropriate interpersonal behavior.

⤫

RESEARCH METHODOLOGY

Paradigms for research using the more traditional treatment versus-control-groups designs have been discussed in detail elsewhere (Bergin, 1966; Goldstein, Heller, and Sechrest, 1966; Kiesler, 1966); only the evaluation of treatment as reported in case studies is dealt with here. As is the case with traditional play-therapy evaluation reports, the vast majority (96 per cent) of the papers on behavior therapy of children here reviewed are case studies which describe modification of the behavior of individual subjects or of small groups of children displaying similar problem behaviors. Some writers have concluded that demonstrations of therapeutic efficacy with single cases represent no scientifically acceptable evidence at all. For example, Breger and McGaugh (1965) have argued that the behavior therapists' reliance upon single-subject therapy evaluations necessarily creates doubts about their claims of therapeutic success, and that, therefore, most of the reported successes "must be regarded as no better substantiated than those of any other enthusiastic school of psychotherapy" (p. 351). This criticism has application only insofar as the methods used by therapy researchers studying individual subjects fail to meet the criteria usually applied to laboratory "free operant" studies. The "single organism, within-subject design" (Dinsmoor, 1966) has been extensively described elsewhere (Bachrach, 1964; Honig, 1966; Sidman, 1960, 1962). Only a few of the major features are taken up here. The contention here is that use of this method in therapy evaluation can powerfully demonstrate behavior control if certain specified procedures are followed. For instance, adequate base-line measures of the occurrence of the problem behavior (and, when applicable, frequency of prosocial responses) should be collected over a period of time long enough to provide reliable rate information. Obviously, these data should be collected in a rigorous, planned manner and not retrospectively recounted by the child's parents or teachers, as is frequently done in both traditional and behavior-therapy case studies. The therapist-experimenter should also provide a specific and detailed description of the treatment procedures, which should include sufficient data to permit replication by other investigators. Included should be information on the total number of treatment sessions, the length of each session, description of the spacing of sessions over time, and the total time span of the therapeutic intervention. The nature and extent of contacts with parents, teachers, and other involved individuals also ought to be provided. This body of information allows the reader to make comparisons regarding the efficiency and power of various treatment techniques. The work of Paul (1966), Lang and Lazovik (1963), and Lang, Lazovik, and Reynolds (1965) provides a high standard for the description of treatment procedures. Paul also presented a useful analysis of problems and alternative stategies in the design of therapy-evaluation studies.

Therapy-process data on the rate of occurrence of the behavior under investigation should be collected during every treatment session. Continuous data collection during therapy aids both in precise identification of the variables controlling the child's behavior and in the evaluation of treatment efficacy (Reyna, 1964).

A technique refinement not often observed is the systematic variation of the treatment reinforcement contingencies. After substantial and apparently reliable behavior modification has taken place, the reinforcement contingencies should be altered temporarily, for example reversed, so the problem behavior is once again reinforced or the prosocial response, instated through positive reinforcement, extinguished. Correlated changes in the observed response rate provide a convincing demonstration that the target behavior is unmistakably under the therapist's control and not due to adventitious, extratherapeutic factors. This design feature is extremely important, if not essential, when $N = 1$, as Sidman (1960) and Dinsmoor (1966) have pointed out. The problem of the feasibility of such reinforcement-contingency reversals in clinical research is a knotty one, but this procedure should have high priority when the report is presented as a research study and the method described is to be taken seriously as an effective treatment technique. If the problem behavior precludes the reinstatement of natural contingencies, a number of substitute techniques might be considered. Use of a yoked control treated identically to the treatment subject with the exception that the active therapeutic ingredient is not systematically administered should prove useful in desensitization studies where contingency reversal is not feasible. Demonstration of behavioral control also might be accomplished by breaking the target behavior into subunits, for example on the basis of response magnitude or object, and independently manipulating the separate units (a technique suggested by Florence R. Harris). Less desirable substitutes for complete contingency reversal include the following control techniques: contingency changes that have predictable effects on response emission, for example, schedule changes; contingency reversal for a limited aspect of the target behavior and/or for the target behavior under limited, discriminable conditions.

Unfortunately, all of the previously discussed experimental control procedures are undermined if the accuracy of the rate measures is open to question. As in all psychotherapy research, extreme care must be taken to assure that truly objective behavior observations and measures are used. Since therapists are notoriously unobjective observers when the validity of their favorite treatment technique is in question, the best procedure would require either automatic recording of the target behaviors or the use of observers who are naive regarding the treatment procedure. Two additional refinements used by Brackbill (1958) in her study of the extinction of the smiling response in infants seem highly desirable for use in therapy evaluation also. First, sound-film recordings should be made at several points in the treatment process to permit independent and, if necessary, repeated observer reliability checks. Such a film record would also be useful to therapists wishing to learn techniques not adequately described in the published report. Another impressive design feature used by Brackbill was the establishment of high inter-observer reliability prior to the inception of the study proper, a procedure rarely, if ever, followed in the child-therapy research literature where observer reliability is typically shaped while the behavior modification is proceeding. A possible result is that the observations made early in therapy lack reliability.

Lest the state of affairs in the reliability department look too black, it should be pointed out that the types of behaviors usually dealt with by behavior therapists are well defined, easily observed, and difficult to mistake, for example, the incidence of temper tantrums, enuresis, or speech deficit. Therefore, observer bias should affect the results less seriously than in cases of variables less rigorously defined, such as lack of positive self-regard, covert hostility, or high anxiety. Nevertheless, investigators should not ignore Rosenthal's convincing demonstrations (1963, 1964) that experimenter bias can distort results even when seemingly very unmistakable response classes are under study.

One further therapy-evaluation procedure which should be undertaken in single-case as well as in treatment versus control group designs is a follow-up analysis of the stability of the behavior modification. A series of follow-up evaluations over a period of time, perhaps several years, would provide much-needed information concerning "symptom substitution" and generalization effects and would be a highly desirable design feature. Naturally, it is proposed that any follow-up data collection be made in a form more rigorous than the all too typical therapist's phone call to the child's parents or teacher, a procedure very likely to be subject to the Hello-Goodbye effect (Hathaway, 1948); the persons contacted for information feel it is only polite to assure the therapist that he had helped the child, whether or not any change in behavior is actually observable.

Unfortunately, many of the behavior-therapy studies reviewed here fail to meet most of the assessment standards suggested in the evaluation paradigm and thus represent no improvement over the traditional clinical case study in terms of experimental rigor. Nevertheless, in contrast to the play-therapy case-study literature, there are a small but growing number of carefully designed behavior-therapy case studies which meet most, if not all, of the suggested evaluation criteria and which convincingly demonstrate the power and efficiency of behavioristic treatment approaches (Allen, 1964; Doubros and Daniels, 1966; Harris, 1964; Wahler, 1965). While it is still possible to argue the merits of the theoretical bases for behavior-therapy techniques, careful application of the "single organism, within-subject design" should leave little question about the method's effectiveness.

II

BEHAVIORAL APPROACHES
TO MENTAL RETARDATION

CHRISTMAS IN PURGATORY IS THE PROVOCATIVE TITLE OF A photographic essay by Blatt and Kaplan (1967) showing several state institutions for mentally retarded children and adults. There, in somber black and white photographs, retarded persons are shown to exist in a shadowed world made by their keepers. Although the deadening and harmfully poor care too often given the retarded and the mentally "disturbed" has been discussed for two thousand years, one need only read the personal account of Clifford Beers (1908), or the discussions by Bockoven (1963), Ullmann and Krasner (1965), Dain (1964), or Ullmann (1967) to realize that current modes of patient care remain largely primitive in character and negative in effect. We are only beginning to accept the very old idea that perhaps much of what we have considered to be the patients' own condition of internal disturbance or irreversible mental limitations is after all produced or at the least sustained by the very environment designed to help them. Pinel's question, "How are we to distinguish between the exasperation caused by the chains, and the symptoms peculiar to the illness?" though voiced in the nineteenth century, still awaits an answer. The chains in modern institutions are not forged steel, but patients are nevertheless restrained by a complex web of differential reinforcement which sustains withdrawn passivity and socially maladaptive or bizarre behavior, i.e., the very behavior which, as Ullmann and Krasner (1965) suggest, may serve as an artificially created justification for continued stay in the institution. Severely psychotic or retarded persons are especially subject to this differential reinforcement; for them the staff member may have such low expectations that he abandons any attempt to teach even simple self-help behavior and instead shapes up and maintains severely dependent behavior. Institutions may thus become, as Patterson (1963) noted, vast "teaching machines" that help to maintain patients as patients.

There has recently been more recognition that patient behavior is dependent to a great extent upon the nature of the institutional environment, and that modifying specific aspects of the environment can modify even severe behavior. As scientific observation of human behavior has been augmented, a good beginning has been made in analyzing the factors operating upon specific patients and in systematically controlling those variables with the aim of modifying the patient's behavior. The classic work of Ayllon (1963) and Ayllon and Michael (1959) has demonstrated effectiveness in modifying, through relatively simple environmental manipulation by ward staff, even severely psychotic behavior.

Institutions for the mentally retarded are faced with bizarre and seemingly subhuman behavior by many of their charges. Until recently, institutional staff members paid little attention to the science of human behavior provided by psychology, and thus did not believe that much could be accomplished. The institutions were, and many still are, pessimistic places for inmates thought to have such gross intellectual and motor limitations that they could not learn normal, adaptive, human behavior. After all, what can we hope to do with a fifteen-year-old girl who operates on a seven-month social level? (Chapter 8.) What of a sixteen-year-old mute boy who vomits eight or nine times a day, and is regularly joined by other patients in consuming the vomitus? (Chapter 6.) What of a twenty-six-year-old man who lies on the floor and cries because he fears stairs? (Chapter 6.) The task accepted by the institution, to "help" such people, is formidable. Lacking a scientific method, the institution reaches only continued failure which, in time, erodes an original optimism and produces the cynicism of pessimistic, economy-minded custodial care.

Attempts have recently been made to utilize conditioning principles in modifying the behavior of severely retarded children. Fuller (1949) and Rice and McDaniel (1966) have attempted conditioning procedures even with profoundly retarded, vegetative patients. Rice and McDaniel point out that even profoundly retarded children with severe metabolic defects, who "function on a near-zero behavioral level," were found to respond differentially to a limited array of basic reinforcers.

Luckey, Watson, and Musick (1968) utilized an electric stimulator belt worn by a severely retarded six-year-old boy in aversive conditioning to inhibit chronic vomiting. The authors report rapid control over the behavior and no recurrence during a 93-day follow-up period. They also noted a general improvement in the child's over-all behavior, with his becoming "increasingly amenable to self-care training."

In another important study, Baer, Peterson, and Sherman (1967) approached higher-level behavior of retarded children. Through systematic training utilizing food and verbal rewards, they established imitative behavior in retarded children who previously were "without spontaneous imitative behavior, either vocal or motor." The authors suggested that social imitation, an important learning medium for most children, may characteristically be lacking in mentally retarded children. Thus the educational implications of teaching children how to imitate may be of considerable value, basic to the task of teaching complex social behavior to retarded children.

The papers reproduced in this section report a variety of behavioral approaches to retarded children. Dependent, regressed, and even grossly bizarre behavior may inadvertently be reinforced and maintained by well-meaning and too often overburdened staff. This point is made by Blackwood and his colleagues, by Whitney and Barnard, and by Hundziak, et al., who utilized the direct-care staff of attendants and nurses to carry out training programs. These authors describe their efforts to modify basic behaviors such as eating, vomiting, toilet and phobic behaviors of severely retarded children.

Minge and Ball employed ward technicians to teach limited self-help skills to six girls whose IQ's ranged from 10 to 24. It is clear from the results that it is possible to teach self-help skills to even profoundly retarded children.

Esposito describes his attempts to overcome long-standing deficits in motor behavior of retarded children. He reports part of a larger project aimed at introducing behavior modification approaches into a state agency for retarded children.

Doubros, working with higher-level retardates, attempted to alter nonverbal behavior, such as general social cooperation, through the continued repetition of socially appropriate and positive verbal statements in weekly therapy sessions. The appropriate verbalizations were "drilled" during therapy sessions, and the child's correct verbalizations were reinforced by the therapist's attention. Although Doubros' article reports an essentially exploratory attempt, it suggests that highly reinforced, appropriate verbal phrases might become important cues for later appropriate behavior in high-level, retarded children.

The use of conditioning procedures to modify significantly even the most bizarre behavior of retarded children, as well as higher-level verbal and social behavior, offers potentially powerful teaching or therapeutic tools. Continued demonstrations of learning-theory approaches will, hopefully, lead to a relatively well-delineated technology which can easily be taught to direct-care staff and thus become an integral part of the institution's environment. In this way "therapy" may be moved from the relative exclusiveness and mystery of the clinician's office to the more powerful domain of the teacher, nurse, and attendant.

⊰ 6 ⊱

Operant Conditioning of Social Behaviors in Severely Retarded Patients

Ralph O. Blackwood, John E. Horrocks, Tina F. Keele, Marcel Hundziak, & Judith H. Rettig

A number of laboratory studies have indicated that severely retarded patients respond to operant conditioning about as well as lower organisms and normal human subjects. Ellis, Barnett, and Pryer (1960) found that defectives of the type usually labeled "untestable" (seldom included in psychological experiments because of their extremely limited skills) actually adapt readily to operant conditioning procedures and that even subjects of lowest intelligence are sensitive to changes in schedules of reinforcement. Both Orlando and Bijou (1960) and Spradlin (1962) also report that severely retarded children respond to operant conditioning procedures. In each of the studies cited above, however, the investigators found that the behavior of the retarded patients was a little less reliable or less sensitive to the controlling conditions than that of lower organisms. In other words, the evidence indicates that the recently developed principles of teaching, based on reinforcement principles, could apply to severely retarded patients but with somewhat less precision in behavioral control.

The study reported here was carried out at the Columbus State School on patients diagnosed as severely or profoundly retarded. These patients were part of a special treatment unit with a patient-staff ratio of 10:1. In addition, the unit had the full-time services of a psychiatrist, a physician, and a psychologist.

Preliminary exploratory observations indicated that much of the ongoing behavior of the patients was under control of easily identifiable reinforcers. In the dining room the strongest reinforcers seemed to be food, as would be expected. The responses which were most often and most consistently reinforced by food seemed to occur with the highest frequency. For example, patients would reach across the table for other patient's food before eating their own. Aggressive patients were reinforced by receiving more food. Most patients indiscriminately crammed food into their mouths at a high rate, hardly chewing at all. This behavior was consistently reinforced, since it enabled patients to consume more in an apparently competitive situation. Patients who ate slowly had their food stolen and were punished by receiving less food, despite constant supervision. Nearly all the patients had learned a rather complex set of operant behaviors which were effective in getting them to the table. A number of mealtime responses were under stimulus control of the signal that the meal was ready. When a meal was announced, most patients walked down the hall, made the correct turn at a four-way intersection, entered the correct door and sat down in front of a food tray, perhaps snatching some food before seating themselves. It was apparent that these patients were not learning socially acceptable eating habits, but it was also clear that they had learned certain complex behaviors which produced immediate unconditioned reinforcers.

On the ward, one of the strongest reinforcers was the attention of attendants and nurses, whether they were approving or censuring. The fact that attention given by staff members is a most important reinforcer is consistent with the findings of Ayllon and Michael (1959) on psychiatric wards. Since the attendant-patient ratio was low and the frequency of destructive or socially disruptive behaviors was comparatively high, attendants spent much time and energy attempting to terminate or to prevent undesirable behaviors. Thus, the very patients who exhibited little or no undesirable behaviors and who caused no trouble were usually ignored and deprived of the reinforcing attention. On the other hand, a patient who screamed, who attacked another patient, or who engaged in other unruly, disturbing, or harmful behaviors often received immediate attention. No matter how busy an attendant might be with ward duties, certain behaviors were not permitted.

By rearranging the contingencies of reinforcement on the ward, the experimenters reduced or eliminated several undesired behaviors.

≈

CASE 1. SHAPING EATING BEHAVIORS

An attempt was made to shape socially acceptable eating habits in subject, S-1, who had some of the most unacceptable eating habits on the ward. He crammed food into his mouth at a very high rate, using both hands and swallowing the food without chewing. He often stood up and quickly reached across the table to snatch food. When there was no more food, S-1 sat drooling and stared into space or at the serving line with food on his face, his shirt front, his trousers, and on the floor around him.

S-1 was an eighteen-year-old male who had been at the institution for three and one-half years. The diagnosis was chronic brain syndrome associated with intracranial infection with mental deficiency. On the Vineland Social Maturity Scale he received a Social Quotient of 13. Daily medication for S-1 was Stelazine, 20 mg., and Thorasine, 400 mg.

During the training period S-1 was taken to a special room for two meals each day. At first M & M candies were used to shape the use of the spoon. Although the subject had not been observed using a spoon in the dining hall and attendants reported that he could not use a spoon, it was obvious from the speed with which he developed skill with the spoon that he had previously been taught its use. The candies were put one by one into a dish so that S-1 could eat them with the spoon. Initially, taking food with the hands was a strong response. Extinction was accomplished by removing the candy as soon as S-1 started to release the spoon or lift his free hand. By the end of the first training session S-1 was skillful with the spoon.

For the second meal, a tray was prepared and brought to the experimental room. When S-1 was brought into the room, he rushed toward the tray of food and had to be restrained. He was seated at the table across from the tray but made repeated and forceful attempts to stand up and reach the food. The tray of food was put out of sight; an empty tray was set before the subject and the training with the candies was repeated. When the desired response pattern became stable, small bits of food were substituted for the candies. As might be expected, in the beginning this disrupted the neat responses with the spoon and S-1 again attempted to use his hands. As in the first training session, each time S-1 started to use his hands, the tray was pulled away. Before the session was over he was eating food neatly with his spoon. As acceptable eating behaviors were shaped, more pieces of food at one time were put on the tray until eventually S-1 ate with his spoon from a full tray of food.

To develop a slower rate of eating, each time S-1 reached for another spoonful after he had taken a mouthful of food, the tray was immediately pulled away. After a few sessions of this training S-1 began to eat slowly, to chew his food, and to look around the room and laugh.

S-1 usually arrived at the experimental room before the tray of food was brought in. At first he tried to rush to the door and, when the tray arrived, he rushed to it and tried to take the food. When forced to remain seated, he turned around in his chair and faced the door, waiting and drooling. To shape more acceptable habits, an experimenter stood on the opposite side of the table from the door. Each time S-1 looked or turned away from the door he was given a piece of candy. Soon the desired response, sitting with his face toward the table, was produced. The desired posture was maintained by use of a roughly estimated variable interval schedule with a mean interval of approximately twenty seconds.

The experimenters observed that when no adequate timer was available and the intervals had to be estimated, it was very difficult for the experimenter to prevent his own behavior (i.e., presentation of reinforcement) from coming under the stimulus control of the behavior of the patient. There are few changing environmental stimuli, other than those produced by the patient, to serve as "clocks"; therefore time is difficult to estimate. On the other hand, there is a strong tendency for the experimenter to estimate time intervals by the most important stimulus change in his environment, the degree of approximation of the patient's behavior to the undesired response. The experimenter waits for some undetermined interval to pass and, in the meantime, the subject makes a closer than average approximation to the unwanted response. This tends to be a discriminative stimulus controlling the experimenter's own response. The experimenter is "reminded," by S's response, of the passage of time and rewards the subject. The experimenter is rewarded by a temporary reduction in random responses as the subject consumes the reinforcer. The long-term effect is an inadvertent shaping of subcriterion approximations of the undesired response.

In less than two weeks S-1 was coming into the experimental room, sitting down without being told, waiting for the tray, and eating slowly with his spoon from a full tray of food. The task of maintaining the proper contingencies of reinforcement, however, was too difficult even for two experimenters. Sometimes it was impossible to prevent undesirable responses from being reinforced with food. Hence, reinforcement errors were made which resulted in undesirable behavior. Three persons, well trained in operant conditioning procedures might have handled the task efficiently. But such intensive treatment for two or three meals each day over a period of weeks or months would not be economically feasible.

The decision was made to discontinue attempts to control eating behavior. However, during the dining room observations it had been found that only a few of the patients were receiving more than one helping of food. Often a larger, quicker patient took most of a weaker patient's food. The patients were weighed; a few were found to be overweight and many underweight. Diets were prescribed; two helpings for all those underweight and one helping for the overweight. After this, most of the underweight patients gained weight. Also, during the following weeks there was a noticeable decrease in mealtime noise and disorder.

⋈

CASE 2. TEACHING A PATIENT TO COME WHEN CALLED

S-2, a twenty-two-year-old male, was regarded by the attendants as one of the least likely to learn anything. He was diagnosed as profoundly retarded with chronic brain syndrome associated with birth trauma. This subject's Binet-Infant IQ was 11. S-2's medical record reported an abnormal EEG and neurogical abnormalities characterized by increased tonicity of muscles in all extremities, hyperactive deep tendon reflexes, severe ataxia, and a mask-like expression of the face. His daily medication was Compazine, 30 mg., Thorazine, 300 mg., and phenobarbital, $1\frac{1}{2}$ grains. The S spent most of his time sitting on the floor or walking around aimlessly picking up and eating rags, wood, plaster, feces, cigarette butts, etc.

Although some of the attendants claimed that S-2 obeyed a few simple commands, he would not approach E when called and attendants failed to demonstrate any ability to control his behavior. In attempting to teach S-2 to respond to his name, E stood in front of him and called his name, but the S did not approach. Then E held a colorful piece of candy in the S's line of vision. He immediately approached the E and took the candy. After four trials the E, rather than the candy, became the discriminative stimulus; each time E came within sight of S-2 the S approached and followed E about the ward. In order to make the calling

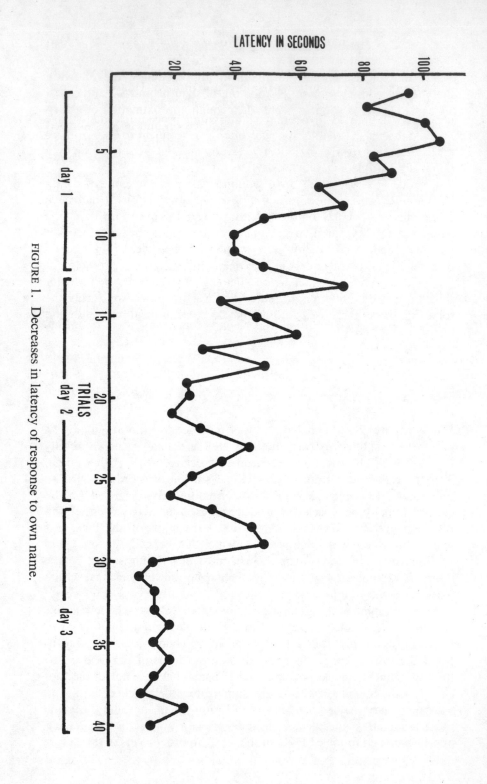

FIGURE 1. Decreases in latency of response to own name.

of S's name the discriminative stimulus for approaching E, the following shaping procedure was used. E stood out of sight behind S-2 and called his name. Then, as soon as S-2 made a rough approximation of a turn toward E, the candy was held in his line of vision and he was allowed to take it. Only three half-hour sessions were required to train S-2 to come from across the room when called by his name. Figure 1 shows response latencies starting with the second trial on which S turned and took the candy in response to the verbal stimulus alone.

⊁

CASE 3. ELIMINATING CONDITIONED AVOIDANCE BEHAVIORS

When S-3, a sixteen-year-old male, was transferred to the ward under study his hair was very long. Attendants in the ward from which he had been transferred reported that he would not allow them to cut his hair. This boy has been committed to the institution at six years of age because his parents found him unmanageable. On the Vineland Social Maturity Scale S-3 received a Social Quotient of 13. He was diagnosed as severely defective due to uncertain cause with the functional reaction alone manifest. S's daily medication was Thorazine, 100 mg., and Dilantin, 3 grains.

When the attendants tried to cut S's hair with electric clippers, S-3 jumped from the chair and ran away. It was learned that S-3 had previously been restrained on the rare occasions when his hair was cut. A shaping procedure was undertaken to get S-3 to sit still during hair cutting. One E dispensed reinforcement while the other handled the clippers. First the clippers, turned off, were brought within a few feet of S-3 and he was rewarded with candy, praise, and withdrawal of the clippers. On each repetition the clippers were brought a few inches closer. Any time S-3 made any move to avoid the clippers, E dropped back a few inches and again slowed the rate of advance. On a few occasions avoidance responses suddenly became strong and several times S-3 jumped out of his chair and ran to the other side of the room. However, he came when called and sat down, being reinforced for this cooperation with candy, praise, and a pat on the shoulder. After a few trials he allowed the clippers to touch his hands. It was possible rather quickly to progress to circling his head with the clippers and then to rubbing them over his head. He was rewarded on a rough variable interval schedule during this time. The mean interval was approximately 15 seconds.

The clippers were then turned on and S-3 was rewarded again when he let the buzzing clippers come closer, when he handled the clippers, when he let them circle his head, and finally, when he let them be rubbed over his head. Less than 25 minutes after beginning the shaping procedure, S-3 allowed his hair to be cut.

The haircutting was interrupted for several minutes. When E attempted to use the clippers again, S-3 had recovered some of his avoidance responses. Since it was only a short time since he had eaten a heavy breakfast, further work was postponed until a time when deprivation would make candy a more effective reinforcer. An hour before lunch, training was initiated again. S-3 came when called and sat down. The silent clippers were brought slowly to his head as he was intermittently reinforced. He made no observable responses, and when the clippers were turned on the procedure was equally successful.

Four days later, when the clippers were tried on S-3 just before dinner, he smiled, cooperated perfectly, and made no avoidance responses. Although no further treatment was given, the attendants reported that S-3 cooperated well during the next haircut. Eight months later, a check with attendants indicated that S-3 had continued to cooperate nicely during haircutting.

 measured

CASE 4. ELIMINATING FEAR OF STAIRS

An experiment was carried out with S-4, a twenty-six-year-old severely retarded subject who, when the elevator failed, refused to go down the stairs even though this meant a long delay before he could eat. According to the records, S-4 had been unable to sit without support until the age of two years, began to pull himself to a standing position at the age of three years, first walked unassisted at the age of five years, and was not bladder or bowel trained until ten years of age. The mother was extremely overprotective, making no attempt to help S-4 in ambulation and bladder or bowel training until the ages mentioned. According to the records, the mother kept the subject in a baby buggy until beyond the age of five years. The parents had S-4 committed at the age of twenty-one after he had become increasingly difficult to manage because of temper tantrums and violent behavior toward other members of the family.

At the time of the experiment S-4 talked "baby talk" and cried often but fed and dressed himself. On the Binet he received an IQ of 22. His diagnosis was severe cultural-familial mental retardation. He was receiving no medication. S-4 was overweight, ordinarily asked for second helpings at every meal, and begged for candy between meals but on the day the experiment was initiated he had refused to go down the steps to get to the dining hall. Instead, he sat on the floor, crying. It was learned that in the past he had been forced to walk down the steps in spite of the fact that he cried loudly all the way down. This time, however, his sitting on the floor frustrated the usual tactics and the attendants left S-4 behind.

Using candy as reinforcers, cooperative behavior was shaped by getting S-4 to stand, to walk to various parts of the room, and to come when called. Then he was "baited" down the steps. That is, E stood a few steps ahead of S-4 holding candy and allowed S to take the candy when he came close enough to reach it. After lunch training was initiated. For the first few trials S-4 was reinforced on each landing, then on each floor, and finally he was reinforced for descending or ascending all the way. The subject moved one step at a time, holding tightly to both railings and crying all the way. Initially, it took him more than three minutes to go from the third floor to the ground floor but eventually he was able to reduce this to 50 or 60 seconds. Also, S's crying gradually decreased in frequency, was finally eliminated altogether, and, concurrently, he became more relaxed in his movements while on the stairs. Figure 2 shows S's progress in stair climbing.

A check with the attendants six months after termination of treatment indicated that, since the treatment, S-4 had continued to use the steps without trouble.

CASE 5. CONTROL OF REGURGITATING RESPONSE

The attendants nominated S-5 as the patient with the most repulsive behaviors. On returning from a meal, S-5 almost invariably went to one side of the room, repeatedly vomited, and then consumed the vomitus. Other patients joined S-5 in consuming the vomitus.

S-5 was a sixteen-year-old mute patient, diagnosed as profoundly mentally retarded, with encephalopathy due to mechanical injury at birth. According to the records of his childhood, he sat up at about seven months of age, stood at about a year, and walked at about a year and a half. Also, at about 18 months of age S-5 began to say two words, "ouch" and "Mom." Toilet training was unsuccessful and he was slow in learning to eat. As he grew older, S-5 became extremely

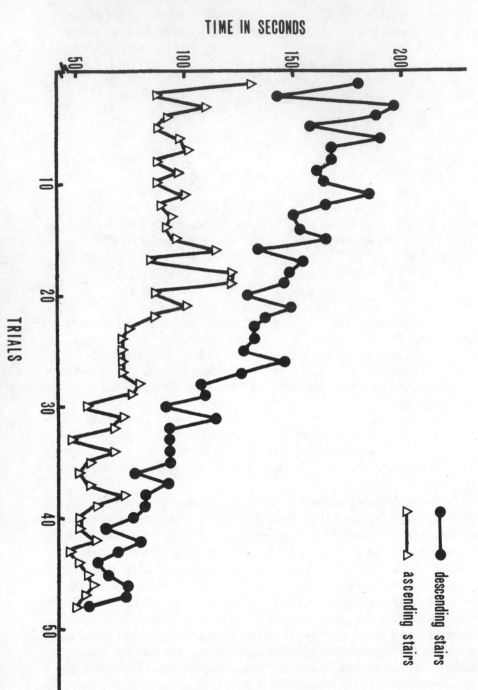

FIGURE 2.   Changes in the rate of stair climbing.

destructive, throwing things and attacking other children. The parents kept him in a separate room from which all breakable objects had been removed. At the age of seven, S-5 was committed to the institution and placed in a custodial ward.

At the time of the experiment S-5 was physically well developed and very active; he walked or ran around the ward almost constantly and occasionally attacked patients or attendants by striking or biting them. At other times he smashed windows or simply bit on his own hand. S-5 was not toilet trained, often refused to wear clothes, and ate bits of plaster, paper, feces, sticks, or anything else available. However, he came for medicine when called and obeyed a few other simple commands. The vomiting behavior was first reported about six months before the experimental treatment was initiated. Prior to treatments the attendants were asked to keep a record of the frequency of the subject's vomiting responses over a five-day period; S-5 averaged nine vomiting responses per day. However, there is some reason to believe that this figure is conservative. The attendants had nothing to gain from keeping accurate records and, furthermore, they had other important duties which they were under pressure to perform.

The treatment was at first carried out by E and a research nurse but was later administered by attendants under the supervision of E. The treatment procedure was to apply an aversive stimulus to the vomitus in order to prevent its consumption from acting as a reinforcer, and at the same time to strengthen behaviors which were incompatible with vomiting using candies as reinforcers. Also, vomiting was punished with a time out; a 2- to 5-minute period during which no reinforcers were given. Cayenne pepper was used as the aversive stimulus, being sprinkled liberally on the vomitus as soon as possible after the regurgitating response.

In the beginning the behaviors which were incompatible with the undesired responses were reinforced on a fixed interval of one minute. However, S-5 quickly formed a temporal discrimination, returning to E just before the end of each interval. On the first attempt to use a variable interval schedule S-5 returned just before the end of each minute interval and, if he was not reinforced, tended to vomit immediately or respond aggressively. When the aggressive behaviors occurred, S's face and chest sometimes flushed and he often struck his fist against his own teeth or bit his knuckles.

S-5 quickly learned to come when called but he developed what might be called "begging responses." These were eliminated by shaping the response of walking away from E and staying away until called. This behavior was quickly developed by reinforcing successive ap-

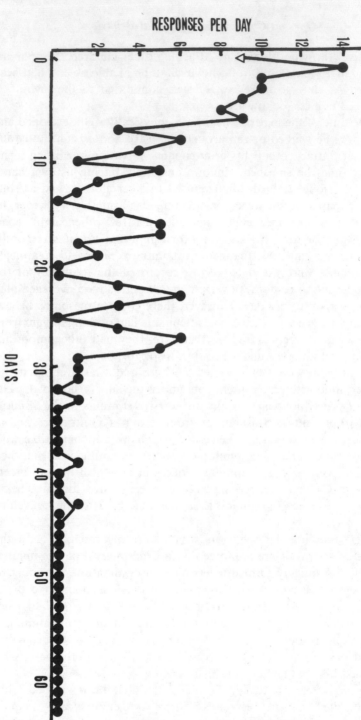

FIGURE 3. Increasing control over regurgitating response.

proximations of the desired response. In fact, using the calling of S's name as a discriminative stimulus, it was easy to shape his behavior so that he would walk to any part of the ward.

It became obvious that the probability of vomiting was very high just after each meal but gradually weakened until, after 30 to 45 minutes, there was very little likelihood of the response occurring. However, when a variable interval schedule with a one-minute mean interval was used, the vomiting response was under control during treatment but returned to full strength just after the end of the 45-minute treatment period. Therefore, what might be called an expanding variable interval schedule was used. This schedule started as a variable interval schedule with a 15-second mean interval but the mean interval was expanded in steps until after 45 minutes the mean interval was 5 minutes.

With several such adjustments in the treatment, control was gradually gained over the vomiting response. Figure 3 shows the progress made. After complete control was gained over the response, control was maintained for 19 days. At the end of this time, treatment was turned over to nontrained attendants and control over the response was lost, returning to approximately the original strength.

In view of the success with individual patients, a controlled study was planned to investigate the possibility of training attendants to use reinforcement with large groups of patients. However, no significant difference was found between experimental and control groups in improvement in basic social skills. A *post hoc* insight suggests that no differences should have been expected as traditional, rather than operant, methods of training and supervision were used to maintain attendant behaviors. Even if attendants were operantly trained to manipulate the reinforcement contingencies on the wards, problems of understaffing and staff turnover might prevent an effective program. On the other hand, it would be possible to develop mechanical and electrical equipment to program contingencies of reinforcement and train patients in basic social behaviors. The large initial investment required to develop such automated equipment would be more than repaid, later, by reduced costs of caring for severely retarded patients.

⊱7⊰

Operant Conditioning
in Toilet Training
of Severely Retarded Boys

Marcel Hundziak, Ruth A. Maurer, & Luke S. Watson, Jr.

Training of severely mentally retarded institutionalized patients in basic social skills is one of the most important and difficult problems confronting those concerned with habilitating these individuals. The application of operant conditioning techniques in toilet training of severely retarded boys at the Columbus State School is described here.

Clinical observations made on a unit for severely retarded boys showed that (1) eliminations occurred according to a relatively constant physiological rhythm, usually every $1\frac{1}{2}$ or 2 hours; (2) the patients responded to a conventional training schedule without special reinforcements by restricting eliminative acts to toilet facilities; (3) the reinforcements (praise and candy) seemed to increase motivation to use the bathroom facilities; (4) proper training of patients on living units was difficult because of overcrowded and inadequate facilities.

These observations were confirmed in a pilot study involving six severely retarded boys. The pilot study unit also served as a proving ground to test and develop a training device to be employed in the main project.

From the *American Journal of Mental Deficiency*, 70:1 (July 1965), 120–124.

This study was partially supported by a grant, #MH 06583–01, from the National Institute of Health, United States Department of Health, Education, and Welfare, Washington, D.C.

96

The purpose of the present study was to test the efficacy of operant conditioning techniques in toilet training of severely mentally retarded boys. The study, although independently conceived, followed essentially the principles later outlined by Ellis in the article on toilet training of severely defective patients (1963). The conditioning schedule used consisted of reinforcing with food, light, and a tone, each eliminatory response, i.e., Ss were rewarded on a continuous reinforcement schedule.

An attempt was made to test the following hypotheses: (1) The subjects toilet trained with the application of operant conditioning techniques and a special reinforcing device will show greater progress in the use of the commode for defecation and urination, as shown by the behaviors measured, than subjects toilet trained according to the conventional approach. (2) The elimination habits established through operant conditioning will be transferred and maintained at the original living unit.

⤫

METHOD

Subjects

All Ss lived in a large unit for 50–60 severely mentally retarded, physically non-handicapped boys between the ages of seven to fourteen years, whose social quotients were between 8 and 33 as measured by the Vineland Social Maturity Scale.

The Ss were selected by a regular nurse on the basis of information obtained from the unit matron and through actual observation confirming the occurrence of soiling and wetting in each candidate. The 29 Ss then were randomly assigned to three groups: an operant conditioning group (8 subjects), a conventional training group (8 subjects), and a control group (13 subjects). The number of Ss later was reduced to 26. One subject was dropped from the operant conditioning group for medical reasons. Two Ss were dropped from the conventional training group for administrative reasons.

Apparatus

A reinforcement device was used to reward eliminative responses. It was a 5' 2½'' high, 2½' wide, and 2' 1'' deep portable box and housed a Gerbrands Universal Feeder, a tone oscillator, and three colored electric bulbs. Whenever the Ss urinated or defecated in the commode, the attendant would press a control button connected to the reinforcement device dispensing a piece of candy through a food pan at the front of the box and simultaneously emitting light and tone.

An automatic "elimination" switch also was developed as a part of the study. The switch was installed in a commode to be activated by each defecation or urination. However, it proved too unreliable and was not used in the experiment.

Procedure

As a part of the program the Ss belonging to both the operant conditioning group and the conventional training group spent seven hours a day, five days a week, on special training units. The training was done by attendants. All Ss in these two groups were placed individually on the commode every two hours and whenever the eliminative need was indicated overtly by them or when physiological signs of approaching elimination, e.g., restlessness, were intercepted. In the operant conditioning group each defecation or urination in the commode was rewarded immediately through the use of the electrically operated candy dispenser which was located beside the commode.

The Ss belonging to the conventional training group were not rewarded by the candy dispenser. With this group, however, the attendant was instructed to approach the Ss in the traditional manner known to her from the work done in the institution. In general, the conventional toilet training on other units of the institution consisted of taking the children to the bathroom several times a day, scolding them for soiling, and praising them for successful use of bathroom facilities. Candy was given to the children occasionally but not in any relation to the training program.

The control group Ss (13 boys) remained on the living unit 24 hours a day with 25–30 other severely retarded, non-toilet trained boys. No organized routine was maintained to subject the patients to a toilet training program during the experimental period.

A period of adjustment to unfamiliar surroundings was allowed for subjects who belonged to the two special training units. Their initial reactions to the training units were characterized by disorganization of behavior with symptoms of irritability, hyperactivity and/or withdrawal. Toilet training proper was started after two weeks, when initial confusion subsided and it appeared that the Ss had adapted to the training unit environment. The training period lasted 27 days.

Each of the three groups: the operant conditioning group, the conventional training group, and the control group, was observed before and after training. The operant conditioning group and the conventional training group were observed at the special training unit while the control group was observed at the original cottage. In addition, to test transfer of acquired toilet habits to the living unit, a second post-training observation was done for the operant conditioning and conventional training groups at the original cottage. Observations were made independently by raters who, for $5\frac{1}{2}$ hours each day for three consecutive days, recorded the frequency of all incidents of incontinence and use of bathroom facilities for each child. Precautions were taken to make sure that the raters were not informed about specific group assignments of individuals *S*s.

＞＜

RESULTS AND DISCUSSION

Considering the small number of *S*s in each group and the low score frequencies there was serious doubt as to the normality of the distribution, and inspection of the data appeared to verify this suspicion. Therefore, the median and interquartile range were selected as descriptive statistics, and the Sign Test (Siegel, 1956) was used to assess differences between pre- and post-training group scores.

Tables 1 and 2 show the median and interquartile ranges for pre- and post-training defecation and urination difference scores for the three groups. A one-tailed test was used to evaluate the pre- versus post-training observations for the operant conditioning and conventional groups while a two-tailed test was used for comparing the pre- versus post-training observations for the control group and for the test of transfer of acquired toilet habits to the living units.

The operant conditioning group showed a significant increase in the use of bathroom facilities for both urination and defecation (.016 and .031 levels respectively). The conventional training group showed no significant change in toilet habits. The control group showed a significant increase in the use of toilet facilities for urination (.032 level) but no significant increase for defecation.

The findings support hypothesis No. 1 by revealing that the operant conditioning group advanced more in training than did the two other groups. The test of transfer of acquired toilet habits showed that the use of bathroom facilities for urination and defecation at the original cottage did not decrease significantly as compared with the post-

TABLE 1. Medians and Interquartile Ranges of Difference (Pre- and Post-Test) Scores for Defecation in Toilet

Groups	Q_1	Median	Q_3
Operant conditioning	0	1	3
Conventional training	0	0	.5
Control	0	0	1

TABLE 2. Medians and Interquartile Ranges of Difference (Pre- and Post-Test) Scores for Urination in Toilet

Groups	Q_1	Median	Q_3
Operant conditioning	2	9	10
Conventional training	−.5	1	2.5
Control	0	1	3

training findings at the special training unit. Support is herewith furnished in favor of hypothesis No. 2.

The findings of the study seem to support the following conclusions: (1) the operant conditioning technique is useful in toilet training of severely retarded children; (2) the operant conditioning technique is superior to the conventional method in the toilet training of severely retarded children; (3) the ability to use the commode acquired by the subjects through operant conditioning was transferred and maintained at the original living unit.

The analysis of the data revealed in addition some interesting trends that deserve a more detailed discussion.

A numerical increase (although not significant) in the rate of use of toilet facilities for defecation and urination also was observed in the conventional training group showing a positive response to the conventional toilet training program.

The numerical increase in the rate of use of toilet facilities for elimination observed in both experimental training groups did not affect significantly the incidence of soiling and wetting on the floor. This means that the subjects continued the old pattern of eliminative habits dissociating the situation in the toilet from the classroom situation. This complication in the training process probably could be eliminated by installation of provisional commodes in classrooms and by gradual transfer of commodes to restrooms once the eliminative habits were acquired.

Most subjects used the toilet facilities in a passive manner, and only when they were prepared by the aide for the eliminating function. Clinical observation revealed that only one subject (operant conditioning group) spontaneously learned to indicate his eliminative needs and to seek the toilet facilities on his own.

The experiences of the investigators seem to confirm the theoretical elaborations of Ellis (1963) on the application of reinforcement principles in toilet training of severely retarded patients. The investigators feel that training readiness rather than a certain CA (between 12–35) as proposed by Ellis (1963) should serve as one of the selection criteria for toilet training of severely retarded *S*s. The toilet training readiness depends essentially on the ability of the central nervous system to exert sphincter control and is related only indirectly to the CA. Neurological examinations done by one of the investigators showed that soiling and bed wetting among the severely mentally retarded patients were correlated highly with the degree of damage to the central nervous system. The toilet training readiness is manifested by the ability of the subjects to withhold the eliminations for longer periods of time and by development of a more or less constant rhythm of elimination.

The investigators regret that modest means and limited time did not allow them to extend the study for a longer period of time and to expose the subjects to a training program operating for 24 hours a day. Eventual transition to a variable ratio reinforcement schedule and weaning off candy also was considered in the future. In view of these shortcomings the present study properly should be regarded as an exploratory attempt which will hopefully be followed by more elaborate work.

~ 8 ~

Operant Learning Theory
and Nursing Care
of the Retarded Child

Linda Rae Whitney & Kathryn E. Barnard

In the study described here, attention is directed toward the observation and analysis of spoon-feeding behavior; the effect of satisfaction versus deprivation in the reinforcement process; the effect of positive and negative reinforcement; and finally, scheduling of reinforcement. Data are presented on the child's skills in dressing, toilet, bathing and grooming, ambulation, and communication, since these are areas in which nurses help provide care to the retarded child.

The subject, Ann, was admitted to Fircrest School for the Retarded in November, 1963, at the chronological age of fourteen years four months. According to the physician's diagnostic examination, Ann was mentally retarded and had spastic paralysis. She was functioning at the one-year-old level. Ann's developmental history was uneventful except for her mother's hospitalization during the prenatal period for a unilateral salpingectomy and oophorectomy. Birth was full term and uncomplicated; so was the postnatal period. Her lag in motor development was noted as not holding her head up until she was fourteen months old, sat alone at twenty months, and had not, according to the physician's progress notes, ever walked alone. Ann had been institu-

From *Mental Retardation,* 4:3 (June 1966), 26–29, a publication of the American Association on Mental Deficiency.

tionalized at an early age and was reported to be a very destructive child who tore up bedding and her own clothing, induced vomiting, smeared feces, and took food from other residents.

Ann was one of 80 girls placed according to functional level in a wing of the institution for residents who were severely or profoundly retarded and were nonambulatory. There was one counselor to every fifteen residents.

The nurse obtained current information on Ann's self-help skills by observation and interview with attendant counselors working directly with Ann. Although the investigator primarily focused on the use of reinforcement techniques to teach feeding skills, other self-help skills were noted on a continuing basis to determine any changes which might occur.

The nurse utilized the Gesell developmental guide to assess Ann's motor functional level. Now, aged fifteen years, Ann was noted to function at approximately a seven-month level. She could sit unsupported, grasp, release, and bring objects to her mouth.

OBSERVATION

During three meals, the investigator sat in an unobtrusive area on the ward and observed Ann's response to the usual ward routine. She was fed by older, more capable, mentally retarded residents who held a dish of food under her chin and spoon fed her from one dish at a time. Ann sat unsupported, looked directly ahead, and ate her entire meal, making no attempt to grasp the spoon or dishes. Following the second meal, however, Ann was seen to crawl toward another less capable resident, take her toast and handle her dishes with random carelessness. This incident promptly evoked the attention of a counselor, who smiled and said, "That's not a nice girl." She placed Ann in a wheel chair in the corner of the room. Following the third meal, Ann crawled to the food cart and handled the food. A cleaning lady said. "There goes our gal again." Counselors looked around, smiled and placed Ann in a crib with high side rails.

From this series of observations, the nurse recognized that no attempt was being made to encourage self-help feeding, although Ann demonstrated motor abilities necessary for self-help. In addition, the response of the staff to Ann's behavior seemed to strengthen the behavior it followed.

The counselors reported that Ann frequently removed all of her clothing when left alone in a wheel chair, bed, or enclosure on the wing. The nurse noted that the counselors approached Ann most frequently when she removed her clothing, less frequently when she was dressed appropriately. When the ward was understaffed on weekends, the rate of Ann's undressing reached as high as 10 to 20 times daily.

Ann was not toilet trained. Attendant counselors routinely placed her on the toilet after meals and restrained her because, if left alone, she would crawl about the bathroom. Counselors reported that she frequently handled her feces and "made a mess" on the ward. On one occasion it was noted that Ann was restrained in the bathroom and left for fifteen minutes.

Her bathing and grooming was carried out entirely by the counselors. On three occasions the nurse took Ann to the sink to feel the water and she quickly withdrew her hand. If given a brush, Ann would take it with a forceful tug and throw it on the floor. She allowed counselors to brush her hair, however, and squealed when she looked at herself in the mirror.

The counselors reported that Ann was usually restrained in her wheelchair or kept in bed. When left alone she would crawl from the ward. The investigator and the physician on staff noted that Ann could walk with assistance. She had a knee contracture of 10–20 degrees which limited her range of extension and was associated with balance difficulties. Therefore, although her balance seemed integrated, she was unable to take independent steps.

Ann responded to simple verbal commands, such as "lift your leg," "get up," "sit down." The only articulation of sound that she emitted was a small rhythmic cry at infrequent intervals when she seemed pleased with some activity (looking at herself in mirror). She was not able to combine words or sounds to express ideas. She seemed to make her needs known by approaching counselors and pulling on their arms, removing her own clothing, taking food from others, and handling her feces; all these behaviors evoked attention from the counselors.

❤

REINFORCEMENT PROCEDURE

A program to initiate self-help skills of feeding was based on the principles of operant learning theory. Ann was taken to a private room and left alone with a full tray of food. The nurse observed the child to determine her degree of independent function at mealtime in the absence of intervention. During three meals Ann haphazardly overturned her dishes and brushed her tray to the floor. She was observed to look about the room, to crawl down from the chair, to approach, on hands and knees, overturn dishes and pick them up, suck from them, and release them. She did not, at any time, demonstrate correct spoon feeding in the absence of specific environmental contingencies.

The nurse arranged to be with Ann in the private room and provided specific contingencies of positive and negative reinforcement during the next six meals. After conferring with the physician, the nurse reduced Ann's diet to 1,000 calories.

Ann was seated in a chair in front of a low table, the nurse seated to her right side. Dishes were placed one by one in the far right corner of the table. Spoon-feeding behavior was developed by successive approximation. The nurse placed the spoon between the child and the food and tapped it on the table. Initially, as soon as the child looked at the spoon the experimenter responded by feeding her a bite of food. Progressively, more advanced behavior was required of the child before food was given. Ann had to not only look at the spoon but make some gesture with her right arm in the direction of the spoon. Finally, looking, reaching, and grasping the spoon were required before food was forthcoming.

Ann displayed the behavior of reaching persistently with both hands for the bowls of food and/or throwing her spoon on the floor. When this inappropriate behavior was demonstrated food was immediately withdrawn from her reach and the nurse firmly placed the child's left hand under the table and said "no." The specific conditions of food being presented only for appropriate behavior and withdrawn for inappropriate behavior were continued at 8:30 A.M. for six consecutive days. The spoon was a discriminative stimulus in this situation. The nurse's response of withdrawing the food and the child's hand when inappropriate behavior was exhibited weakened the behavior it followed. The presentation of food for behavior in contact with the spoon strengthened the behavior it followed.

After five consecutive sessions of precise reinforcement consequences, Ann demonstrated the ability to spoon-feed herself in a private room with no intervention by the nurse. She was observed through a one-way mirror and was noted to take 82 spoonfuls of food, progressing from one dish to the next. Whereas she formerly took heaping teaspoons of food and stuffed food into her mouth, she now took smaller amounts of food on the spoon and behaved in a more orderly manner. She did spill some of her food in the process of feeding, but she seemed to prefer the spoon to the hand as a tool for self-feeding. For example, when Ann did spill food she used her spoon to scrape it from bib to mouth and did not finger-feed.

Counselors on the ward reported that Ann's behavior in other areas had also changed. For example, she would sit quietly in her chair awaiting the experimenter each morning. She no longer removed her clothing, except for her shoes and stockings. She did not play with her feces nor did she take food from other residents. Without observing the precise environmental stimuli in response to the child, one cannot determine why these behaviors decreased in frequency. The nurse did note, however, that the counselors began to ask questions about Ann and approached her more often than they had before the experimental intervention.

After the sixth session, that in which the child demonstrated the ability to spoon feed herself, the nurse withdrew systematic reinforcement conditions. Food was no longer contingent upon the child's correct feeding behavior. The nurse informed the staff that she would not be back to feed Ann for about five days. Ann was to be fed as she was before the nurse began working with her. The purpose of this period was to determine if the precise consequences of positive and negative reinforcement were, in fact, responsible for the acquisition of spoon feeding.

It was difficult for the staff to understand the need for this step. "If Ann could feed herself, why wasn't this enough to show the effect of positive and negative reinforcement?" they asked. "What will happen if Ann 'unlearns' the behavior and won't be able to feed herself again?"

After seven days had elapsed, the nurse returned to the ward and approached Ann. Ann was in bed. When approached, she screamed loudly in monosyllables and reached out and firmly pulled the experimenter's uniform and attempted to reach for the experimenter's nursing cap. All of the sheets were off her bed on the floor. She sat naked looking out on the ward, her clothes thrown in a heap on the floor.

The nurse dressed Ann. An attendant was asked to bring the tray of food to the experimental psychology laboratory. The attendant walked beside Ann. As the experimenter assisted her to walk, Ann reached out, grabbed a dish of fruit and threw it on the floor and then turned to the experimenter and smiled. In the private room she demonstrated behavior similar to that of the pre-reinforcement period. The spoon was not used. Food was taken from the bowls by finger and by sucking, utensils were thrown on the floor.

During the next ten sessions the experimenter accompanied Ann in the feeding situation and set up precise contingencies of continuous positive and negative reinforcement for feeding behavior. Spoon feeding was rapidly reinstated under these conditions. A high frequency of spoon-feeding behavior was exhibited during the first session, which indicated that relearning was easier than the initial learning.

In order that Ann's spoon-feeding behavior would not be inadvertently extinguished when the nurse could no longer be with the child each day, the nurse began to fade out her participation in the spoon-feeding activity, and a counselor on the wing was taught to use the same techniques. The child was noted to continue spoon feeding at a high frequency when the counselor used these techniques consistently and immediately.

✖

RESULTS

Four months after the initiation of spoon feeding, the following changes were noted in Ann:

The counselor working with Ann had used reinforcement techniques to teach the proper method of grasping and releasing the cup. Even after spoon feeding was learned, she continued to reach persistently for her milk at the beginning of each meal, drank the entire amount and threw the glass on the floor. Milk was divided into four portions and proper release to the table required. Milk was removed when inappropriate throwing was exhibited. Techniques of fading were utilized. The counselor placed her hand over the child's, initially, as the glass was grasped and released, later the counselor faded out her participation in the activity.

Ann was then transferred to an ambulatory area. In this living unit she was seated at a table with other girls. It was observed that Ann waited until grace had been asked (delayed reinforcement) and then fed herself independently. On occasion she attempted to take food from other residents, but this behavior declined in frequency from that of the pretraining period.

Ann walked with assistance one-half hour every day after breakfast for four months. Later she walked unaided and pedaled a tricycle independently; she still needed help in mounting and dismounting the tricycle. The behavior of walking and riding the tricycle seemed to be reinforced by the social approval and approach of the staff as they observed Ann attempting this new activity. The activity itself may have had reinforcing value to this child. The opportunities for imitating walking were greater on the ambulatory ward and it was anticipated that ambulation would continue to improve.

By scheduling toilet training to coincide with Ann's pattern of elimination and staying with her during this time, some success was noted. The contingency of staying with her during the time she was on the toilet seemed to provide a positive reinforcement for attempts to toilet train.

While Ann did not learn to dress herself, her pattern of undressing declined to the point where she took off only her shoes and stockings.

✂

DISCUSSION

Analysis of the initial baseline data indicated that Ann's not using a spoon was being maintained and even strengthened by her being fed and receiving social reinforcement from the counselors when she grabbed food from the other children and the food cart. These observations led to the assumption that both food and social response were reinforcing to Ann's behavior.

The withdrawal of the continuous reinforcement schedule after the sixth session (food as a positive reinforcement for spoon feeding; removing the food and Ann's hand from the table and saying "no" as a negative reinforcement for her inappropriate behavior) demonstrated that the use of positive reinforcement was the factor responsible for the maintenance of spoon feeding.

Ann was placed on a 1,000-calorie diet to insure that her level of satiation for food was not interfering in the effectiveness of food as the primary reinforcer. Breakfast was delayed till 8:30 A.M. for the same purpose. According to operant principles these two measures should increase the strength of the reinforcer.

A continuous schedule of reinforcement was initiated in this study. Each time Ann successfully approximated spoon feeding she was immediately reinforced with food. The literature indicates that continuous reinforcement provides a schedule which most rapidly institutes a behavioral response; however, by abruptly withdrawing continuous reinforcement, an emotional response could be expected. Ann demonstrated an emotional response by screaming and taking off her clothes during the period when the experimenter withdrew the reinforcement. The use of interval or ratio scheduling in which the reinforcement is offered at preplanned times or after an established number of successful responses provides a means of increasing the probability that a skill will be continued with less emotional response when the reinforcement is withdrawn.

The removal of Ann from the usual ward environment provided a situation which was less distracting and in which the dependent variables could be controlled.

The case study of Ann augments a rapidly growing body of evidence that the systematic use of reinforcement provides a sufficient, and perhaps a necessary, basis for establishing skills in the child who is not developing self-help skills in the normal sequence of child development.

Certainly it is necessary to go through the steps of observation, evaluation of the observation, formulation of meaning of the observed data, and, finally, application of intervention appropriate to the desired results. In applying the theories involved, the contingencies operating in the environment are altered to reinforce the type of behavior desired. The actual change — whether it be building up a feeding repertoire or eliminating an undesirable behavior — has to take place within the child. The nurse-therapist cannot make this change, but can create the conditions which increase the probability of its occurrence.

FURTHER IMPLICATIONS

Eliminating Behavior

There has been some report in the literature that extinction of undesirable behavior in the retarded individual is difficult to achieve. A graduate student was working with a child diagnosed as brain injury, with severe behavioral problems that, according to the diagnostic team, were not primarily the result of cerebral dysfunction. The student went into the home to collect data on the child's hyperactive, destructive behavior. She sought to determine when it occurred, how often, and its magnitude in relation to what was happening in the environment.

In this case, utilizing the theory in the home situation presented a more difficult task than working in the institution. There was evidence of resistance from the family in cooperating with the program of reinforcement, especially when the child began to show fewer undesirable behaviors, such as throwing the phone.

It was hypothesized that this child's aggressive, destructive behavior provided an object on which the parents could project their feelings of anger. Parents often find it unacceptable to dislike a child because he is slow or retarded. It is possible that tantrums and self-destructive and object-destruction behavior provided the parents with a reason for their unacceptable feelings.

In consulting with public health nurses, we have found aspects of this theory useful. In one case where the child was presenting "extreme temper tantrums," according to the mother, the nurse asked the mother to help in the observational phase by recording the tantrum behavior. She recorded the time of the tantrum, how long it lasted, what had happened immediately before, and how the tantrum was handled.

The mother recorded the behavior for one week. Tantrums seemed to occur in the morning when the child arose and when she was getting ready to go to school. In analyzing the data, the nurse found that instead of the high frequency of tantrum behavior the mother had initially reported, there was an average of two tantrums a day. These data led to the hypothesis that specific observation by the mother provided an objective tool by which she could look at her daughter's behavior and work with it. On the fifth day the duration of the tantrum had decreased to 5 minutes, compared with 45 minutes on the first day. The mother described having clothes and the dressing procedure more organized by the fifth day.

Educational Implications

We at the University of Washington have begun to explore how the application of reinforcement can be included in the curriculum of undergraduate and graduate students. From the results of Whitney's study (1965), we are certain that this framework can be incorporated into the nursing function with respect to evaluation and programming behavior of the retarded individual. Our next step is to explore how this can best be taught to students. We have developed some assumptions: that the student learns to use the techniques of this theory by being exposed to the basic principles of the theory, and by observing the process of reinforcement before applying it. In accord with these assumptions we are planning a series of teaching films on the observation of behavior, evaluation of developmental readiness, and programming a schedule of reinforcement.

~ 9 ~

Teaching of Self-help Skills to Profoundly Retarded Patients

M. Ronald Minge & Thomas S. Ball

Until recently it was thought widely that profoundly retarded persons could not benefit substantially from teaching efforts, regardless of the method used (Stevens, 1964). However, a recent study by Bensberg, Colwell, and Cassel (1965) has suggested that the profoundly retarded can be taught self-help skills by using a combination of operant and classical conditioning in a one-to-one technician-patient relationship. In this study, the tasks to be taught were divided into smaller, incremental steps for easier acquisition, and correct responses were reinforced systematically. The techniques employed are outlined in Bensberg's handbook for ward personnel (1965).

While this study demonstrated the utility of a conditioning approach in the teaching of self-help skills to profoundly retarded patients, it apparently suffered from an important methodological limitation. Bensberg et al. relied on changes in ratings to measure improvement. While their modified Vineland Social Maturity Scale did show such improvement, it represents at best an indirect measure of the development of skills, and one that can be influenced greatly by experimenter or teacher biases.

It was felt that more direct and objective measures of profoundly retarded patients' behavior would demonstrate more clearly their ability to learn self-help skills. An investigation was undertaken at Pacific State Hospital to explore this possibility. The teaching techniques used were modeled after those of Bensberg et al., but in the present

From the *American Journal of Mental Deficiency*, 71:5 (March 1967), 864–868.

111

study a step-by-step program for teaching the tasks was developed and employed. The use of this program helped to objectify the experiment by controlling the nature and order of instruction. It also made it possible to determine objectively the patients' daily progress and to develop an evaluative system directly related to the program. Further, it allowed close analysis of the program itself, revealing patients' difficulties with any of its steps, making constant evaluation of the program possible. Finally, it helped technicians focus upon objective improvement, gave them a logical basis for proceeding to the next step, and insured continuous collection of relevant and easily manipulated data.

The self-help program, which was developed and tested in a pilot study, concerned these eleven skills: attention, coming to the technician, sitting down, remaining seated, standing up, removing shirt or dress, removing pants, removing socks, putting on shirt or dress, putting on pants, and putting on socks. Each of these tasks was broken down into component parts for incremental acquisition at a pace consistent with patients' abilities.

≍

METHOD

Subjects.   Six girls were chosen as *S*s because they were among those with the fewest self-help abilities in the hospital. Their diagnoses, chronological ages, intelligence quotients (from the Kuhlmann Test of Mental Maturity), and social quotients (from the Vineland Social Maturity Scale) are shown in Table 1. They had resided in the hospital from one and a half years to seven and a half years, and at the time of the study were part of a ward group of eleven girls.

TABLE 1.   Diagnosis (Dx), CA, IQ, and SQ or Experimental *S*s

S	Dx	CA	IQ	SQ
M.Ra	encephalopathy	10.3	19	26
M.Re	encephalopathy	15.0	10	10
V.G.	encephalopathy	9.3	10	15
S.T.	mongolism	8.5	24	27
M.H.	undifferentiated	12.3	14	19
D.T.	undifferentiated	11.5	19	11

In general, the behavior repertory of the six Ss prior to training was quite limited. They generally paid little attention to anyone and responded to such simple commands as "Come here" only part of the time. None was toilet trained and none used words to communicate. Their dressing skills were minimal, as none made any attempt to dress or undress at appropriate times. One girl slapped herself frequently and slept a great deal, and another actively resisted directions by throwing herself to the floor.

Procedure. The three technicians who had taken part in the pilot study of the program were temporarily assigned to the ward and group which contained the six Ss. Two worked in the morning and the third worked in the afternoon. They assumed the regular duties of caring for the group of eleven girls and also carried out the training program. Supervision from the psychology department was made available to them.

Programmed self-help training was given for two months. During this period each S was taught in two fifteen-minute sessions per day. The training procedure followed the program and technicians worked with one S at a time. In the teaching of each skill S first was given a simple verbal direction and a sufficient gesture or actual tug to insure her correct response. Correct responses were reinforced with food plus a statement of praise such as, "Good girl."

As the first steps were mastered, the cues were diminished and more complex responses were required for reinforcement to be given. For example, the following sequences were followed in teaching S to stand up and to take off her pants:

Standing up

I. Stands up, with technician providing
   a. a gentle lift under arm or shoulder plus spoken direction.
   b. a light touch and gesture plus spoken direction.
   c. upward gesture plus spoken direction.
   d. spoken direction only.
II. Stands up with technician at least 5 feet away, giving
   a. upward gesture plus spoken direction.
   b. spoken direction only.

Undressing: Pants

I. Use elastic-banded cotton pants. Child should be seated, with pants nearly off; over one foot only. She removes them, with technician
   a. placing patient's hands on pants and helping pull them off, plus spoken direction.

    b. pointing to pants, plus spoken direction.

    c. giving spoken direction only.

II. Patient is seated with pants at both knees. She removes them, with technician

    a. pointing at pants, plus spoken direction.

    b. giving spoken direction only.

III. Patient either seated or standing, pants all the way up. She takes them off when the technician

    a. points at the pants, plus spoken direction.

    b. gives spoken direction only.

S was kept at each step in the program until she had demonstrated mastery of it by responding correctly to four of the first five directions given her in a session. That is, *S* was tested in each session, and progression to the next step depended on her passing the test without immediate prior practice.

At first *S*s were given food reinforcement in addition to their meals. However, after two days it became apparent that they often did not attend or respond to directions. In order to increase attention and motivation, *S*s were required to earn breakfast and lunch in the training sessions. They were given a spoonful of the meal after each correct response and then were allowed to finish the meal after the training session. A meal was completely withheld on the several occasions when *S*s clearly were not motivated sufficiently to respond. On a few occasions two consecutive meals were withheld. This practice produced increased responsiveness and facilitated learning, as *S*s typically made more correct responses after missing a meal. They were allowed to eat as much as they wished in subsequent meals. The evening meal was not used to reinforce behavior. (The use of meals as reinforcers apparently did not affect *S*s' weight, as their weight changes were about the same as for previous months.)

Due to the short duration of the experiment, simple articles of clothing were used to teach dressing skills. T-shirts were used in lieu of dresses at first, as they were manipulated more easily. As *S*s developed their ability to handle the shirts, they were graduated to simple dresses. Cotton panties and ankle-length socks were also used.

Behavior changes resulting from the training program were measured in three ways. First, a situational test of the eleven skills covered by the program was devised. The eleven situational test items and the terminal steps for each task in the program were quite similar. *S*s were given each direction five times and the correct responses were rewarded with a bite of food. The tester was a technician familiar to the *S*s and the test was administered after they had been fed their regular meal. Responses were scored by another person. The test was administered at three intervals: just before the training period commenced, after one month, and at the completion of training.

The second measure of behavior changes compared the experimental group's pretraining and posttraining scores on the situational test with those of a control group over the same period. The control group was comprised of five girls from a different ward. They were equated as closely as possible with the experimental group with respect to CA, MA, SA, diagnosis, and length of hospital residence. The control Ss did not receive special training during the 60-day period, but were given the usual care and training generally afforded patients at the hospital.

The third measure of behavior changes used the program itself. Ss were tested at the beginning of each session to determine their readiness to progress to the next step and their daily scores showed their rate of progress.

✂

RESULTS AND DISCUSSION

All Ss' situational test scores progressively improved from the first to the second and third administrations. The total mean scores on the pretraining, midtraining, and posttraining tests were 7.88, 14.13, and 19.75 respectively. The difference among them, as evaluated by analysis of variance, was significant at the .001 level ($F = 15.06$; $df = 2,10$).

The three mean scores for each test item are shown in Table 2. The scores increased for every item with one exception: remaining seated. This item differs from the others in that it (a) requires inactivity rather than active behavior and (b) was established fairly well in Ss' repertory even before training began. It may be that Ss did less well on this item because they were reinforced systematically for actively responding to all other cues but reinforced for inactivity in this case. Ss did not develop the last three self-help skills to any great extent because they did not progress to these steps in the two-month training period.

The second measure of change compared the test scores for the experimental group with changes made by an equated control group. The experimental group's total mean scores on the pretraining and posttraining tests were 7.88 and 19.75. The corresponding scores for the control group were 13.40 and 14.60. The difference in amount of change, as evaluated by a t test, was significant at the .01 level ($t = 3.90$; $df = 9$).

TABLE 2.   Comparison of Situational Test Scores on Three Administrations

	Mean Number of Correct Responses		
Item	*Pre-Training*	*Mid-Training*	*Post-Training*
1. Look at me	2.00	4.17	4.33
2. Come here	1.83	3.50	3.50
3. Sit down	1.33	2.83	3.67
4. Stay seated	3.83	3.33	2.17
5. Stand up	1.50	2.50	3.67
6. Dress off	0.00	1.67	2.83
7. Pants off	0.00	.17	2.67
8. Socks off	0.00	0.00	2.50
9. Dress on	0.00	.67	.83
10. Pants on	0.00	0.00	0.00
11. Socks on	0.00	0.00	.50

The third means of evaluating behavior changes was essentially phenomenological. Progress through the 36 major substeps in the program was plotted as a cumulative frequency curve. In this way *S*s' rate of progress could be determined and difficult steps identified. The average acquisition curve for the six *S*s is shown in Figure 1.

It is evident from Figure 1 that the group continued to gain new self-help skills throughout the two months of training. This is in contrast to the earlier finding that patients attained a plateau of learning after one month (Bensberg et al., 1965). It is possible that the present study used smaller and more appropriate program steps, thereby facilitating learning. It appears vital that steps be made consonant with patients' abilities, so that their interest and progress might be maintained. In this study the very rapid rate of acquisition did decrease after the first 16 days. Many *S*s experienced particular difficulty with the fourteenth and eighteenth substeps. The former required *S* to completely remove a dress when given only a spoken direction. The absence of other cues likely made this step difficult for all *S*s, as profoundly retarded patients' ability to discriminate and respond to verbal stimuli alone appears quite limited. One *S* remained at the thirteenth step for 35 days.

In the other difficult step the technician handed a dress to *S* with the bottom opened toward her. She was required to put the dress on without

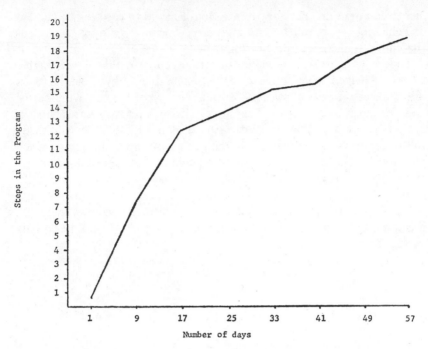

FIGURE 1. Mean number of steps achieved in the program in eight-day periods.

assistance. It may be that the number of fairly complex movements required was puzzling to *S*. Initially, it was difficult for several *S*s even to grasp the dress, and several sessions were spent teaching this often-assumed skill of grasping. One *S* stayed just below this step for 36 days, until the end of the training period.

Another probable reason for the decrease in the initially rapid rate of acquisition was that *S*s demonstrated in the pretraining situational test that they were able to perform some of the skills taught in the first eleven program substeps, but they were very inconsistent.

It is evident from the three measures of change that it was possible to teach self-help skills to profoundly retarded patients. *S*s' behavioral improvement also was obvious from a descriptive standpoint. By the end of the training period they appeared far more attentive and all were amenable to many simple verbal instructions. They had greatly improved their ability to dress and undress for bedtime and showers. The incidence of such behaviors as tantrums and aggression against self was greatly reduced, as *S*s found that misbehaviors were not reinforced with increased attention. They apparently had learned to earn reinforcement by behaving appropriately, and such direct means of getting rewards as snatching food were largely extinguished.

The technicians who used the program reported that it was highly useful. It helped them to teach skills systematically by breaking tasks into substeps for easier mastery and also enabled them to evaluate Ss' daily progress in an objective manner. The technicians carried out the program without difficulty and with little need for supervision. By following the program they became more aware of conditioning principles and generalized their use to the teaching or extinguishing of other behaviors. A programmed learning approach to the teaching of skills to the retarded thus seems very useful and practical in an institutional setting. While the present study involved profoundly retarded patients, it is quite likely that appropriately modified programs would be equally useful for patients with greater abilities.

~10~

Stair Ascending-Descending Behavior in Trainable Retarded Preschoolers

Fred G. Esposito

Four trainable retarded children, ages five to seven, in a state-operated Regional Center program were conspicuous for poor posture, awkwardness of gait, reluctance to run, fear of heights, and general ineptness with regard to position and motion in space. They balked at ascending and descending from their bus, bidding to be carried each time. They dropped to all fours when facing an inclined plane such as a moderately steep ramp or hillside. Stairs, too, were negotiated on all fours. Each refused to jump or alight from a height of more than three inches. This behavior had been consistently observed over the previous year and a half in the center's program. An exploratory program was improvised to help overcome their difficulty in negotiating stairs, ramps or hillsides.

A fifteen-foot long, two-foot wide, wooden ramp; an up-down, three-step (standard riser $8\frac{3}{4}$ inch) stairway; a soft gym mat; blocks and cookie bits (Pecan Sandies) made up the materials.

The objective was to program each child so that his ultimate behavior would be walking erect, unaided, up the stairway and down again. A systematic desensitization/reinforcement paradigm was used.

The first phase involved setting up intermediate subgoals which were approximations of the ultimate objective. Each child was tested to see if he would walk the ramp merely as it rested horizontally on the floor. Each child was allowed to step up the ramp thickness ($2\frac{3}{4}$ inches),

119

walk the ramp length and then to the mat which rested at approximately the same height as the ramp. Intermittent cookie reinforcers were linked with a teacher aide who verbally praised and bear-hugged, terminating with a rolling frolic on the mat while the child was securely embraced by the aide.

Three children mastered this task within 8 trials, seeming to crave the terminal activity and foregoing the cookie reinforcer. This procedure was maintained until each child attained the criteria of non-phobic repetition of specified behavior, during 15 seconds of observation. At this point, a block ($1\frac{3}{4}$ inches) was placed under one end of the plank, resulting in a mild incline. Again the same procedure and criteria were invoked. When the high end of the ramp reached one stair height (fourth session), the blocks were removed and the actual stair served as the high end of ramp support.

Each aide initially bear-hugged the child as he pivoted at ramp-top poised to negotiate the drop to the mat. The aides became adroit at gradually withdrawing their participation in the drop: From a bear-hug dropping together, to holding-less-than-bear-hug, to holding two hands, to holding one hand, to no-hand support and mere verbal stimulus accompaniment, and then to autonomous jumping by the child. Each child continued within the outlined procedure until he could autonomously walk the inclined ramp and jump from the third step. At this point the ramp was removed and a wooden block, the width and depth of the stairway, but only half each stair's riser height, was placed on the floor before the first stair. Again the child emitted foot-raising behavior to the box height and was reinforced even if "all fours" were employed. Only two of the original four children demonstrated this operant behavior. Systematically they were reinforced if only one hand and two feet were used, then no hands. The jump to the mat from this level brought the primary and secondary reinforcers from the aide.

In time the criteria were raised in terms of step level, and the children were successively reinforced at higher step levels, up to the top of the three steps.

The next phase, deemed relevant in terms of developing motor and spatial self-sufficiency, involved the elements and sequencing of elements of descent from height; first, descent from ramp, second, descent from stairs, which progressed to descent from the top step—much the converse of the program of ascent described above.

Within 16 sessions, three of the four trainable retarded children performed at criterion with the third-step level for both ascent and descent. The fourth child was lost to the program because of a family summer vacation.

External criteria confirmed results in that the bus driver, teachers, and aides observed autonomous bus embarking and disembarking daily by the three subject children. Observations made over the next several weeks indicated that the children continued their newly-learned behavior, and, with practice, seemed to become increasingly capable of negotiating stairs, ramps, and hills. Their new skills had apparently quite easily generalized to all stairs and ramps in the building, the steps of the buses, and the hillside around the building.

One of the unexpected dividends of this project was that the children were introduced to falling, rolling, and tumbling on mats and found it so reinforcing that gymnastics has become one of the most sought-after activities by the children. Now, with shouts of "me do," "me do!" they roll, jump, and laugh on the mat, obviously enjoying this new facet of program activity.

~ 11 ~

Behavior Therapy with
High Level, Institutionalized,
Retarded Adolescents

Steve G. Doubros

Despite voluminous experimental work in the area of learning, only within the last few years have principles derived from the laboratory begun to find their practical and ultimate application to therapy (Dollard and Miller, 1950; Wolpe, 1954; Wolpe, 1964; Eysenck, 1964). Behavior therapy can be defined as a systematic manipulation of the patient's behavior, according to learning principles, to help the patient exert appropriate and socially condoned control over his overt behavior. Disturbed demeanor is assumed to be the outcome of persistent and ineffective emotional habits which are primarily manifested by anxiety. The establishment of these maladaptive habits follows a developmental sequence of faulty learning in the course of everyday human interactions and experiences. To assume that neurotic patterns are learned implies that they may also be unlearned.

Watson (1930) presented evidence to show that self verbalizations underlie all thinking. These internal verbal responses may lead to appropriate or inappropriate modes of thinking and action, depending upon the nature of previous reinforcing operations. The intimate relationship between verbal and motor behaviors is evident in many ethnic groups where speech is often accompanied by hand gestures of various kinds.

From *Exceptional Children*, December 1966, pp. 229–232.

The use of the speech musculature for the control of disturbed behavior has been recently emphasized by Luria (1961), who attempted to develop a training technique whereby speech manipulation brings about a change in the cognitive processes. Speech is gradually reshaped and reconstructed along new lines by the excitation of new verbal patterns and the inhibition of old unadaptive ones. Salter (1964) has also developed a conditioned reflex therapy along similar lines.

The aim of behavior therapy with high level mentally retarded adolescents is twofold: (a) to generate self control and (b) to increase socially acceptable behaviors. There is reason to believe that retardates subscribe to the same laws of learning as normal individuals do. The only apparent difference between the two populations seems to be in the acquisition and maintenance of conditioning patterns.

An extension of the laboratory situation into the therapist's office would suggest that the neurotic symptomatology is equivalent to the dependent variable, whereas behavior manipulation during therapy is equivalent to the independent variable. No one would deny that the exact nature and specification of these two variables are very elusive in the therapeutic setting. Crude as the expressions of these variables may be, generalization of beneficial therapeutic effects to other areas outside the therapist's office (behavior amelioration) constitutes the best pragmatic criterion of therapeutic success from many points of view.

In line with behavior principles, the assumption is made that the retardate's impractical, unadaptive verbal and motor behavior can be modified for the patient's benefit by a deliberate and systematic manipulation of his verbal system. Talking it out techniques are often incapable of changing the patient's conduct. The presence of functional speech in the retardate is an important asset within his personality structure. Often, the motor, perceptual, and cognitive areas are adversely affected by central nervous system defects and, hence, they are not readily amenable to environmental manipulation with regard to general social adaptation. As a result, verbal manipulation becomes the only avenue through which behavior control can be progressively established.

><

OUTLINE OF THERAPY

The present investigator has developed the following blueprint for behavior therapy:

1. Definition and specification, by observation and cottage reports, of the behavior constructs to be modified.

2. Review of the social and developmental history for clues regarding the development of these patterns of behavior.
3. Reconditioning of the patient's verbal system through the application of the following learning principles: (a) continuous and immediate social reinforcement (i.e., attention, interest, praise) of any verbalizations that have sound underpinning; (b) withdrawal of social reinforcement following self defeating, unadaptive verbalizations; (c) repetition of critical verbalizations by the patient at the therapist's request or demand; (d) use of imaginary, threat inducing situations for the purpose of enabling the patient to reduce anxiety and find appropriate solutions to his problems; and (e) constant probing into the patient's daily behavior and systematic encouragement to think problems out (self verbalizing), instead of acting them out.

During the course of therapy, appropriate verbalizations are selectively reinforced by making them contingent upon social rewards at the therapist's discretion. When the therapist asks his patient to repeat critical phrases related to his behavior difficulties in the cottage, the probability of establishing new verbal motor connections is increased. By continuous and unrelenting repetition, new verbal themes become firmly established. The speech musculature serves as a medium or a ground for building new verbal motor associations. Concurrently, incompatible or socially unacceptable verbal habits and actions are gradually eliminated by prompt and constant withdrawal of social reinforcement.

The patient is also asked to memorize verbalizations commensurate with social norms and regulations (e.g., it is important that I have friends, I must do my cottage duties, people like me when I like them). Each therapy session often becomes an exercise in memorization of critical, appropriate verbal patterns. Verbal drilling is continuous, social reinforcement is prompt, and withdrawal of attention is immediate. The course of therapy resembles a process of deliberate and systematic teaching of new verbal response classes. The therapist shows a willingness to listen to the child only when he shows responsible behavior during the therapy session. The sessions afford opportunities, not only for the learning of appropriate verbal themes, but also for the unlearning of neurotic patterns.

It is hoped that once a few discriminate verbal cues for acceptable behavior have been established during the therapy sessions, they will eventually lead to expected verbal and motor behaviors in other extralaboratory settings. However, more often than not, the institutional setting does not provide the consistent and immediate social reinforcement necessary to sustain the emotional improvements accomplished during therapy. The patient may be treated differently by the personnel of the various areas that he attends during the day. For this reason, it is necessary that the other training areas be informed of the therapist's program with the patient in order to coordinate the therapeutic goals. Ultimately, there is reason to believe that the retardate's disturbed thinking will be modified by the repetitive teaching of a practically new language.

TWO ILLUSTRATIVE CASES

Roger, a tall, thin, thirteen-year-old boy, was admitted to the institution because of suspected mental retardation and overt, antisocial behavior. At school, he was aggressive, stole a bicycle, had erratic school attendance, and was "sickening polite and somewhat paranoid, obnoxious and sarcastic." He also had trouble "keeping his hands off of girls" and, on at least one occasion, requested sexual intercourse with his adoptive mother. He had threatened the family with a knife, attempted to blow up the family's mobile home, and broken into other homes in the neighborhood. Intellectually, he functioned on the borderline level of retardation (WISC full scale score of 81).

The psychiatric diagnosis at the time of admission was borderline mental retardation, based partly upon emotional deprivation and partly upon neurotic emotional disturbance characterized by aggressive acting out, poor impulse control, marked feelings of inferiority, low self esteem, and mild to moderate depression. Because of his extremely poor social functioning, he was placed in a closed cottage.

Behavior therapy began three months after admission and was continued for a period of six months in weekly 45-minute sessions. The goal of therapy was to make him conscious of his aggressiveness to the point where modification of such behavior could be effected. In the initial stage, the therapist discussed with him the meaning of the word aggression and the possible reasons for such demeanor. Behavior manipulation was later instituted through social verbal reinforcement (e.g., "that's correct") when present or future actions were described by the patient in socially acceptable terms. When abusive or undesirable language was used in describing such events, practically all social verbal reinforcement was withdrawn. For example, when Roger talked of people around him as being helpful and understanding, instead of critical and uncooperative, the therapist nodded his head approvingly and made a positive reply. Upon the patient's use of profane statements, the therapist either turned his face away or remained silent for many seconds.

Roger was asked on many occasions to repeat certain statements made by the therapist about previously discussed topics. When such statements were repeated by the boy, verbal reinforcement was prompt and immediate. Imaginary, threat inducing situations were occasionally introduced to present Roger with opportunities for learning coping responses to enable him to deal with such situations in the future. Questions such as "What would you do if someone accused you of stealing something you hadn't stolen, called you a bad name, or hit you without any excuse?" were asked.

Answers were then discussed, and suggestions were made as to how these situations should be handled by the patient in the future. The therapist would often say: "To feel anxious and angry at other boys accusing you of things you haven't done or hitting you when you are not to blame is natural. But to express your feelings by hitting them back, instead of talking about these things, will get you into more trouble. You must learn to ask the aides to help you. You must learn to control yourself. Please repeat what I just told you." It was felt that by having the boy repeat and imitate such verbalizations, a process of self instruction in responsible actions was being learned.

Despite some early resistance to therapy, Roger gradually became more cooperative. Satisfactory social interaction was always rewarded by the therapist's attentive listening and intermittent comments of approval. When Roger came late to therapy, this action was completely ignored at first; but the therapist deliberately extended the time allotment at the end of the session in order to make up for the time lost at the beginning of the hour. Figure 1 is a graphic presentation of Roger's behavior progress preceding, during, and following therapy. The dependent variable in this case is expressed by the frequency of restrictions and isolations.

Following therapy and a sizable improvement in social adjustment, Roger was transferred to an open cottage. The following comments were taken from nursing staff notes one month after the termination of therapy: "He has made good adjustment...functions well in all activities." It became apparent that the emotional gains obtained in therapy generalized to other training and treatment areas.

Carl, a twelve-year-old boy, was admitted to the institution with a diagnosis of encephalopathy due to prenatal injury, asphyxia at birth, and postnatal injury associated with a convulsive disorder and behavior

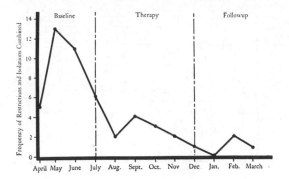

FIGURE 1.　Behavior improvement based on frequency of restrictions and isolations.

reaction. Upon admission, the nursing staff described him as a very sick boy. He stayed away from the cottage, got into trouble going to training areas, and was destructive and socially aggressive. In the cottage, he was "selfish, sassy, and unruly." His intellectual performance was well within the borderline level of retardation (IQ of 75), and he had a moderate speech defect. Carl was in an intensive treatment cottage when therapy began.

Therapy consisted of both playroom and office sessions on a weekly basis for a period of about eleven months. All social verbal reinforcement was contingent upon the description of socially compatible self verbalizations and constructive social play activities. Attending responses by the therapist were withheld when Carl showed such inappropriate behaviors as baby talking, shouting, and moving around the room. Carl was frequently asked to repeat socially acceptable verbalizations (e.g., I must learn to like others, you are not supposed to sass the aides, school is good because you learn a lot of things). In order to sensitize him to his inappropriate behavior and to strengthen social controls, he was also asked to write repeatedly the sentence "I must behave myself." Coming to therapy on time meant not only a verbal reward of praise by the therapist, but also an occasional material reward, such as candy. With progress in behavior therapy, socially cooperative activities increased in frequency, while antisocial acts became less and less prevalent. Figure 2 gives a pictorial view of this improvement.

Upon termination of therapy, Carl was functioning on a relatively adequate social level in almost all of his adjunctive and training areas. The nursing staff notes described him as a person who "has improved a lot. Most of the areas agree that Carl has settled down and has been

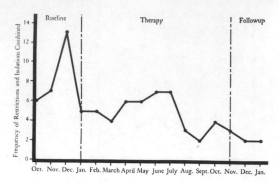

FIGURE 2.   Behavior amelioration based on frequency of restrictions and isolations.

able to accept what training we have to offer.... He came to accept rules and regulations well enough to function in the group with co-operation and mannerly display.... He is functioning more independently and is no longer a behavior problem." He was discharged from the institution a month after the termination of therapy.

Despite the obvious limitations of using a dependent variable of restrictions and isolations as a criterion for therapeutic success, it is nevertheless important to realize that it is one of the few objective measures available in an institutional setting. Even if we discount this criterion, the fact that both of these patients improved sufficiently to be transferred to an open cottage or dismissed from the institution affords adequate observable evidence of the success of the behavior therapy.

III

MODIFICATION

OF PSYCHOTIC BEHAVIOR

THIS PART BEGINS WITH A RECENT REVIEW ARTICLE BY ROBERT Leff. Clearly, as illustrated by Leff's article, most of the behavior modification approaches with children have been based on positive reinforcement in an operant framework, while relatively little use has been made of techniques based on the respondent conditioning paradigm. Although many psychologists, particularly Skinnerians, object to the use of aversive control of behavior, some, such as Lovaas et al. (1964), Ball (1965), and Tate and Baroff (1966), report success using aversive stimuli — for example, painful electric shock — to control severely disruptive behavior. In Chapter 13, Tate and Baroff point out that some behaviors, such as head-banging, can be so severe and persistent that permanent physical damage may result. Under such conditions it can be understood that aversive control, itself apparently less severe than the child's own behavior, might be justified. In this regard, Marshall described the toilet training of an autistic child much as Hundziak et al. described with retarded children, and reported success using a candy-dispensing apparatus immediately to reinforce appropriate elimination in the toilet. It is interesting to note that Marshall's use of negative reinforcement, five seconds of darkness, to control the child's masturbating, seemed to increase rather than decrease the unwanted behavior. Later the removal of salt, a "favorite" of the child, did seem to be an effective negative reinforcer. Marshall reports success in bringing about toilet training and in teaching the child's mother to continue the training.   ·

The speech development of autistic children is considered to be an important prognostic indicator (Kanner, 1948; Eisenberg, 1956; Hewett, 1965; Rimland, 1964). That is, those who fail to develop speech by about their fifth year typically show little subsequent clinical improvement. Brown (1960) found that even with psychotherapy autistic children who had no speech by age three remained withdrawn and severely disturbed. This suggests that speech and other improvements may be related to some other factor which interferes with development, and also suggests a causal relationship; that is, speech development at an early age is necessary as a basis for later social learning. Lovaas, Berberich, Perloff, and Schaeffer, and Hewett attempt to develop speech in autistic children so that future therapy and the children's development will be facilitated; these authors and others have clearly demonstrated that speech can be developed through reinforcement procedures even in severely psychotic, previously nonverbal children.

The chapters by Browning and Davison deal with higher-level social behavior. Browning reduced stuttering in a nine-year-old schizophrenic boy. Inferring that stuttering seemed reinforced by both the attention given to it and the anxiety reduction which occurred at the end of a stuttered phrase, Browning utilized both operant shaping and reciprocal inhibition techniques. His use of progressive relaxation, based on Jacobsen's (1928) work is of particular interest because there are few papers which report the use of reciprocal inhibition with psychotic children. In this collection, only those articles by Browning, Graziano, and Graziano and Kean utilized "relaxation" with psychotic children.

Davison's paper describes an attempt to program social learning sequences for an autistic child. Using Ferster's thesis that for autistic children there has been a failure in developing generalized secondary reinforcers and the children thus respond almost exclusively to primary reinforcement, Davison used college students as "nontraditional" therapists, to apply the specified reinforcement and develop more socially cooperative behavior in the autistic child.

The paper by Graziano is a brief overview of a program developed to treat the multiple behavior problems of autistic children in a group rather than an individual setting. Attempts were made to program the daily environment to utilize the many potential reinforcers, to develop new, secondary reinforcers, and to shape and maintain adaptive behavior including speech, academic achievement, social cooperation, and the control of aggressive behavior. As in Davison's work, the program was carried out by subprofessional staff who were trained in relatively short time.

One of the approaches used in this group behavior modification was based on the concept of reciprocal inhibition, and utilized "programmed relaxation" modeled after Jacobsen's (1928) work. This attempt to use reciprocal inhibition with autistic children is described by Graziano and Kean. The authors suggest that, contrary to the apparently accepted opinion in this field, relaxation training of psychotic children might be a potentially useful and effective therapeutic technique.

In the final paper, Ney reports a controlled study with twenty schizophrenic children, comparing the effectiveness of treatment by operant conditioning with treatment by traditional play therapy. After 50, forty-five-minute treatment sessions by nurses, the operant conditioning group had gained more speech and improved more in social behavior, as measured by the Vineland Scale, than did the traditional play therapy group. Ney's study, like the DeLeon and Mandell paper, is one of the few available which attempt controlled comparisons of behavioral and psychodynamic therapies with children.

This Part presents a variety of behavioral approaches to severely psychotic children—from focus on basic behaviors of individual children, to attempts at an integrated, social-learning, group behavior therapy program. The selections point out the need for careful planning or step-by-step programming, the potential use of nonprofessional or nontraditionally trained therapists, the possibilities of more direct involvement of the parents, the possible effectiveness of using reciprocal inhibition with psychotics, and the possibility of developing social group behavior therapy programs in which the multiple problem behaviors of several children are dealt with simultaneously in a programmed environment.

⊰12⊱

Behavior Modification
and Childhood Psychoses

Robert Leff

Over the course of the last 15 years, various types of behavior modification, that is, modification procedures which are directed primarily at the behavioral symptoms of a psychological disorder, have been effectively used in a wide variety of applications. Grossberg (1964) reviewed the large body of literature that has rapidly accumulated in this general field. More recently, an increasing number of investigators have been devoting their attention to experimental inquiries into the efficacy of behavior modification with the most severe of the childhood disorders—the childhood psychoses, including early infantile autism. Virtually all of the methods employed in this work to date are direct derivatives of the operant-learning procedures which have been established in the comparative laboratories.

The primary behavior disorders of childhood which characterize the subjects of the research discussed in this review have been labeled variously childhood schizophrenia, early infantile autism, and symbiotic autism. According to Bender (1953), childhood schizophrenia is a disorder of the entire organization and maturation of behavior processes.

From *Psychological Bulletin*, 69:6 (1968), 396–409.

The author expresses his gratitude to Justin Aronfreed, James Geer, Harvey Winston, and Julius Wishner for their helpful critical comments. This work was done during the author's tenure as a United States Public Health Service Predoctoral Fellow and was supported by National Institute of Mental Health Grant No. 5 Tl MH-8209.

Manifest in such primary disturbances of function is a "global insta-
bility and poor integration of the control and direction of behavior at
all levels [p. 415]." Also typical of these cases are pan-anxiety and
secondary disturbances in the basic perception of the self as an object
in the psychological world, including perturbations in body image,
identity, and orientation to the objects and forces of the external world.
On the more specific level of symptomatology, the schizophrenic child is
often subject to somatic complaints, shows abnormal EEG activity, and
indulges in bizarre regressive behavior, repetitive motor actions, and
tantrums. Also noted are speech and thinking disturbances.

Early infantile autism is a diagnostic entity, first described by Kanner
(1943) and eventually recognized by him and his co-worker (Eisenberg,
1957, p. 79) as "the earliest possible manifestation of childhood schizophrenia." The criteria that Kanner proposed for diagnosis of this
"disturbance of affective contact" with other persons are: (a) definite
early onset, before the age of two; (b) demonstration of at least selected
age-appropriate intellectual abilities; (c) early preference for extreme
"self-isolation" or "aloneness"; and (d) obsessive insistence on the
preservation of "sameness" in the environment. In addition, there are
several subordinate, distinguishing features of this childhood disorder,
reviewed by Rimland (1964), among which are (a) the low incidence of
psychotic progenitors and the lack of clinically detectable hallucinations
or delusions in autistic versus schizophrenic children, (b) the very
frequent fetishlike preoccupation with mechanical objects, and (c) the
extremely high and peculiar incidence of extraordinary spatial memory
and musical ability.

Rimland (1964), on the basis of these and other factors enumerated
in his book, maintains that autism deserves the status of a separate and
unique diagnostic category. He deplores the practice of misnaming true
autism "childhood schizophrenia," and the more frequent indiscriminate
use of the autism diagnosis to include cases which do not meet Kanner's
(1943) original criteria. To some extent, Kanner, himself, may have
become responsible for the trend toward a diluted concept of autism
when, in 1956, he isolated as the pathognomonic, primary symptoms
of autism only the extreme self-isolation and the obsessive insistence
on the preservation of sameness (Eisenberg and Kanner, 1956). Com-
pounding the effects of Kanner's implied reduction of the stringency of
criteria for autism is the observation that there apparently is a great
deal of overlap in symptomatology between the early autistic and
childhood-schizophrenic syndromes. Finally, it appears possible that
several of the studies reported here may have confused the diagnoses
somewhat, while others have employed mixed samples of autistic and

schizophrenic children. All the children dealt with here, however, are quite clearly severely disturbed (psychotic), and all seem to respond similarly, on the whole, to the treatments applied. Thus, at least within the present context, that is, that of the effects of behavior-modification techniques with the primary disorders of childhood, differential diagnosis will not be considered a crucial issue.

Instead, major emphasis will be given to the problem of the efficacy of the behavior-modification procedures discussed. Traditional psychodynamic methods of therapy, in all their diversity, have failed to demonstrate any reasonable degree of efficacy with psychotic children. In 1956, Eisenberg reported a follow-up study of 63 autistic children, and, in 1957, after a thoughtful review of the literature on childhood schizophrenia, he concluded that there was little or no reason to believe that any of the techniques employed to that date, including classical psychotherapy and electrical and chemical shock, had been shown to have beneficial effects on the patients treated. On the other hand, the rapidly growing body of literature reporting positive results of behavior-modification methods attests to the potential power of this "new" therapy. Many investigators have reported successful therapeutic manipulation of the behavior of hospitalized psychotic adults (e.g., Ayllon and Haughton, 1962; Ayllon and Michael, 1959; King, Armitage, and Tilton, 1960; Sherman, 1965). In addition, the deviant behavior patterns of normal, neurotic, and retarded children have been shown to be readily amenable to the control of various operant-training procedures (Baer, 1962; Bijou, 1957; Harris, Wolf, and Baer, 1964; Lazarus, Davison, and Polefka, 1965; Wolf, 1965).

No such application of the established principles of operant learning to the specific problems of the autistic or schizophrenic child appeared in the literature until 1961. The appearance in that year of two papers (Ferster, 1961; Ferster and DeMyer, 1961a) gave major impetus to subsequent research in this field. In these publications, Ferster presented his thesis that autism, like any other behavioral phenomenon, is best understood and treated within the framework of a social-learning theory. The autistic child is not seen as qualitatively different from the normal one; rather, he is distinguished from the normal organism only by the relative frequency of occurrence of all the performances in his repertoire. Thus, for example, the autistic child engages in a great deal less behavior which influences his social environment, and a great deal more behavior intended to influence only the physical environment than does the normal child.

Though Ferster regards lack of positive reinforcement (especially parental attention) as the fundamental agent in the production of many autistic deficits, he also recognizes that a consistent program of active restriction of a child's behavior may produce the severely limited behavioral repertory that is characteristic of the autistic child. Illustrative of this type of etiology is Ferster's (1965a) recent description of a mother who appeared, on casual observation, to be continuously involved in normal interaction with her child. Closer observation, however, indicated that the mother's only true interactive behavior with her son was comprised of restrictions of the boy's attempted manipulations of his environment. Thus, Ferster (Ferster and DeMyer, 1961a) stated that:

> all of the basic processes by which new performances are generated, strengthened, maintained, eliminated, punished, suppressed, or controlled by special aspects of the environment are relevant to an analysis of how a particular history could produce a weak, positively maintained repertoire (p. 344).

The next logical step in the consideration of an appropriate behavior-modification program, therefore, consists of an arrangement of reinforcement contingencies so as to establish conditioned and then generalized reinforcers, many of which are social in nature. Most investigators would agree that the primary goal of this modification, whether it be predominantly accomplished through the use of positive reinforcement or avoidance-learning techniques, is to render other human beings "meaningful in the sense of becoming rewarding to the child" (Lovaas, Benson Schaeffer, and Simons, 1965, p. 108).

The focus of this paper will be upon operant training, since it has been employed far more extensively with psychotic children than the desensitization or "deconditioning" techniques that are more closely associated with the principles of Pavlovian or classical conditioning. The term "operant training" refers to a diversity of procedures that have been derived directly from principles of behavior that were established in the basic operant-research laboratory. Both appetitive and aversive paradigms are used. In the former type of procedure, reinforcement contingencies are arranged in order to produce new behavior (shaping) or to modify existing behavior via, for example, the method of successive approximations.

Aversion therapy is another class of treatments, one component of which is passive-avoidance training. This method incorporates the traditional concept of punishment, where noxious stimulation regularly follows undesired behavior. Positive-reinforcement withdrawal or deprivation will be subsumed under this category of passive-avoidance techniques, consistent with the view of withdrawal of positively reinforcing stimuli as one form of aversive contingency. Active-avoidance learning, on the other hand, involves situations in which the attenuation or elimination of aversive stimuli is made contingent upon desired, adaptive responses.

In the studies conducted thus far with psychotic children, positive reinforcement and/or avoidance techniques are the methods upon which the behavior modifiers have relied most heavily. Typically, modification goals have been relatively circumscribed and clearly specified. Since most of the work is recent, there has been little opportunity for adequate long-range follow-up reports. This precludes the possibility of fruitful analyses of extended therapeutic efficacy in terms of percentages of patients who met a long-term criterion of improvement. But such longitudinal outcome criteria would not be appropriate for many of the studies reviewed because they were not addressed to the issue of long-duration change. Furthermore, group-statistic criteria are not necessary for a rigorous demonstration of the potency of operant-training methods.

The operant approach leads, instead, to a research design in which evaluation of results is accomplished by means of successive experimentation with the same organism. The subject thus becomes his own control in a program that has carefully specified target behaviors and modification goals. Typically, the subject's "base-rate" behavior, recorded prior to the application of the modification procedure, is compared with behavior measures taken after the introduction of experimental manipulations. An evaluation of outcome may subsequently be achieved by temporary discontinuance of the modification procedure (i.e., return to base-rate conditions), followed by reinstatement of the procedure.* Systematic variation of behavior in accordance with the changing experimental conditions provides conclusive evidence of efficacy.

Since much of the work reviewed has been reported in preliminary and case studies, complete demonstrations of experimental control such as that outlined above were not often incorporated. The outcomes, then, of a good deal of this work must be evaluated with respect to the degree to which the results reflect dramatic changes in behavior that appear to be reasonably permanent and to contribute substantially to the adaptation of the children so treated. The studies are grouped according to the type of basic procedure used — positive reinforcement, active avoidance, or passive avoidance.

---

* An alternative design recently presented by Browning (1967) also uses a self-control procedure, but avoids some of the practical drawbacks of the above-described method when it is applied in the setting of a residential treatment center.

OPERANT-TRAINING TECHNIQUES

Positive Reinforcement

It should be recognized, of course, that the great majority of experiments reported in this review incorporate *some* positive-reinforcement contingencies in their procedures, but the studies grouped here are distinguished by their sole reliance upon positive reinforcement. Ferster and DeMyer (1961a) showed that the response patterns emitted by two schizophrenic children who were exposed to fixed-ratio (FR) and variable-interval (VI) schedules under nonverbal reinforcement approximated the characteristic functions obtained with animals and normal humans under such schedules. In addition, a conditioned, or "generalized" reinforcer (coin) was established. The children failed to learn on a multiple schedule (FR-VI) and had great difficulty in a relatively simple transfer-of-training task, where learned discriminative control could not be maintained upon introduction of a new, slightly different apparatus. Nevertheless, both subjects exhibited more experimentally controlled behavior and less tantrum activity with increasing exposure to the automatic environment.

In 1962, Ferster and DeMyer further demonstrated the practicability of controlling key-press behavior in two autistic children through nonverbal intermittent-reinforcement schedules. The children, who eventually performed discriminative acts quite well for intermittent food reward, nevertheless exhibited very restricted behavioral repertoires, in that their operant activity was largely uninfluenced by a wide variety of available stimuli which are reinforcers for normal children. Both these demonstration experiments were informative because they showed that conventional learning technology is adequate for the experimental analysis of this previously refractory disorder.

Metz (1965) obtained "generalized imitation" in two schizophrenic children using conditioned verbal and nonverbal reinforcers ("good" and tokens) in a gradual shaping procedure which began with the experimenter passively "putting the subject through" the action he was to imitate later and rewarding him with food and verbal praise ("good") after each passive demonstration. The experimenter's guidance was progressively withdrawn ("fading" technique) until eventually only an occasional verbal reinforcement was necessary to maintain imitative performances. The problems encountered in this program involved slow learning rates and strong tendencies toward "superstitious" responding, based on inadvertently administered rewards during training. In addition, occasional "regressive" behaviors occurred, that is, responses previously appropriate were emitted in subsequent situations where they were inappropriate. More than balancing the effects of these setbacks, however, were Metz' (1965) observations that: (a) many imitative responses "persisted and increased, in a context of reward for imitation, *without specifically being rewarded*" (p. 397, italics added); (b) the frequency of inappropriate, ritualistic, and emotional behavior (tantrums) decreased as appropriate activity increased; and (c) these withdrawn, autistic children eventually "expressed joy or delight upon 'solving' a problem...sought the model out whenever he appeared on the ward...etc." (p. 398).

Two comments are in order here. First, this investigator enjoyed a greater degree of control over the motivational states of the subjects than is usually possible, since the subjects were deprived of their breakfast daily, and their lunch consisted solely of the reinforcements earned in the experiment. The second point, this one made by the author, limits the interpretation of the results somewhat since no control subjects or procedures were run, and, in light of the diverse extra-experimental experiences undergone daily by these institutionalized children, no strong inference can be made that the increased generalized imitative performance was the specific result of the operant-training procedures.

In an interesting experiment by DeMyer and Ferster (1962) that was conducted on the ward, rather than in a laboratory, new social behaviors were taught to eight schizophrenic children (aged two to ten) by the regular hospital staff of nurses and attendants, who had received explanatory lectures on the basics of operant learning. Each worker spent a great deal of time with the child according to regular hospital routine, but, in addition, each of these "experimenters" had the task of discovering those particular adult behaviors which were especially reinforcing to each of the children involved. Such reinforcers ranged from verbal praise and reassurance to holding the child, playing music, and dancing. When the worker to whom the child seemed most responsive was found, he began the shaping program that constituted the "therapy" of this study. The authors, in conjunction with each worker, decided what sort of behavior was to be shaped with each child, and the worker spent one-half hour a day, three or four times a week, engaged in these activities.

This individually tailored program clearly represents a departure from the less personal and more formally organized tactics employed in other behavior-modification studies and comes closer to the love-oriented techniques of psychoanalytic therapies. Since most of the workers relied heavily on bodily contracts, such as holding and rocking the children, the therapy was more practicable with the younger children, and, indeed, the children under six showed the greatest positive effects. Results were reported in terms of individual improvements for each child, with the general conclusion that "there were classes of behavior which definitely seemed to improve as a result of this therapy and other, more general behavior changes, not directly attributable to the specific procedures employed" (DeMyer and Ferster, 1962, p. 460). The authors did not fail to mention the inherent difficulty of evaluating these results due to the subjects' numerous uncontrolled contacts with other institutional personnel during the course of the study. But it is noteworthy that untrained, nonprofessional workers probably did accomplish some important behavioral changes in the appropriate direction.

That the strategy of employing inexperienced nonprofessionals in operant-training programs for severely disturbed children can be successful has been further demonstrated in a study by Davison (1965). Here, four college undergraduates were given one month of classroom training in the basic concepts of social reinforcement and operant learning. The undergraduate "therapists," working in teams of two, then applied their newly learned techniques to modifying the behaviors of two autistic children. They returned daily reports to the author-supervisor, and he in turn made suggestions and changes during the course of the program. Working conditions in the day-care center at which this experiment was performed were far from ideal. The psychotic children were exposed to the student therapist for less than 15% of their waking hours for a total of only 4 weeks. Also, as a result of unanticipated situational problems with the children, the author was prevented from carrying out his postmeasure of behavioral change as originally planned. Since the pre- and postmeasurements were quite dissimilar, the only firm conclusion that was warranted was that "the therapists *probably* were able to control the child better after the treatment" (Davison, 1965, p. 148). (The more successful team achieved an average increase of about 40% in the number of commands obeyed). Of course, the failure in experimental rigor involving measures and the limitations imposed by uncontrolled institutional settings limit interpretation of these results. But one highly significant implication of this work is that intelligent, highly motivated students may be trained in a very short time to execute a behavior-control program that requires the application of learning principles to the manipulation of psychotic behavior in children.

Perhaps most universally characteristic of children who are labeled schizophrenic is their withdrawal from interpersonal relationships. It has become a classically noted feature of childhood schizophrenia that very little physical contact occurs between afflicted children. Yet,

Hingtgen, Sanders, and DeMyer (1965) observed that their six schizo-phrenic subjects did eventually engage in such behavior, despite the fact that reinforcement was never made directly contingent upon social contacts. The children were seen experimentally for one session per day, 5 days a week. They were first taught to press a lever to obtain coins on a fixed-ratio (FR) schedule of reinforcement. Then the six subjects were paired into three teams, the members being taught, through nonverbal shaping procedures, to emit cooperative responses, that is, they were eventually required to alternate their bar presses in order to obtain rewards, one subject's response allowing the other subject to obtain reinforcement. The results indicated that it was possible to shape these alternative cooperative responses in early childhood schizophrenics within an average of 23 sessions. (However, it must be noted that each of the subjects here had received several months of pre-experimental operant training.) This cooperative behavior is clearly attributable to the training program employed.

However, as mentioned above, it was also noted that other, more general behavior changes occurred as the experiment progressed. The increase in physical contact activity between the children was one of the most striking of these changes. Children who typically behaved as if they were unaware of the presence of other humans were now seen to direct a good deal of their attention and their activity toward another child, within the confines of an experimental setting. As the experiment-ers have noted, their subjects were exposed, during the remainder of each experimental day, to play therapy, psychotherapy, occupational therapy, music therapy, and so forth. Yet it seems likely that the ob-served increase in forms of social interaction which were not directly reinforced was also primarily due to the experimental manipulations, since the behavior referred to increased in the experimental room, but not on the ward.

If it is accepted that the experimental manipulations incidentally established certain situation-specific social interactions, then a critical evaluation of this result becomes necessary. Such an evaluation will be facilitated by a closer examination of the types of interpersonal behavior which occurred. While some of the contact actions involved one subject's guiding the hand of the other to the lever, there were other "cooperative" interactions of a less passive nature, in which one subject would slap or otherwise attack the other in order to rouse him to action. It is obvious that behavior such as this may be called "co-operative" only within the context of this experiment, that is, a subject who forces his teammate to act in order to render his own actions effective in securing reinforcement is not cooperating or "operating jointly with another" in the usual sense of that definition. Rather, he is coercing another solely in order to further his own ends — in this case, the acquisition of material rewards.

The above analysis is not meant to imply that the so-called cooperative behavior is of no potential value in an operant-learning approach to a therapeutic training program for psychotic children. Though the physical prompting of a teammate cannot be classified as true cooperative behavior, it does entail reality testing and the tacit recognition of other human beings as significant mediators of desired ends. Action taken with reference to the instrumental value of others is indicative of an adaptiveness that is characteristically absent in the autistic or schizophrenic behavioral repertoire. Thus, the elicitation here of such adaptiveness through the use of reinforcement-contingency techniques suggests that these operant-training methods may constitute a fruitful approach to the problems of the primary behavior disorders of childhood.

Indeed, a follow-up study by Hingtgen and Trost (1964) provides added support for this inference. In an attempt to induce more general behavioral changes, the authors made provision for the direct reinforcement of vocal and physical interactions between four young nonverbal schizophrenic children. After an average of 46 sessions, the two pairs of children (who had all had approximately one year of previous experience in operant-learning procedures) exhibited a low but stable rate of interactive behavior. This level of contact action was significantly greater than that measured in a series of pre-experimental toy-play observations in which the subjects participated. Moreover, in line with the authors' expectations, physical contact and vocal behavior were observed to increase in the ward setting, as well as in the home.

Further evidence for the power of operant-training methods is provided by the work of Hewett (1964, 1965). This author has been able to engineer and maintain a consistently enforced training program with his hospitalized subject population. In the course of one year of daily individual training, a thirteen-year-old autistic boy who had not developed useful speech was taught a 55-word sight vocabulary (Hewett, 1964). This was accomplished by using gumdrop reinforcers for correct matching of visually presented words with corresponding pictures. Eventually, picture cues became unnecessary, and the child could select any word card on the verbal command of the teacher. Finally, the subject was taught the alphabet and was required to write out any requests that he wished to make of the hospital personnel.

In connection with the author's long-term goal — the socialization of this psychotic child — there were other behavior modifications which accompanied those described above. The author described the subject's growing interest in his education and his increasing conformity to his teacher's instructions, even under conditions of decreasing reinforcement. The child showed enjoyment of his work by emitting laughter and other vocalizations. He also frequently initiated new learning tasks by bringing the teacher pictures whose symbolic designation he was eager to master. Finally, the subject gave definite indications that the teacher had acquired secondary reinforcement value for him. The child began to look directly at the teacher's face, rather than only at his hand (the immediate reinforcement-delivery mechanism), and drew simple sketches which symbolized events of great importance in his life.

All of these changes, and especially the latter ones which represent the definite attempts of a previously intractable autistic child to communicate with his adult teacher, are behavior modifications which were not directly reinforced in this child's educational program. In the absence of even rudimentary control procedures, it would be unwarranted to attribute these changes solely to the operant-reinforcement program per se. The author, for instance, did not describe the extraexperimental daily activities engaged in by the subject. Nor did he characterize in any detail the nature of the teacher's behavior toward the child, that is, it cannot be ascertained from this report whether the relationship between the teacher and child was warm and solicitous or mechanically impersonal. These variables could conceivably play an important role in the behavior-modification program. Such deficiencies in descriptive information notwithstanding, it seems likely that the dramatic general improvements shown by this child were largely the outgrowth of the experimental manipulations. In strong support of this statement is the fact that the subject had remained virtually inaccessible to all previous socialization attempts during the first 13 years of his life. Only when reinforcement became reliably contingent, through human mediation, upon certain goal-directed behaviors did the child acquire rudimentary communication skills. And it would seem that in large measure the acquisition of these skills facilitated the further socialization of this autistic boy.

Several other papers which describe therapeutic programs for psychotic children are of direct relevance here. Though the practitioners involved are psychodynamically oriented, they have explicitly incorporated basic tenets of reinforcement theory in their therapies. Weiland and Rudnik (1961), for example, made an eight-year-old autistic boy's receipt of his favorite toy contingent upon his verbalization of the word "ball," thus widening the child's vocabulary until he was eventually singing songs. The authors stated:

> In the ideal therapeutic program, the total environment of the child
> should be organized to allow all of his gratifications to be offered by

some single person who could erect such barriers as to make it impossible for the child to achieve these gratifications by himself (autistically)....Gratification without asking for the assistance of his specific worker(s) would not be permitted, while withdrawal would be obstructed by the persistent efforts of the worker. The child would be offered certain activities or objects which were known to be of high desirability to him. These would be given, however, only if the youngster specifically asked the worker for them (p. 560).

Thus would these workers establish the secondary or generalized reinforcing power of other human beings for the schizophrenic child.

Dubnoff (1965), who successfully treated a child who had been diagnosed as "early infantile autistic" by Kanner, similarly mentioned that such a child in her therapeutic program "is expected to verbalize his demands before they are gratified.... Only appropriate behavior is gratified" (p. 386). This kind of therapy seems a long conceptual way from the all-accepting, permissive, and indiscriminately rewarding type of treatment advocated by some psychoanalysts (e.g., Bettelheim, 1952, 1965). However, despite this apparent gulf that seems to exist between behavior-modification approaches to therapy and the more traditional psychodynamic model, it seems probable that the most successful therapeutic strategy will evolve from a close collaboration between the two.

An example of such a collaboration is provided in two recent papers by Ferster (1965a, 1965b) who described a program in which he cooperated with the clinical director of a treatment center for autistic children. Ferster stated that in the course of their work together, he was continuously impressed by the underlying similarity of their two superficially disparate approaches. In describing his previous investigations of the phenomena of operant learning, Ferster (1965a) stated that his "customary approach to an experiment is essentially clinical." That is, procedures in his animal and human experiments "are carefully designed to meet the repertoire of each individual subject; there is a day-by-day interaction with the experiment in which each procedure derives from the results of previous procedures" (p. 14). Conversely, emphasized Ferster, careful observation of the clinical director's therapeutic activity revealed that:

many of her procedures consisted of direct and forceful manipulation of the milieu directly contingent upon the child's behavior [1965b, p. 3]. She places limits on the child's behavior, gives or withholds food, attention and automobile rides and toys [1965a, p. 14].

It is in practices such as these that many therapists, either wittingly or unwittingly, often make effective use of the basic principles of operant learning. The evidence suggests that therapeutic potency is a direct function of the degree to which these principles are *systematically* applied.

Positive Reinforcement and Passive-Avoidance Learning

Lovaas, Freitag, Gold, and Kassorla (1965) performed a series of well-controlled experiments, the results of which supported many of the implications about children's psychotic behavior derived from the findings of earlier studies. In their first study, Lovaas and his co-workers increased the "appropriate music behavior" and simultaneously decreased the seriously self-destructive behavior of a nine-year-old schizophrenic girl. In acquisition periods, music was played and social reinforcements (smile and "good") were delivered only following appropriate behaviors, such as clapping in rhythm. Significantly, control or extinction periods were also run, during which music was again played, but no social rewards were forthcoming. Appropriate changes in the subject's behavior from acquisition to extinction periods revealed that the behaviors in question had come under experimental control.

A second study, this time using a bar-press response, confirmed the finding of the first study, that is, frequency of self-destructive behavior is a function of the presentation and withdrawal of reinforcement for other behaviors in the same situation. The third study reported in this article demonstrated the tremendous importance of the parental or adult "attention" variable. The authors showed that delivery of sympathetic comments ("I don't think you're bad") contingent upon the occurrence of self-destructive behavior *increased* the frequency and magnitude of such undesirable behavior over levels of performance obtained in base-line control sessions, which were interspersed among experimental sessions. Furthermore, a reduction in tantrum and destructive behaviors was observed in sessions in which the experimenter was nurturant and attentive to the subject *except* when the subject indulged in tantrum or destructive behavior, at which times he was ignored. Such results make it difficult to escape the authors' conclusion that the types of self-destructive acts they examined are best understood "as learned, operant, or instrumental behavior" (Lovaas, Freitag, Gold, and Kassorla, 1965, p. 79).

Wolf, Risley, and Mees (1964) described their rather dramatic therapeutic intervention into a case which had proven intractable to conventional therapies. They used shaping procedures with a food-deprived hospitalized schizophrenic boy of $3\frac{1}{2}$, who was characterized by severe self-destructive behavior and refusal to wear eyeglasses (which were necessary to save his sight) and to sleep at night. Using bits of food as reinforcement and isolation from all social contacts as punishment (analogous to time out from positive reinforcement), these therapists were highly successful in decreasing the child's tantrums and increasing his eyeglass wearing to an acceptable level. When the child began to throw the glasses, isolation, made contingent upon such throwing, effectively reduced this unwanted behavior. Subsequent eating-habit problems were similarly eliminated. The child (who had complex but noncommunicative verbal habits at the outset) was trained to imitatively name pictures and use pronouns correctly in social speech. Verbal stimuli such as "no" came to suppress undesirable nonverbal behavior, probably as a result of frequent pairing with the experience of being sent into isolation. Perhaps most impressive is the authors' account of the mother's report, 6 months after the child's return home: "Dicky continues to wear his glasses, does not have tantrums, has no sleeping problems, is becoming increasingly verbal, and is a new source of joy to the members of his family" (Wolf et al., 1964, p. 312).

Risley and Wolf (1964) used shaping procedures based on ice-cream-bite rewards and incorporated prompting and fading procedures in a program of therapy with a six-year-old autistic child. They succeeded in enlarging the child's verbal repertoire from echolalic speech to appropriate picture naming and eventually to appropriate answers to questions such as, "What's your name?" and "Where are you going?" Unique in this study was the follow-up procedure conducted with the child's parents. The mother, who had observed several laboratory sessions, was instructed and supervised in the basic operant techniques so that she could continue the therapy at home. Though she manifested an early tendency to urge and prompt the child too frequently, she soon came to understand the necessity for strict adherence to a schedule of contingent rewards and in this manner was able to make remarkable progress with the boy. Praise became an effective reinforcer, though not quite as effective as food was in motivating learning. Tantrum screaming, formerly a serious problem, was reduced greatly by sending the child to his room whenever he engaged in such "atavistic" behavior. Chanting, repetitive verbalizations were converted, through gradual shaping and imitative learning, into meaningful sentences. The authors concluded on an optimistic note, stating that seven other sets of parents are effectively working with their disturbed children in this way.

A talkative (but uncommunicative) schizophrenic child who met criteria of (a) being in no individual therapy, (b) having no known physiological damage, (c) receiving no medication, and (d) accepting a candy when offered to her was chosen by Davison (1964) as the subject in an experiment which used previously inexperienced undergraduates as behavior modifiers. The students received training similar to that described in Davison (1965). They saw the psychotic child in the uncontrolled environment of a day-care center where they occupied only 8 of the child's 25 weekly institutional hours. According to the author, "the crux of this therapy was to utilize play situations for the differential reinforcement and extinction of various behaviors" (p. 150). The extinction referred to, as in other studies, was a sort of time-out procedure, in which the positively reinforcing therapists withdrew a certain distance from the subject if the subject misbehaved. The results of the short "therapy" indicated that both therapists had achieved a markedly greater degree of control over the subject than they had had at the outset in terms of the number of commands issued to the child that were obeyed.

But, in addition, and somewhat to the author's surprise, the child also obeyed an equally high percentage of the standard commands given by both a nonprofessional worker who spent a great deal of time with the child and a college student never before seen by the child. The author tentatively concluded that the child had become, as a result of the behavior therapy, more responsive to adults in general. Other positive features of the results were the incidental apparent desensitization of several phobic fears, and the fact that adults seemed to have acquired the status of generalized reinforcers to whom the child was attracted. Finally, the "extinction" procedures evidently eliminated at least two deviant behaviors—kicking and pouring sand on others. It is tempting to conclude that the behavior-modification program was responsible for all these changes, but there was obviously insufficient control of the child's activities to warrant any strong conclusions of this nature.

Ferster and DeMyer (1961b) described the salutary effects of prochlorperizine administered to an autistic child who was required to perform a matching-to-sample discrimination task. Correct matches enabled the child to get a wide variety of reinforcers; incorrect matches were followed by short time outs from positive reinforcement. Analysis of results indicated that matching to sample was significantly better under drug than under placebo conditions. However, since the authors' only statement about the effects of the drug was that it "increased the amount of his behavior," it is difficult to tell whether the improved matching performance was due specifically to the drug's psychological effects or whether it was merely a function of the child's hyperactivity. If it were the former, such a drug might prove to be an important educational aid in behavior-therapy programs for psychotic children.

Positive Reinforcement and Active-Avoidance Learning

Hewett (1965) reported that he was able to teach a mute autistic child 32 words over a 6-month period using a paradigm that combined both reinforcement and active-avoidance procedures. The four-year-old subject, sitting in a special teaching booth, was exposed to a variety of reinforcing stimuli when he responded correctly, but was subjected to isolation in the darkened booth if he failed to respond correctly on cue. In preliminary training, the child was required to perform a series of imitative acts, such as touching appropriate facial features. Subsequently, an undifferentiated vowel sound that was frequently uttered by the child was used as the basis for the verbal learning program. The method of shaping, using successive approximations and the fading technique that was previously described in connection with Metz' (1965) paper, was employed. Ward personnel and the child's parents observed many of these procedures and continued to require the newly learned words from the child, reinforcing him only at appropriate times. Though the subject's acquired speech did not approach normal language, Hewett (1965, p. 935) was justified in stating that the child "generalized an experimentally acquired vocabulary to the larger environment and uses it to verbally express his needs (e.g., 'I want toilet.')." The successful training given to this child is particularly impressive in view of the extremely poor prognosis that is typical for the psychotic child who fails to develop language by the age of four or five.

The last study reviewed here was conducted by Lovaas, Benson Shaeffer, and Simons (1965). Schizophrenic twins were given escape-avoidance training in a room with an electrified-grid floor. The children were first physically guided, then more and more required to initiate the approach response when they heard the experimenter's command, "Come here!" At first they responded in order to escape painful shock, but they soon learned that a low-latency response (less than 5 seconds) would enable them to avoid shock. In addition, the children were shocked whenever they began to emit tantrum behavior. These procedures resulted in a long-lasting response tendency to the "come here" command (9–10 months passed before extinction began to occur) and good suppression of the tantrums. Pairing the word "no" with shock gave it the status of a conditioned suppressor, demonstrated by its reduction of the frequency of a child's bar press for positive reinforcement.

In a second part of this study, the subjects received further shock-avoidance training with a portable subject-mounted shock apparatus.

The children, who were required to hug and kiss the experimenter, showed increased affectionlike behavior as a result of training. Nurses who rated the subjects immediately after the avoidance sessions, but who were unaware of the purpose of the experiment, described the children as more dependent upon adults, more responsive and affection seeking, and more anxious and fearsome. They saw the children as less happy and content, but emitting less pathological behavior. It is well known that professional raters of such general classes of behavior as those preceding often have difficulty in agreeing upon what they observe. Relatedly, it was also explicitly pointed out by Harris et al. (1964) that teachers, nurses, and attendants who are direct participants in shaping procedures often produce completely fallacious estimates of behavior change resulting from such procedures (as checked against objective records). Admittedly the nurses in the present study were not involved in the therapy procedures nor, say the authors, did they know about them. Yet it would seem appropriate to use caution in accepting such nonprofessional, nonitemized behavior ratings.

The last experiment reported by Lovaas, Benson Schaeffer, and Simons (1965) in this article described children's learning to press a bar for candy and the sight of the experimenter's face. Accompanying this was shock-escape training in which the subjects had to go to the experimenter. Eventually, the subjects pressed the bar for the sight of the experimenter alone, without showing any generalized increase in activity resulting from the shock sessions. Here again, one has the nurses' informal observation of a perhaps generalized tendency resulting from this training. The children, who previously showed only immobility when hurt, now sought out other human beings when hurt in a variety of extraexperimental situations.

❧

DISCUSSION

The results of these studies indicate that behavior-modification techniques may be extremely useful tools in the education and rehabilitation of psychotic children. None of the investigators whose work was reviewed here would claim that they have cured their subjects. But many can justifiably state that they have equipped their subjects with several of the basic skills and habits necessary for the most rudimentary of adjustments to their social environment. Furthermore, behavior "therapists," guided by social-learning models which are more parsimonious than traditional psychodynamic theories, have been able to effectively control, and in several cases eliminate, much of the undesirable and maladaptive behavior of these children. Results such as these, achieved with types of patients that had formerly proven largely intractable to other therapeutic approaches, are sufficient to warrant further exploratory research in this area.

An examination of what appear to be the potential advantages of the behavior-modification methods described here is in order. One such advantage may be the speed with which these procedures work. Davison (1964), for example, working under the poorest of nonlaboratory conditions and seeing the subject for only a short time each day, achieved significant control over the child in 4 weeks. Exemplified also in Davison's (1964, 1965) work, as well as that of others (e.g., DeMyer and Ferster, 1962; Risley and Wolf, 1964), is the fact that such programs can apparently be executed by rapidly trained nonprofessional workers and continued in the home by parents. If this is generally the case, it might eventually be feasible for a small core of professional therapist-trainers to supervise simultaneously many therapeutic workers in behavior-modification programs with large numbers of clients.

An instructive outcome of this behavior-modification research has been the demonstration that certain types of behavior, previously conceptualized by psychodynamic theories of psychopathology as complex reactions to internal states, are more realistically and profitably conceived as socially learned and maintained acts. An example of the rapidly achieved benefits of such reanalysis was the above-described virtual elimination of self-destructive tantrums without recourse to harsh, suppressive punishments. Such tantrum behavior was found to be maintained by adult attentiveness to it and was eliminated by withdrawing attention or merely by occupying the child with incompatible behavior (Davison, 1964; Lovaas, Freitag, Gold, and Kassorla, 1965).

The foregoing discussion of the potential assets of operant-learning therapeutic models is based on evidence from a variety of essentially clinical studies. It is obvious that further demonstration of the adequacy and efficacy of behavior modification with psychotic children is necessary. Future investigations must employ better controlled procedures and long-term follow-ups with larger subject populations in order to relate general as well as specific enduring results to the techniques used. Negative side effects of treatment procedures must be recognized and evaluated by competent observers. A major problem concerns the generality of therapeutic effects. Although several of the above studies reported "generalized," long-lasting results, most of the behavior changes accomplished have been relatively limited ones.

The restricted nature of the behavior changes reported in these studies is, of course, not surprising. When a program of behavior modification is planned, it is usually designed with a carefully specified goal or set of goals in mind. Certain undesirable behavior must be eliminated; adaptive skills and habits must be imparted. The aims of this sort of procedure contrast sharply with those of various orthodox therapies which direct their efforts at more molar goals, such as attitude change and the modification of personality traits. Yet, the authors of several of the studies reviewed here (Hewett, 1965; Lovaas, Benson Schaeffer, and Simons, 1965; Metz, 1965; Risley and Wolf, 1964; Wolf et al., 1964) reported that positive, generalized changes did accompany the more circumscribed changes resulting from their experimental manipulations. Phenomena like these raise important questions concerning their determinants, for it seems clear that the task of greatest ultimate significance will be the development of those procedures that have maximal catalytic effects in appropriate or adaptive directions.

Perhaps the simplest hypothetical explanation for the unique success of behavior-modification techniques specifies that much of psychotic (and especially autistic) deficit is due to the disturbed child's *inability to learn under ordinary circumstances*. Whether it is due to organic malfunction or parental influence, early failure to solve extremely simple problems would be expected to interfere with subsequent learning. Such interference would, in turn, be expected to increase exponentially, with successive failures producing progressively greater decrements in learning skills.

It follows, then, that the infant with such a developmental history would be for the most part helpless to organize or adapt to his environment and would therefore tend to withdraw from interaction with his surroundings. If this sort of etiological conception is accepted, then it may be hypothesized that behavior-modification methods achieve their striking effects simply because they order the environment sufficiently so that even the most severely impaired child can successfully manipulate it. Once the subject begins to experience manipulative successes, it is possible that a facilitation process may begin, whereby an eventual approximation to normal intellectual growth can occur.

Presumably spurring such growth would be the child's recognition of and orientation toward varied sources of reinforcement to which he was previously unresponsive. In their recent discussion of the role of behavior modification in producing generality of adaptive change, Baer and Wolf (1967) have conceptualized this therapeutic process as one in which initial modification of certain of the subject's key behaviors promotes his "entry into natural communities of reinforcement" that were hitherto ineffective in influencing his behavior. Thus, for example, after having received appropriate language or motor training from an adult, a socially isolated or immobile psychotic child might suddenly "discover" the reinforcement potential of his agemates or of activities that are available to him. It would be expected that behavior emitted with reference to such new communities of reinforcers would be instrumental in the consolidation of earlier changes and in the amplification and extension of therapeutic gains that were achieved in the laboratory.

It seems likely that the process by which widespread changes are accomplished must make use of motivational and learning or cognitive factors which are relatively novel in the experience of the psychotic child. That is, it is hypothesized that (a) the sensation of "mastery" resulting from successful control of the environment, and (b) the establishment of learning sets or "strategies" in such children interact in a manner that is crucial to the child's eventual general improvement. It would seem important, in this context, to avoid the use of the term "generalization" to describe nonspecific, adaptive change, since the phenomenon under discussion has little in common, structurally, with stimulus or response generalization. That is, the broader behavior and attitude changes that may result from behavior-modification procedures cannot properly be described in terms of their location on any true generalization gradient, except insofar as one refers to a continuum of "adaptiveness" or "improvement" to describe the nature of the change. Knowledge of the determinants of this process of nonspecific, adaptive change will obviously be invaluable in the construction of efficacious therapeutic methods.

A promising approach to the problem would seem to be one that emphasizes the establishment of learning and behavior strategies or, in operant terminology, complex response chains with general applicability, as opposed to an approach that emphasizes discrete response learning. Operationally, the teaching of such learning strategies may take the form of training in a small number of increasingly complex response chains. Alternatively, and perhaps more basically, such training may depend heavily upon the teacher's ability to modify the child's typical attentional behavior, that is, it may be of central importance to first teach the child to orient toward a variety of potential reinforcement sources and "reinforceable" types of behavior that are appropriate and adaptive in character, but toward which he was generally indifferent prior to training.

The preceding discussion of the modification of behavior of childhood psychotics is, of course, highly speculative. But while the evidence to date is inconclusive, it certainly is strongly suggestive. The implication of these data is that effective new techniques of therapeutic behavior modification may be developed from the basic principles of operant-learning technology. If such techniques do prove to be statistically successful, it appears that they will have the additional virtues of simplicity and easy communicability. With these qualities, operant methodology could facilitate the realization of widely available, rapidly effective therapy for at least one area of psychopathology, that is, the psychoses of childhood.

13

Aversive Control
of Self-injurious Behavior
in a Psychotic Boy

B. G. Tate & George S. Baroff

There have been many attempts to explain self-injurious behavior (Cain, 1961; Dollard et al., 1939; Freud, 1954; Goldfarb, 1945; Greenacre, 1954; Hartmann et al., 1949; Sandler, 1964). It has been labeled masochism, auto-aggression, self-aggression, and self-destructive behavior. The present authors prefer the term self-injurious behavior because it is more descriptive and less interpretive. Self-injurious behavior (SIB) does not imply an attempt to destroy, nor does it suggest aggression; it simply means behavior which produces physical injury to the individual's own body. Typically SIB is composed of a series of self-injurious responses (SIRs) that are repetitive and sometimes rhythmical, often with no obvious reinforcers, and therefore similar to stereotyped behavior. Common types of SIB are forceful head-banging, face slapping, punching the face and head, and scratching and biting one's body.

A patient who emits SIRs at high frequency and/or magnitude is particularly difficult to work with because the behavior interferes with the production of more desirable responses and there is always the risk of severe and permanent physical injury, e.g., head and eye damage. Usually such patients must be physically restrained or maintained on

From *Behavior Research and Therapy*, 4 (1966), 281–287, Pergamon Press.

heavy dosages of drugs. Lovaas et al. (1964), however, successfully employed punishment in the form of painful electric shock to dramatically reduce the frequency of SIRs in several schizophrenic children. Ball (1966) used the same technique with a severely retarded girl and achieved similar results.

The present paper describes two punishment procedures used to control SIB in a psychotic boy. In Study I, punishment was withdrawal of human physical contact contingent on a SIR. In Study II, punishment was response-contingent painful electric shock. Following a description of the subject, the procedures and results of Studies I and II are presented, followed by a report on related behavioral changes and a general discussion.

SUBJECT

Sam was a nine-year-old blind male who was transferred for evaluation and treatment on a research basis from an out-of-state psychiatric hospital to Murdoch Center, a state institution for the mentally retarded. At the age of five he was diagnosed as autistic and was hospitalized. For the next four years he received group and individual psychotherapy, and drug therapy with no long-term benefit. Drugs were used in an effort to control self-injurious behavior, screaming, and hyperactivity.

The SIB began at about the age of four and consisted of face slapping. By age nine, his SIB repertoire included banging his head forcefully against floors, walls, and other hard objects, slapping his face with his hands, punching his face and head with his fists, hitting his shoulder with his chin, and kicking himself. Infrequently he would also pinch, bite, and scratch others.

At age eight, bilateral cataracts, a complete detachment of the left retina, and partial detachment of the right retina were discovered. An ophthalmologist has suggested that the cataracts were probably congenital but were not noticed until they matured and that the retinal detachments were likely caused by head-banging. The cataract in the right eye was removed soon after its discovery, leaving Sam with some light-dark vision and possibly some movement perception.

Upon arrival at Murdoch Center, Sam was assigned a room in the infirmary and drugs were immediately discontinued. Casual observations were made for the first two weeks while he was adapting to his new environment. Following the adaptation period, eighteen 30-min.

daily observation periods were conducted during which a female research assistant held Sam, tried to interest him in games, and ignored all SIRs. These observations yielded a median daily average SIR rate of 2.3/min. (range: 0.9–7.9/min.). A second type of observation consisted of 5-min. periods four times a day at random intervals. Over a 26-day period the median daily average SIR rate was 1.7/min. (range: 0.3–4.1/min.). SIB, therefore, was a frequent form of behavior observed under a wide variety of situations.

Observations also revealed the following: Sam had a firm hematoma approximately 7 cm. in diameter on his forehead — a result of previous head-banging. His speech was limited to jargon and to approximately twenty words usually spoken in a high-pitched, whining manner and often inappropriately used. He was not considered autistic at this time because he obviously enjoyed and sought bodily contact with others. He would cling to people and try to wrap their arms around him, climb into their laps and mold himself to their contours. When left alone and free, he would cry, scream, flail his arms about, and hit himself or bang his head. When fully restrained in bed he was usually calm, but often engaged in head-rolling and hitting his chin against his shoulder.

―

STUDY I: CONTROL BY WITHDRAWAL AND REINSTATEMENT OF HUMAN PHYSICAL CONTACT

Early observations of Sam strongly indicated that physical contact with people was reinforcing to him and that being alone, particularly when he was standing or walking, was aversive. Study I was undertaken in an effort to learn if a procedure of withdrawing physical contact when a SIR occurred and reinstating the contact after a brief interval during which no SIRs occurred could be used to control Sam's SIB.

Procedure

Study I began on the fourth day following the end of the 26-day observation period mentioned. During the three weeks preceding the commencement of the study Sam was restrained in his bed except for morning baths given by attendants and for daily walks around the campus and through the infirmary corridors with two female research assistants (Es). During the walks Es held Sam's hands and chatted to him and to each other and ignored SIRs.

Study I consisted of twenty daily 20-min. sessions run at the same time each day by the same Es. There were five control sessions (SIRs were ignored), followed by five experimental sessions (SIRs were punished), five control sessions, and five experimental sessions.

Control sessions consisted of a walk around the campus with the two Es who chatted with Sam and with each other. Sam walked between them, holding onto a hand of each. When he emitted SIRs the Es ignored them.

Experimental sessions were identical to the control sessions except that when Sam hit himself, Es jerked their hands free so that he had no physical contact with them. The timeout from physical contact lasted 3 sec. following the last SIR. At the end of 3 sec., Es allowed him to grasp their hands and the walk resumed. No comments were made to Sam when a hit occurred—the only responses to the SIR were withdrawal of contact and cessation of talk if Es were talking at the time.

All sessions began when Sam left his room and entered the corridor leading outside the building. The same route around the campus was followed each day. Each session ended while he was outside the building, but the procedure for the particular session was continued until Sam was returned to his room, undressed, placed in bed, and restrained— usually about 12 additional min. Records were kept by one E who silently marked the SIRs on a piece of paper during the walks.

Results of Study I

Virtually all of the SIRs made during the sessions were chin-to-shoulder hits. On a few occasions Sam would punch his head with his fist during punishment but he rarely withdrew his hand from an assistant and hit himself.

Figure 1 presents the average SIRs per min. for each day of the study. The median average rate of SIRs for the first 5 control days was 6.6 responses per min. and sharply declined to a median average of 0.1 responses per min. for the following 5 experimental days. The response rate recovered somewhat (median average = 3.3) during the second 5 control days and decreased again during the second 5 experimental days (median average = 1.0). The unusually high rate of SIRs on the second day of the second control run was associated with a temper tantrum which lasted about 15 min.

On the experimental days an interesting change in Sam's behavior occurred which was noticed by both Es and the authors. On control days Sam typically whined, cried, hesitated often in his walk, and

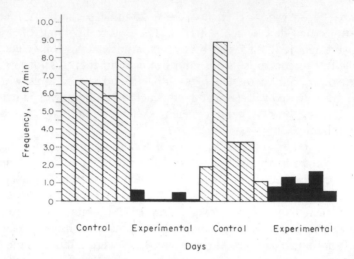

FIGURE 1.   Effect of the punishment procedure of Study I on the daily average frequency of SIRs. On experimental days SIRs were followed by withdrawal of human physical contact and reinstatement of contact after a minimum interval of 3 sec. On control days the SIRs were ignored.

seemed unresponsive to the environment in general. His behavior on experimental days was completely different—he appeared to attend more to environmental stimuli, including the Es; there was no crying or whining, and he often smiled. A brief discussion of this change in behavior appears at the end of the paper.

The results of this study indicate that the relatively simple procedure of controlling the contingencies of this chronic SIB produced a dramatic reduction in its frequency. Of interest also are the relative effects of punishing the SIR and ignoring it. These results do not, of course, mean that long-term effects would be the same.

ᗊ

STUDY II: CONTROL BY ELECTRIC SHOCK

Although the SIB could be reduced by response-contingent withdrawal of physical contact, it was decided that the risk of completely destroying the right retina by further head-banging was great enough to preclude the long-term use of this method. Parental permission was then obtained for the use of painful electric shock.

The shock apparatus was a stock prod (Sears & Roebuck Number

325971) similar to the one used by Lovaas et al. (1964). The prod was a cylinder 58 cm. long and 3 cm. in diameter containing seven D cells and an induction coil. With fresh batteries approximately 130 V were available at the two 0.48 cm. diameter terminals, 1.24 cm. apart, projecting from one end of the prod. Shock was administered by turning the induction coil on and touching the terminals to the bare skin of the patient.

Study II began 46 hours after the termination of Study I.

Procedure

For 24 min. prior to the administration of electric shock, Sam was allowed a free-responding period. The authors, accompanied by a physician, entered Sam's room, talked to him pleasantly and freed his hands, leaving him lying in bed with both feet restrained. They remained close to his bed while an assistant in an adjoining room recorded each SIR. After 24 min. of observing and recording the free-responding behavior, it was explained to Sam that if he continued to hit himself he would be shocked, and the shock would hurt. A shock of approximately 0.5 seconds duration then immediately followed each SIR. No more comments were made to Sam concerning the shock which was delivered to the lower right leg.

The contingent shock period was continued for 90 min. After the first two shocks were administered. Sam's feet were untied and he was placed in a sitting position in bed. The authors talked pleasantly to him and encouraged him to play with toys. Approximately 1 hour after the first shock he was placed in a rocking chair for 30 min. Sam was then returned to his bed and left alone unrestrained, while being observed for another 90 min. over closed-circuit television. Contingent shock was continued, but there was a delay of 30–35 sec. between the SIR and the administration of punishment (time required to reach Sam's room from the observation room).

Shock was continued on subsequent days and was sometimes delivered immediately and sometimes delayed 30 sec. depending on whether the therapist was with Sam or observing him on television. At night he was restrained in bed at the wrists and ankles with cloth restraints.

Results of Study II

As soon as Sam's hands were released for the 24-min. free-responding period he began hitting his face with his fists. The intensity of the SIRS immediately increased as a temper tantrum developed during which he screamed, flailed his arms about wildly, twisted his body about, hit his face and head with his fists, hit his shoulder with his chin, and banged his head with great force against the iron side rail of the bed. The head-banging was so forceful that it was necessary to cushion the blows by placing the authors' hands over the bed rail. The average rate of SIRs during the 6-min. temper tantrum was 14.0 per min. During the next 18 min. he became calmer and the average rate dropped to 2.0 responses per min.

During the first 90-min. contingent shock period a total of only five SIRs were emitted (average rate = 0.06 responses per min.). The shocks produced a startle reaction in Sam and avoidance movements, but no cries. The authors talked to him, praised virtually all non-injurious responses, and generally behaved pleasantly. When led from the bed to the rocking chair, he immediately began crying and flailing his arms. A SIR was promptly followed by a shock and he became calm. A few seconds later he was sitting in the chair and smiling with apparent pleasure. At the end of the 90-min. period Sam was returned to his bed and left in it free while being observed over closed-circuit television. Throughout the second 90-min. observation period he remained quietly in bed posturing with his hands. Four SIRs were emitted and were followed by delayed shocks. The SIR rate had decreased from 2.0/min. in the last minutes of the free responding period to 0.04/min. At the end of the period a meal was offered which he refused. He was then restrained for the night.

The following day Sam was free from 9:00 A.M. until 2:30 P.M. All of this time was spent in bed with toys except for 1 hour in the afternoon during which the authors encouraged him to rock in a rocking chair and walk around his room. Twenty SIRs of light intensity occurred during the $5\frac{1}{2}$-hour period (average rate = 0.06 responses per min.). Four of these were followed by immediate shock and the other sixteen by delayed shock.

On the second day following the commencement of shock Sam was free from 8:00 A.M. until 4:30 P.M. There were only fifteen SIRs during the entire day (average rate = 0.03/min.) but most of these occurred during one brief period of agitation at noon. He was out of bed about 3 hours being rocked, walked, and entertained with toys.

In the ensuing days Sam's daily activities were gradually increased until he remained out of bed 9 hours a day. He was still restrained at night because of limited personnel available to check him. He began attending physical therapy classes for the severely retarded 3 hours a day where he was encouraged to play with a variety of toys. He now apparently enjoys walks, playground equipment, and playing "games" involving following directions and making discriminations, for example, various objects (ball, book, music box, etc.) are put on a table across the room and he is asked to bring a specific one to E. He is more spontaneous in his activities than he was when he arrived and he is now capable of walking and running alone without clinging to people.

Punishment of SIRs with shock was continued and the decline in rate progressed. Since the beginning of shock 167 days have elapsed. The last observed SIR was emitted on day 147.

⤙

OTHER CHANGES IN BEHAVIOR

Sam's intake of food and liquids had undergone an over-all decrease since his admission although there were wide day-to-day fluctuations. Three months after his admission (5 days before the use of shock), his weight had decreased by 14 pounds (20 per cent). On days when he ate nothing he usually held great quantities of saliva in his mouth for hours — emptying his mouth only by accident or when forced to. In the 36 hours preceding the commencement of shock, Sam ate only a small portion of one meal and drank only 400 ml. of liquids. Supper was refused on the day shock was first administered. The following day he drank a small quantity of milk and ate some cereal for breakfast, but all other liquids and food were refused during the day — he had started saving saliva again. In addition he was posturing with his hands most of the day (posturing had been observed before any treatment began).

On the second day following the commencement of shock he refused all food during the morning. At 2:00 P.M., he was again offered juice which he refused. He was then told firmly to drink but he would not open his mouth. It was then discovered that a firm command followed by the buzz of the stock prod (but no shock delivered), would cause him to open his mouth and take the juice, but he then held it in his mouth without swallowing. Again, a command and a buzz produced swallowing. The sequence of "Drink," and "Swallow," was repeated until he had consumed all of the juice. Verbal praise and affectionate pats were used to reinforce each desirable response. With this procedure, command-buzz-reinforcement, he also drank a glass of milk and ate some ice cream. This was the most food he had consumed in 4 days. Only one shock was actually administered — buzzing of the prod was sufficient the other times. This procedure was continued for the evening

meal and the following day. On the third day he began eating spontaneously and has continued, although there are still occasions when he has
to be prompted. In the following 15 days he gained 10 pounds and his
weight continues to increase, but at a normal rate.

The posturing was stopped in similar fashion. When, for example,
Sam held his hands up instead of down by his sides, he was told firmly
to put his hands down, and if he did not, the buzzing of the prod was
presented. The act of holding saliva in his mouth was stopped by telling
him firmly to swallow and sounding the prod if he did not obey. The
same procedure was effective in reducing his clinging to people.

＞＜

DISCUSSION

Both punishment procedures effectively reduced SIB in this psychotic
boy. Aversive control by withdrawal of physical contact was immediately
effective both times it was used.

Aversive control by painful electric shock also reduced the SIB
immediately and has remained effective over a 6-month period. In
addition, it was found that eating behavior could be reinstated, posturing could be stopped, and saliva-saving and clinging could be terminated
by firm commands followed by the sound of the shock apparatus if
there was no compliance, and followed by social reinforcement if
compliance occurred. Over the 6-month period since the inception of
shock, its use has decreased. Part of the beneficial effects of punishment
by shock obviously were derived from the more stimulating environment provided him following the initial treatment—an environment
which could not have been provided had the SIR rate not been suppressed
to avoid injury. A secondary gain was probably derived from the marked
positive change in behavior of attendants and nurses toward Sam. It
should also be noted that punishment by electric shock prevented
accidental reinforcement of SIRs. Before any treatment began it was
sometimes necessary to interfere with SIRs by holding Sam's arms,
a procedure which may have been reinforcing to him. No deleterious
effects of the shock were observed.

An intriguing area of speculation is how to account for the complete
change in behavior observed on experimental days of Study I and
observed often after shock was delivered in Study II. One plausible
explanation for the difference in behavior is that the whining, crying,
and SIB belong to the same response class and the suppression of SIB
also suppresses these other behaviors. Once the undesirable behaviors

are suppressed the more desirable ones, e.g., smiling, listening, attending to the environment, and cooperating with others can occur.

Another conjecture is that both types of punishment produce a general arousal in the central nervous system which results in increased attention (Hebb, 1955). Attention to the external environment could account for the cooperative behavior, smiling and apparent listening. This idea is further supported by the immediacy of the punishment effect—not only did SIB, whining, crying, and negativistic behavior cease abruptly, but within seconds the more desirable behaviors emerged.

14

Acquisition of Imitative Speech by Schizophrenic Children

O. Ivar Lovaas, John P. Berberich, Bernard F. Perloff,
& Benson Schaeffer

For the great majority of children, the problem of teaching speech never arises. Speech develops within each child's particular environment without parents and teachers having to know a great deal about how it occurs. Yet, in some children, because of deviations in organic structure or prior experience, speech fails to develop. Children with the diagnosis of childhood schizophrenia, especially autistic children, often show little in the way of speech development (Rimland, 1964). The literature on childhood schizophrenia suggests two conclusions regarding speech in such children: first, that the usual treatment setting (psychotherapy) in which these children are placed might not be conducive to speech development; and second, that a child failing to develop speech by the age of 5 years remains withdrawn and does not improve clinically (Brown, 1960). That is, the presence or absence of speech is an important prognostic indicator. It is perhaps obvious that a child who can speak can engage in a much more therapeutic interchange with his environment than the child who has no speech.

The failure of some children to develop speech as a "natural" consequence of growing up poses the need for an increased knowledge of how language is acquired. A procedure for the development of speech in

From *Science*, 151:3711 (February 11, 1966), 705–707. Copyright 1966 by the American Association for the Advancement of Science.

previously mute children would not only be of practical importance but might also illuminate the development of speech in normal children. Although several theoretical attempts have been made to account for language development, the empirical basis for these theoretical formulations is probably inadequate. In fact, there are no published, systematic studies on how to go about developing speech in a person who has never spoken. We now outline a procedure by which speech can be made to occur. Undoubtedly there are or will be other ways by which speech can be acquired. Furthermore, our procedure centers on the acquisition of only one aspect of speech, the acquisition of vocal responses. The development of speech also requires the acquisition of a context for the occurrence of such responses ("meaning").

Casual observation suggests that normal children acquire words by hearing speech; that is, children learn to speak by imitation. The mute schizophrenic children with whom we worked were not imitative. Thus the establishment of imitation in these children appeared to be the most beneficial and practical starting point for building speech. The first step in creating speech, then, was to establish conditions in which imitation of vocal sounds would be learned.

The method that we eventually found most feasible for establishing verbal imitation involved a discrimination training procedure. Early in training the child was rewarded only if he emitted a sound within a certain time after an adult had emitted a sound. Next he was rewarded only if the sound he emitted within the prescribed interval resembled the adult's sound. Toward the end of training, he was rewarded only if his vocalization very closely matched the adult's vocalization—that is, if it was, in effect, imitative. Thus verbal imitation was taught through the development of a series of increasingly fine discriminations.

✼

SUBJECTS

The first two children exposed to this program are discussed here. Chuck and Billy were six-year-old in-patients at the Neuropsychiatric Institute at UCLA. These children were selected for the program because they did not speak. At the onset of the program, vocal behavior in both children was restricted to occasional vowel productions with no discernible communicative intent. These vowel sounds occurred infrequently, except when the children were tantrumous, and did not resemble the pre-speech babbling of infants. In addition, the children evidenced no appropriate play (for example, they would spin toys or mouth them). They engaged in a considerable amount of self-stimulatory behavior such as rocking and twirling. They did not initiate social contacts and became tantrumous when such contact was initiated by others. They evidenced occasional self-destructive behavior (biting self, head-banging, and so forth). Symbolic rewards such as social approval were inoperative, so biological rewards such as food were substituted. In short, they were profoundly schizophrenic.

><

PROCEDURE

Training was conducted 6 days a week, 7 hours a day, with a 15-minute rest period accompanying each hour of training. During the training sessions the child and the adult sat facing each other, their heads about 30 cm. apart. The adult physically prevented the child from leaving the training situation by holding the child's legs between his own legs. Rewards, in the form of single spoonsful of the child's meal, were delivered immediately after correct responses. Punishment (spanking, shouting by the adult) was delivered for inattentive, self-destructive, and tantrumous behavior which interfered with the training, and most of these behaviors were thereby suppressed within one week. Incorrect vocal behavior was never punished.

Four distinct steps were required to establish verbal imitation. In step 1, the child was rewarded for all vocalizations. We frequently would fondle the children and we avoided aversive stimulation. This · was done in order to increase the frequency of vocal responses. During this stage in training the child was also rewarded for visually fixating on the adult's mouth. When the child reached an achievement level of about one verbal response every 5 seconds and was visually fixating on the adult's mouth more than 50 per cent of the time, step 2 of training was introduced.

Step 2 marked our initial attempt to bring the child's verbal behavior under our verbal control in such a manner that our speech would ultimately stimulate speech in the child. Mastery of this second step involved acquisition of a temporal discrimination by the child. The adult emitted a vocal response—for example, "baby"—about once on the average of every tenth second. The child was rewarded only if he vocalized within 6 seconds after the adult's vocalization. However, any vocal response of the child would be rewarded in that time interval. Step 3 was introduced when the frequency of the child's vocal responses within the 6-second interval was three times what it had been initially.

Step 3 was structurally similar to the preceding step, but it included the additional requirement that the child actually match the adult's vocalization before receiving the reward. In this and in following steps the adult selected the verbalization to be placed in imitative training from a pool of possible verbalizations that had met one or more of the following criteria. First, we selected vocal behaviors that could be prompted, that is, vocal behaviors that could be elicited by a cue prior to any experimental training, such as by manually moving the child through the behavior.

An example of training with the use of a prompt is afforded in teaching the sound "b." The training would proceed in three stages: the adult emitted "b" and simultaneously prompted the child to emit "b" by holding the child's lips closed with his fingers and quickly removing them when the child exhaled; the prompt would be gradually faded, by the adult's moving his fingers away from the child's mouth, to his cheek, and finally gently touching the child's jaw; the adult emitted the vocalization "b" only, withholding all prompts. The rate of fading was determined by the child; the sooner the child's verbal behavior came under control of the adult's without the use of the prompt, the better. The second criterion for selection of words or sounds in the early stages of training centered on their concomitant visual components (which we exaggerated when we pronounced them), such as those of the labial consonant "m" and of open-mouthed vowels like "a." We selected such sounds after having previously found that the children could discriminate words with visual components more easily that those with only auditory components (the guttural consonants, "k" and "g," proved extremely difficult and, like "l" and "s," were mastered later than other sounds). Third, we selected for training sounds which the child emitted most frequently in step 1.

Step 4 was a recycling of step 3, with the addition of a new sound. We selected a sound that was very different from those presented in step 3, so that the child could discriminate between the new and old sounds more easily. To make certain that the child was in fact imitating, we randomly interspersed the sounds of step 3 with the sound of step 4, in a randomized ratio of about 1 to 3. This random presentation "forced" (or enabled) the child to discriminate the particular sounds involved, in order to be rewarded. There was no requirement placed upon the child in step 3 to discriminate specific aspects such as vowels, consonants, and order of the adult's speech; a child might master step 3 without attending to the specific properties of the adult's speech. Each new introduction of sounds and words required increasingly fine discrimination by the child and hence provided evidence that the child was in fact matching the adult's speech. All steps beyond step 4 consisted of replications of step 3, but new sounds, words, and phrases were used. In each new step the previously mastered words and sounds were rehearsed on a randomized ratio of 1 to 3. The next step was introduced when the child had mastered the previous steps—that is, when he had made ten consecutive correct replications of the adult's utterances.

One hour of each day's training was tape-recorded. Two independent observers scored the child's correct vocal responses from these sessions. A correct response was defined as a recognizable reproduction of the adult's utterance. The observers showed better than 90 per cent agreement over sessions. When the child's correct responses are plotted against days of training, and the resulting function is positively accelerated, it can be said that the child has learned to imitate.

The results of the first 26 days of imitation training, starting from introduction of step 3, have been plotted for Billy (Figure 1). The abscissa denotes training days. The words and sounds are printed in lower case letters on the days they were introduced and in capital letters on the days they were mastered. It can be seen that as training progressed the rate of mastery increased. Billy took several days to learn a single word during the first 2 weeks of the program, but a single day to master several words during the last 2 weeks. Chuck's performance was very similar to Billy's.

After 26 days of training both children had learned to imitate new words with such ease and rapidly that merely adding verbal responses to their imitative repertoire seemed pointless. Hence the children were then introduced to the second part of the language training program, wherein they were taught to use language appropriately.

The imitation training took place in a rather complex environment, with many events happening concurrently. We hypothesized that it was the reward, given for imitative behavior, which was crucial to the learning. To test this hypothesis, the adult uttered the sounds as during the training and the children received the same number of rewards as before. However, the rewards were contingent upon time elapsed since the last reward, regardless of the child's behavior.

The data show a deterioration in imitation behavior whenever rewards are shifted from response-contingent to time-contingent delivery. It is concluded, therefore, that reward immediately following correct, imitative behavior (and withholding of reward following incorrect responding) is a crucial variable in maintaining imitative behavior in these children. The same finding has been reported by Baer and Sherman (1964) who worked with imitative behavior in normal children.

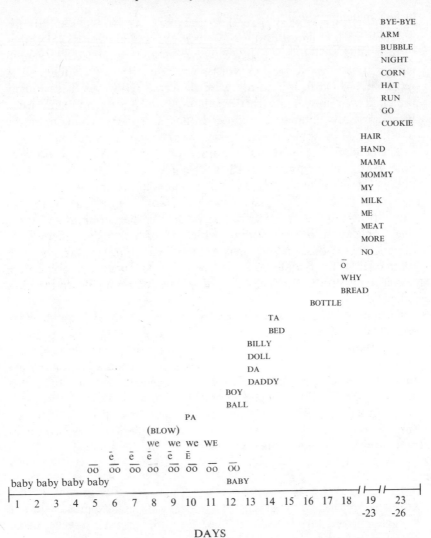

FIGURE 1.   Acquisition of verbal imitation by Billy. The abscissa denotes training days. Words and sounds are printed in lowercase letters on the days they were introduced, and in capital letters on the days they were mastered.

Since the child was rewarded whenever he responded like the adult, *similarity* was consistently associated with food. Because of such association, similarity should become symbolic of reward. In other words, imitative behavior, being symbolic of reward, should eventually provide its own reward (Baer and Sherman, 1964). To test this hypothesis, both children were exposed to Norwegian words which they were unable to reproduce perfectly when first presented. The adult simply stated the Norwegian word and the child always attempted to repeat it; no extrinsic rewards were delivered. However, occasionally the child was presented with English words which the adult rewarded when correctly imitated. This procedure was necessary to maintain the hypothesized symbolic (learned) reward function of imitation.

The children improved in the imitation of the Norwegian words over time. It is as if they were rewarded for correct behavior. In view of the data pointing to the need for rewards in maintaining imitative behavior, and in the absence of extrinsic rewards, we would argue that the reward was intrinsic and a function of the prior imitation training. There is one implication of this finding which is of particular interest for therapeutic reasons: children may be able to acquire new behaviors on their own. (This finding contrasts with the frequent stereotype of a conditioning product, namely, that of an automaton unable to function independently.)

Currently, three new schizophrenic children are undergoing the same speech training program as Billy and Chuck. After 3 days of training, one of these children achieved a level of imitative behavior similar to that shown by Billy and Chuck after 26 days. It should be pointed out that schizophrenic children are a very heterogeneous group with respect to their speech histories and symptomatology in general, and that Billy and Chuck had failed in development to a profound degree. Insofar as one works with such a diverse population, it is likely that numerous procedures could be helpful in establishing speech.

15

Teaching Speech
to an Autistic Child
through Operant Conditioning

Frank M. Hewett

The autistic child is a socialization failure. One of the major character-istics of autism which both illustrates and perpetuates this failure is defective speech development. The nature of speech peculiarities in autistic children has been described by Kanner (1948) and according to Rimland (1964) lack of speech is found in almost one-half of all such children. The follow-up studies of Kanner and Eisenberg (1955) indicate that presence or absence of speech by age five has important prognostic implications. Almost without exception the autistic child who reached his fifth birthday without developing speech failed to improve his level of socialization in later years. Even with psychotherapy, autistic, atypical children who had no speech by age three were found by Brown (1960) to remain severely withdrawn and generally unim-proved.

While intensification of speech training efforts with younger autistic children would seem a logical therapeutic maneuver, such children are characteristically poor pupils. Conventional teaching techniques are seldom successful because of the autistic child's profound withdrawal and preference for self rather than other-directed activities.

From *American Journal of Orthopsychiatry,* 35:5 (October 1965), 927–936. Copyright 1965, the American Orthopsychiatric Association, Inc.

❦

BACKGROUND

The staff of the Neuropsychiatric Institute School at the University of California, Los Angeles, has been exploring operant conditioning techniques for teaching communication skills to autistic children. Reading and writing have been taught to a twelve-year-old autistic boy who had never developed speech (Brown, 1960). Recently a four-and-a-half-year-old, nonverbal autistic boy was the focus for a speech-training program.

In operant conditioning, the pupil learns to produce a given response (e.g., vocalization) following presentation of a cue or discriminative stimulus (e.g., teacher's prompt) in order to obtain a desired reward or positive reinforcement (e.g., candy). In a similar manner he learns to avoid responses which lead to an undesirable consequence or negative reinforcement (e.g., isolation).

Operant conditioning techniques have been successful in increasing the frequency of vocalizations in normal infants and reinstating speech in nonverbal schizophrenics. An attempt to initiate speech in an autistic child is described by Weiland (1961) who withheld a desired object (e.g., ball) until the child produced the word, "ball."

Speech training with animals has long involved conditioning procedures. Hayes (1951) established a three-word vocabulary in his famous chimpanzee, Vicki, by making receipt of food contingent on vocalization. These vocalizations were later shaped into words by manipulating the lips of the chimp until closer and closer approximations of the desired words were obtained.

Mowrer (1950) has written extensively on teaching birds to talk. According to Mowrer it is essential that the trainer's appearance become associated with positive reinforcement. He draws a parallel between this and the mother-child relationship during infancy. The mother's voice acquires secondary reinforcement value and is imitated because of its close association with food gratification and removal of pain. In a like manner presentation of food and water to birds becomes the basis for teaching speech as these positive reinforcements are paired with the trainer's presence and his verbal cues.

❦

THE SUBJECT

Peter is a four-and-a-half-year-old Caucasian boy diagnosed as autistic at age two. He failed to develop speech although he said "Da-da" and

"Ma-ma" during his first year. All attempts at speech ceased at one-and-one-half years and Peter was nonverbal when admitted to the Children's Service of the Neuropsychiatric Institute (NPI). Peter preferred to be left alone during infancy and became upset when picked up or cuddled. He was described as "too good," a young child who sought repetitive, mechanical activities rather than social interaction. At about age two Peter began to develop marked oppositional tendencies and became hyperactive, aggressive and uncontrollable in his behavior. His mother was constantly chasing him out of the street and away from danger. Peter's interest in mechanical gadgets increased and he developed an unusual degree of fine motor coordination. Recent neurological and laboratory tests were negative, and Peter's medical history has been uneventful. His hearing has also been judged as unimpaired. Peter has an older brother and sister who are normal.

PROCEDURE

In planning the program of speech training, provision had to be made for gratifying and controlling Peter. Gratification and control are basic ingredients in all effective learning situations. Children learn those tasks which prove rewarding and which are taught in a systematic and structured manner. Autistic children, left to their own devices, are highly selective learners who obtain gratification by bizarre, inappropriate means; set their own limits, and consequently learn a restricted number of socialization skills. Before such children can be trained, the teacher must discover ways of providing gratification and establishing control. With respect to the latter, Phillips (1957) has emphasized the importance of consistent and direct intervention of the autistic child's demands if behavioral changes are to be effected.

Food and candy are generally effective positive reinforcers, although autistic children may be quite variable in their preference. Peter was apathetic about food but displayed a consistent desire for candy as well as other positive reinforcers to be described later.

Candy, however, would not control Peter's behavior. He was highly distractable, and his attention could only be engaged for brief periods with the promise of a candy reward. In an effort to reduce extraneous stimuli to a minimum and to introduce negative reinforcement as a lever for establishment of control, a special teaching booth was constructed for Peter. The booth was divided into two sections, joined by a movable shutter ($2 \times 2\frac{1}{2}$ feet) which could be raised and lowered by the teacher.

The teacher occupied one-half of the booth and Peter the other half. Each section of the booth was four feet wide, three and one-half feet in length, and seven feet high. The only source of light came from the teacher's side and was provided by two spotlights which were directed on the teacher's face. When the shutter was down, Peter's side of the booth was dark. When it was raised, light from the teacher's side flooded through the opening and illuminated a shelf in front of Peter. To the left of the shelf was a ball-drop device with a dim light directly above it. This device consisted of a box into which a small wooden ball could be dropped. The ball rang a bell as it dropped into the box and was held inside the box until released by the teacher. When released, the ball rolled out into a cup at the bottom of the box where it could be picked up. This ball-drop device was Peter's "key" for opening the shutter. When the ball was released into the cup, he picked it up and dropped it into the box. At the sound of the bell, the teacher raised the shutter and initiated contact between the two of them.

In this setting the teacher not only provided candy and light as positive reinforcers but also used music, a ride on a revolving chair, color cartoon movies and a Bingo number-matching game which Peter liked. Isolation and darkness served as negative reinforcers and were administered when Peter failed to respond appropriately within a five-second period. Pilot trials with Peter and four other autistic children revealed the positive reinforcers to be effective in varying degrees and that all subjects would "work" to avoid isolation and darkness.

The training program with Peter can be divided into four phases: introduction, social imitation, speech training and transfer.

PHASE ONE: INTRODUCTION

When Peter was brought by his parents for admission there was a noticeable lack of separation awareness on his part. Despite the fact that he never had been away from home before, he walked away from his parents and into the ward without any visible reaction. Peter immediately was isolated in a room with an individual nurse where he remained for the first week of hospitalization. He was only taken from this room at mealtimes, when he accompanied the teacher to the teaching booth where he was fed. Peter quickly learned the mechanics of the booth. During this introductory phase he obtained each mouthful of food or drink of liquid by using the ball-drop "key." The shutter would be open when Peter was placed in the booth. The teacher fed him a portion of food and then lowered the shutter, releasing the ball into the cup. Peter picked the ball up and dropped it into the opening. At the sound of the bell, the shutter opened bringing the teacher's lighted countenance into view and providing another mouthful of food for Peter. This process was repeated mouthful by mouthful and sip by sip for one week.

By the third day of this first phase the teacher held food or liquid out for Peter but did not deliver it until eye contact was established. This first task of looking the teacher directly in the eye before getting food and drink was learned quickly, and immediate eye contact upon presentation of food was established 83 per cent of the time by the twentieth feeding.

The initial phase served not only to introduce Peter to the booth environment in which speech training would later be attempted, but also to acquaint him with the teacher. At first the teacher often would encounter resistance as he attempted to lead Peter from his ward room because of the change in activity involved. But by the fourth day of this phase Peter responded to the teacher's verbal command and walked to the door to meet him. During the course of his feeding sessions Peter remained in his chair directly in front of the teacher 57 per cent of the total time on the first day to 90 per cent on the day of the final feeding.

Throughout this paper, references are made to various positive reinforcers such as candy and food as providing necessary gratification for Peter. The teacher-child relationship which began at this early stage is not discussed. It is definitely felt, however, that the teacher acquired secondary reinforcement properties through constant association with primary reinforcers as described by Mowrer. While no attempt was made to control the teacher's facial expressions, physical contact with Peter and verbalization, these undoubtedly played an increasing role in motivating and controlling him as the training process progressed.

><

PHASE TWO: SOCIAL IMITATION

Once Peter had been introduced to the booth, he was removed from isolation on the ward and allowed to participate in activities with the other children. Twenty-minute social imitation training sessions (in the booth) were held both morning and afternoon. During these sessions Peter learned to follow simple verbal directions and to imitate the teacher's hand movements. A variety of positive reinforcers was used at the beginning of this phase so that candy, the most potent reward, could be used during the speech-training phase.

Peter learned to place his hand on the teacher's face in order to obtain a segment of childrens' music. The music would continue so long as Peter kept his hand on the teacher's head. Peter appeared to enjoy testing this routine by quickly withdrawing his hand and replacing it to see if he could change the pattern.

The next task given Peter was that of clapping his hands in imitation of the teacher. Such a response would be rewarded by a single rotation of a motorized chair on which Peter sat. The hand-clap imitation proved a difficult task for him, and the shutter frequently was lowered because he was inattentive or failed to respond within the five-second limit. Once Peter learned the imitative hand-clap, another response was introduced. This required him to place both of his hands on his face in order to see a sequence of a color cartoon movie shown on a small screen to his right. This response was learned in one day. Additional social imitation training was done with the revolving chair as a reward. Peter readily learned to touch any part of his head (e.g., ear, nose) in imitation of the teacher. Each correct response within a five-second time limit earned a single rotation of the chair.

This phase was accomplished during the first month of the training program. Only those responses which Peter gave in direct imitation of the teacher were rewarded, and random responses were ignored. The main goal of this phase was to develop a reciprocal imitative relationship as a basis for speech training.

⊷

PHASE THREE: SPEECH TRAINING

Peter had begun to vocalize spontaneously during phases one and two. He emitted 23 random spontaneous vocalizations on the first day of the booth feeding, and 79 random vocalizations during the final feeding day. In addition, music appealed to Peter, as it does to many autistic children, and he had been heard humming parts of familiar childrens' songs. He also had spontaneously hummed a few bars of the tune used as music reinforcement during phase two. The teacher selected the first three notes of this tune as the initial response in the speech-training phase, and candy was introduced as a positive reinforcer. A small lighted window was placed on Peter's side of the booth. A piece of candy could be dropped behind the glass where it remained in view until the teacher flipped it out to Peter.

The speech-training phase began with the teacher's placing a piece of candy behind the window and flipping it out. Peter was immediately drawn to this source of candy. Another piece of candy then was placed behind the window where it remained in view while the teacher hummed the first notes as an imitative cue. Peter was resistant to responding and only after several shutter drops did he imitate on cue and receive his candy reinforcement.

Once this response was established, the teacher began work on the first word. Peter had randomly made a shrill, undifferentiated vowel sound (ē-oö) during his spontaneous vocalizations in phases one and two. The teacher produced this vocalization and expected Peter to imitate it on cue for a candy reward. This was quickly established and actual speech training was under way.

Shaping this undifferentiated vowel sound into a word was the task at hand. The method of *successive approximation* described by Isaacs was used. The word "go" was selected for shaping because it denoted action and would lend itself to meaningful transfer in phase four. The teacher began by providing an imitative cue slightly in the direction of "go-o-o-o-o." Peter willingly approximated it. On successive trials, the teacher's cue moved more and more toward the word "go." The shaping of this word was accomplished dramatically in two days, and Peter consistently produced a well-articulated "go" on cue in order to obtain candy.

Overoptimism in such cases is inevitable but seldom warranted. Establishing the first conditioned word may be deceivingly simple, but retaining it is another matter. For five days, Peter readily responded with an imitative "go" to receive candy and quickly transferred this response to make the revolving chair "go." On the sixth day, however, he refused to respond appropriately. Instead of "go" he produced the vocalization, dä-dē. For the next seven days he refused to say "go."

Peter would be given five seconds to respond. If an inaccurate response was given, the shutter was dropped and a five-second penalty of isolation and darkness was administered. If the next trial produced the same response, an additional five-second increment was added and a penalty of ten seconds ensued. This increase was cumulative, and longer and longer periods were spent with Peter and the teacher separated. At the close of the penalty period, the ball was released, Peter dropped it into the box, rang the bell, and contact with the teacher resumed.

A power struggle had begun. In an effort to resolve it, the teacher went back to providing the undifferentiated vowel sound (ē-oö) as a cue. But Peter did not respond. The major concern at this time was that the teacher would become an aversive reinforcer and that the positive relationship previously established would be negated. It was decided to wait out this resistance and to handle each inaccurate response in the prescribed manner. Finally, on the eighth day Peter began to imitate the undifferentiated vowel sound. This was quickly shaped back into the word "go," and at no time in the program did Peter display this marked resistance again.

In our previous pilot speech conditioning with autistic children, introduction of the second word often eliminated the initially learned word from the child's repertoire. It was, therefore, with some concern that the second word "my" was introduced in connection with a Bingo number-matching game which Peter liked. In order to obtain a Bingo marker, Peter was held for successive approximations of the word "my." This word was selected for its usefulness in denoting possession in the later transfer phase. During training on the new word, careful attention was given to systematically reviewing the previously learned word "go," and Peter discriminated well between the two words. The giving of an alternate reinforcer for the new word (e.g., Bingo marker) instead of candy appeared important in aiding discrimination.

The speech-training phase lasted six months during which time Peter acquired a 32-word vocabulary: go, my, see, candy, shoe, key, I, want, hi, bye-bye, mama, daddy, water, toilet, food, eye, ear, nose, mouth, hair, Peter, fine, please, juice, cracker, cookie, milk, Johnny, Marguerite, yes, no, school.

Once the first two words "go" and "my" were learned, Peter's speech became echolalic and he readily attempted to imitate all words the teacher said. However, improvement of his articulation of the 32-word vocabulary was emphasized rather than the building of a larger vocabulary.

Following the acquisition of "my," candy reinforcement was provided on a periodic basis for all new words learned.

Photographs were taken of Peter, his mother, father, brother and sister and he learned the name for each picture. In addition, pictures of Peter eating ("food"), drinking ("water") and going to the bathroom ("toilet") were used as cues. An attempt was made to break the echolalic pattern of Peter's speech, and he learned to answer the direct questions: "How are you? What's your name?" The technique used to teach Peter the appropriate responses to these questions (e.g. "Fine" and "Peter") was developed by Lovaas. First, Peter was given both question and answer for imitation (e.g., "How are you fine"). Gradually the teacher faded the question portion by saying it softly and quickly while emphasizing the answer (e.g. "How are you, FINE!"). Peter soon made a clear imitation of "fine" while paying less and less attention to the question. In a single training session, he learned to respond appropriately to these two direct questions.

The speech-training and transfer phases overlapped as Peter was required to use his conditioned words in a meaningful social context from the beginning of phase three.

PHASE FOUR : TRANSFER

As soon as Peter had learned the word "go," transfer from the teaching booth to the hospital ward was emphasized. Each day when the teacher arrived Peter was required to say "go" as the teacher turned the key in the ward door lock to take him out for a training session.

A ward nurse later was brought into the teaching booth with the teacher. She immediately gained Peter's cooperation for social imitation tasks and the word "go." After working several sessions the nurse held Peter for the word before he was taken through the dining room door and out of the ward on walks. Peter was enrolled in the preschool program with another teacher, and she also participated in several booth-training sessions. Later Peter was required to say "go" in order to enter the schoolroom door. He also was held for "my" before he could obtain a desired object during school periods.

As Peter's vocabulary began to increase, he was required to ask for water, the toilet and food by preceding these words with the phrase, "I want." Also receipt of each periodic candy reinforcement was contingent on "I want candy." Such items as juice and crackers served in the preschool also were given to Peter only when he asked for them. These words were not introduced in the booth. Verbal imitation generalized from the teacher and the booth to other adults and even children in the ward environment.

The children in the preschool became very interested in Peter's attempts at speech and provided constant reinforcement of his words by prompting him. One older boy would hold a toy car at the top of a slanting block runway and let it "go" only when Peter directed him verbally. Peter proved a willing participant in such games.

The major effort during the transfer phase was undertaken with Peter's family. When Peter was permitted six-hour visits twice a week during the seven months of the program, he was not allowed to go home overnight. His parents knew that speech training was being attempted with Peter but not the exact nature of the program. On one occasion, however, while he was on a walk and his parents were moving more slowly than he desired, Peter spontaneously said, "go."

Once he had mastered the 32-word vocabulary Peter's parents were allowed to observe a training session through a one-way vision screen. Most of Peter's training sessions at this point were held outside the booth since he no longer needed the controlled teaching environment. Later both parents were brought into the room and directly observed the training session. Peter performed well with his parents at his side.

When the teacher pointed to Peter's mother and asked "Who's this?" Peter immediately said, "Mama," and took the photograph of his mother and placed it on her lap. He responded in a like manner for "Daddy." His parents then took the place of the teacher and evoked Peter's verbal repertoire using the photographs, Bingo game, candy, and water. The transfer from teacher to parents was uneventful.

After this introduction to the speech program, Peter's parents (and occasionally his brother and sister) joined the teacher for weekly training sessions. Peter also was sent home on weekend visits, and the parents were advised regarding ways in which his newly acquired speech could be used at home. The entire family became involved in reinforcing his speech.

From this point on, Peter had great difficulty separating from his parents and often cried and clung to them as he was to report back into the hospital. Once the parents had left, Peter was given to long periods of crying on the ward. These reactions were in marked contrast to the detachment and apathy he exhibited upon separation following visits during early stages of the program.

A notable event occurred when Peter spontaneously imitated his mother's saying "money" and subsequently added, "I want money," in order to get coins to operate a vending machine. Shortly thereafter he approached the ward nurse saying, "I want toilet," or, "I want school," at the appropriate time, and his conditioned speech began to take on properties of meaningful language.

Peter remained in the speech-training program for eight months following phase three. For most of that period he participated as an outpatient, living at home, and attending the NPI School three times weekly for a two-hour preschool program and 40-minute, speech-training sessions. His speaking vocabulary grew to 150 words, and he demonstrated an insatiable desire to learn new words and phrases. Reading lessons also were introduced at this time as a means of enlarging his vocabulary. At the time of discharge, Peter was returned to the care of the referring psychiatrist, enrolled in a private nursery-kindergarten, and placed with a speech therapist who had observed the speech-training procedures in the NPI School.

><

DISCUSSION

In reviewing the significance of the conditioned speech which Peter acquired during the program it is important to consider the difference between speech and meaningful language.

Speech can be defined as articulated vocal utterances which may be the basis for communication, but meaningful language implies expression of thought and emotion in an appropriate and integrated manner. Birds may acquire speech but not true language skills.

Peter's rapid acquisition of words in association with visual and auditory cues is viewed as an important stage in the development of language. Although he did not systematically acquire the readiness for speech as does the normal child whose socialization experiences from early infancy are intimately involved with words, Peter learned to value and use word symbols. He also generalized an experimentally acquired vocabulary to the larger environment and used it to express his needs verbally (e.g., "I want toilet," or, "I want water").

How successful Peter will be in expanding his speech and converting it to truly meaningful language remains to be seen. That a sizeable communication breakthrough has occurred between an isolated, autistic boy and the social environment, however, cannot be denied.

Not only did this breakthrough make Peter more aware of his social environment, but it also altered the reaction of others toward him. This was clearly seen when nursing staff sought him out for verbal interaction, providing cues for imitation and holding him for speech before granting requests. Although many problems exist between Peter and his family, his newly acquired speech seems to hold promise for improving their relationship and facilitating limit-setting at home.

Goldfarb et al. (1956) have suggested that the response of others to the speech defects of schizophrenic children actually may reinforce such defects. Thus, the nature of the relationship between a nonverbal schizophrenic child and the environment may not be conducive to improved socialization. Meeting the needs of such a child by responding to his primitive and often bizarre attempts at communication may merely make an unsocialized existence more rewarding. In addition, the nonverbal schizophrenic child may be perceived as so atypical and difficult to reach that others develop less personal and involved means of relating with him.

The speech-training program described in this paper represents an intensive effort to establish the vital link of speech and language between a nonverbal, autistic boy and his environment during the critical period of early childhood. Peter's success in acquiring the beginnings of spoken language appears to warrant further investigation of operant techniques for establishing communication skills in autistic children.

❧ 16 ❧

Behavior Therapy for Stuttering in a Schizophrenic Child

Robert M. Browning

The purpose of this study was to devise a treatment procedure which would be effective for the elimination of stuttering in a schizophrenic child. A secondary objective was to demonstrate the effectiveness of selecting treatment procedures in consideration of behavioral characteristics of the patient as well as their appropriateness in a residential treatment setting.

There are numerous studies in the literature which have established that various behavioral modification techniques can effect changes in stuttering (Flanagan et al., 1958; Rickard and Mundy, 1965; Goldiamond, 1965; Case, 1960; Sheehan, 1950; Sheehan and Voas, 1957; Walton and Mather, 1963). However, there is a paucity of studies demonstrating the practical application of these techniques, which would involve meeting the requirements of economy, long-term effects, and a minimum of deleterious effects on other aspects of the patient's treatment program.

This case study was designed to meet the requirements of practical application. For example, certain behavioral characteristics of the subject in this study which had to be considered in the development of his treatment program were those which warranted the diagnosis of childhood schizophrenia. Such behavior made it predictable that noxious stimulation (e.g., Flanagan et al., 1958) would not be advisable since it was known that such conditions would increase the S's general

From *Behavior Research and Therapy*, 5:1 (1967), 27–35, Pergamon Press.

withdrawal, and would be expected to contaminate E as a social reinforcer in S's residential treatment program. Negative practice was also discounted as a possible method since the S's speech was replete with moderately severe speech blocks which are not reliably controlled by this method (Fishman, 1937).

Residential care necessitates a requirement of economy, which in this instance meant a minimum scheduling of professional staff time. The behavioral program herein was devised so that the majority of treatment time involved educational and child-care worker staff in such a way that it would not deter from their scheduled duties. Since a residential program must either produce long-term effects, or make techniques available to the parents so that they may control the child's behavior following discharge, a treatment technique was designed to incorporate simple procedures which the parents could be instructed to administer.

The format of this paper will be to present the treatment program while also elaborating on the rationale for each successive step as it satisfied the requirements of personality characteristics of S, economy, coordination with S's total treatment program, and long-term effects.

METHODOLOGY

Subject

S was a nine-year-old Caucasian male who had been in residence at the Children's Treatment Center for 3 months prior to the inception of this study. His diagnostic status at date of admission was schizophrenic reaction, childhood type, and the behavior which merited this label would be considered moderate. An accompanying diagnosis of psychomotor seizure disorder was established at seven years of age as evidenced by neuropsychological evaluation and repeated EEG's which confirmed the presence of temporal lobe foci. Moderately severe stuttering had characterized S's speech since he was four and one-half years old, and he had never received formal speech therapy. Although all the conditions responsible for S's acquisition of stuttering are not known, it was learned that S commanded an unusual amount of parental attention when he stuttered. It was also observed that cottage staff at the Treatment Center would tolerate and attend to S's stuttering. These observations implied that two reinforcement conditions were contingent upon S's stuttering: the social reinforcement of attention from the listener, and the hypothesized anxiety-reduction associated with completion of a stuttering response (Sheehan, 1950). The treatment program was designed so that these reinforcement contingencies would eventually be reversed; attention and anxiety-reduction would be contingent upon correct speech rather than stuttering.

It has been reported that a major difficulty in the control of stuttering is the generalization of treatment effects to the patient's social environment (Rickard and Mundy, 1965). This difficulty of generalization of treatment effects was expected to be intensified with this S since a deficit in stimulus generalization is a behavioral correlate of brain-damaged children (Mednick and Wild, 1961). The treatment program incorporated procedures which would assist the generalization of treatment effects.

Procedure

This study incorporated the recommendations of a same-subject design in which S serves as his own control (Sidman, 1961). The treatment procedure was a series of nine steps, some of which were conducted simultaneously and some successively. Three steps were extinction periods devised to check on the efficacy of each successive treatment condition. The last extinction period enabled E to directly replicate the final phase of the study in which cottage staff were entirely responsible for the training and in which the previously mentioned reinforcement contingencies for S's speech were reversed. The following is an elaboration of each step and the rationale governing the choice of each of the treatment conditions and its particular order.

Step 1: *Operant level, days* 1–8. The behavioral baseline of stuttering was determined by the percentage of words stuttered or blocked during twice daily 3-min. speech samples obtained by the research assistant. The morning recording was of free speech and was obtained prior to breakfast. The afternoon recording was obtained after school and was derived from reading passages from texts selected at S's grade level. The reading selections were never repeated so as to control for any spurious reduction of stuttering resulting from adaptation effects (Bloodstein, 1948; Sheehan, 1950). During the latter part of the study the conversation and reading samples were alternated between morning and afternoon, and eventually these samples were reduced to only one per day. The speech samples afforded a continuous comparison of treatment effects with the original operant level of stuttering. The research assistant obtained all speech samples and was never involved in the treatment program. The measure of stuttering was simply the percentages of words emitted during the speech sample which contained a speech error, with no distinction given to duration of blocks or number of sound and word repetitions. This coarse grouping of speech errors was a necessity because of the time involved in a precise analysis of speech errors, but it did afford a rigorous baseline for testing treatment effects.

Step 2: *Relaxation training, days* 9–17. The second step of this study was to train *S* to relax according to the procedure incorporated in studies on reciprocal inhibition (Wolpe, 1958). A shortened version of the procedure used by Lang and Lazovik (1960) was employed in this study. *S* was brought to *E*'s office for 10-min. daily sessions for training in the technique of progressive relaxation. During these sessions *S* was not allowed to speak while in the office. If the necessity for speech arose *S* was to signal *E* with his hand at which time he would be taken into the hall to speak. This was devised to prevent *S*'s stuttering being associated with the stimulus characteristics of *E*'s office. As will be seen in the next step, the treatment program was scheduled to ensure that only correct speech occurred in *E*'s office. The rationale for relaxation training was to make available to *S* a response which would later be used to counter-condition the anxiety associated with speech.

Step 3: *Successive approximation to normal speech, days* 18–53. The third step was the most crucial in the study, since it involved the acquisition of four types of behavior which were to be acquired before cottage staff could be used exclusively in *S*'s treatment program. The most obvious behavior to acquire was correct speech as a response available to *S*. This was accomplished by training sessions which progressed from initially silent rehearsals of one word to more difficult speech tasks which eventually progressed to spontaneous conversation with *E*.

The second training regimen involved the reinforcement conditions which would be used to control *S*'s speech. It was known that token rewards were highly reinforcing to *S*, but it would be inconvenient for *S*'s speech to be under the control of token reinforcers at the time of his discharge. Thus, during this step of the study, correct speech responses evoked during the training sessions in *E*'s office were always paired with token rewards as well as verbal reinforcement in the form of praise. Marbles were the token rewards; they were valued at 1 cent each, and *S* used them to purchase toys from a toy cafeteria. This procedure was devised to strengthen the reinforcement condition, and hopefully by pairing verbal reinforcement with token rewards, the former would acquire a stronger and more consistent reinforcing value then formerly. This procedure would also assist in generalization of reinforcers since the verbal praise would be more comparable to the reinforcement conditions which teaching and cottage staff would use when they were responsible for the program.

Suppression of the anxiety associated with stuttering (by counter-conditioning) was the third type of behavior to be acquired during Step 3. Since the speech training trials were designed to progress at a difficulty level which almost assured errorless performance, inter-trial relaxation periods were utilized to associate anxiety-reduction with correct speech. These relaxation intervals were initially directed by *E*'s instructions, but eventually *S* was responsible for inducing the relaxation response. The duration of these relaxation periods progressively diminished during this phase of the study. Furthermore, *S* was reinforced for responding to his speech errors as discriminative stimuli to cease speaking, to relax, and then to complete the speech task successfully. One may interpret this response sequence as a self-control technique, i.e., stuttering was reinforced only when it served as a discriminative stimulus to evoke the incompatible response chain of relaxing and speaking correctly. As will be evident in the treatment procedure utilizing cottage staff, this response chain had to be available to *S* for him to profit from their training regimen.

The fourth training goal of Step 3 was to compensate for the expected deficit in generalization of treatment effects. When *S* was able to converse without error with *E*, the training sessions were conducted in settings which progressively approximated *S*'s daily environment. To illustrate, sessions were initially conducted in the office, then with *S* standing up, then with the door open, and finally, while walking around the grounds. When cottage staff finally assumed responsibility for the speech correction program, *S* already had the experience of speaking correctly in the environment in which staff were associated.

This third treatment step could be summarized as the following: (a) successively approximating normal speech through graduated speech tasks which guaranteed a minimum of error, (b) reinforcing correct speech through anxiety-reduction and token rewards while simultaneously attempting to increase the effectiveness of verbal reinforcement by pairing this with the token rewards, (c) reinforcing stuttering as a discriminative stimulus to evoke a relaxation response which was incompatible with the anxiety previously associated with speech, (d) conducting the speech training sessions under conditions which gradually approximated *S*'s environment. The following is an outline of each speech training session of Step 3. The days on which speech training sessions were held are noted in sequential order. Throughout these sessions, all trials which *S* completed without stuttering, and those trials which he corrected an error before completing the verbal task, were followed by token and verbal reinforcement.

OUTLINE OF DAILY SPEECH TRAINING SESSIONS DURING STEP 3

Day 18. Five trials of silently rehearsing one word ("I") as directed by *E*, with 15-sec. inter-trial relaxation periods directed by *E*.

Day 21. Five trials of silently rehearsing two words ("I am") were alternated with four trials of saying aloud the two words when directed to do so by *E* and with 15-sec. inter-trial relaxation periods also directed by *E*.

Day 23. Ten trials of silently rehearsing three words ["I am (*S*'s name)"] and ten trials of saying these words aloud as directed by *E* with 45-sec. inter-trial relaxation periods directed by *E*.

Day 24. Same as Day 23 but with four words ["I am (*S*'s first and last name)"].

Day 25. Same as Day 24 but with five words ("I am nine years old").

Day 28. Twenty trials in which *S* repeated five- and six-word sentences after *E*, and spoken at *E*'s signal with 30-sec. inter-trial rest periods also directed by *E*.

Day 29. Twenty-eight trials of six- to eight-word sentences repeated aloud after *E* and at *E*'s signal with 15-sec. inter-trial relaxation periods directed by *E*.

Day 30. Twenty-six trials in which five- to eight-word questions after *E* and at *E*'s signal with 30-sec. inter-trial relaxation periods directed by *E*.

Day 31. Sixteen trials in which *S* repeated after *E* four- to nine-word sentences at *E*'s signal with 30-sec. inter-trial relaxation periods also directed by *E*.

Day 32. *S* was asked twenty different questions, whose answers he silently rehearsed, then spoke aloud with one- to four-word replies. He signalled *E* by raising his hand that he was ready to speak and when he dropped his hand he would speak, which was the same signal *E* had used. All trials were followed by 45-sec. inter-trial relaxation sessions directed by *E*. The last three trials were conducted with *S* standing up rather than sitting down in a reclining chair as he had done previous to this time.

Day 35. Twenty-four trials in which *E* asked *S* questions and *S* replied at *E*'s signal. Forty-five-sec. inter-trial relaxation periods were used, relaxation initiated by *S*.

Also initiated on this date were the instructions that he could obtain marbles from either staff or *E* by approaching and initiating conversation. For every correct sentence he would get one marble from that staff member. This order was in effect from Day 35 to Day 45 as a test run. During that interval only eleven sentences were elicited, which suggested that this method was not effective since *S* was avoiding speaking.

Day 36. Twenty-three trials of spontaneous speech in which *S* signaled when he was ready to speak by dropping his hand (which was the same signal previously used by *E*) with 45-sec. inter-trial relaxation periods directed by *S*. At this time there was also initiated a rule that henceforth, whenever *S* stopped speaking at a block and relaxed and then began the sentence over again and completed it successfully, he would receive a token reward, but if he did not succeed on this instruction, then he would not receive a reward.

Day 37. Same as previous day with nineteen trials.

Day 42. Sixty-three trials of spontaneous speech with sentences ranging from one to fifteen words. This session was carried out while walking around the grounds.

Day 43. Same as above, eighty-three trials.

Day 44. Same as above, forty-two trials.

Day 45. Sessions were carried out in the office, same as above with forty-one trials.

Day 46. Same as above with forty-three trials.

Day 49. Same as above with thirty-two trials.

Day 51. Same as above with twenty-five trials.

Day 53. Twenty-five trials. Spontaneous speech carried out while walking around on the grounds.

Step 4: *Extinction period, days* 54–73. The fourth step of the study was a nontreatment interval scheduled to determine if there were any stable treatment effects as reflected in the daily speech samples.

Step 5: *Continuation of Step* 3 *plus staff as social reinforcers of S's speech, days* 74–81. The fifth step was a continuation of the daily sessions with *E*, with speech tasks at the same difficulty level as the last sessions of Step 3, i.e., spontaneous conversation both in *E*'s office and while walking on grounds.

Also initiated during this step was the employment of staff as reinforcers for correct speech. Staff were requested not to respond verbally whenever *S* made a speech error. As soon as *S* repeated his statement correctly, i.e., without stuttering or blocking, they were to praise him and to continue their conversation with him. It was often necessary for staff to afford *S* cues of his stuttering, which varied from a slight turn of one's head when *S* made an error, to a direct request such as, "Why don't you try to say that again?" The rationale for this response contingency by staff was as follows: *S* would become quite irritated if one did not attend to his speech. When staff would not respond, this placed *S* in an immediate conflict. However, *S* had acquired correct speech in *E*'s office which afforded him a response which not only reduced the anxiety elicited by staff's refusal to respond, but which was verbally reinforced by staff. At this time, the reinforcement contingencies, which were suspected to be sustaining *S*'s stuttering, were reversed. Whereas *S* previously received attention for stuttering, he now only received attention and verbal interaction from others for correct speech. Whereas speech-induced anxiety was previously reduced by completion of the stuttered verbal response, the anxiety was sustained and continued to be associated with the stuttering response since he was not allowed to continue speaking until he restated the response correctly. Presumably, only at the time of successful completion of the response would anxiety-reduction occur. Sheehan (1950) experimentally demonstrated the effectiveness of the procedure of requiring a stutterer to repeat a phrase until it was errorless before continuing to a new response.

S continued to be seen by *E* during this phase of the study so as to increase the probability that he would have correct speech available and not respond to this conflict situation by withdrawal in the form of mutism. Such withdrawal would be expected of the schizophrenic child who did not have readily available a response for a recurrent conflict situation.

Step 6: *Extinction period, days* 82–86.

Step 7: *Staff as social reinforcers of correct speech, days* 87–112. During the period of the seventh step, staff members were used in the control of *S*'s stuttering. This was the same procedure as in Step 5, with the exception that *S* was no longer seen by *E*.

Step 8: *Extinction period, days* 113–119. During the week allotted to the eighth step, nontreatment was included, to determine if cottage staff had been responsible for the control of *S*'s stuttering, and if there was any consistency of treatment effects thus far.

Step 9: *Replication of Step 7, days* 120–140.

❥

RESULTS

Table 1 contains the means and standard deviations of the percentage of words stuttered or blocked as derived from the daily speech samples for each of the nine steps of the study. Inspection of Figure 1 reveals the daily percentages of errors present in *S*'s conversation and reading speech samples throughout the study. Reference to both table and chart show that the effects of successive approximation to normal speech in *E*'s office (Step 3) did not generalize to *S*'s daily speech as sampled in the cottage, although his reading errors did decline from the operant level. *S* seldom made errors under the conditions of relaxation and reinforcement utilized during these training sessions in *E*'s office; only eighteen uncorrected stuttering errors occurred in the speech tasks of Step 3.

During Step 5, in which *S* continued to be seen by *E* while staff made their attention and verbal reinforcement contingent upon correct speech, there was a marked reduction of *S*'s stuttering. The extinction period which followed Step 5 occurred while *S* was on a 5-day home visit. Only one speech sample was obtainable during this interval, and it was taken immediately upon his return to the Treatment Center. As can be seen in the Table, *S*'s stuttering rate was again almost identical to that which was observed to occur in the operant level, which indicated that the treatment procedure was effective in controlling his speech, although these effects had not generalized to his home.

The final step of the study was to use staff members exclusively, and at this time *S* demonstrated the greatest diminution of stuttering. One major difficulty was found in using staff members as social reinforcers for correct speech. The staff had been accustomed to *S*'s extensive stuttering and long speech blocks for several months. It was observed that they would request *S* to repeat a stuttered or blocked response, provided that speech error was quite obvious, if not comparable to the operant level errors. They frequently failed to correct mild speech errors, which during the last steps of the study characterized *S*'s speech. The result of this failure is that staff were inadvertently reinforcing a low level of stuttering. Unfortunately this was on a variable schedule since some staff members were more compulsive than others in following

TABLE 1.　Mean per cent words stuttered or blocked for each of the nine steps as derived from daily reading and conversation speech samples

Step	Reading		Conversation	
	M% Stuttered	S.D.	M% Stuttered	S.D.
1.　Operant level	21.47	2.81	22.61	3.91
2.　Relaxation training	17.47	2.95	19.52	2.15
3.　Successive approximation to normal speech	13.75	3.26	23.13	3.39
4.　Extinction period	14.48	3.13	19.50	1.61
5.　Continuation of step 3 plus staff as social reinforcers	8.34	2.12	10.28	2.78
6.　Extinction period*	—	—	21.03	—
7.　Staff as social reinforcers	5.49	2.68	7.95	3.50
8.　Extinction period	3.56	1.45	8.18	.36
9.　Staff as social reinforcers	2.81	.72	4.18	2.43

* Only 1 sample available

this management order of requesting S to repeat an incorrect response until he was correct. Other residential centers using this technique should be alerted to this problem, and possibly train their staff to discriminate speech errors.

✂

DISCUSSION

The effectiveness of combining several behavior modification techniques was demonstrated in this study. Precise information on the relative effectiveness of each technique was not established. Previous research has demonstrated that several procedures can effect fluctuations in the incidence of stuttering, but for a method to be applicable to a clinical setting, it must provide long-term effects. The procedure described herein does not necessarily guarantee such long-term effects, but it is sufficiently simple to that S's parents could easily be trained to reinstate the training procedure, and extinguish the stuttering responses.

　　The approach of this study may be applicable to other residential settings in which one treatment goal is to improve the speech of psy-

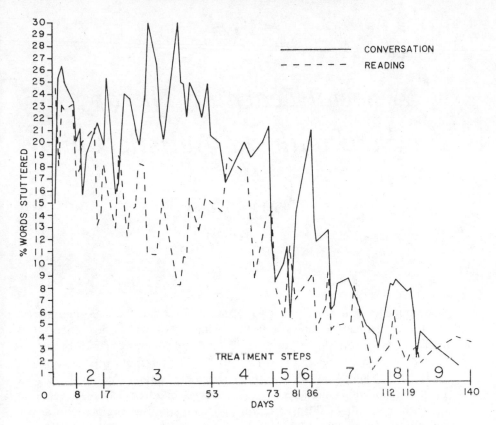

FIGURE 1.   Per cent words stuttered in daily reading and conversation
  speech samples throughout the nine treatment steps.

chotic children. The approach can be simplified in this manner: first
the response of correct speech is made available to the patient, then the
conflict associated with speech tasks is intensified for the stutterer by
not responding to him unless he speaks correctly. Thus, whereas stuttering was previously an avoidance response which was presumably
reinforced by the anxiety-reduction contingent upon the completion
of a verbalization, anxiety persists to be associated with stuttered responses, and anxiety-reduction and social reinforcement now follow
only correct responses. The danger of this approach is to demand
correct speech from *S* when such responses are not available to him.
Such circumstances could most likely result in random behavior and
increased anxiety. With the schizophrenic child one would expect that
these circumstances would guarantee increased withdrawal, if not
mutism.

~17~

A Social Learning Therapy
Program with an Autistic Child

Gerald C. Davison

Since Lindsley and Skinner (1954) reported for the first time a method
for the experimental analysis of the behavior of psychotic patients,
many investigators have successfully utilized operant conditioning
procedures to manipulate the behavior of adult psychotics (e.g., King
et al., 1957; Ayllon and Michael, 1959; King et al., 1960; Ayllon, 1963).
The behavior of both normal and retarded children has also been
shown to be readily controllable through such conditioning procedures
(e.g., Bijou, 1955, 1957, 1958; Bijou and Baer, 1960; Baer, 1961, 1962b).
Ferster (1961) and Ferster and DeMyer (1961a, b) have extended these
techniques to the behavior of autistic children, demonstrating that
even their behavior could be shaped by operant techniques. Successful
conditioning of verbal behavior in both normals and psychotics has
also been reported (Krasner, 1962).

Aside from a recent report by Wolf et al. (1964), however, the studies
which deal with psychotic behavior have initially restricted themselves
either to shaping up behaviors such as pulling a plunger, or to extinguishing behaviors like hoarding towels. If the principles are powerful,
considerably more complex behaviors should be manipulable. Moreover,
most work with psychotics has been conducted in residential settings,
where the investigators have been able to exercise the kind of control
which is assumed to be necessary for a truly effective operant reinforcement program. Especially with psychotic children, however, it is seldom

From *Behavior Research and Therapy*, 2 (1964), 149–159, Pergamon Press.

possible to institute a treatment program which involves all, or even a large percentage of, the patient's time: aside from the scarcity of in-patient facilities, parents are reluctant to give up completely the custody of their children.

This report deals with the limited treatment of a psychotic child in a day-care center. The author first trained nonprofessional personnel in the principles of social learning (predominantly operant) therapy. He then conducted a "therapy-experiment" in order to explore the feasibility and effectiveness of such a program in a treatment setting that was far from ideal, although quite realistic.

THEORETICAL RATIONALE

The syndrome of "early infantile autism" was first isolated and labeled by Kanner (1943) as involving a specific constellation of symptoms. More recently, Ferster (1961) has subjected these behaviors to a functional analysis, which logically proceeds through the following steps: the specification of the syndrome at a behavioral level; the assumption that behavior is shaped and maintained by environmental contingencies; an analysis of how behavioral deficits like those in autism are associated with certain environmental contingencies, prima-rily nonreinforcement; and finally, an analysis of parental variables which could provide such reinforcement contingencies.

The most important aspect of his thesis for the present program is that there has been a retardation in the development of secondary and generalized reinforcers in their control over the child's behavior. Thus the child responds almost exclusively to primary reinforcers. The general plan of this study was to follow Ferster's reasoning, but to use human therapists to set up the contingencies for and to dispense the primary (and later, secondary) reinforcements. It is contended that human beings can shape a much wider range of behaviors than can a machine, as well as function as models for teaching complex patterns of behavior more quickly than is possible through the purely operant technique of successive approximations (Bandura and Walters, 1963).

METHOD

In an earlier report (Davison, 1964), it was demonstrated that one could train intelligent, ambitious undergraduates in about four hourly meetings to carry out a behavior-control program which requires the application of learning principles to the manipulation of psychotic behavior in children. The present program was conducted during an academic quarter at the same private day-care center. This center was in a very small, dilapidated house with five rooms and about an acre of land. The building was surrounded by a high fence; within the inside play-area were swings, a sand-box, a jungle-jim, and a "dinosaur" (a jungle-jim constructed to resemble a dinosaur). The house itself was well supplied with various toys suitable for children aged three to ten. In the area outside the fence was a large wooded field with a tree on which a swing had been made out of an old automobile tire. About 15 children, ages three to fourteen, would be brought there on weekdays by their parents, from 9.30 A.M. until 2.00 P.M., where volunteer-workers, primarily housewives with college degrees, supervised their play activities. The directors of the center described their program as "milieu therapy."

Both the academic commitments of the students and an agreement not to interfere unduly with the ongoing program at the center made it impossible to utilize more than eight of the child's 25 hours spent each week at the center. This amounted to less than 15 per cent of the child's waking hours. Moreover, the physical set-up, as will be seen in the case study material below, made it very difficult to work undisturbed with the child. Two students worked with the child, one during the mornings two days a week, the other during the afternoons.

The crux of the therapy was to utilize play situations for the differential reinforcement and extinction of various behaviors. Despite their training in operant conditioning theory and demonstrations of the many contingencies which could arise in the course of actual treatment, it was clear that the many moment-by-moment decisions would have to be made by the students themselves; the author, if you will, provided the proper "set." It was pointed out also that each primary reinforcement was to be accompanied by a smile and a laudatory phrase, along with a remark to the effect that obeying the therapist had earned the candy. Each worker wrote up a detailed behavioral report of the happenings of each session, stressing the trouble spots. These reports enabled the author to monitor the treatment. (For more complete details of the training, the reader is referred to Davison, 1964.)

The assumption was made only that the child's behavior had probably been shaped as theorized by Ferster (1961) and, at any rate, could be brought under significant control by a social learning therapy. A little girl was chosen on the basis of four criteria: (1) she was not in individual psychotherapy; (2) she had no known physiological damage; (3) she was not on medication; and (4) she accepted an M & M candy when it was offered to her. She was a pretty, frail-looking nine-year-old child. She was very talkative (although communicating little), and was characterized by withdrawal, various ritualistic behaviors, apparent hallucinatory activities and general disobedience. Because the aim was to test the limits of a short-term program, there was no inquiry made into the background of the child.

><

"OBJECTIVE" INDEXES OF THERAPIST-CONTROL

"Therapist-control" was defined as the percentage of commands obeyed by the child with each therapist without the use of candy-reinforcements. A "Control for Familiarity" was a worker, familiar to the child, who could be tested at the same time the therapists would be tested, the important difference being that, between the pre- and post-measures, she would not have made use of our techniques. As will be seen, a compromise had to be made because of practical problems.

Inasmuch as earlier work in this setting had shown the fruitlessness of preparing a list of commands beforehand, the author decided to construct the commands on the scene, the idea being that similar conditions could be re-created for the post-measurement. Fortunately, this child's behavior was characterized by general withdrawal, not by tantrums and other deviant behaviors which would necessitate intervention. As a result, it was possible to obtain with both therapists, and with the control, very meaningful measures.

Each measurement was taken in the same way. The author and the respective worker "interacted" with the child for 15 min., that is, they made efforts to speak with her and show her things. Then it was announced that "a game" would be played. Standing not more than three feet away, the author then instructed the worker to ask the child to do various simple motor tasks, e.g., "Take this book, Give me that doll," and others. Each command could be repeated twice, the child being considered to have failed an item if she did not obey by the second repetition. Since these behaviors were of a very simple nature, there were no problems of scorer-reliability. The choice of commands was made on the scene and was determined both by the materials available and by the child's position, viz., if she were standing near a doll and oriented toward it, she was asked to pick it up. In order to increase the number of observations, several of the commands were given more than once. (It was, in fact, possible to duplicate the command-schedule of Therapist B with the Control.)

Results of the Pre-measures

With Therapist A, the child obeyed none of 23 commands.

With Therapist B, the child obeyed 1 out of 17 commands.

With the Control for Familiarity, the child obeyed 2 out of 17 commands.

The conclusion from these pre-measures was that neither the therapists nor the Control had any significant control over the child's behavior.

Results of the Post-measures

Nearly seven weeks later, as had been planned in the beginning, the author returned to the center for post-measures. Academic commitments made it feasible to repeat the measures first with Therapist B. Complications arose, however, which must be discussed in reporting the post-measures.

Up to the time the author arrived, the child had been behaving as usual, i.e., obeying practically every instruction of the therapist, without candy-reward. However, upon seeing the author, she began to withdraw, sob and become generally intractable, saying that she did not like the author, that she did not want him around. As might be expected, the post-measure showed no improvement over the pre-measure. Moreover, the therapist could not even get her attention with M & M's — a state of affairs that had not held since the very beginning of treatment (see case material below).

An attempt was made to get *some sort* of post-measure inasmuch as the case study material clearly indicated that the therapists had, indeed, acquired a significant amount of control over the child, which one should be able to tap with these "objective" measures. The alternative was to have the therapists execute the list of commands by themselves. In order to exclude subjective biases as much as possible, both therapists were told to play with the child as usual for half an hour, taking care toward the end of this period to bring her into the area where the pre-measures had been taken. They were then to decide when to begin and to take the measures without delay or interruption. Once again, for both therapists, the area was relatively quiet, so that the post-measures were judged to be meaningful indices of post-therapy control:

With Therapist A, the child obeyed 20 out of 23 commands.

With Therapist B, the child obeyed 15 out of 18 commands.

In an attempt to "save" the pre-measures, the author returned to the center two days later with Therapist B. This time the child was not at all disturbed by the author's presence, but was indifferent to him as had been the case for the pre-measures. The results showed that:

With Therapist B, the child obeyed 15 out of 17 commands.

In the strictest sense, the Control for Familiarity was lost, for this volunteer-worker had stopped coming to the center soon after the start of the present program. It was possible, however, to enlist the assistance of another worker who had spent even *more* time with the child — at least six months. Not more than 15 min. after the immediately preceding measurement session with Therapist B, the following results were obtained:

With the Control for Familiarity, the child obeyed 17 out of 17 commands.

The first conclusion could be seen as an unfavorable one: the child could be controlled as well by a worker who was very familiar to her after the treatment program as by workers who, in addition to having become familiar, had followed an operant conditioning program *designed* to increase the degree of therapist-control. However, the assumption could also be made that, during the seven weeks of therapy, adults in general had acquired secondary reinforcing power for the child. Although the author had assumed that, to effect this, a new adult would have to either follow his own operant regime with primary positive reinforcement, or at least be present while the child was being manipulated by an operant-therapist, this hypothesis of "spontaneous generalization" seemed to merit testing.

On the same day as the two preceding measures, therefore, the author brought to the center a female undergraduate who was totally unfamiliar to the child. After interacting for only five minutes (because of practical considerations), the author and this student executed the command-schedule of Therapist B (and the Control for Familiarity) and obtained these results:

With the Control for Generalization, the child obeyed 14 out of 17 commands.

Discussion

A comparison of the pre-measures of each therapist with his own post-measures indicated that both had acquired significantly more control over the child. The data from the Control for Familiarity, however, did not justify concluding that this increase was necessarily a result of the therapy-program, although one could surely argue that the operant regime had achieved its results far more quickly than did the milieu therapy. The Control for Generalization, on the other hand, strongly suggests that, as a result of this therapy, the child had learned to pay attention to adults and to obey their instructions, i.e., the child had become generally more manageable, indicating even greater success than had been anticipated.

＞＜

CASE STUDY MATERIAL

Throughout the treatment program, it became increasingly apparent to both the author and the therapists that the most valuable data were being collected in the reports which each therapist wrote up following a therapy-session. It is in these reports that one could see the steady development of therapist-control and the kinds of plans that were made along the way to handle various contingencies. In as complex and true-to-life setting as was found at this day-care center, along with the severe practical limitations, one has to rely on descriptive data. The objective measures suggest very strongly that the program had the desired effect. The following case report tells *how* this came about. (Subjectivity in these data was minimized by restricting the reporting to *descriptions of behavior*.)

The numbering of the sessions below denotes the therapist and his (or her) session with the child.

Sessions A-1 and B-1. The therapists were given an orientation to the center, and the author used various ongoing situations to illustrate further the mechanics of the operant techniques. The pre-measures were taken, after which the author demonstrated with the child the use of M & M candies as incentive and reinforcement. The child remained very much withdrawn, unwilling to do anything more than take a few steps for a candy. She strayed off to familiar workers during most of these two sessions, although by the end of B-1, the therapist had managed to coax her near the swing.

The initial strategy was to concentrate on very simple tasks, like merely walking toward the therapist, in order to achieve some frequency of reinforcement.

Session B-2. For the first half of this session, the child refused to do things like sit on a chair or pick up a block (which were, incidentally, two of the items from this therapist's command-schedule). The therapist managed to get the child outside and, after several attempts, guided her onto the swing; however, for about 15 min. she would not stand up from it. Toward the end of the session, the child became much more obedient, doing things like picking up sticks. At one point she threw them away; the therapist pointed out to her that, in order to get a candy, she must hand him the sticks gently; the child obeyed this instruction and received a reinforcement. When it was time to leave, the child begged the therapist to stay a bit longer, telling him that she liked him. By making his presence for a few more minutes contingent on her obeying him, the therapist was able to persuade the child to do several things which she had earlier refused to do.

Session A-2. This session began much better, the child expecting the therapist. She obeyed several simple commands as long as they did not take her out of the vicinity of the worker who had acted as the Control for Familiarity. When the child began to throw things about carelessly, the therapist pointed out what *should* be done, and the child complied for candy-reinforcement. In order to remove the distraction of the other worker, the therapist carried the child to the Dinosaur, where they played for several minutes. The child kept running off to the other worker, however, so the therapist waited a few minutes before going after her in order to minimize the chances of reinforcing her for leaving. It was noticed that the child was fascinated by her reflection in the windows, and the therapist was able to get her to do various things while watching herself. In a field outside the fence, the child displayed severe avoidance reactions to mushrooms, saying that she would not touch them out of fear of being poisoned; repeated attempts with candy were unsuccessful in persuading the child to touch the plant. By the end of the session, she was remaining continuously with the therapist.

Session B-3. The child was rewarded with candy for coming to the therapist as soon as he arrived. Although obedience was good for several simple tasks, the therapist was unable for half an hour to get the child off the swing; threats of withdrawal, actual withdrawal and frequent offers of candy were of no avail. When the child finally tired of the swing, the therapist took her outside the fence, where good control was possible with fewer candies. Later on, the child agreed to climb onto the first rung of the Dinosaur, a behavior in which she would not engage earlier in this session. They also played catch, candy-reward becoming intermittent.

A general shift in strategy was made: the therapists were to concentrate on making reward intermittent along with introducing more difficult activities. Recalcitrance was to be dealt with by increasing the number of candies and/or by reducing slightly the difficulty of the command, e.g., if she refused to pick up three rocks, the idea was to get her to pick up at least two.

Session A-3. The child stayed with the therapist throughout (and continued to do so, with both therapists, for the remainder of the program). With primary reinforcement intermittent, the child obeyed virtually every command. Defiant behaviors, like throwing sand, were handled as already noted. A pocket mirror was introduced to furnish reflections for reinforcement. She climbed two rungs onto the jungle-jim for the first time. The therapist managed to keep her playing at clay a little while longer than she wanted to. The child also carried across the yard a piece of plywood which she had earlier refused even to touch.

A combination of the mirror and the increasing effectiveness of secondary and generalized reinforcers reduced sharply the need for candy-reinforcement.

Session B-4. It was found that the frequent tumult at the center made it generally difficult to control the child, so that all the succeeding sessions were conducted, for the most part, in the woods and field outside the fence. It was once again impossible to lead her away from the swing once she had consented to swing on it. They played catch today for a much longer period of time, reward being only a peek in the mirror at the very end. At the end of this session, as with most of the following, the child was very reluctant to leave the therapist to go home.

Session A-4. Up to the time the therapist arrived today, the Staff had been unable to get the child into the bathroom; the therapist managed this contingency without any difficulty. It was reported that the child jumped off a fallen tree stump which she had earlier been afraid to do. She also touched a mushroom with her shoe. The handling of a third fear was also noted: whereas she had earlier refused even to sit near the therapist while he was blowing up a balloon, on this day she could be coaxed even to touch it, in fact also finding that she could see her reflection in it.

There continued to be few occasions on which she did not obey immediately without either candy or the mirror; in these few instances, the promise of candy brought compliance.

Session B-5. The difficulty in getting her off the swing today was successfully handled by promising a peek into an especially large mirror, namely the outside mirror of the therapist's car. The end of the session made possible a very powerful withdrawal of reinforcement for disobedience: when she once again would not leave the swing, the therapist announced that he would leave the premises. This was done in spite of her entreaties for him to remain.

Session A-5. On a walk today she shivered in fright when seeing two horses about 30 feet away on the other side of the fence. Reassurances stopped her shaking. She also touched an inflated balloon much more readily. No more than three candies and the same number of peeks in a mirror were needed to maintain perfect control.

Session B-6. While looking for pitch on trees, the child agreed to swing on the tire swing outside the fence. Unfortunately, she bumped her nose on it and began to kick the therapist. He managed to distract her with another task. Outside of this incident, control continued to improve.

Session A-6. The child was bothered by a rather strong wind, and was generally unmanageable for the first half of the session. The introduction of more candy, however, brought her under control, and by the end of the day she had even been coaxed to touch the previously feared balloon.

Session B-7. On a walk, the therapist persuaded the child (with candy) to put her head through the tire swing on which she had bumped her nose in Session B-6. At the swing inside the fence, however, control was difficult to maintain as the child teased another who was trying to swing. Aside from this incident, however, she obeyed nearly every command, without candy.

At this point, the therapists were told to keep her away from this inside swing inasmuch as their control over her was not yet great enough to handle this contingency.

Session B-8. Today the child jumped off a stump over two and one-half feet high without insisting that the therapist hold her hand; earlier she would not jump more than one foot off the ground unless she was held. She also teetered on a board, a behavior which she had been afraid to engage in earlier. She agreed to *sit in* the tire swing, for a candy. The mirror was reported to have lost its effectiveness as a reinforcer.

The difficulty in preventing her from kicking became too great merely to ignore, for the therapist had to step out of the way lest he be hurt. The plan to handle this problem was as follows: the therapist was to walk off briskly to a distance of at least 25 feet; if the child ran after him, he was immediately to give a simple command so as to reinforce her both for running after him and for obeying an instruction. This was to be repeated if necessary.

Session A-7. This session was one of the most difficult of the entire program. The child kicked and swore, teased others, and obeyed very little. She became fascinated by another child eating some clay, and the therapist was unable to get her away from this scene for more than a few minutes at a time. Even the frequent offer of candy was relatively ineffective. The aforementioned plan to control kicking had not yet been put into action.

The assumption was made that some crisis at home had caused this trouble, and, since we were not in a position to control this, the plan was simply to carry on and see.

Session B-9. The strategy against kicking was put into operation as follows. After obeying very nicely at the outset, the child kicked the therapist when he told her to hand him something. He strode off quickly, the child running after him and pleading for him not to go. He then gave her a simple instruction, at which she kicked him again. He walked off again, the child trailing and imploring. Another instruction met with a petulant "No," at which the therapist strode off a third time. At this point the child picked up the object she had been told to and ran after the therapist quickly to give it to him. After this two-minute episode, there was no more kicking for the remainder of the session. Excellent control was the case thereafter, with activities including jumping off stumps and swinging in the tire swing five times (an earlier limit being three times), this time the child not even insisting that the therapist hold her hand. Several new tasks were done as well, one of them bouncing a ball back and forth with the therapist.

Session A-8. After playing in the sand-box for a while, the child kicked sand at the therapist, at which point the withdrawal technique was again used. (It should be noted that this is a different therapist from the one immediately above.) The effect was as planned, the child promising not to kick anymore. On a walk, the child *touched* and *smelled* a mushroom — a considerable improvement over Session A-2.

Session B-10. When the child persisted in throwing a ball at some other children, the therapist withdrew. There was no more trouble for the remainder of the session. Other activities included jumping off stumps and playing in the tire swing.

Session A-9. Occasional kicking and pouring sand on another child were immediately extinguished by withdrawal of the therapist.

Session B-11. After playing catch for a while, the child kicked the ball away, saying that she did not want to play anymore. The therapist succeeded in getting her to throw it one more time before stopping. An unsuccessful attempt was made to persuade her to climb onto a stump that was taller than she. There was more swinging in the tire.

More trouble with kicking was reported, and it was decided to lengthen the time of withdrawal.

Session A-10. When tired of playing ball today, the child docilely handed the ball to the therapist, saying "I'm tired."

Session A-11. Once again she informed the therapist pro-socially that she did not want to play ball anymore. She also climbed higher on both the Dinosaur and the jungle-jim than she ever had. On a walk today she exhibited none of her earlier fears of horses (cf. Session A-5).

Sessions B-12, A-13, B-13. The post-measures were taken.

⤬

DISCUSSION

Several things may be noted from these case study data:

1. Whereas the child initially would stray off from the therapists, by Session A-3 she always remained with each therapist.

2. Activities which she initially would not do even with the offer of a candy, she was doing for no candy at all before the end of the program.

3. The deliberate use of extinction procedures was shown directly to have eliminated at least two isolable deviant behaviors, viz., kicking and pouring sand on others.

4. Pro-social behaviors were substituted for anti-social behaviors, e.g., handing the therapist the ball when tired of playing, instead of kicking it away.

5. Improvement did not follow a monotonic function, due at least in part to the treatment having been restricted to no more than eight hours per week.

6. Several avoidance behaviors, probably motivated by actual fear, were apparently eliminated.

The last point is important enough for more detailed discussion. The reports of the various fears at first passed unnoticed, until one of the therapists pointed out that he had managed to coax the child to jump from a height which she had earlier been quite afraid of. Instructions were then given the therapists to note such occurrences more carefully, the result being the frequent mention of fears and their undoing, as has been seen above.

It is suggested that these fears were eliminated by their having been reciprocally inhibited through the evocation, in the presence of the feared objects, of emotional states antagonistic to anxiety (cf. Jones, 1924; Wolpe, 1958). These pleasant states, it is contended, were aroused both through the dispensing of primary positive reinforcement and through the presence of a person who had come to be associated with these affective states. Similar cases with children (albeit nonpsychotic) have been reported by Lazarus (1960) and by Lazarus, Davison, and Polefka (1965).

><

CONCLUSIONS AND IMPLICATIONS

The success of the program with this single child indicates that operant techniques are appropriate — perhaps even peculiarly appropriate — to manipulating the behavior of psychotic children. The advantages of a case study, supplemented by more objective assessment procedures, lie in the detailed idiographic description of the complex development of a single patient's reaction to therapy. As helpful as such data are for formulating better procedures and for generating fruitful hypotheses, it must not be forgotten that they do not, by themselves, provide scientific verification of the theories on which they are based.

On the more positive side, the use of operant conditioning in a setting where almost everything is uncontrolled might have been predicted to have disastrous consequences in terms of partial reinforcement (Ferster and Skinner, 1957). That this did not occur here may be due to the child's having been able to discriminate among workers, such that she was put on a different reinforcement schedule entirely when the student-therapists were working with her. However, the fact that she was very obedient with the Control for Generalization offers difficulty for this explanation, especially since it is certain that no one else had been following a similar regime with her. Perhaps the author, after the disturbance he caused at the first post-test, became a discriminative stimulus for the new schedule of reinforcement.

Even if one were to generalize from this single case, however, it would be premature to conclude that the therapy had "cured" the child, that is, that it had changed the response-patterns to approximate more nearly what is regarded in our society as normal. Although one *assumes* that a therapy of this nature can, over a much longer period of time and directed toward a wider range of behaviors, bring about truly basic and enduring changes (as appears to have happened with Wolf et al., 1964), it must be made clear that the child's behavior was still very deviant at the end of the program. The gains that she had made were considerable, but even while obeying virtually every command, for example, she was emitting verbalizations which could only with great difficulty be considered healthy.

There is something very positive to say for this kind of program, in spite of its limitations. Even under very poor conditions, trained undergraduates were, in fact, able to acquire a significant degree of control over a psychotic child in a very short time. It is hard to conceive of a therapy which does not presuppose at least that the patient pay attention to the therapist and follow his instructions, whether they be to press levers or to free associate. Especially with psychotic children does this pose a problem, and any procedure which enables the therapist to achieve a working measure of control over his patient's behavior merits consideration from practitioners of any persuasion.

⤝ 18 ⤞

Programmed Psychotherapy

Anthony M. Graziano

Most of the reports of behavior therapy with children have described what are basically research attempts with one or two children as subjects, and have been focused on discrete or single-problem behaviors. Patterson and Brodsky (1966) point out that the rapidly-developing field lacks reports of over-all success with children who present *multiple* problem behaviors. The realities of the clinic are such that multiple and not single-problem children are referred.

Another area which seems to have been little investigated thus far is a group behavior therapy approach, in which social-environmental programming is carried out to take advantage of the social contingencies which so readily occur in groups. This paper briefly describes an attempt to modify the multiple behavior deficits and surpluses of psychotic children, using a group behavior therapy approach in which the social environment is carefully programmed.

This work began early in 1963 when I was asked to develop a therapy program for four autistic children (Graziano, 1963). Exploratory rather than definitive, it is based on clinical observations and limited experimentation. Its major assumptions are:

1. Observed behavior and not inferred dynamics is the content of therapy.

2. Adaptive and maladaptive behavior is learned and, as Dollard and Miller (1950) note, "should be unlearned by some combination of the same principles by which (it was) taught."

Paper presented at the Eastern Psychological Association, Boston, Massachusetts, 1967.

This work was supported in part by grants from the State of Connecticut Department of Mental Health, Division of Community Services.

3. If the focus is on learning, then the task must be teaching.

4. To modify complex human behavior one must analyze it into its more specific response constituents and then elicit and reinforce those constituents in carefully planned sequences of successive approximations.

The four autistic children were observed in order to determine their gross *behavioral deficits* in various response classes such as verbalizations, object manipulations, cooperative behavior, and so on. A range of response constituents in each response class was identified and techniques sought to elicit and reinforce those responses step by small step, strengthening those which more nearly approximated the complex behavioral goal. Such carefully planned sequences of constituent responses and immediate reinforcement of behavior which successively approximates the complex behavioral goal are the basic elements of programmed learning. Hence the title, *Programmed Psychotherapy*.

Planned in detail for each individual, the programs are applied in group settings. We assume the group provides more stimuli and rewards, increases imitative learning and vicarious reinforcement, and facilitates positive transfer by more closely approximating the "normal" world.

Because behavioral concepts afford parsimonious explanations and straightforward techniques, they can be effectively and inexpensively taught to selected nonprofessionals including parents. Our group workers must be efficient reinforcing agents — i.e., mature, friendly, calm, gentle but firm, and intelligent enough to adhere to the rational, planned program. Constant active involvement and sharp alertness is required to stimulate and immediately reinforce emerging adaptive behaviors. The parents of our children have been readily trained to use behavior modification techniques. In three cases, in fact, we have trained and supervised parents as therapists to carry out the major therapy at home. We believe that the training of parents as therapists is an area of potentially vast significance.

In our original group two unresponsive boys, ages five and nine, had no interaction, no speech, and few vocal sounds. Two years earlier, one had broken his arm and reacted so little that his parents were unaware of it for several hours.

Another boy, age six, totally ignored people, never played with toys, but did eat dirt, buttons, and clay. Hyperactive and loud, he rapidly circled the room screaming, screeching, and shouting his entire vocabulary "no," "fire," and "help." Prone to sudden destructive outbursts, he attacked with feet, fists, nails, and teeth. His quietest and most controlled behavior consisted of shredding books and tearing the heads and limbs from dolls.

The girl, age six, was literally always on her toes, hopping from foot to foot, holding a small doll against her nose and crooning bits of TV commercials. Well coordinated, she accelerated like a track champion, dashing away in unpredictable directions. She spun wildly, bounced, jumped, snapped her head back and forth, and emitted ear-splitting screams. The most violent child in the group, she frequently "destroyed" the room.

Aloof and alone, they had no social interaction. All had short attention spans. Three were head-bangers, with long, destructive tantrums. Only one was toilet trained. None used toys appropriately, none showed academic skills, and none had useful, communicative speech.

As Rimland (1964) noted, prognosis for autistic children is closely linked to speaking ability. Eisenberg (1956) and Kanner and Lesser (1958) reported that sixteen of thirty-two autistic children who had useful, communicative speech at age five later achieved "fair" to "good" social adjustment while only one of thirty-one "nonspeaking" children reached even the "fair" level. When our group began none of the children had "useful, communicative speech." Hence, according to available criteria, their prognoses were very poor.

In viewing their gross behavioral deficits it appeared that therapeutic progress would occur most readily through the acquisition of new, adaptive behavior, rather than decrement of existing, maladaptive responses. Our therapeutic starting point, then, was to *stimulate and reinforce a high rate of responding to us* and then, through planned sequences of successive approximations, selectively reinforce increasingly adaptive responses. However, because they ignored nearly all stimuli, we had to rely on trial and error to discover effective stimuli and rewards. Accordingly, we touched them, held them, talked, offered objects, etc., until they finally made their first consistent response to us; whenever we came near, they retreated!

The constant stimulation was apparently noxious, and by moving away they effected the *cessation of noxious stimulation* which, presumably, reinforced their moving away. The same reinforcement was used to teach them to reach a hand toward us, touch us, accept proffered objects, move toward other people, and approximate words. That is, when the response occurred we removed the noxious stimuli, ourselves. In a few weeks they had acquired a variety of entirely new responses to us. However, they became increasingly aggressive and difficult to control because, in developing the new, high response rate, *all* behavior, including aggressive responses, had been reinforced.

Having achieved the desired high rates of responses, we began to differentially reinforce adaptive responses, such as verbal behavior, while letting maladaptive behavior weaken and diminish. More rewards were needed and "snack time" was initiated as a *reward-dispensing social situation*. Initially the children ignored snack time but, with bits of cookies and sips of juice, their approaches to the table were reinforced. Finally, all four were seated together and the time increased to our imposed twenty-minute maximum.

During snack many social and verbal responses were reinforced by *food as a primary reward* which also gave secondary reinforcing value to the social stimuli. Snack time soon acquired its own high, positive reinforcing value.

To develop the secondary reinforcing value of verbal stimuli, verbalizing and the primary reward, food, were carefully paired, and the children's attention to general verbal stimuli increased. In the same manner we also developed the reinforcing value of specific phrases such as "good work" and "good job" to serve as verbal reinforcers.

When both general and specific verbal stimuli had acquired secondary reinforcing value, a major therapeutic sub-goal had been reached; previously, in order to reinforce adaptive behavior we had to be near the child to present physical rewards such as food. If he were beyond arm's reach we could not reward him. However, once *verbal reinforcers* had been developed, we could *reinforce at a distance*, presenting verbal rewards from the farthest point in the room. Gradually, dependence on primary rewards decreased as use of verbal rewards increased. Interaction with the autistic children was eventually nearly all on a verbal level.

Once a verbal level of interaction had been achieved, we set out to teach the children to control maladaptive behavior through their own use of verbal mediators. One technique was to encourage *rote repetition of behavioral "rules"* such as "we don't throw things," "we don't hit," and "we don't bite people." With reinforced repetition of these rules, the following sequence was observed: The rules were repeated but without apparent effect on behavior. Later they verbalized the rules while engaged in the prescribed behavior. Then they began to delay the maladaptive behavior for longer periods of time as they verbalized "we don't hit," etc. The overt verbalizing gradually diminished to a whisper, then to silent mouthings of the phrases, and finally, dropped out entirely, while its stimulus control of aggression remained. For the past year aggressive and destructive behavior has been rare.

With the children's increased general responsiveness and continued verbal development, *social imitation and vicarious reinforcement* increased. It was now possible to reinforce at a distance, and also to reinforce one child's adaptive behavior and expect another child to learn it through vicarious conditioning.

An *automatic reinforcing framework* as a steady background was developing. Now, nearly all behavior occurring during the sessions was reinforced in some manner and care was needed to *prevent the occurrence of maladaptive responses* lest they, too, be reinforced. Stimulus conditions were manipulated so as to maximize adaptive responses. When, however, maladaptive responses did occur, they were stopped immediately by use of mild physical restraint, removal from the room, repetition of verbal admonitions and withdrawing or withholding positive reinforcement. In contrast to catharsis techniques, maladaptive behavior was not allowed to occur.

It was assumed, when snack time had reached approximately twenty minutes, that enough reward value had been acquired to generalize to another table-and-chair situation, "school time." The transition to and subsequent development of "school time" is shown in Figure 1. The group now consists of six autistic children, with a certified schoolteacher, in a structured classroom for three hours daily, five days per week. The children, originally with no academic skills, are now reading, writing, and doing arithmetic. Two of the children are achieving at second and third grade level which, in one case, is only one year below expected grade placement, based on chronological age.

These originally aloof and later aggressively embattled autistic children, with such poor prognoses for social adjustment, are now

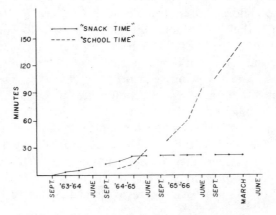

FIGURE 1.   Transition to, and subsequent development of, "school time" from "snack time."

interacting in cooperative, verbal, social situations for at least six hours daily in various table-and-chair situations such as school, playground activity, field trips, etc.

As predicted, there has also been a measurable increase in verbal behavior. Tape recordings were analyzed for two children over a two-year period and show a marked increase in verbal responses (Figure 2). While adaptive verbal behavior increased, the maladaptive vocal behavior such as screaming did not decrease. This suggests some success in teaching adaptive behavior but relative difficulty in decreasing existing maladaptive responses.

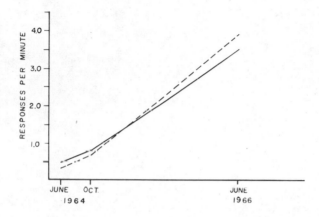

FIGURE 2.   Frequency of appropriate verbal responses of two autistic children over a two-year period.

The last illustration concerns a four-year-old, nonverbal autistic girl who never seemed to approach people. Except for crying, her most consistent behavior was a stereotyped wrist-rubbing followed by putting an entire fist in her mouth. While generally unresponsive to external stimuli, she did respond to the sound of a small music box. This music box was then used as a reinforcer in nine half-hour training sessions and (a) wrist-rubbing decreased to nearly zero and (b) she not only stopped moving away from the group worker, but actively moved toward and stayed with her. For the first time in her life this child had made positive moves toward another person and had maintained a noticeable reduction of wrist-rubbing.

This paper has briefly described some of the concepts and methods used in our program and has focused on the acquisition of adaptive behavior. Other techniques were also employed in attempts to decrease maladaptive behavior and included reciprocal inhibition, mild physical restraint, partial isolation, removal of positive reinforcers, and extinction trials. A larger monograph describing this program is in preparation.

~ 19 ~

Programmed Relaxation
and Reciprocal Inhibition
with Psychotic Children

Anthony M. Graziano & Jeffrey E. Kean

Systematic desensitization in the treatment of neuroses is based on the principle of reciprocal inhibition, which Wolpe (1958) describes as follows: "if a response incompatible with anxiety can be made to occur in the presence of anxiety-evoking stimuli it will weaken the bond between these stimuli and the anxiety responses."

Wolpe used Jacobson's (1938) muscular relaxation as the major response antagonistic to anxiety. For each patient a hierarchy of anxiety-producing stimuli is carefully determined through testing and interviews, and then relaxation training is provided. When able to relax deeply on instruction, the patient "pictures" the stimuli in the anxiety-arousal hierarchy beginning with the least arousing and progressing, over several sessions, to the most anxiety-provoking. Relaxation is prepotent over the first few items in the hierarchy and since the patient cannot be both relaxed and anxious simultaneously, anxiety as a response to these stimuli is progressively dampened.

Developed for treating neurotics, reciprocal inhibition is not con-

From the *Proceedings,* 75th Annual Convention, American Psychological Association, 1967, pp. 253–254.

This study was supported in part by a grant from the State of Connecticut Department of Mental Health, Division of Community Services.

sidered useful for psychotic conditions. Eysenck and Rachman (1965) asserted that such behavior therapy might alleviate "neurotic habit patterns" in some psychotics but for "many, perhaps most, psychotic patients, the procedures of behavior therapy cannot be applied." Cowden and Ford (1962), however, reported success with hospitalized adult schizophrenics in desensitization of phobic behavior in one and compulsive behavior in another.

Except for phobias or enuresis there has been little systematic investigation of reciprocal inhibition techniques with children. As Eysenck and Rachman (1965) stated:

> The success of reciprocal inhibition therapy depends on the appropriate choice and skillful manipulation of the inhibitory response. The inhibiting response which has been most commonly used in the treatment of adult phobics is relaxation. For obvious reasons, it is not possible to use relaxation with many children, especially young ones (p. 210).

It appears that reciprocal inhibition is most effective with adult neurotics, less so with nonpsychotic children, and of no use with psychotic children. However, our exploratory clinical work suggests that relaxation and desensitization may be potentially significant techniques with psychotic children.

An earlier paper (Graziano, 1967b) described "programmed psychotherapy" with a group of autistic children. The approach focuses on observed behavior rather than inferred dynamics and assumes that complex human behavior is best modified by specifying terminal behaviors, analyzing them into response constituents, and then eliciting and reinforcing those constituents in carefully planned sequences or "programs" of successive approximations. Planned in detail for each child these programs were applied in groups in order to maximize stimuli and rewards, increase imitative learning and vicarious reinforcement, and facilitate positive transfer to the "normal" world.

The group began in 1963 with four autistic children, three boys, ages five, six, and nine, and a girl, six, all with lifelong patterns of extreme aloneness and preservation of sameness. They had no social interaction; three were head bangers with frequent long, destructive tantrums. None used toys appropriately, showed academic skills, or had useful communicative speech. At home all had feeding problems and were totally aloof or uncontrollably wild. According to criteria described by Rimland (1964), these children had very poor prognoses for improvement.

A major therapeutic task, acquiring adaptive social behavior, was approached through sequences of reinforced successive approximations in structured social groups. In less than 2 years they acquired a large repertoire of adaptive behaviors including speech and sustained cooperative interaction.

A second major task, however, reduction of overlearned maladaptive behavior such as aggressive outbursts, was not so readily achieved. In contrast to Eysenck and Rachman (1965), we found the acquisition of adaptive behavior more readily occurring than the decrement of maladaptive behavior. Our use of mild physical restraint, extinction, and repetition of "rules" appeared effective in reducing the duration and intensity of outbursts, but their *frequency* remained high.

Although they had learned socially adaptive behavior and their characteristic wild outbursts were shorter and less intense, a wide range of minor stimuli still elicited sudden high excitement leading to violent outbursts, increased stimulation, and continued interference with acquisition of adaptive behavior. Tense, even when quiet, with rigid, spastic-like movements, they appeared always ready to react violently. Seeking to reduce the frequency of excitement, we attempted reciprocal inhibition using muscular relaxation as the response antagonistic to generalized excitement. As in Wolpe's approach this required both training in relaxation and systematic desensitization.

The autistic children apparently had no behavioral referent for the concept "relax"! Consequently the training sessions were highly structured, brief, and presented on a concrete behavioral level with much practice and reinforcement. Verbal reinforcers such as the phrases "good work" and "good job," laboriously taught earlier in the program, were now used as the major reinforcers for the appropriate behaviors.

For 3 days preceding training the children were told about "relax time," and the first session was introduced with, "O.K., now it's relax time." With the lights out and the children lying on a mat as instructed, the therapist soothingly told them to close their eyes and pretend they were lying in bed where "it is nice and comfortable," to breathe easily and be calm, settled, and relaxed. After two minutes of quiet, attentive cooperation by the four children, one child walked away, the therapist ended relax time, and the usual program continued.

On succeeding days, with the children lying, sitting, or standing, the therapist paired gentle manipulation of arms, legs, and necks with verbal instructions to relax. Any response approximating relaxed behavior was given immediate verbal reinforcement and eventually the children relaxed on verbal instruction alone.

Daily relaxation training became a regular part of the program from November 1965 to June 1966, with 105 sessions totalling nearly 15 hours, with a mean of 7.1 min.

The criteria of relaxation were: five consecutive sessions in which the child was cooperative, quiet, and visibly "loosening" on instruction. Three of the children reached these criteria in 25, 32, and 43 sessions respectively. The fourth child attended only 25 of the first 93 sessions and then reached criteria on Session 94. Thus, three children after the Session 43 and all four after Session 93 were successfully relaxing. As the sessions lengthened from a mean of 4.4 min. for the first ten to 12.7 min. for the last 10 sessions, cooperation, involvement, and enjoyment visibly increased. The children were now easily reporting their bodily states of relaxation or tension. During 105 training sessions only three excitement responses occurred and it appeared that relaxation training was, in fact, antagonistic to excitement and was successfully damping it.

The most interesting finding was that, in addition to the decrease of excitement response during relaxation training, there was an unpredicted and marked decrement of the generalized excitement response throughout the whole day. When they had reached relaxation criteria the children were emitting so few high excitement responses that systematic desensitization was not necessary. Apparently there had been an "unsystematic" or spontaneous desensitization, and the generalized high excitement response had effectively been inhibited. Innumerable observations of the children spontaneously practicing, and verbalizing relaxation procedures throughout the program and at home further suggest that there was considerable generalization of the relaxation training.

By September 1966, there were three relaxation sessions daily, to train new children and maintain the relaxation response for those already trained. As seen in Figure 1, the generalized high excitement response with its subsequent aggressive episodes virtually disappeared soon after all children had reached relaxation criteria.

The autistic children learned to perform muscular relaxation in a small group situation and gave behavioral indications that the activities were reinforcing for them. As planned, relaxation came under the control of many stimuli including verbal instructions.

The most significant hypothesis generated by this exploratory project with psychotic children is: carefully structured training in physical relaxation without formal desensitization sequences, significantly reduces the generalized response of high excitement, and the resulting relaxation generalizes beyond the training situation. With psychotic children relaxation training alone appears to bring about a major, constructive modification of behavior. It may be that systematic desensitization is necessary to modify specific patterns such as phobias, but the generalized excitement response of psychotic and other severely

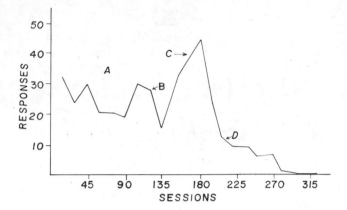

FIGURE 1. Decrement of high excitement responses after initiation of relaxation training. (A) baseline measures of excitement responses; (B) initiation of training in relaxation; (C) three children reach criteria (43 days); (D) fourth child reaches criteria (94 days).

disturbed children might be effectively modified simply by general training in relaxation.

If future research under better controlled conditions supports this hypothesis, then programmed relaxation without desensitization training might be a significant therapeutic technique with hyperactive children. Furthermore, relaxation training is an uncomplicated, parsimonious technique, applicable in groups, and easily taught to and used by persons other than highly trained psychotherapists.

~ 20 ~

Operant Conditioning
of Schizophrenic Children

Philip Ney

Since the early descriptions by Kanner (1949), Bender (1947) and Mahler (1952), childhood schizophrenia has become an increasingly fascinating area of investigation.... Characteristically, schizophrenic children are difficult to teach. This fact is borne out by the frequent parental reports of the child's negativism and by Anthony (1958) who found them very hard to condition. Goldfarb (1965), though not a behavior therapist, states, "the schizophrenic child needs to experience people who are different from himself, and who will respond to each of his actions by predictable approval and disapproval, by reward and punishment." Other authors see the schizophrenic child's behavior as explainable through learning theory. Thus operant conditioning would seem a logical therapeutic tool...(and) there is...need for a controlled study to determine how successful operant conditioning really is.

~

EXPERIMENTAL DESIGN

We are starting with the null hypothesis that there is no difference between the results of treatment with operant conditioning and play therapy. The sample consists of twenty of the twenty-five schizophrenic

From *Canadian Psychiatric Association Journal*, 12 (1967), 9–13.

boys housed in a newly established ward of The Woodlands School. Most of these were found within the school and were failures of previous therapies. They were diagnosed in accordance with the English Working Parties' nine points (Creak, 1961). Though their illness varied in severity, they all had at least six of the nine points. All had very poor emotional relationships and apparent retardation. Because some of the parents had long ago lost interest in their institutionalized children and were not available to give a history, we had to substitute with practical tests of the child's behavior. For example, one method used to determine whether the child had "illogical anxiety" was to lift him onto a high, narrow platform. Many, rather than being anxious, appeared to enjoy their precarious stance. Preoccupation with a particular object was tested by seeing if in five trials the child would go to the bottom of a box of toys for his string. We hope to report these tests and findings at a later date.

The children in the sample were matched for sex (they were all males), age, signs of organicity, duration of previous hospital stay, amount of speech, and Vineland score. The matching is fairly good because we had a large population of schizophrenics within the hospital community from which to draw. They were randomly assigned to either operant conditioning or play therapy treatment groups.

The children were treated in especially rebuilt rooms, providing what was hoped were optimum conditions for learning. Each was treated forty-five minutes, five days a week by a nurse's aide and a nurse as the co-worker. The nurse's aide was alone with the child in the treatment room while the co-worker assisted her from behind a two-way mirror of an observation room between the two treatment rooms.

Differences in therapist were controlled by having the same two nurses treat a pair of children, one child by each method. The treatment rooms were identical. In each treatment room there were two mirrors to facilitate the child's gaining self-awareness (Hughes, et al., 1965). The amount of individual attention was the same for both children. The nurses were instructed to spend equal time with each of their two children while in the day room. Prior to the beginning of the experiment there was a two-month period of evaluating the patients and of instructing the staff.

The operant conditioning took place in four basic areas of behavior called stages. These were self-awareness, emotional relationships, imitation of adult behavior, and communication. Each of these stages had twenty-five phases beginning with very simple behavior such as touching a soft toy and gradually shaping this response to a show of affection toward the nurse. Self-awareness was shaped from the simple response of the child glancing at a mirror to his naming body parts and identifying himself in a picture. Adult imitation began with copying the therapist's arrangement of blocks and ends with expressive body movements. Any spontaneous nonverbal expression, feeling and later any sound, was shaped into words and finally a dialogue with the therapist. The basic difference between this and other techniques is that instead of conditioning specific bits of behavior, we are conditioning basic attitudes. Instead of words we condition the child to understand it is safe to communicate. This could be called "conditioned insight." The result was that a number of children began talking before we conditioned for words.

The positive reinforcement was a small candy delivered by a dispensing machine strapped to the child and activated by the co-worker. The machine still had some bugs. Instead of using it the therapist gave the candy, taking her cue from the observer. At the time she said, "That's a good boy." We hope this social reinforcement will facilitate generalization into everyday situations. This method gives fairly quick reinforcement and prevents the common problem of reinforcing any intervening behavior after the correct response. The negative reinforcement would have been the shunting of the candy, which was offered in a small window of the dispenser, into a sealed compartment. Instead the therapist said, "No, Johnny" and turned her back on him for 30 seconds. The number of correct responses was calculated and plotted on a graph. The desired behavior was most quickly established by a fixed ratio of one hundred per cent rewards (Das, et al., 1965).

Two stages were conditioned together, self-awareness and emotional relationships, then imitation of adult behavior and communication. This allowed the child to choose between two responses. Our previous observation was that having a choice decreases the child's negativism which occurred usually as soon as he perceived we were trying to teach him a specific response. Much atavistic behavior occurred with the moves to new phases, so that smooth conditioning depended on the very gradual shading of contingencies.

The essence of our play therapy is similar to that described by King (1964). It is in understanding the child's free play with toys in sand as an expression of his thoughts and as symbolic of his conflicts. When the conflict of a predominant or recurrent segment of play is understood, it is interpreted, and the child is reassured as to what is permissable behavior. Regression is allowed, but not encouraged. The nurses are instructed to interact as real people and not to just reflect the child.

Observations were made before, midway through a course of fifty sessions, following termination of treatment and on follow-up. Since speech is so fundamental in treatment — it is also a fundamental prognostic sign (Eisenberg, 1957) — it is the chief variable measured. Also attempts are made to note changes in symptomatology, particularly emotional relationships. Vineland and other psychological scores are compared. The assessing psychologists are blind as to which child is in which group.

><

RESULTS

The preliminary results tend to show operant conditioning as the more effective treatment. Although there was change in both groups, the increase in the amount of speech for the children in the operant conditioning appeared greater than that of the play therapy group. There is a great deal of intragroup variability, with some children conditioning much faster. This phenomena is not related to age, intelligence, or severity of the illness, but probably to the skill of the therapist. The next step is a period of two months without specific therapy. The sample will be reassessed and crossed over. A second fifty therapy sessions is planned.

><

DISCUSSION

The results of this experiment have left us with more questions than answers. The superiority of operant conditioning may be due to a host of factors, such as the fact that no verbal instruction is required, the nurses are being taught to respond predictably to the child as recommended by Goldfarb, or to other uncontrolled factors, such as bias of the nurses in their preference for one kind of treatment, and operant conditioning technique being easier to learn. Unanswered is the question of whether it is possible to condition two responses in the same session. So far it seems feasible and, in providing the child with a choice, it does help overcome his negativism. One also wonders if it is possible to initiate spontaneous, genuine affect by conditioning a show of affect. It does appear that the conditioned show of feeling by the child awakens a genuine response in the nurse which in turn evokes a genuine feeling of attachment in the child.

There seems no doubt that schizophrenic children are difficult to condition. This is more likely due to their psychological negativism or neurological dysfunction than to their apparent lack of intelligence. Finally the whole question of crucial stages in development comes up. These children were all well behind, not learning to talk at the critical age, but some have made remarkable progress.

➤

SUMMARY

Though there is little agreement concerning the diagnosis, incidence, or etiology of childhood schizophrenia, until recently most authors agree there is no effective treatment. Operant conditioning is reported to succeed where other therapies have failed. Twenty children diagnosed according to Creak's criteria in two groups matched for age, sex, duration of stay, Vineland score, and amount of speech were treated by either interpretive play therapy or operant conditioning. Emotional relatedness and self-identity, then imitation of behavior and speech were conditioned with the positive reinforcements of candy. Tested before, during and after fifty 45-minute sessions, those in the operant-conditioning group had gained more speech and improved more on Vineland score. The relative efficacy of operant conditioning may be related to the greater ease with which the staff learned this technique and the need of these children for predictable routines. The experiment will continue with a crossover complex.

IV

MODIFICATION
OF ANTISOCIAL BEHAVIOR

TRADITIONALLY THE INTERVENTION IN JUVENILE ANTISOCIAL behavior has largely been based on punishment, meted by various social agents. In the past, punishment has involved inflicting physical pain through flogging, branding, and mutilation (Burchard, 1967), and it is still basic to our current practices of withdrawing most sources of personal reinforcement through incarceration of the individual in special agencies such as jails and juvenile correction centers. In contemporary society there still seems to exist strong social approval for punitive action in response to juvenile antisocial behavior.

In some programs, however, more humanitarian treatment approaches, based largely on psychoanalytic theory, have been applied. According to Burchard (1967) these programs emphasize the alleviation of internal disturbance through the establishment of "close, accepting interpersonal relationships enabling the individual to 'work through' his problems." In order to establish this type of relationship, a warm, permissive, nonthreatening, and nonpunitive situation was required. As a result the psychoanalytically oriented programs fostered a highly permissive, indiscriminately reinforcing climate in which even the negative behavior was allowed expression and was undoubtedly, although unintentionally, reinforced. Although there have been vast improvements in a humanitarian and moral sense, the permissive, psychoanalytic programs have not been clearly validated as effective in altering antisocial behavior.

With the re-emergence in the past decade of behavioral approaches to children, the effectiveness of a permissive, indiscriminantly reinforcing climate, and dependence upon development of a "relationship," have been questioned. Instead, the behaviorally oriented worker focuses directly on the task of modifying antisocial behavior, using a variety of behavioral methods. Although the behavior therapist may utilize punishment in differential reinforcement techniques, he relies primarily on the use of positive reinforcement. One of the major differences, in fact, between the two approaches in their actual implementation is the degree of emphasis placed on adaptive behavior. The psychodynamic view tends to emphasize the inferred pathology and indiscriminantly reinforces all behavior, while the behavioral approach clearly emphasizes adaptive behavior and differentially reinforces it. There is thus a far less morbid and vastly more positive emphasis than in the psychodynamic programs.

We seem to have swung back to a middle position regarding the use of punishment—i.e., from earlier programs which were nearly completely punitive, with indiscriminate punishment of all behavior, to the more humane psychodynamic programs which offered permissiveness and the indiscriminate reinforcement of all behavior. Both are extreme approaches which fail to discriminate between adaptive and maladaptive behavior. In contrast, the behavioral focus not only emphasizes the positive development of adaptive behavior but also carefully discriminates between adaptive and maladaptive behavior and utilizes differential reinforcement procedures.

The papers in this section all describe behavioral approaches to antisocial juvenile behavior. In the first selection Burchard discusses his residential training program for mildly retarded adolescent boys with antisocial behavior. Operant conditioning principles are used to differentially reinforce prosocial behavior and weaken antisocial behavior. The author concludes that specific antisocial behavior can be modified in this intensive training behavioral program. Further work will be needed, as Burchard indicates, to generalize such behavioral changes to the child's eventual natural community outside the institution.

Robert Schwitzgebel used individual interviews to differentially treat two matched groups of delinquent boys on four classes of behavior: hostile statements, positive statements about other persons, prompt arrival at work, and socially desirable behavior. Positive and negative social reinforcement, such as attention and show of interest, small cash bonuses and gifts of food, was given on variable schedules. Schwitzgebel found that positive social reinforcement for prompt arrival time, positive statements about other persons, and two of the measures of socially desirable behavior were associated with significant improvement in those behaviors. After discussing some of the design weaknesses, the author indicates that interviews using operant conditioning approaches successfully developed "dependable and prompt attendance" and other social behaviors in these characteristically impulsive juvenile delinquents. Schwitzgebel concludes that operant conditioning approaches are demonstrably effective with delinquents, but that a tradition-bound clinical profession has thus far failed systematically to use the knowledge in the majority of treatment programs.

Fineman's report (Chapter 23) describes his use of an immediate-reward point system for modifying antisocial behavior in a short-term detention center. Although this study presents no quantitative assessment, it does suggest the feasibility of the merit point system for these children, and the approach merits testing in similar institutions. A repetition is needed of Fineman's work on a larger scale and with quantitative evaluation of results.

Wetzel describes his use of behavioral approaches to eliminate the compulsive stealing of a mildly disturbed ten-year-old boy. He used nonprofessional staff in arranging the reinforcing contingencies for acceptable, nonstealing behavior. It is interesting to note that the "therapist," the person who controlled and administered reinforcement, was one of the institution's cooks, selected because she was one of the few persons to whom this boy had made positive approaches. Wetzel reports a cessation of stealing which had been of long duration and resistant to attempts to change it, and attributes the behavioral change to the negative reinforcement administered by the experimenter. Dinsmoor, accepting Wetzel's results, i.e., markedly improved behavior, questions Wetzel's explanation of it. Dinsmoor's behavioral analysis suggests that several factors other than those specified by Wetzel might have been operating and accounted for the measured behavior change.

These two chapters present interesting analyses of complex maladaptive behavior without reference to traditional psychodynamic interpretations to which stealing, as a "symptom," is usually subjected.

Welsh describes his attempts to control the obviously dangerous behavior of setting fires. As the author points out, the child's family cannot easily wait while a therapist devotes weeks or perhaps months to develop "rapport," in order eventually to remove the fire-setting "symptom." It is important to modify this behavior quickly and then, with danger less imminently at hand, approach the modification of the child's other maladaptive behaviors. Welsh describes two cases in which he has utilized a therapeutic strategy based on the idea of stimulus satiation, and his apparent success suggests that stimulus satiation may be translated into potentially useful therapeutic techniques, and warrants further investigation under better controlled research conditions.

Systematic Socialization:
A Programmed Environment
for the Habilitation
of Antisocial Retardates

John D. Burchard

With respect to the treatment of the individual who repeatedly displays antisocial behavior, several programs claim to have achieved behavioral change by using the dynamics of the interpersonal relationship and group interaction occurring within the institutional setting (Aichorn, 1935; Bettelheim, 1950; McCorkle, 1958; Polsky, 1962; Redl and Wineman, 1952). Although these programs differ they all have some characteristics in common. In the first place each is derived from, or closely associated with, psychoanalytic theory. The emphasis clearly is placed on psychic or psychodynamic processes rather than overt behavior. Second, it is felt that internal disturbances can be modified through the establishment of close, accepting interpersonal relationships enabling the individual to "work through" his problems. Thus, the programs involve considerable permissiveness, acceptance and reward

From *The Psychological Record*, 17 (1967), 461–476.

This project is supported by a Mental Health Project Grant (1 R20 MH02270–01) from the Department of Health, Education, and Welfare, and by Murdoch Center, a state institution for the mentally retarded in North Carolina.

(reinforcement). Individuals are encouraged to express themselves freely and openly and within very broad limits; punishment and censure are avoided. It is hypothesized that since internal conflict developed out of previous punitive interpersonal relationships, any response to antisocial behavior which involved punishment would make the individual more defensive (suspicious, hostile) and less capable of developing adaptive interpersonal relationships. Thus, it is assumed that antisocial behavior must occur with impunity.

These treatment programs which rely heavily on the use of reinforcement and permissiveness are in sharp contrast to "programs" they replaced. With respect to punishment the pendulum has swung to the opposite side. In the past most efforts to modify or eliminate antisocial behavior involved punishment. Whether for purposes of revenge, deterrence, or social protection, the individual was either punished by inflicting physical pain (flogging, mutilation, branding, etc.) or by being placed in an institutional environment where most sources of gratification and reward were removed. While punishment may be justified logically on the grounds of seeking revenge, there is a dearth of empirical evidence to support the claim that punishment serves the purpose of deterrence. Recent studies show that observation of a model receiving punishment for socially unacceptable behavior has a deterrent effect on the subsequent behavior of college and nursery school students in a similar situation (Bandura, Ross, and Ross, 1963; Lefcourt, Barnes, Parke, and Schwartz, 1966; Walters, Leat, and Mezei, 1963). Such studies do not, however, provide objective evidence that punitive treatment of delinquents and criminals deters delinquent or criminal behavior in others.

Preventive detention or imprisonment does offer social protection against the life prisoner who remains in prison. The majority of individuals, however, sent to correctional institutions and prisons are later returned to society to continue their depredations. Furthermore, many individuals who receive punishment are apt to be more hostile and bitter after serving sentences and are returned to society more criminally competent and dangerous than prior to their commitment. Thus, some of the new treatment programs have attempted to eliminate punishment and establish permissive, accepting institutional environments.

It generally is agreed that an institutional setting which creates a punitive atmosphere or one in which all but undesirable behavior is ignored (custodial prison or correctional institution) generates hostility to, and lack of cooperation with, rehabilitative goals. That is not to say, however, that all forms of punishment are ineffective or fail to render the results for which they were intended. Recent evidence indicates that while punishment can eliminate certain behaviors, consistency, intensity, timing, and duration are important (Azrin and Holz, 1966; Church, 1963; Solomon, 1964).

In considering whether or not to use punishment or reinforcement the main consideration should be the effect each has on the behavior being modified. Programs which indiscriminately reinforce or punish behavior do little to prepare the individual to meet the exigencies of the social environment and its contingencies outside the institution. Case histories of many delinquents suggest that the previous conditioning history of antisocial behavior is characterized by indiscriminate punishment (rejection, disapproval, whipping, etc.) and indiscriminate reinforcement (love, affection, attention). While permissive treatment programs may result in a positive reinforcement contingency (relationship) between the resident and the therapist it does not necessarily follow that the resident learns from this relationship how to cope more effectively with the contingencies that will occur in the noninstitutional environment (Eysenck, 1965).

By conceptualizing antisocial behavior as behavior acquired, maintained, and modified by the same principles as other learned behavior, it is conceivable that an individual can learn constructive, socially acceptable behavior by being placed in an environment where the behavioral consequences are programmed according to principles of operant conditioning. Instead of administering an excess of reinforcement or punishment on an indiscriminate, noncontingent basis, behavior would be punished or reinforced systematically on a response contingent basis. This had been the objective of the Intensive Training Program at Murdoch Center.

The Intensive Training Program is an experimental residential program in behavior modification for mildly retarded, delinquent adolescents. Utilizing techniques based on principles of reinforcement, punishment, and programmed instruction a standardized program involving mostly nonprofessional staff has been developed to teach delinquent retardates practical skills (personal, social, recreational, educational, and vocational) which are essential for an adequate community adjustment and for reducing or eliminating antisocial behavior.

Residents and Staff. Residents are selected for the ITU on the basis of age (10–20), IQ (above 50) and the amount of antisocial behavior displayed in the institution. Twelve residents presently are in the ITU. Table 1 lists age, years at Murdoch Center, months in the ITU, and a brief description of characteristic antisocial behaviors which occurred prior to their transfer into the ITU.

TABLE 1.

Characteristic Forms Antisocial Behavior Displayed at Murdoch Center During Year Prior to Transfer to ITU

Resident	Age	Years at Murdoch Center	Months in ITU	Approximate Academic Level	Characteristic Forms Antisocial Behavior Displayed at Murdoch Center During Year Prior to Transfer to ITU
1	18	6	16	5th grade	Property damage in excess of $1,000, AWOL 11 times, fights, excessive profanity, expelled from school and job assignment
2	16	2	16	Pre 1st grade	Stealing from staff cars and residents' lockers, AWOL 3 times, arson with minor property damage, expelled from school and job assignment
3	13	5	15	1st grade	Arson with minor property damage, breaking and entering, theft from staff and peers, expelled from school
4	17	3	16	Pre 1st grade	Arson with minor property damage, theft from staff and peers, AWOL one time, expelled from job assignment
5	16	4	16	Pre 1st grade	Theft of straight razors, radio, tractor, property damage, choking resident with rope, fights, breaking and entering, expelled from job assignment
6	12	1¼	13	Pre 1st grade	Constantly disobeying staff, no major infractions, expelled from school
7	15	5	11	Pre 1st grade	Constantly disobeying staff, no major infractions, expelled from school
8	19	4	9	Pre 1st grade	Theft of tent and hatchet, knives, bicycle, cigarettes, breaking and entering, arson causing property damage in excess of $1,000. AWOL 5 times, expelled from job assignment
9	16	¼	3	5th grade	Knocking down older resident causing broken leg,* constantly disobeying staff
10	13	1	4	Pre 1st grade	Theft from staff, masturbating dog, attempt to set residents' clothes afire, hitting CP with wet towel, refused to attend school
11	15	¼	1	3rd grade	AWOL three times, accomplice in theft of two cars†
12	17	7	1	2nd grade	Breaking and entering, theft from staff, property damage, AWOL four times, frequently truant from school, expelled from job assignment

All the residents have obtained intelligence quotients within the mildly retarded range (50–70) with the exception of one (9) whose IQ was within the borderline range. One resident (4) was attending school on a regular basis. The residents who were assigned institutional jobs (1, 2, 3, 4, 5, 7, 8, 11, 12) were either expelled for displaying antisocial behavior or worked on an irregular basis due to behavior problems displayed elsewhere.

    * While in state mental hospital.

    † While living in community.

The staff consists of nine unit instructors, workshop instructor, classroom instructor, research assistant (all classified as attendants), project director, teacher, and social worker. University students participate in the program periodically. There are two unit instructors on duty each day from 6:30 A.M. until 11:00 P.M., and one on duty at night. The remaining staff works on weekdays between 8:00 A.M. and 5:00 P.M.

A high school education is required for the position of instructor. Some have further education, but none has completed a full year of college. Instructor training consisted of one week of class lecture and discussion, and one week of demonstration and participation in reinforcement techniques. Informal, on-the-job training involving individual discussion and bi-weekly meetings of the staff is a continuing process.

Reinforcement Procedures. Reinforcement procedures are based on operant conditioning principles (Ferster and Skinner, 1957; Michael and Meyerson, 1966; Skinner, 1953) used to develop voluntary behaviors of humans in a variety of institutional settings (Atthowe and Krasner, in press; Ayllon and Azrin, 1964, 1965; Birnbrauer, Wolf, Kidder, and Tague, 1965; Burchard and Tyler, 1965; Cohen, Filipczak and Bis, in press; Girardeau and Spradlin, 1964). The steps included defining the behaviors to be reinforced, selecting an effective reinforcing stimulus, and programming the reinforcement contingencies.

There are two independent criteria for selecting behavior to be reinforced. One involves selecting behaviors which produce a physically identifiable change in the environment that can be reliably observed and reinforced. To facilitate observation and reinforcement of these behaviors the environment is arranged so that these responses can occur only during a specified time interval and within a designated area (Ayllon and Azrin, 1965). Examples of such behaviors are the time a resident spends sitting in his seat during the school or workshop periods. The purpose of this criterion is to permit an analysis of the effects of a given reinforcer.

Due to the complexity of the situation and the limitations on the staff it is impossible to record and reinforce the occurrence of many behaviors which are necessary as part of the habilitation of the resident. Therefore, the second criterion is to select behaviors which provide the resident with a behavioral repertoire which will produce reinforcement in a community environment. Behaviors which are selected are maintaining a job, staying in school, budgeting money, buying and caring for clothes, buying food and meals, cooperating with peers and adults, and so on. For these behaviors an analysis of specific effects of reinforcing stimuli was not performed.

Previous studies have demonstrated that verbal reinforcement (praise, approval, etc.) is not an effective reinforcer for individuals frequently displaying antisocial behavior (Cleckley, 1955; Johns and Quay, 1962; Quay and Hunt, 1965). Therefore, immediate reinforcing stimuli are nonverbal conditioned reinforcers consisting of aluminum tokens. Tokens are delivered promptly by staff members upon the occasion of selected responses and can be exchanged for various items and privileges listed in Table 2.

To minimize stealing, pressuring, and the development of undesirable reinforcement contingencies between residents, each resident is assigned a number, and only those tokens stamped with his number can be

TABLE 2.

Reinforcement Available for Tokens*	Tokens†
Meals	5
Commissary	
Food items: candy, cake, coffee, crackers, gum, peanuts, pies, potato chips, and soda pop	5–10
Smoking articles: cigarettes, cigars, flints, lighters and lighter fluid, matches, pipes, and pipe tobacco	2–100
Grooming and hygienic articles: combs, deodorant, hair cream, shampoo, shaving cream, shoe shine equipment, soap, talcum powder, tooth brushes and toothpaste	3–30
Other commissary items: books, fishing equipment, key chains, kites, models, locks, string, and writing accessories	2–100
Clothing Articles: shoes, pants, and shirts	25–1000
Recreation activities: ball games, riding bicycles and go-carts, fishing, hiking, recreation with non-Intensive Training Unit residents (unsupervised by ITU staff), movies, skating, swimming, and trampoline‡	10–190
Miscellaneous: bus tickets for trips to town and visits home	90–1500

* In most instances the value of a token is equivalent to the value of a penny. With the exception of meals, and some recreational activities the number of tokens required for items or activities is roughly equivalent to its monetary value.

† Upon making each purchase a resident is required to fill out a purchase order with his name, the date, the day, the time, the items and the appropriate cost. If the purchase order is filled out correctly one token is subtracted from the cost of each item.

‡ Residents may exchange tokens for money and make any "reasonable" purchases while they are in town.

exchanged for reinforcement. Most reinforcing items and privileges are available for all residents in the institution on an infrequent, non-contingent basis. Generally the reinforcement schedule is as nearly continuous as possible.

Punishment Procedures. Punishment procedures are based on the operant conditioning principles of punishment developed from previous research (Azrin and Holz, 1966). The objective was to develop a punishing stimulus which could be administered immediately following the response, and which was of short duration but of sufficient intensity to decrease the frequency of response. This is in contrast to some institutional situations in which responses are not punished until they become extreme, and then the punishment is of long duration (restriction or seclusion) and involves much litigation and reconciliation (attention) on the part of staff.

Steps in developing punishment procedures were similar to those involved in the development of reinforcement procedures and consisted of defining behaviors to be punished, selecting effective punishing stimuli, and programming punishment contingencies. Behaviors selected for punishment are those which usually meet punishment in the community; these include fighting, lying, stealing, cheating, physical and verbal assault, temper tantrums, and property damage.

Unlike objective behaviors selected for reinforcement, specific behaviors to be punished are not defined in terms of specific, identifiable change in the physical environment that occurs within a specifically designated time or place. (The behaviors which have been selected for punishment are under the control of a wide variety of stimuli, most of which would not be present at any arbitrarily designated time or place. However, it would be possible to program the environment so that some of those stimuli were present and then analyze the effects of the punishing stimulus as specific identifiable responses occurred. This is presently being done under laboratory control.) It is impossible to observe the occurrence of all punishable behavior and if all such behavior were observed, it would not be punished with perfect consistency. It was felt, however, that the consistency was sufficient to proceed with an analysis of the punishing stimuli that were utilized.

The punishing stimuli consist of two verbal responses, "time out" and "seclusion," which signify the loss of positive reinforcers (tokens) and removal from the immediate environment — a combination of response cost (Weiner, 1962) and time out from positive reinforcement (Wolf, Risley, and Mees, 1964). The difference between time out and seclusion is primarily one of intensity with seclusion involving a greater loss of tokens and a more extreme and prolonged removal from the environment.

Time out is contingent upon most offenses which cannot be ignored and which do not involve violence. Whenever a staff member says "time out" to a resident, he is charged four tokens and is required to sit in the time out area, a row of chairs at one side of the dayroom. Minor disruptive behavior while in time out is ignored; however, the resident remains in time out until his behavior is appropriate for three to five minutes.

Seclusion is contingent upon fights, physical assault, significant property damage, disruptive behavior in time out which cannot be ignored, or refusal to go to the time out area. Whenever a staff member says "seclusion" the resident is charged 15 tokens and taken out of the unit to a nearby seclusion room. This is an empty room approximately 8' × 16' with one outside window. The window is covered by a heavy metal screen with the shade behind the screen drawn. The resident remains in seclusion until he is quiet for approximately 30 minutes. If the resident goes to seclusion in an orderly fashion and stays there the minimum period of time he is reinforced with five tokens upon his return to the unit.

The staff is instructed to administer the punishing stimuli in a matter-of-fact manner, and all litigation is ignored until after the termination of the time out or seclusion period to minimize any uncontrolled reinforcement contingencies that might exist (i.e., attention). The punishing stimuli are administered immediately after each punishable response occurs and are programmed on a continuous basis as much as possible.

In order to effect the response cost which is charged at the presentation of the punishing stimuli, the Behavior Credit System was devised. A behavior credit (BC) sheet is posted on a bulletin board in the unit for each resident, similar to those shown in Table 3. The columns represent days of the week and the rows represent number of BCs. In order to earn a BC or to maintain the maximum number of BCs (seven), a resident has to pay the response cost he has been charged during the day. Each resident has until the end of the day to pay the debt he has accumulated during that day. If he does not do so he loses one BC.

In order to create incentive to earn BCs and thus to pay the response cost associated with his punishment, prices and privileges are partially determined by the number of BCs a resident has. If a resident has seven BCs (the maximum number), all reinforcers cost their regular price (see Table 1), the resident has free access to the yard area outside

TABLE 3.   Sample behavior credit sheets for two consecutive weeks

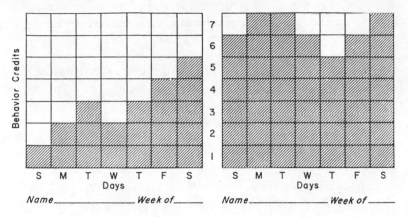

Name_____ Week of_____   Name_____ Week of_____

the unit, and he can buy the following privileges: (a) a trip to town (90 tokens), and (b) one hour recreation time with non-ITU residents (girls). Each hour costs 15 tokens; 10 are returned to the resident upon his prompt return to the unit at the end of the hour.

Residents with 3, 4, 5, or 6 BCs are required to pay an additional 5 tokens for every item they purchase (e.g., each meal costs 10 tokens). Residents with 0, 1, 2 BCs are required to pay an additional 10 tokens for each item (e.g., each meal costs 15 tokens). Residents with less than 7 BCs are not eligible for "outside" privileges.

✕

EXPERIMENT I

The purpose of the first experiment was to analyze the effect of the reinforcing stimulus (the token) on the frequency of two specific responses. Although all residents express a desire to have tokens which they readily exchange for a variety of items and privileges, this does not demonstrate that administration of the token, contingent on a given response, actually increases the frequency of that response.

Response

The two responses selected for this experiment consisted of sitting at a desk during workshop and during school. The reasons for selecting these particular responses were: (1) The responses could be recorded reliably by a relatively untrained person who merely started a clock when a resident was in his chair, and stopped it when he was not. (2) The responses could not take place without the observer being present. Both school and workshop sessions were two hours each weekday, with school taking place in the morning (9–11 A.M.) and workshop in the afternoon (2:45–4:45 P.M.). (3) The environment could be arranged so that the response was a free operant. Within each two-hour time interval the response was free to occur for any duration. Attendance in both school and workshop was voluntary. However, the only way a resident could earn tokens during that time was by going to school (workshop). (4) The responses were similar to behavior which occurred outside the Intensive Training Unit with relatively low frequency. As noted above only one resident was attending school on a regular basis and none of the residents had worked satisfactorily or regularly on a job assignment.

Procedure

The design of the experiment was based on an A-B-A type of analysis with reinforcement contingent on the response during the first phase, non-contingent during the second phase, and then contingent again during the third phase. Each phase lasted five consecutive days. The experiment was conducted on two separate occasions, first for school behavior and later for workshop behavior.

The schedule of reinforcement for phases one and three was twofold in both the workshop and the school. One schedule was based on the amount of time the resident spent sitting in his assigned seat. He received one token for every 15 minutes accumulated on his clock. Because the school and workshop were in session for two hours each day, the maximum daily tokens a resident could earn for each session was eight.

The second schedule was based on specific tasks which the resident could perform while he was in the school or workshop, such as completing a page of arithmetic problems or assembling a certain number of objects. Although the type of school task varied from day to day, the type of tasks performed in the workshop remained constant each day. The number of tokens a resident earned on this schedule varied between 0 and 50.

On each day in Phase 2 each resident received the average number of tokens he had received each day during the five days of the first phase. On the first day of Phase 2 all the residents were told the following: "From now on you will receive your school (workshop) tokens five minutes before you go to school (workshop). You will receive about the same number you have been earning in the past. We would like you to keep going to school (workshop) but you will not receive any tokens while you are there. Here is the number of tokens each of you will receive." (The amounts were read and the list was posted on the bulletin board.)

Phase 3 was similar to Phase 1 with the administration of tokens contingent upon the time each resident spent in school (workshop) and the number of tasks he completed while he was there. (Because of home visits and transfers into the program after the experiment was underway, those residents who contributed to the school data [1, 2, 3, 4, 7, 8, 9, 10, 11] were not the same as those who contributed to the workshop data [1, 3, 4, 7, 9, 10, 11, 12].)

Results and Discussion

The lower graphs in Figures 1 and 2 show that when reinforcement was noncontingent (Phase 2) decline in school and workshop performance was immediate and near zero throughout the five-day period. The reinstatement of contingent reinforcement in Phase 3 resulted in an immediate increase in school and workshop performance to a level similar to that in Phase 1. The upper graphs show that reinforcement was relatively constant across all three phases.

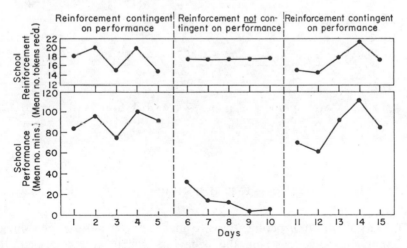

FIGURE 1. Mean number of minutes of school performance by nine residents.

The absence of overlap between the contingent phases (1 and 3) and noncontingent phases (2) demonstrates that the token had a reinforcing effect which was greater than any other reinforcement that occurred in either the school or the workshop. The generality of the reinforcing effect of the token is further demonstrated by the fact that individual graphs are very similar to the graphs for the entire group. For each resident there was a marked decline in school and workshop performance in Phase 2, followed by an increase in performance during Phase 3 that is similar to the level obtained in Phase 1.

With respect to reactions of residents during the experiment, the instructions preceding Phase 2 seemed to coincide with their definition of happiness. During the last two days of Phase 2, however, several residents asked if they could go back to earning their tokens in school (workshop) because they thought they could earn more tokens that way.

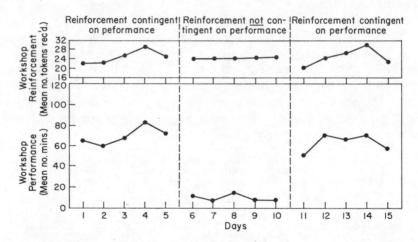

FIGURE 2.   Mean number of minutes of workshop performance by eight residents.

EXPERIMENT II

The purpose of this experiment was to analyze the effects of a punishing stimulus (response cost) on the behaviors which were punished. If punishment is defined as the removal of a positive reinforcer contingent on a given response (Skinner, 1958) the data provided in Experiment

I demonstrate that contingent removal of tokens (response cost) does involve punishment. If, however, punishment is defined in terms of a consequence of a behavior that reduces the future probability of that behavior (Azrin and Holz, 1966), then it is uncertain whether or not response cost, as used in the ITU, is punishing. Therefore this experiment attempts to ascertain the effects of response cost on the future probability of certain responses.

Responses

The responses consisted of various antisocial behaviors (stealing, lying, cheating, fighting, property damage, and physical and verbal assault). The staff was instructed to use time out whenever a particular response could not be ignored, and to use seclusion whenever time out was inappropriate. The staff was instructed to ignore such behaviors as disobeying the request of a staff member, name calling and profanity unless such behavior precipitated a fight.

Except for extreme instances of violence and rage the time out procedure was used first. If a particular response in time out could not be tolerated or if a resident refused to go to time out, then seclusion was used. Although responses were not defined as objectively as those in Experiment I, the staff had been using time out and seclusion for approximately one year prior to this study and were familiar with the procedures involved.

Procedure

The design is the A-B-A type of analysis used in Experiment I. Each of the three phases lasted seven consecutive week days. During Phase 1 response cost was contingent upon the antisocial responses which resulted in time out (a loss of four tokens) and seclusion (a loss of 15 tokens). Therefore, the number of tokens each boy had to pay each day for his behavior credit depended upon the number of times he went to time out and seclusion that day. During Phase 2 the response cost was noncontingent. The number of tokens each boy had to pay for his behavior credit during this phase did *not* depend upon the number of times he went to time out and seclusion each day. Rather, the daily behavior credit cost for each resident was the average number of tokens he had paid each day for his behavior credit during Phase 1.

At the beginning of Phase 2 the residents were told that they would be paying a fixed number of tokens for their behavior credits. Although they kept the staff busy by asking many questions about the procedure, the initial statement made to them was as follows: "From now on the number of tokens you have to pay for your behavior credit will be the same each day. Each of you will be charged about the same amount you have been paying in the past. Here is the amount each boy will have to pay. (The charge for each boy was read and the list was posted on the bulletin board.) It doesn't matter how many times you go to seclusion or time out, behavior credit will always cost you that many tokens each day."

Phase 3 was similar to Phase 1 with response cost contingent upon the antisocial responses which resulted in time out and seclusion. There were eight residents who contributed to the data in this experiment (1, 3, 4, 6, 7, 9, 10, 11).

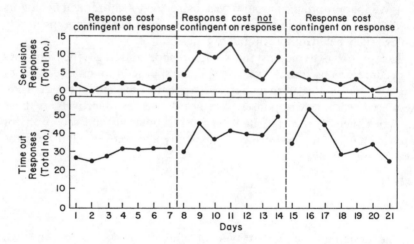

FIGURE 3.   Total number of seclusion and time-out responses by eight residents.

Results and Discussion

Figure 3 shows that time out and seclusion responses were not brought under complete experimental control by the manipulation of the response cost contingent. Although responses generally increased during the noncontingent phase, there was some overlap between contingent and noncontingent phases indicating that other uncontrolled variables were influencing the occurrence or the recording of the responses.

Variables which may have contributed to the uncontrolled effect could be a function of the data collection system (responses too subjectively defined, staff inconsistency, etc.) or of the punishment contingency (too much delay between response and response cost). Nevertheless, effects of these variables should have been relatively constant across all three phases. A more plausible explanation for the overlap between the contingent and noncontingent phases is that the verbal discriminative stimuli which defined the change from one phase to another were ineffective. Although the residents were told that the cost of their behavior credit would or would not depend upon the number of times they went to time out or seclusion, it may be they had to experience the change before it affected the frequency of the responses. Also, the increase in the frequency of responses resulting in seclusion during Phase 2 probably prevented the occurrence of a greater number of responses which would have resulted in time out. As the amount of time a resident spends in seclusion increases, the opportunities to go to time out decrease.

Without further experimental manipulation additional speculation regarding the incomplete experimental control seems unwarranted. Nevertheless, the data that were obtained in Experiment II, together with data demonstrating the reinforcing effects of the token, do provide evidence in support of response cost as a punishing stimulus.

CONCLUSION

The over-all objective of the Intensive Training Program is to develop effective techniques for teaching the antisocial retardate a repertoire of socially acceptable behavior which will enable him to survive outside of an institutional environment. The first step was to determine effective reinforcing and punishing stimuli which could be used to increase or decrease the future occurrence of behaviors. Experiments I and II provide evidence in support of the contingent presentation or removal of tokens as reinforcing and punishing stimuli respectively. Further research is being done to enhance the effectiveness of these stimuli, especially with respect to their effects on different individual behaviors. At the same time programs are continually being developed which utilize the contingent presentation and removal of tokens to teach a wide variety of practical behaviors (reading, writing, time telling, using public transportation, buying and washing clothes, and using a telephone).

Thus far the emphasis in the program has been on the acquisition or elimination of specific behaviors by trying to place the resident in an environment where maximal behavior modification can occur. A second objective is to develop methods for bringing modified behaviors under the control of more natural contingencies. Although frequent and immediate administration of a material reinforcer (token) may be an effective way to increase or maintain behavior, the probability of such a consequence occurring outside of the ITU is extremely remote for most behaviors. The same is true for behaviors which result in the removal of tokens. Although it is impossible to determine the uncontrolled contingencies which will exist outside of the ITU, it is probable that the presentation and removal of material reinforcers (money) will occur only after a considerable amount of behavior (vocational) and/or time (weeks) has taken place. Therefore, if behavior is to persist in the community, other consequences will have to become reinforcing such as infrequent praise and social approval or performing a behavior which is part of a chain of behaviors that has resulted in reinforcement in the past.

As behavior is modified in the ITU the contingencies gradually are modified in the direction of those which would exist if the resident were living in the community. Obviously, it is not completely possible to simulate a noninstitutional environment within an institution. Therefore, as soon as the contingencies within the ITU have become as "natural" as the situation will permit, the resident will be placed in environmental settings (work placement, halfway house, boarding house, etc.) which provide a closer approximation of the community.

The above outline for phasing the residents into the community is largely theoretical. Contingencies and schedules of reinforcement and punishment will be modified on an individual basis, depending upon a resident's response to a given program.

Whether or not the controlled environment and the systematic reinforcement and punishment contingencies which exist in the Intensive Training Program will facilitate the habilitation of antisocial retardates must await further experimental analysis. The program has demonstrated, however, that specific behaviors can be modified, at least on a temporary basis. It is also apparent that gross antisocial behavior can be brought under control, and that a variety of practical behaviors can be learned.

~ 22 ~

Short-Term Operant Conditioning
of Adolescent Offenders
on Socially Relevant Variables

Robert L. Schwitzgebel

The elimination or modification of unwanted behavior is a frequent goal of psychotherapy. Although assessment of psychotherapeutic effectiveness is an extremely complex matter, there seems to be rather general agreement that orthodox clinical procedures have not proven very effective in dealing with adolescent behavior disorders. One of the most well-known, extensive, therapeutic and research efforts, the Cambridge-Somerville project (McCord, McCord, and Zola, 1959; Powers and Witmer, 1951), had but marginal success. An evaluation of results based on psychological tests, school adjustment reports, and court records 3 years after termination showed no significant difference between treatment and control groups.

The recidivism rate for juvenile parolees in the United States ranges from 43 % to 73 % of the original reformatory commitments (Arbuckle and Litwack, 1960, p. 45). Southerland and Cressey (1960, p. 43), for example, noted that about 72 % of the offenders admitted to reformatory in Massachusetts in 1957 had been in correctional institutions previously. Teuber and Powers (1951) found that psychiatric treatment of delinquents resulted in no significant difference in the number of court appearances. Meese (1961) conducted a study involving younger

From the *Journal of Abnormal Psychology*, 72:2 (1967), 134–142.

adolescent offenders in weekly conferences with a counseling and guidance orientation. After treatment, the experimental group did significantly poorer than the control group in terms of measurable anxiety, academic achievement, and reading skill. Apparently the treatment procedures were not only unhelpful but to some extent iatrogenic. A review by Shannon (1961) concludes that "research indicates that no group or profession has demonstrated the ability to effectively deal with deviant behavior; research shows that treatment results in no greater improvement than that which accrues by simply leaving persons with a behavioral problem alone" (p. 35).

There are now over 100 published studies which have used the free operant method with humans. Several comprehensive reviews are readily available (e.g., Bandura, 1961; Bandura and Walters, 1963; Krasner, 1958). The most common S populations have been college students and psychiatric patients. The outstanding exceptions, from the point of view of the present research, have been the rare reports of studies involving criminal offenders as Ss (e.g., Cairns, 1960; Johns and Quay, 1962; Kadlub, 1956; Lykken, 1957). All of the experimental Ss in these studies were incarcerated at the time of the research, and none of the procedures had a therapeutic orientation. The large majority of human operant studies to date have been conducted in "artificial" settings (e.g., laboratory cubicles, hospital wards). This, of course, raises the question as to what extent the results and principles can be generalized to common social interactions; although Azrin, Holz, Ulrich, and Goldiamond (1961) have dramatically demonstrated that "the importance of extending the procedures of operant conditioning to 'real life' situations should not be allowed to override the elementary considerations of experimental control (pp. 29–30)." With but few exceptions, the behaviors which have been most frequently studied (e.g., plural nouns, lever pulling) may also be considered rather "nonsocial."

In 1958 a small clinical research project studying the dynamics of hostility hired seven adolescent male delinquents to participate in interviews and to take a series of psychological tests (Slack, 1960). A mutual acquaintance of the E and the delinquent, in most cases a social worker, served as a referral contact. Once the delinquent could be persuaded to come to the office a few times the probability of establishing a treatment relationship was fairly high. How to initiate cooperative attendance without the use of referrals, however, remained a problem. For this reason, the original procedure was altered by going directly into areas of high crime rate and hiring Ss from amusement centers, pool halls, and street corners (Schwitzgebel and Kolb, 1964). A storefront was established as a meeting place.

The responses of *S*s were tape-recorded during each interview session, and *S*s were paid the customary wage of $1.00 an hour. After six or seven interviews, it was noticed that most *S*s seemed to enjoy the interviewing and testing, and thus the procedure was gradually modified toward therapeutic ends. Each *S* participated in an interview procedure involving psychoanalytic, client-centered, or a directive counseling orientation. The *S*s were seen an average of three times a week for a period of approximately 9 months. A follow-up study of the first 20 *S*s (Schwitzgebel, 1964), 3 years after termination of employment, showed that the number of arrests and months of incarceration of the employees was about one-half that of a matched control group. Casual inspection of the data suggested that the degree of "unorthodoxy," directness, and concrete expression of feelings on the part of the *E* — regardless of professed theoretical bias — seemed to bring about the most substantial change in *S* behavior. The present study was designed as a partial test of this observation. It was hypothesized that therapeutic intervention which provided planned differential consequences for typical interview behaviors would result in different "treatment" outcomes.

METHOD

Subjects

The initial contact to recruit *S*s was made by two *E*s who met prospective *S*s, without prior knowledge or arrangement, on a street corner. The nature of the contact was informal but direct. The prospective *S* was told that *E*s were from a university, that they were doing research, and that they needed people to help them with their work. It was explained that the purpose of the research was to find out what teenagers think and feel about things, how they come to have certain opinions, and how they change.

In the course of this explanation, *E*s would offer to take the prospective *S* and several of his friends to a nearby restaurant of their choice and buy them refreshments. It was made explicit, however, that one of the "qualifications" for the job and for going to the restaurant was that the person had a court or police record and, preferably, had spent some time in prison. (At this point, some *S*s voluntarily produced probation cards, tattoos, knives, bicycle chains, and an accurate knowledge of the state penal system as evidence of their qualifications to serve as research *S*s.) Although *S*s were often suspicious that *E*s were policemen, detectives, homosexuals, gangsters, or even escaped mental patients, they would usually go to the restaurant. Informal conversation in the restaurant about topics of the boys' interest would be followed by an invitation to visit the office.

Forty-eight Ss were employed and assigned to one of three matched groups: two experimental groups and a control group. The Ss in the experimental groups participated in 20 interviews over a period of 2–3 months. Control Ss ($N = 14$) participated in only two interviews spaced over the same amount of time. Due primarily to the inability to locate control Ss for the final interviews, the final effective N was 35. The mean age for these 35 Ss was 16.2 years with 9.1 years of completed schooling and an average of 1.4 years probation. Seven Ss had been incarcerated an average of 1.6 years.

Definition of Response Categories

To determine what specific effects social reinforcers might have, Experimental Group I ($N = 9$) received positive consequences for statements of concern (positive statements) about other people and for dependable and prompt arrival at work. Experimental Group II ($N = 12$) received negative consequences for hostile (negative) statements about people and positive consequences for socially desirable nonverbal behavior giving evidence of tact or employability.

1. Positive statements. "Positive statements" or "statements of concern" were interpreted as any verbalization of sympathy for another person or any comment raising another person's status (cf. Bales, 1950) directed toward a specific individual or individuals. For example, a general statement, such as "Us crooks are good people" (which was, in fact, made), was not scored as a positive statement. However, "Joe is a good guy," did satisfy the criterion. The scoring was done in terms of "units" rather than separate sentences or general topics. Sentences were assumed to be too difficult for a judge to count accurately, and general topics occurred so infrequently that they could not provide a discriminative measurement. A "unit" was defined as any continuous series of statements (disregarding the usual conversational interruptions). If, for example, an S talked about Joe's being a "good guy" for 5 minutes, it was scored only as one unit. If, on the other hand, the S talked about Joe for several minutes, changed the topic, and then later reverted to talking about Joe, he would receive a score of two units.

2. Negative statements. Negative or hostile statements were defined as expressions showing antagonism, or which decreased another

person's status. Again the verbalizations were required to refer to a particular person or persons, and were scored in units. The intention and meaning of a statement was taken into account in scoring, and not merely its structure. A statement negative in structure might be made, for example, toward a friend, but the intention and tone of it might clearly imply playfulness or even admiration. Such statements were not scored as hostile units.

3. Arrival at work. "Arrival at work" was measured by the regularity and promptness with which an *S* arrived at the laboratory for his interview. The *S*s who arrived within 5 minutes of the appointed time were considered as having arrived on time. For *S*s who arrived later, a record was made of the difference between the appointed time and the arrival time. Failure to arrive at all was assigned a value of 60 minutes, since *E*s were not required to wait longer than 1 hour. On this basis, an average time discrepancy was computed for each *S*.

4. Socially desirable behavior. "Socially desirable behavior" was measured by a standardized series of test situations presented to each *S* while having refreshments at a restaurant. The purpose was to measure *S*'s social behavior in terms of general employability. The test situations included the following:

(a) Each *S* was told that he could order a maximum of $1.00's worth of food. The amount of food ordered and the attitude of *S* was observed.

(b) The *E* would begin playing with a small Chinese puzzle. At *S*'s request, the puzzle would be given to *S*, and the total amount of time spent working on the puzzle was recorded.

(c) A small sum of money (between 25 and 40 cents) was secretly placed on the floor by *E*. The *S*s were ranked on the basis of the amount of money retained.

(d) The *S* was offered the last stick of gum or the last cigarette of a pack. The *S*s were grouped as to whether or not they accepted the offer.

(e) The *E* purchased, in addition to individual requests, food which could be shared by the group (e.g., French fried potatoes, a large pizza, potato chips). The proportion which *S* ate of the total amount was noted.

(f) During the initial and final interviews, *S*s were invited to play what was called "the poker chip game." This game required that within a 5-minute period an *S* thinks of all the "bad" things he could do. For each item he named he was given a poker chip, which could be cashed in at the end of the game for 3–5 cents each. After 5 minutes had passed, the chips were counted and the earnings tallied. The *S* was then required to think of all the "good" things he could do. (The tasks were assigned in this order since the latter was more difficult.) One rule of the game was that negative suggestions (e.g., *don't* let the air out of tires) did not count as a "good" behavior. It was necessary for S to think of something positive or constructive, not simply prohibitive. Again, a 5-minute limit was set, and the chips counted.

This provided, for experimental purposes, a measurable index of S's ability to "free associate" and to verbalize possible actions related to the concepts of "good" and "bad" behavior. The Ss appeared to enjoy the game and often asked to play it again during work sessions. This was not permitted since practice effects had not been determined. A comparison of the number of chips received for each of the two tasks gave what was referred to as a "thought-count ratio." Variations in this ratio were observed before and after the employment period.

During the actual treatment or employment period, desirable social behaviors were not sharply defined in advance. The Es observed individual Ss and attempted to reinforce those operants which indicated cooperativeness, tact, or sustained effort at a task. Behaviors specifically rewarded by Es included, for example, voluntarily picked up Coke bottles around the laboratory, leaving a note in advance when unable to come to work, returning change when accidentally overpaid, unexpectedly bringing food to share with E, and helping to repair a tape recorder.

Schedule and Types of Consequences

The main task assigned to each experimental S consisted of his talking into a tape recorder about anything he wished. The tone of the work sessions was informal and friendly, but Es tried to avoid giving direction to the content of the conversation. Ideally, S and E interacted in a manner best described as "client-centered counseling." The single purposeful exception to this procedure was the differential consequences following the specific behaviors previously indicated. Control Ss received no special, planned consequences except a cash bonus following the initial interview. All experimental Ss came to the laboratory two or three times a week for 1 hour for the required total of 20 hours.

When an E consciously attempted to alter the frequency of a specific behavior of an S by the delivery of a prescribed consequence, this constituted for this experiment a legitimate reinforcement attempt. Positive consequences consisted of verbal praise, small gifts (e.g., cigarettes, candy bars, and cash bonuses in amounts varying from

25 cents to $1.00); negative consequences were inattention and mild verbal disagreement. All reinforcement attempts were delivered on a variable interval—variable ratio schedule. It was assumed that this would be the most convenient and natural schedule to administer, and possibly the only feasible schedule to use where *E* was also required to maintain an active interest in the content and feelings expressed by the *S* (cf. Azrin et al., 1961).

The attempt to shape dependable and prompt attendance at work among Experimental Group I *S*s may serve to illustrate the reinforcement procedure. An *S* might arrive, for example, 30 minutes late for the third meeting. The *E* would welcome him and mention that this was much better than 2 days before when he was an hour late. For the "good effort" the *S* was given a 50-cent bonus. The next appointment might find *S* arriving within 15 minutes of the scheduled time — hoping perhaps for a 75-cent bonus. The *E* would be likely to say nothing about his arrival, but the *S* might call attention to the fact and ask about his bonus. It would then be explained that an employee could always expect to receive the basic wage, but that bonuses depended entirely on the amount of money the *E* happened to have and on his feelings at the time. The *S* might be disappointed until, later that hour, he received a 50-cent bonus for, say, mentioning that he was worried about his aunt in the hospital. He might then realize that he could never be sure what he might receive a bonus for, or what the bonus would be, but the whole thing seemed to be an interesting game.

Each *S* received an average of six explicit reinforcement attempts on each of two variables. This average was depressed by the fact that many fewer negative consequences were given than positive (cf. Figures 1 and 2). At least two factors combined to account for this unintentional discrepancy. First, since the participation of the *S*s depended on their willingness to return for additional interview sessions, interviewers were hesitant to risk antagonizing *S*s. Second, *E*s usually became favorably disposed toward *S*s and were not inclined to intentionally apply aversive sanctions. The following excerpt, taken from an interview with a 15-year-old Negro *S* (Experimental Group II) several days after President Kennedy's assassination, may serve to illustrate an *E*'s rather weak attempt to suppress an *S*'s hostile statements.

S: I had a book report in school. We had to write about him [President Kennedy]. Now I wrote — let me see if I can remember what I said — Oh, there should have been no reason in the world why the President should have been assassinated.

E: Yes.

S: Then I said, Lee Oswald must have been crazy, you know.

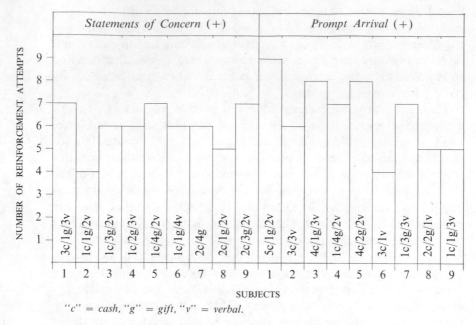

FIGURE 1. Number of reinforcement attempts, Group I.

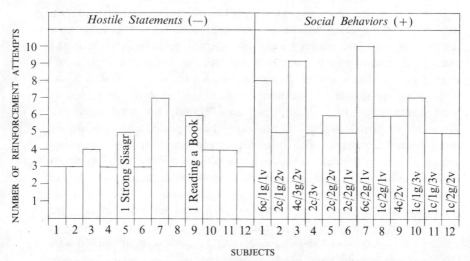

FIGURE 2. Number of reinforcement attempts, Group II.

E: Yes.

S: Then I put it this way. On the morning when Kennedy went to make his speech at Dallas, Texas, I myself had no idea that later on in the day he would be... be, you know, dead.

E: That's right, nobody did.

S: Then I said to myself, it was a blow to everybody; it was a big blow, you know what I mean?

E: Yes.

S: It hurt everybody. I wrote, Lee Oswald is dead now, right?... O.K., he's dead. He paid for his punishment, right?

E: No.

S: O.K., wait. Let me finish. I said to myself, he paid for his punishment....

E: Yes.

S: ... but he paid for it too easy. (*S* then describes various tortures he would like to have inflicted on Oswald.)

E: Yes, the other night I was thinking about that. That's the way you feel even though you know better; you still feel like this.

S: Yes. I know how his brothers feel and his wife especially. (This leads to a discussion about the Kennedy family and the funeral.)

Transfer

In order to test the effects of the attempted conditioning procedure outside the laboratory situation, various behaviors of the *S*s were recorded while in a restaurant of their choosing. One of the two *E*s who made initial contact with a prospective *S* served as a "judge." The judge was primarily responsible for noting the frequency of positive and negative verbal statements of the *S*. The judge was expected to participate in the group, but to remain distant enough to obtain the necessary count. The other *E* had the major responsibility for group interaction and for noting the responses of the *S* to the nonverbal test situations. Postemployment testing was again done in a restaurant, the *S*s particular *E* (who served as a judge on the initial contact) was replaced by another judge. It was assumed that the presence of the *S*s *E* would be less duplicative of natural situations than the presence of a stranger. Judges were randomly assigned to *S*s for postemployment testing. Theoretically, no judge was to know *S*s group assignment. This was practicable with experimental *S*s, but since meeting control *S*s was often a matter of searching, their group assignment was more obvious.

In order to test interjudge scoring reliability, eight persons who served as judges or Es were instructed in advance as to the scoring procedure. A composite tape recording was made from excerpts from the work sessions of five different pilot Ss. The length of the excerpts varied from 5 to 7 minutes and they were selected to yield different frequency counts (between 0 and 9) of positive or hostile verbal units for each S. Judges listened to the tape and independently noted the occurrences and the topics of hostile and positive statements. On the basis of the frequency of these verbal units, each judge then ranked the five Ss on the amount of expressed hostility or expressed concern. The ranking procedure aided in proving some internal check on the validity of scoring, since judges could recognize any discrepancy between the total of scored units and their general impression of a given S. On two occasions such discrepancies arose, but, for purposes of ranking, the original or uncorrected scores were utilized.

The rankings of the five Ss by the eight judges permitted an estimate of interjudge reliability as expressed by the Kendall (1948) coefficient of concordance. The Kendall W coefficient was .84 ($s = 542$) for positive units and .69 ($s = 440$) for negative units, both significant below .01 (Siegel, 1956). Informal periodic spot checks requiring two interviewers to count the number of hostile and positive units from a randomly selected 15-minute interview segment of a single S showed no significant change in reliability. In general, it was not difficult for judges to agree on what constituted a positive or a hostile statement. This particular S population is not usually given to subtlety of expression. The most difficult decisions (accounting perhaps for the somewhat lower W coefficient for hostile units) involved statements which were hostile in content but not in tone or affect. Consider, for example, the following exchange:

S_1: (Describing his being stopped by a policeman for a stolen motor scooter)...I told him we didn't need no permit to drive in Alabama, but he didn't believe me.

S_2: (Slowly, each word emphasized) You dumb —— ! (Both laugh). This type of expression would not formally qualify as a hostile statement although some interviewers would initially tend to score it so. This source of variance was never completely eliminated.

><

RESULTS

The results of the present investigation will be described by noting the effect of the conditioning procedure on (a) arrival time, (b) verbal behavior, and (c) "nonverbal" social behavior.

(a) Arrival Time. The early sessions with almost all Ss brought wide fluctuation in attendance behavior. By the sixth or eighth session differences became more apparent. On the basis of the average time discrepancy computed for each S, Experimental Group I Ss showed an average time discrepancy of 11.2 minutes. Experimental Group II Ss, not conditioned on this variable, showed a 15.6-minute discrepancy. The difference in promptness arrival between the two groups was significant in the predicted direction (Fisher test, $\alpha < .025$). Figure 3 shows the distribution of the Ss based on their mean arrival time for 19

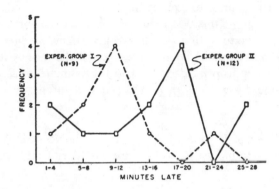

FIGURE 3. Mean arrival discrepancies (latenesses) of experimental subjects for 19 scheduled appointments.

scheduled appointments (the first hour, the initial contact, was unscheduled.) The majority of Ss from Experimental Group I lie within the first three ranges; in contrast, the majority of Experimental Group II Ss lie within the last three ranges.

(b) Verbal Behavior. The mean number of verbal units for each group of both positive and negative statements is presented in Table 1. The most clear change occurred in Experimental Group I where an average of 1.9 positive statements was made during the test period prior to employment, and an average of 4.0 statements was made after employment. A comparison of changes within each group, using the Mann-Whitney test (Siegel, 1956), showed that Experimental Group I Ss had a significantly ($U = 22$, $\alpha = .047$) larger increase in positive statements after employment than did Experimental Group II Ss. A similar comparison of Experimental Group I Ss with Control Ss showed an even more significant ($U = 94.5$, $\alpha = .017$) gain for the Experimental Ss conditioned on this variable.

Experimental Group II Ss, who received negative consequences for hostile statements, showed some decrease in the average frequency of such statements. Although this decrease (from a mean of 5.8 to 3.8) was somewhat larger than in the other two groups, a comparison of the changes within the groups (Mann-Whitney test) did not permit rejection of the null hypothesis at a significance level equal to or less than .05.

(c) Social Behaviors. Only two tests yielded significant results: the amount of food ordered and the "thought-count ratio." No other measured variable was found to distinguish the groups. The amount of time Ss spent working on a puzzle showed a wide variance (from 10 seconds to 6 minutes and 20 seconds) and no clear trend. The majority of Ss in all groups prior to employment did not accept the last cigarette or last stick of gum; this was reversed to about the same extent in all groups on the second testing. Similarly, it could not be predicted on the basis of group assignment what percentage of the money found on the floor would be appropriated by S. And the estimate of the proportion of shared food taken by S proved to be too unreliable to serve as a measure.

TABLE 1.   Average Frequency of Positive and Negative Verbal Units for a 2-Hour Test Period before and after Employment

Group	Positive				Negative			
	Before		After		Before		After	
	M	SE	M	SE	M	SE	M	SE
Experimental I	1.9	±0.6	4.0	±0.9	5.1	±0.8	3.6	±0.7
Experimental II	2.5	±0.6	2.9	±0.5	5.8	±0.7	3.8	±0.6
Control	1.8	±0.4	2.1	±0.4	5.4	±0.6	4.8	±0.5

The average amount of food ordered by Ss before and after employment is shown in Table 2. All groups showed some increase in the amount of food ordered on the second testing; however, Experimental Group II Ss who were conditioned on social behaviors showed the least amount of increase. A comparison of changes within the groups revealed that the increase among Group II Ss was significantly less (Fisher test, $\alpha < .05$) than the increase among Control Ss

The other measure which was apparently influenced by the treatment procedure was the "thought-count ratio." The mean scores for each

TABLE 2.   Average Amount of Food Ordered before and after
Employment

Group	Before		After	
	M	*SE*	*M*	*SE*
Experimental I	$.65	±.05	$.77	±.07
Experimental II	.61	±.06	.64	±.06
Control	.55	±.08	.74	±.07

TABLE 3.   Mean Frequencies of Thoughts about "Good" and "Bad"
Behaviors as Tested in a Game Situation

Group	"Good" Behaviors				"Bad" Behaviors			
	Before		After		Before		After	
	M	*SE*	*M*	*SE*	*M*	*SE*	*M*	*SE*
Experimental I	8.8	±1.6	8.5	±1.8	18.0	±2.1	17.3	±1.8
Experimental II	10.2	±1.0	15.6	±1.6	18.3	±1.6	18.5	±1.1
Control	10.1	±0.9	11.1	±1.0	16.7	±1.3	16.9	±1.1

group on this test are presented in Table 3. Experimental Group II Ss conditioned on socially desirable behaviors increased from 10.2 thoughts about "good" things they might do to an average of 15.6 such thoughts during the 5-minute game-like situation. This gain was significantly greater than that in the Control group $(U = 36, \alpha < .05)$, and it also differed significantly from the slight loss which occurred in Experimental Group I $(U = 25, \alpha < .05)$. Seemingly, the treatment procedure which rewarded positive social behaviors was capable of influencing the ability of Ss to think of ways in which they might act to another person's benefit. The treatment procedures used in the present study had no apparent effect on the frequency of thoughts about "bad" behaviors.

In summary, the treatment procedure as applied in this investigation resulted in significant modifications in two of the four major reinforcement categories; namely, positive statements and arrival time. The frequency of positive statements was significantly increased, and arrival at work sessions became significantly more prompt among Ss specifically conditioned on these variables. The categories of social behaviors related to employability and of hostile statements gave some indication of conditioning effects; however, they were not judged to be significant. Measurement and other procedural difficulties unfortunately complicate the interpretation of these results.

✂

DISCUSSION

Since the frequency of positive statements and of attendance behavior was altered with an average of only six reinforcement attempts, one of the issues raised by the present study would seem to be the adequacy of a "reinforcement" interpretation of the results. It is possible that control over these two operants could have been accomplished by the informative or instructional properties rather than the rewarding or incentive properties of the prearranged consequences. Unfortunately, these alternative hypotheses were not explicitly investigated. It seems somewhat unlikely however that the instructional aspects alone account for the observed changes. The very nature of the S population suggests that these are individuals who do not respond readily to adults' instruction to be prompt for appointments or to talk kindly about other people. Both experimental groups were informed as to the next scheduled appointment and were generally aware of the desire on E's part for promptness, yet performance was significantly improved only in the group receiving consequences. Furthermore, the "burst" of appropriate behavior which often occurs when meaningful instruction or information is initially given to well-motivated Ss, did not occur in this study at the onset of the treatment phase.

The procedures of the present experiment did not permit us to specify with any certainty or preciseness what the effective variables of change were, although several other studies seem to indicate the kind of functional relationships which might be profitably investigated in the future. Ayllon and Azrin (1964), for example, investigating the differential effects of instruction and reinforcement, found that adult psychotic patients would show a sharp rise in appropriate social behavior (i.e., use of silverware at meals) when first instructed. Performance would then gradually deteriorate. Consequences without any instruction yielded steady but marginal improvement. Instruction plus contingent consequences produced a high, steady rate. Other work (e.g., Goldiamond, 1962) has demonstrated the importance of contingency relationships between operant and consequence. Spielberger, Bernstein, and Ratcliff (1966) have claimed that some awareness of the correct response is necessary for verbal conditioning in adults, but that once this awareness occurs, most change is attributable to motivational factors.

The failure to obtain a more profound reduction in hostile statements or clearer transfer effects is believed to be largely a result of procedural inadequacies. Many of the tests or observations in the restaurant proved to be unreliable, and *E*s were somewhat hesitant to apply aversive sanctions to hostile verbal behavior during the interviews for fear that *S* might become angry or not return (cf. excerpt previously cited).

The results of the present study would seem to indicate the therapeutic feasibility of an environmentalistic interpretation of behavior disorders. Anna Freud (1958) has written that, among other things, adolescents are very difficult to get into treatment because they do not cooperate, they miss appointments, they are unpunctual, they cannot or will not introspect, and their rapidly changing emotional patterns leave little energy available to invest in the analyst. These behaviors may be typical, but, in this writer's opinion, can be modified without extreme difficulty. Informal observation after the present study indicated that in a few cases "trying to attend work" had not been completely extinguished even two months after termination of employment. One Experimental Group I *S*, for example, a month and a half after termination, left the following note at the laboratory.

Don

I would like you to call me Phone [deleted]. Because I would like to know if I could Get back into the Business if its okay with you

Dingo

It should be noted that by the twentieth interview the attention of the *E* and participation in the project seemed to become very important reinforcers for most *S*s. Arrival became more prompt in both groups, and this tended to wash out earlier group differences presumably caused by differential treatment. On the other hand, aversive sanctions (when *E*s dared to give them) seemed to become more effective, although significant group differences were never achieved.

The characteristic impulsivity ascribed to juvenile delinquents is likely influenced or determined by the particular type and schedule of reinforcements in the individual's history. To some extent, these may be explicitly programmed. Pigeons, rats, dogs, and other organisms which might normally be considered impulsive "by nature" have been successfully trained on slow-down schedules to inhibit gratification for relatively sustained periods of time. And this has been done, of course, without the advantage of any symbolic verbal control.

The fact that a series of interviews with an operant-conditioning orientation could develop dependable and prompt attendance and certain other social behaviors in juvenile delinquents may not surprise therapists familiar with experimental analysis of human learning. What is more difficult to explain, however, is why this knowledge has not been put to systematic use in the large majority of treatment programs. This may be related to a still broader problem; namely, the extent to which usual clinical assumptions about the "character structure" of delinquency is an artifact of the traditional clinical procedure itself. This should be a problem of continued and judicious investigation.

~23~

An Operant Conditioning Program in a Juvenile Detention Facility

Kenneth R. Fineman

A six-month exploratory program was conducted at the San Fernando Valley Juvenile Hall, Intensive Care Unit. Children assigned to this unit were aged twelve to eighteen and had histories of behavior problems (highly anxious, neurotic, psychotic, homosexual, etc.) that suggested the necessity of intensive care. The problem was the development of a program of sufficient power to enable one or two probation counselors to handle 20 or more such youths, the emphasis being on behavior control. (This is the opinion of the author and not necessarily the opinion of the detention facility.)

~

PROCEDURE

In its most elementary form the procedure involves the giving of "plus," or merit points, for appropriate behavior which includes self-control, degree of participation in group activities, and other responses deemed requisite. This is based on Hewett's engineered classroom (1967). Ss can also be given "minus" points which negatively reinforce inappro-

From *Psychological Reports*, 22 (1968), 1119–1120. ©Southern Universities Press 1968.

priate behavior such as acting out, profanity, fighting, etc. The system in addition to controlling behavior is consistent with the detention facility's policy of providing a means of self-evaluation for the ward in addition to providing the staff with information as to which children can be given responsibilities and special privileges. While other units operated on a merit-demerit system, it was found that the point of difference lies in the present system's emphasis on the immediacy of reinforcement. That is, when appropriate or inappropriate behaviors were identified, they were immediately reinforced. The child was also told what incident elicited which points. Positive points would eventually lead to reward while an accumulation of negative points (at one time) would lead to immediate isolation.

Each morning a list of all children ranked from highest to lowest, based on the addition and subtraction of the previous day's points, was put in the unit's day room. It was made known that high-point men would be rewarded frequently, i.e., be given their choice of various prizes. In reality the actual reinforcement by extrinsic rewards was given only once a month. It was hoped that Ss would not get caught up in a game of points and that eventually the counselor would take on secondary reinforcing properties.

With this in mind the counselors were advised to give plus or minus points immediately contingent upon the specified behavior. It was also advised that the bulk of points be "plus" points. If the child seemed incorrigible, the counselor would reward something he did right and try to shape further appropriate behavior.

DISCUSSION

Lack of quantifiable dependent variables preludes any definitive statement of results. However, interviews with the unit counselors and supervising Deputy Probation Officers were taken as valued judgments in determining the success of the program.

Highest praise came for ease of group control, an attenuation of the previous amount of profanity and aggressiveness, as well as an augmentation in group participation. Soon after its inception the system seemed to function without specific rewards, i.e., Ss continued to work for points even though rewards were quite infrequent (about once a month). The only likely reward was social reinforcement coming from counselors and peers when listings were given on the merit ladder each morning.

The effectiveness of the system, including the fact that extrinsic reinforcers (other than social praise) were rarely used, might be interpreted in terms of the short-term detention facility. Being basically a treatment-oriented detention facility the average stay was relatively short, about 2.5 weeks. One might want to test the power of the system on a residential delinquent group to see the relative effectiveness after temporary change due to the "Hawthorne" effect. On the other hand, it appears that the system might be effective for a short-term facility with a great deal of turnover.

~24~

Use of Behavioral Techniques in a Case of Compulsive Stealing

Ralph Wetzel

Several investigators have demonstrated the effectiveness of behavioral techniques in the modification of so-called deviant behaviors. These demonstrations have involved settings varying from the hospital (Ayllon and Michael, 1959; Wolf, Risley, and Mees, 1964) and the nursery school (Harris, Wolf, and Baer, 1964) to the clinician's office (Wolpe, 1958) and the home (Boardman, 1962). Likewise, the modifications have varied from the establishment of new behavioral repertoires to the elimination of whole classes of behavior.

An important feature of many demonstrations is that the change in behavior is often accomplished by relatively untrained, nonprofessional individuals. Hospital attendants, nursery school teachers, parents, and others have all been effective in the modification of deviant behaviors heretofore considered the domain of highly skilled and usually highly paid professional individuals. Usually these nonprofessionals have received very little special training. The implications for the efficient use of consultant time, the reduction of treatment costs, and the dispersion of therapeutic effectiveness are obvious. Bandura (1962b) has pointed out that the professional individual can best spend his time instructing others in the application of behavioral principles and the work of several authors has suggested some very practical and ingenious consulting procedures (Philips, 1960; Williams, 1959; Wolf, 1965).

From *Journal of Consulting Psychology*, 30:5 (1966), 367–374.

The efficiency of behavioral techniques usually depends upon the control of specific response contingencies and has been most successfully applied in controlled environments. Outside of the laboratory, hospitals appear to provide the best control although the nursery school studies of Harris, Wolf, and Baer (1964) demonstrate the achievement of control in a relatively free environment. Boardman (1962), in spite of the relative lack of control in the "natural" environment of a young boy, was able to significantly modify aggressive acting-out behavior using behavioral techniques, and Wolf (1965) has shown that parental cooperation can provide excellent control of specific behavior in the home.

In his discussion of Boardman's demonstration, Bandura (1962) is critical of the use of punishment for several very valid reasons and suggests that it is more desirable to remove reinforcers maintaining the target behavior and reinforce alternative behaviors. However, his suggestion becomes more difficult to implement as the environment becomes more natural. In these situations there are probably multiple reinforcers controlling a behavior, many of which cannot be identified, much less controlled. On the school ground, for example, behavior which is under the control of other children is often difficult to handle because the situation requires modifying the behavior of several other individuals. Further, the natural environment frequently prohibits the use of potentially effective reinforcement contingencies. Although there are certain behaviors upon which parents and teachers may make meals contingent (such as handwashing), the use of food as a reinforcer is generally restricted. Thus, the general use of behavior principles in the more open, natural situation is often hampered by the existence of these multiple reinforcers and by a restriction in the range of reinforcers available for modifying the target behavior.

The present study further demonstrates the use of behavior principles in the modification of a deviant behavior. The "compulsive" stealing of a ten-year-old resident of a home for mildly disturbed children was successfully eliminated over a $3\frac{1}{2}$-month period. Records indicate that the behavior had been a source of difficulty for at least 5 years. The behavior "therapy" was carried out in a field situation and made minimal use of professional time. The study demonstrates the use of nonprofessional individuals in the modification, observations, and recording of behavior and indicates some of the hazards involved in so doing. Hopefully it also suggests some solutions to the problems involved.

=

SUBJECT AND HISTORY

The subject, who will be called Mike, was a Mexican-American boy, age ten at the beginning of this study. He first came to the attention of professional individuals when school authorities expelled him from the first grade and referred his mother to a child guidance clinic. He had already long been a disciplinary problem to his mother who found him "impossible." She had had many complaints of stealing and destructive behavior from neighbors but was unable to exert any control over Mike. She most frequently resorted to locking Mike in his bedroom, but he usually tore open the screen and escaped through the window. On one occasion he left after setting fire to his bed. The father was hospitalized for a chronic condition resulting from a war injury and the family was considered by caseworkers as "marginal." The mother had four children, little money, and was described by the psychiatrist at the guidance clinic as "inadequate."

In the first grade Mike continued to steal, was destructive of school property, disturbed other children, and made no academic progress. At the child guidance clinic, at age seven, he was given a psychiatric and psychological examination. He was described as a nonpsychotic, anxious, "slow learner" with "poor impulse control." His Stanford-Binet IQ was 78. He was diagnosed "passive-aggressive personality, aggressive type, severe." A special education class was recommended from which Mike was expelled one month later because the teacher was unable to handle him. He was placed in a foster home by the public welfare agency.

In the first half of his eighth year, Mike alternately lived in foster homes or under juvenile detention. The complaints from the foster homes were consistently about his stealing and destruction (in one home he chopped up a dining room chair with an ax). Due to his inability to adjust to foster homes and the undesirable effects of his long-term detention residence, Mike was made a ward of the court at age eight and one-half and was placed in the Children's Home, a residential treatment center for mildly disturbed children. The records of Mike's first few weeks at the Children's Home indicate the absence of destructive behavior but a high rate of tantrum behavior, bedwetting, and stealing. In his first interview with the consulting psychiatrist he complained of being picked on by the other children and accused of stealing. He admitted that he just could not stay out of their lockers. The psychiatrist felt that he had "many qualities of a full-blown psychopath" but that he was essentially workable and looking for controls. He was described by the staff as "charming," with little conscience and showing a tendency to "project his faults to others."

During the ensuing nine months Mike was described as making some adjustment to the home. He saw a caseworker once or twice a week, entered special classes of a nearby public school, and gradually established some relationships with the staff. The latter were almost exclusively with the women child care workers with whom he made himself ingratiating and useful. He was variously described by them as "a charmer," "adorable," and "a manipulator." At the same time there was a noticeable reduction in the staff reports of tantrums and daywetting.

His relationships with the other children at the home remained poor, apparently because he continued to steal. More and more the discussions with his caseworker took up the topic of stealing. The casework notes record Mike saying such things as, "I know I shouldn't steal people's things. I know it's wrong, so I am not going to do it." He complained about his inability to get along with "Englisher kids" because they picked on him for stealing. In spite of his complaints and promises, however, the incidence of stealing increased and spread to the school. He frequently brought home from the school toys, books, and assorted objects from the teacher's desk and the school bulletin board.

Various attempts were made to curb the stealing. It was noted, for example, that he frequently gave the objects he stole to another person. Suspecting that he was buying affections, his caseworker spent several sessions discussing Mike's need for affection with him and suggesting to Mike that his stealing enabled him to win affection from others. Mike usually replied by saying he was sorry and that he would not do it again. Another time a child care worker suggested that Mike might derive some satisfaction from the attention his stealing brought and thought they should "simply see that he returns what he takes." This plan was never put into effect although it had merit.

At the end of his first nine months in the home, Mike showed definite improvement in all behaviors except stealing and bedwetting. His stealing was by far the most serious since it had prohibited his establishing rewarding relationships with his peers and had alienated most of the staff. At this time, his behavior was described as "klepto-mania" in his records. The case work notes of this period reflect the general pessimism over his stealing:

> Mike has come to me almost every day saying, "I didn't steal at school," sometimes he has and sometimes he hasn't. I feel our sessions are a "front." He simply wants me to feel he is trying even though he isn't.
>
> The optimism expressed in the last summary in regard to Mike's "sticky fingers" was apparently premature since soon after the end

of October he started stealing both from school and again from the home (whenever a closet was left open) and from the other children.

After nine months in the Children's Home, Mike was recommended for foster home placement. It was the general consensus that his behavior had improved considerably and that his stealing represented a bid for affection. It was hoped that the latter would improve in a home atmosphere with a "loving maternal figure." He was described as "a chronic bedwetter with occasional wet pants... seeking out women and relating to them in an immature way.... Lovable but often like a little pack rat." He was placed with a Mexican-American family described as "exceptionally warm," living on the Arizona desert with three boys and horses.

One can only speculate what happened in the foster home. Five months later the Children's Home received a letter from welfare stating that "Mike's behavior in his foster home suggests further deterioration in his capacity to adjust" and requesting that he be readmitted. He entered for the second time at the age of nine years, ten months.

After readmission, the frequency of stealing appeared to be greater than ever before. It was reported at staff conferences that he was stealing nearly every day and on each shopping trip. The other children had begun to blame him for every missing article and, according to staff notes, "the articles are invariably found in his locker, on his person, or located with another individual who states that they are gifts from Mike."

At one staff conference the rationale for the present study was suggested by the author. Though there was not complete agreement about the method, the nearly five-year history of previous failure and the shortage of staff for casework and interview therapy contributed, perhaps, to its acceptance.

➤

METHOD

Training the Staff. Since the individuals in constant contact with Mike, the child care workers, were relatively untrained and unsophisticated in psychological theory and technique, it was first necessary to acquaint them with a few behavior principles. This was done in a series of four $1\frac{1}{2}$-hour conferences. These covered the nature of reinforcement, the effects of behavior consequences, and the recording of behavior. In addition, the film "Reinforcement in Learning and Extinction"

(McGraw-Hill, 1956) was shown. Discussion was focused on the possible application of these principles to Mike's stealing behavior. The reactions of the staff were varied. Some were enthusiastic, others stated that behavior principles are just "common sense," while others stated that the approach was "too scientific," meaning apparently, that it was too remote and "disregarded feelings." The intention was to convey in these sessions three essential points: (a) the consequences of behavior can control the behavior; (b) recording of the behavior is essential to the success of the study; (c) the study is experimental and there may be a period of trial and error. It will be seen that these points were not completely conveyed.

Selecting the Reinforcer. The staff argued that punishment of the stealing was not desirable. Mike had shown himself resistant to the usual consequences of stealing. Scoldings and disapproval by the child care workers, the anger of peers, the return of the objects all had no effect on the stealing rate. The history indicates that assorted punishments (including spanking and isolation) prior to his admission to the home had been ineffective. The general policies of the home, moreover, encouraged only the most minimal and judicious use of punishment. Extinction by removal of the consequences thought to maintain the stealing was also ruled out. There was no question but that a great deal of attention was paid to Mike's stealing. He had developed an extensive repertoire of excuses and explanations which could hold the attention of a child care worker often for an hour. However, the removal of these consequences was difficult. Much of the attention came from peers, school children, and teachers and was difficult to control. An attempt by the supervisor of the child care workers to reduce the attention paid to the stealing had no effect. It was thus decided to withdraw positive reinforcement contingent on stealing.

The initial task was to find a positive reinforcer that could be conveniently and effectively removed. The child care workers agreed that there was nothing Mike cared enough about that he would stop stealing to maintain. An examination of his personal relations indicated that he had no particular rapport with the child care workers but that he did occasionally talk to one of the cooks, a Spanish-speaking Mexican-American woman who seemed fond of Mike. The decision was made to make the relationship with the cook the positive reinforcer.

Establishing the Reinforcer. Since Mike's relationship with the cook, Maria, was casual and tenuous at best, it was necessary to intensify it to give it effective reinforcing value. It was explained to Maria, through a translator, that she seemed to play an important role in Mike's life at the Children's Home and that it would be helpful if she could become even more important to him. It was also explained that she would eventually be asked to help Mike with his principal difficulty, stealing. Maria was very willing and a plan was devised whereby she saw Mike daily. He was invited into the kitchen, prepared Mexican foods, and taken to Maria's home for visits. Maria mended his clothes, took him shopping and to church. In a few days, Mike apparently was looking forward to his visits and Maria, in turn, became especially fond of him.

The Contingency. Maria was told that it was possible she could help Mike with his stealing. It was explained that whenever Mike stole she would be informed and that as soon as possible she was to say to him in Spanish: "I'm sorry that you took *so-and-so's blank* because now I can't let you come home with me tonight." It was emphasized that she should say nothing else, should listen to no explanations or excuses but should turn and walk away. The following day she was to resume her usual warm relationship with Mike and maintain it until the next stealing incident.

Recording Behavior. The child care workers were told that whenever the property of another person, the school, or the home was found on Mike's person, in his locker, or in his room, and it was determined that the property had not been legitimately given to him, they were to (a) record a stealing incident on a daily chart and (b) when the time came, report the incident to Maria. Maria was instructed to keep a record of sessions she missed with Mike because of his stealing.

RESULTS

Once a week the charts were collected and transferred to the cumulative record shown in Figure 1. Each step up represents *one or more* stealing incidents for a given day. The period of observation covers approximately 5 months and 1 week. The 4 days around Christmas which Mike spent out of the home are not recorded since observation was impossible.

It was planned to allow 4 weeks for the relationship with Maria to develop. The child care workers were instructed to continue the recording they had begun in the training sessions during this time. They were told, also, to handle the stealing in whatever way they were accustomed.

The Baseline. The beginning of the record to *b* constitutes the baseline recording. At *a* Mike began his visits with Maria and the

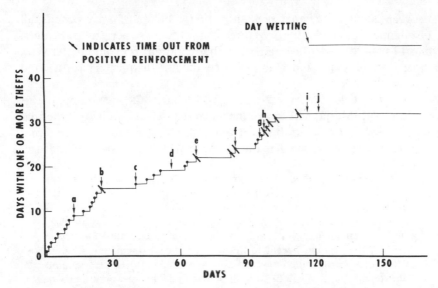

FIGURE 1. A cumulative record showing the effects of withdrawal of a positive reinforcer on the stealing behavior of a ten-year-old boy. The upper right line indicates the absence of day wetting as a substitute "acting-out" behavior.

supervisor of the child care staff began to keep daily records of the interactions between Mike and Maria as well as others. Some quotations from these records will clarify the nature of the relationship between Mike and Maria.

11/10 Began daily hour with Maria — very pleased.
11/11 Went for five hours (in the) afternoon — brought me some homemade tortilla from Maria's.
11/12 Clothes shopping with Maria. Pleased and made certain I marked (them) properly in big letters, happy Maria bought him shirts and took home and shortened sleeves before return — impressed on me what a good mother Maria is. I agreed.
11/13 Related he is teaching Maria English — he really likes to go with her because she has tortillas every day. Liked warm jacket Maria gave him. It was her boy's that he outgrew.

Although there was a reduction in stealing behavior immediately following the beginning of the visits with Maria, the rate soon returned to its original level. Since the record only indicates *one or more* stealing incidents per day, it does not accurately reflect the amount of stealing within days. The following lists the objects stolen in the five incidents between *a* and *b:* *(a)* a ten cent store ring, a ball, a pin, five pencils, all belonging to other children; *(b)* three rolls of toilet paper, three sweaters, and 12 pairs of socks belonging to other children; *(c)* some underwear, three bars of soap, and a model airplane; *(d)* a quarter; *(e)* a child care worker's keys.

The First Contingency. At *b*, 12 days after the beginning of his sessions with Maria, Mike gave the supervisor such a difficult time that she decided to deny him his visit with Maria even though it was premature according to the general program. Her notes are explanatory:

> I left linen closet door open in process of getting towels to boys who went to shower without. Next thing I knew, Mike was having a tooth paste-squirting game all over the room. (He said) he took from closet — I had him clean up. After shower, rash of bandaids appeared all over. Mike admitted taking at same time as tooth paste. Said didn't have p.j.'s. At this point, I went to drawer and pulled (them) out wherein I found a pearl-handled pocket knife which belonged to George, and Playboy magazine. Said he took these from (child care worker's) room when I went into relief room to answer telephone. I recognized with him I was very tired and really should know better than to ever leave a door open... told him I considered this deliberate stealing four times within a half hour and I would tell Maria and he would not go with her Monday.

Since this occurred late one evening, Maria was not informed until the next day nearly 20 hours after the behavior. Hence, the first contingency was hardly contingent, though the supervisor's threat certainly was.

The next day at dinner time Mike went into the kitchen as usual. He was followed by several child care workers who were anxious to see what would happen. They reported that Maria looked "stern" as she spoke to Mike in Spanish. Mike, however, remained in the kitchen and seemed so unaffected that one of the child care workers urged Maria to tell Mike again. Accordingly, Maria repeated the routine, turned and went about her work in the kitchen. Mike wandered into a nearby sitting room where he had been allowed to wait. About 5 minutes later, a child care worker told him he would have to return to his cottage. He was described as "pouty" the rest of the evening and throughout the next day. In the evening, he met Maria in the kitchen as usual. For the next 13 days, no stealing was reported. It was apparently the longest he had gone without stealing at the home.

Removal of the Contingency. A new problem arose in the period represented by the interval *c* to *e* in Figure 1. Mike began to appear with assorted articles which seemed so minor to the child care staff that they were not reported to Maria. Some matches which he said he found, some cookies which "a nice lady had given him," a little Christmas tree from the infirmary all seemed too innocent to report. The child care staff offered two reasons for feeling lenient: (*a*) Mike already seemed better; (*b*) It was so close to Christmas that they hated to deny him his visit. *d* marks Christmas, and it can be seen that, like most children, Mike was especially good the few days on either side of this date.

The Second Contingency. At *e* several articles belonging to other children were found in Mike's locker and he was denied his visit. This was followed by 10 days of nonstealing. At *f*, the supervisor, disturbed at the increasing rate in the previous days in spite of the contingency, urged the child care staff to continue reporting and showed Mike the charts they were keeping, explaining how stealing eliminated his visit for that day.

At *g* the author was called in to consult. Mike had taken his roommate's jacket on one day and his hair brush, the next. The child care workers were concerned about reporting these incidents since it was not uncommon behavior in the home and they did not wish to penalize Mike unfairly. The author discovered at this time that the staff had recently changed, and there were some child care workers who knew little about the program. The next day, Mike stole a pass key, a serious offense, but was not reported. At *h* the final meeting with the child care staff was held at which it was stressed that the contingency must be used consistently and that the recent alternation might make Maria less effective. It was agreed to report the possession of anything not belonging to him. Although this seemed unfair in view of the borrowing behavior of the other children, it was felt that Mike had more to gain by nonborrowing. Beginning at *h* he was denied Maria for possessing someone's clothing and for the two subsequent incidents involving his roommate's hairbrush and some pictures from the school bulletin board. The last incident involved some toys belonging to another child at the home. Although he promised to return them and not "steal again," Maria was denied.

Nonstealing Behavior. In the consulting sessions, stress had been laid on the positive reinforcement of appropriate alternative behaviors. The staff was urged to praise and otherwise reinforce all of Mike's socially appropriate behavior. This proved difficult for nonstealing, however, and the only solution seemed to be to reinforce at certain intervals as long as he did not steal. The problem was resolved on "bank day" when the children bank part of the money they have earned for chores or otherwise accumulated. At *i* instead of banking,

Mike divided his money between two boys, stating that it was to replace some articles he had previously taken and lost and announced that he was "not stealing anymore." It was the first instance of denotable "nonstealing" behavior and was heavily reinforced by the supervisor and child care staff with praise throughout the day.

At *j* a similar incident occurred. Mike took a text book he owned to the public school where the teacher questioned him about it. Mike stated that he had not stolen it but bought it. The teacher, aware of the efforts to help him, verified the story, took Mike to the principal and explained the incident. The principal praised Mike for not stealing and being honest and gave him a set of bird pictures for being a "good boy." The display of these brought praise from the child care staff.

Periodically over the last recorded month, Mike reminded the staff that he had not stolen or lied. Toward the middle of the last recorded month, he asked the child care supervisor to tell Maria he was going to the carnival with the other boys and would not be able to visit with her. His times with Maria have since dropped to two to three times a week. Anecdotal evidence indicates that his relationships with peers have been improving.

Pants Wetting. At a staffing shortly after it became apparent that Mike had improved, it was suggested that he might have begun to wet his pants. A child care worker thought he detected dampness. Many staff members agreed that pants wetting might be a substitute acting-out behavior to replace the stealing. Recording was begun to determine the increase. As Figure 1 shows, there have been no wet pants since the date of the first record.

><

DISCUSSION

If, as suggested, the professional individual is to spend increasing amounts of time instructing others in the application of behavior principles, effective methods of consultation must first be developed. Most often, the individual who is to mediate the change in behavior is unsophisticated in behavioral techniques. In some cases (Boardman, 1962; Wolf, 1965), the "mediator" is simply given a set of specific instructions by the consultant who maintains frequent contact, often by phone, to insure that the instructions are carried out. This can be effective when the number of mediators involved is small (e.g., parents), but is inefficient if the number of individuals involved is large as in the study above, which involved 16 people. It seemed desirable in this case to give the group enough of a foundation in behavior techniques to allow it to function at least semiautonomously. For this reason, the brief training session was instituted.

The training presented several difficulties. The time available and the educational backgrounds of most of the individuals prohibited anything but a rather superficial review of behavior principles. As such, the principles sounded deceptively simple and commonsensical and the systematic characteristic of the techniques tended to be missed. It was difficult, for example, for the child care workers to understand the necessity of reinforcing immediately and consistently. Reinforcement was anything but systematic at the beginning of the program. The study points up the need for long-range staff-improvement programs in behavior principles and techniques if these are to be applied at the institutional level. The development of these can be an important part of the consultant's role.

The training of mediators in the observation and recording of behavior is essential. Accurate records can detect changes in behavior which otherwise might be missed and provide daily feedback on program effectiveness. The use of behavior records presented difficulties for the staff in this study, initially. First of all, record keeping disrupted ongoing routines and was viewed as bothersome. Further, some tended to regard them as a "criminal record" and were hesitant to report stealing incidents for fear of getting Mike into trouble. Eventually, however, the record came to be the principal source of reinforcement to the child care workers since it provided feedback on their effectiveness. Thus, training mediators in record keeping not only provides the consultant necessary information but also provides a source of reinforcement for the mediator himself. The consultant can make his praise contingent on a good record or approximations to it.

Maintaining a systematic program involving several people is made considerably easier if the consultant can find an individual to act as coordinator. For example, in this case the supervisor of the child care workers was invaluable. It is particularly important to be advised of important changes in the environment, illnesses, changes in personnel, and the like. Also, a coordinator can do much toward insuring that records are kept and the contingencies applied. This relieves the consultant from a great deal of "legwork."

If the behavior is to be modified by reinforcement contingencies, the choice of the reinforcer is crucial. The consultant must evaluate the availability of effective reinforcers in the environment and his ability to make them contingent on specific behavior. In situations where the target behavior is maintained by recognizable and controllable reinforcers, extinction coupled with reinforcement of alternate behavior is probably most desirable, as Bandura (1962) suggests. Punishment of the behavior tends to be used more when the consequences maintaining the behaviors are unknown or uncontrollable. Punishment, however, is not only not permissible in many settings but also has several undesirable side effects (Bandura, 1962). Removal of a positive reinforcer, as in this study, is usually not so aversive, often more natural, and within the permissible range. It can also be used when the maintaining consequences are unknown. In all cases special care should be taken to encourage mediators to reinforce desirable alternate behaviors.

The use of relationships as a source of reinforcement has long been a part of behavior modification. "Building rapport" is one way of establishing a reinforcer, as in this study. The consultant should be on the lookout for naturally existing reinforcers in the environment of the target individual. Maria, the reinforcer used in this example, was a "natural." She required no training in how to become reinforcing to Mike. Her usual warmth and interest were entirely sufficient and the training of Maria, upon whom the success of the program rested, took no more than 20 minutes. The important factor was to make the relationship contingent on Mike's nonstealing. Just providing Mike with a warm mother figure, as suggested in his earlier therapy, was not sufficient. Even though his stealing rate dropped immediately after he began his visits with Maria, it quickly rose again. As a mother of a hospitalized patient known to the author recently remarked, "It's not just loving; it's what you love them for."

It is probably desirable to keep generalizability in mind when selecting reinforcers. Mike's nonstealing behavior appears to be coming under the control of the child care worker and peer relationships which may be effective enough to maintain it. Whether or not his nonstealing can be maintained outside of the Children's Home is questionable. However, it can be now stated with some degree of assurance that Mike's stealing is sensitive to its consequences and at least one effective consequence can be specified. Such information should prove useful when future placement is considered for Mike, so that, whatever environment is eventually selected, socially appropriate behaviors leading toward a more rewarding life for Mike can be developed and maintained.

Finally, it should be pointed out that the successful application of behavioral techniques to the modification of deviant behavior probably depends on several conditions not specified by principles of reinforcement. For example, in the middle of this study Mike was shown the charts and informed of how his stealing eliminated a visit with Maria for the day. Although this event was not dictated by reinforcement principles, it very well might have influenced the effectiveness of the contingency. James and Rotter (1958), in fact, have demonstrated that the reinforcing value of a stimulus may be a function of whether or not the subject perceives the reinforcement to depend on his own behavior (skill) or the whims of the environment (chance). Likewise, contingencies imposed in a natural setting tend to generate several changes in the articulation of an individual and his environment well beyond the scope defined by the target behavior. The nature of these changes and their contribution to the outcome are seldom described or evaluated in most studies of environmental manipulation. Thus, though the technique of intervention may be the establishment of a particular reinforcement contingency, several other factors must be considered if the success of the technique is to be evaluated. So far, these additional conditions have been "played by ear" or handled through "clinical intuition." The James and Rotter study and others (Phares, 1957, 1962; Rotter, Liverant, and Crowne, 1961) indicate that conditions which augment or limit the effectiveness of environmental manipulation can be specified and suggest that behavioral principles can be extended eventually into a technology of intervention.

25

Comments on Wetzel's Treatment of a Case of Compulsive Stealing

James A. Dinsmoor

Many of us who study infrahuman behavior in a laboratory setting justify our efforts by assuming that we can develop a systematic body of knowledge that will eventually be useful in the rearing of children, formal education, mental hygiene, clinical diagnosis and treatment, and the broader reaches of social psychology in general. The biological sciences seem to offer a promising analogue, in which the results of laboratory investigations with animal subjects are first checked in field studies and then applied to the clinical practice of medicine. It is only within the last few years, however, that serious attempts have been made to bridge the gulf between the psychological laboratory and the clinical setting. Laboratory investigations have gradually been extended from infrahuman to human subjects, from normal individuals to those classified as deviant, and from such index responses as bar pressing and key pecking to socially significant forms of behavior. It has therefore been extremely gratifying to discover a corresponding stir of interest among our clinical colleagues in the possibility of using learning or conditioning principles in their work. In view of the degree of specialization that has developed in the training of psychologists, the task of combining the two types of skill amounts almost to an interdisciplinary undertaking. It is perhaps natural that laboratory investigators have slighted many of the subtleties and complexities of behavioral modifica-

From *Journal of Consulting Psychology*, 30:5 (1966), 378–380.

tion in a natural setting and that clinical investigators have miscon-
strued the theories and ignored the technical details of laboratory
investigation. These oversimplifications may be expected in pioneering
efforts, although one hopes that continued interaction will bring
greater sophistication to both groups.

In this respect, I view Wetzel's work as a step forward. What may
not be evident to clinical readers is the closeness with which Wetzel
has modeled his study on the single-organism, within-subject design
that has become traditional in recent years in "free operant" studies
of the behavior of rats, pigeons, and monkeys (Dinsmoor, 1966; Honig,
1966). It may be instructive to sketch in the main features of this design,
indicating some of the problems faced in a field investigation and how
Wetzel has handled them.

Although more than one subject is commonly used to replicate the
findings, the main comparison is not made between the performance
of two or more groups of subjects, but between the performance of the
same individual during two or more periods in time. This eliminates
the contribution of individual differences to the comparison, although
it may at the same time raise new problems in dealing with sequence
effects.

The first step is to establish a baseline performance, as a basis of
comparison. For example, the animal may be maintained for a number
of sessions on a given schedule of reinforcement before the schedule
is changed, the level of food or water deprivation is altered, a stimulus
is introduced, or punishment is applied. If the subject behaves in the
same fashion, within narrow limits, for a long time, then behaves
differently when conditions are changed, neither random variation nor
environmental accident seems likely to account for the change in
performance. The evidence becomes even stronger if repeated changes
can be produced in the subject's behavior by repeatedly changing the
experimental conditions.

Wetzel attempts to establish a similar baseline, first, by showing
that the target behavior, compulsive stealing, has been occurring with
a substantial frequency for at least 5 years prior to the beginning of the
study. Wisely, he supplements these indirect data with a period of
direct, quantitative observation. His Figure 1 is plotted in a form
similar to that produced by the automatic recorders commonly used in
operant conditioning laboratories. (The range and sensitivity of this
record could have been increased by following the model even more
closely, plotting the number — rather than merely the presence or
absence — of stealing episodes on each day.) Note that the baseline
frequency is obtained for another 12 days after the visits with Maria

have begun (Points *a* to *b* in the record), in order to rule out the possibility that this factor in itself might have produced a change in the frequency of stealing. The relatively low incidence of stealing from Point *b* to Point *i* suggests that the experimental contingency has been effective, although staff errors in the administration of the procedure make it difficult to evaluate the completeness of this effect. At Point *i* a new contingency, positive reinforcement of behavior viewed as antagonistic to stealing, is introduced. Since very little time has elapsed since the last denial of a visit to Maria, it is difficult to evaluate the contribution of this added variable to the elimination of further stealing. But the long horizontal segment of the record covering the last month and a half of the study indicates that a substantial and persistent change has occurred in the subject's performance.

There are several comments I should like to offer. First, as Wetzel points out, failures by the child care staff to conform to the technical requirements of the program have vitiated to a degree the experimental analysis of the subject's behavior, even though a good deal seems to have been accomplished from a practical point of view. It may be profitable to stress the distinction between using nonprofessional personnel in the practical management of behavior, as advocated by Bandura (1962), and using them in a research study in which the adequacy of the behavioral technique is to be evaluated.

Secondly, it is not clear why Wetzel did not take more energetic steps to explore the possible effects of eliminating some of the natural consequences that may have served to maintain Mike's stealing. Mike's case worker suspected that he was "buying affections." A child care worker suggested that "Mike might derive some satisfaction from the attention his stealing brought." Much of this reinforcement appears to have been under the control of the child care staff, and its elimination might have been as effective as the chosen techniques of adding a new source of reinforcement that could be withdrawn whenever stealing occurred. An abortive attempt does seem to have been made at one point to eliminate some of these reinforcers, but it is not clear whether this attempt failed because the staff did not cooperate effectively in carrying out the procedure or because the procedure did not alter Mike's behavior. No data are offered comparable to those provided for evaluation of the withdrawal technique.

Another closely related question is whether Mike's treatment by the child care staff may not have changed as a result of their training in behavioral techniques and exposure to an illustration of their effectiveness, even though elimination of the natural consequences of stealing was not a part of the experimental program. It is obvious that the child care workers were interested in the program, since several of them followed Mike into the kitchen when the visit with Maria was first denied. Later, between Points c and e on the record, Wetzel notes that the staff ignored (i.e., failed to report) several minor incidents, in view of Mike's improvement and the proximity of Christmas. The tendency to excuse Mike's behavior suggests that less concern may have been felt or expressed, and hence less attention given, than previously. If so, this might have been a contributory factor to the improvement shown in the record. In a laboratory setting it is relatively easy to hold background factors constant while examining the changes produced in the subject's performance by a single experimental operation, but in a natural setting this becomes much more difficult.

The procedure that Wetzel has selected as the experimental operation is one that has recently been receiving considerable attention in laboratory studies. A stimulus during which the usual reinforcement cannot be obtained, sometimes known as an S^Δ or a time out, is made contingent on the subject's behavior. (For a review of the literature, see Leitenberg, 1965.) The contingency that Wetzel has employed, however, i.e., the manner in which the stimulus is related to the target response, differs in one important respect from the conventional laboratory procedure: it is not immediate. With the nonverbal organisms used in the laboratory, delays of more than a few seconds appear to render the contingency relatively ineffective. Indeed, this is to be expected, since other behavior is now more closely associated with the stimulus in time than is the target behavior. The fact that the target response determines when the stimulus is to be delivered is irrelevant. In Wetzel's procedure, a certain amount of time unavoidably elapses between the act of stealing and its detection; the incident is then recorded on the daily chart, but further time evidently elapses before it is reported to Maria; finally, application of the critical stimulus, Maria's denial of the customary visit, must await the next contact with Mike. In many cases, the delay between the act of stealing and the ensuing penalty must amount to several hours.

This suggests two things. First, although the remote contingency seems to have been effective in the present study, the gap may have been bridged by a process that is not available with lower organisms, that is, verbal mediation. In his discussion, Wetzel notes that the relationship between Mike's stealing and the elimination of his visit was explained to Mike "in the middle of this study," but it also seems to have been indicated fairly explicitly by the supervisor the first time the penalty was applied. Verbal mediation of such a contingency may be very difficult to analyze experimentally and to integrate into a systematic theoretical framework. In his analysis of verbal behavior, Skinner (1957, pp. 362 ff.) has attempted to deal with certain forms of instruction, but has not extended this treatment to mediation of the contingency between a response and its consequence. Nevertheless, the efficacy of this technique seems to be attested by the study that Wetzel cites (James and Rotter, 1958).

Secondly, although there is not a great deal of room for improvement in the present instance, an attempt to provide more immediate reinforcement might be indicated in future studies, particularly in cases where the subject may not be readily accessible to verbal techniques or fully capable of generating his own verbal mediation (e.g., autistic children, mental defectives, or psychotic adults).

Finally, I should like to comment on possible ramifications of the experimental treatment. So far as I am aware, there is nothing in conditioning theory that precludes the possibility of symptom substitution. The suggestion that behavioral disorders may develop on the basis of learning principles does not imply that these disorders must necessarily and uniformly be simple in genesis or that no interactions may occur among a variety of symptoms. Such processes as interference between competing responses and the chaining of successive stimuli and responses are quite familiar to the laboratory investigator. I therefore concur with Wetzel's judgment in checking out the possibility of increasing pants wetting, even though no such activity was actually recorded during the period of observation. Correspondingly, I should like to suggest that even a partial and temporary suppression of Mike's stealing by means of the experimental contingency may well have produced broader and more permanent effects in a natural social environment. Removal of this barrier to Mike's acceptance by other children, his teachers, and the child care workers may well have opened up other avenues to attention and affection. That is, the way may have been cleared for the acquisition of various forms of behavior that would be incompatible with stealing and would block its subsequent appearance.

26

The Use of Stimulus Satiation
in the Elimination
of Juvenile Fire-Setting Behavior

Ralph S. Welsh

As most clinicians soon discover, children unlike adults seldom come to the child guidance clinic through their own volition, and seldom do they come equipped with sufficient "intrinsic" motivation to participate willingly in a psychotherapeutic experience.

Many patients are brought to the therapist primarily to relieve the anxiety of the parent rather than that of the child. That is, most children are perceived to be behaving improperly by the parent, and the parent brings the child to the psychologist to effect an alteration in behavior so that the child will then behave normally whether he enjoys his particular mode of adjustment or not.

Such a child may be seen to be a good candidate for traditional psychotherapy, and may respond to treatment after rapport has been established, and a good working relationship has been formed between therapist and patient.

There is a class of behavior, however, that actually may be dangerous to the child and the entire family, and cannot be allowed the luxury of continuing for the next three to six months while the therapist establishes rapport and a good positive transference. Such is the case with the juvenile "firebug," and the early successful removal of the

Paper presented at the Eastern Psychological Association, Washington, D.C., April 1968.

fire-setting behavior obviously has priority regardless of the therapist's orientation. Because of its directness, speed in changing behavior, and lack of necessity for having a patient who is desirous of changing his behavior, stimulus satiation appears to hold considerable promise as a method for the efficient removal of juvenile fire-setting behavior.

Comparative psychologists have been aware of the phenomenon of stimulus satiation for a number of years. It is well known that given a free choice, animals prefer not to repeat responses they have just performed (Heathers, 1940; Riley and Shapiro, 1952). This has been attributed to a kind of fatigue. An early use of stimulus satiation as a psychotherapeutic technique was reported by Dunlap (1930), who called his procedure negative practice. The patient practices an unwanted response (tics, nail-biting, etc.) until it becomes aversive.

Malleson (1959) discusses a technique requiring the patient to visualize feared outcomes until fatigue and boredom develop. Ayllon (1963), on the other hand, was able successfully to eliminate towel hoarding behavior in a patient (a hospitalized schizophrenic female) who was an unwilling participant in the therapeutic process by satiating the patient with so many towels they overflowed her room. One of Ayllon's more difficult tasks was to convince the psychiatrically trained nurses that the technique had some validity. Contrary to their expectations, the symptoms had not returned one year later.

The following case histories, although admittedly anecdoted, report the author's experience with stimulus satiation in the removal of fire-setting symptoms in two children, both seven-year-old males of average intelligence.

><

CASE ONE

The patient was a seven-year-old Caucasian male referred to the out-patient clinic of a midwestern state hospital where the author was then working, for repeated incidents of deliberate fire-setting in addition to other discipline problems in the home, and poor school performance. The most salient finding from the clinical evaluation was the patient's utter fascination with and rapt attention to a lighted match.

The patient was placed in traditional play therapy for six sessions. The parents were seen collaterally each time by a staff social worker. The fire-setting symptoms persisted over this time span. With some misgivings of the clinical director, the therapist was allowed to introduce matches into the therapy hour. Twenty boxes of small wooden matches were obtained. Upon entry into the playroom for the first satiation session, the patient was told that he would be learning how to light matches properly.

Four rules for "learning how to light matches" were put into operation:

1. The match must be held over the ashtray at all times.
2. After taking the match out of the box the cover must be closed before striking.
3. Only one match at a time can be lit.
4. The burning match must be held until its heat is felt on the fingertips, then it must be blown out.

The patient happily began lighting the matches, going through one-and-one-half boxes in forty minutes; some discomfort was shown toward the end of the session.

At the beginning of the second satiation session the patient willingly went right to the matches and began lighting them, but soon became restless and asked to do something else. He was requested to light a few more matches, then was allowed to play with the toys.

At the beginning of the third satiation session the patient was told that he would be practicing with the matches again. He protested, asking to play with the toys first. He had to be forced to sit at the table and light ten matches, then was allowed to finish the session playing with the toys. A conference with the social worker immediately following the session revealed that the parents were now allowing the patient to assist his father in burning trash because, according to the mother, "he no longer shoves sticks into the fire, and no longer has that look in his eyes when the trash burns."

Following the three stimulus satiation sessions, the traditional therapy approach was again followed for four additional months. Some slight improvement was noted in his behavior with his siblings at the termination of the six-month course of therapy, although his school performance showed little change. The fire-setting behavior had not returned.

CASE TWO

The patient was a seven-year-old male referred to the author for individual therapy. The mother initially reported that the child would obtain matches and "burn things." On one occasion he had set fire to his bed and the discovery was made, according to the mother, "just in the nick of time." In addition to the fire symptoms, the patient had a habit of voracious midnight eating, a fear of the dark, a refusal to obey maternal demands, a penchant for climbing telephone poles, and a tendency to lie.

An operant approach was adopted from the first session. The mother was seen briefly prior to each session to explain therapy and to answer her questions.

After the patient had walked into the playroom for the first therapy session, his face broke into a wide grin when told he would be lighting paper matches. Four rules were then specified, the patient being told the rules were to insure safety, although they were also designed to insure fatigue.

1. One match was to be removed from the book at one time, and the cover closed.

2. The lighted match had to be held over the ashtray at arm's length.

3. The extended arm could not be rested on the table or supported by the other arm.

4. Most of the match must burn before being blown out.

During the first three fifty-minute sessions the patient eagerly lit the matches with no apparent sign of losing interest. Attempts to interest him in other playroom activities were without avail. The mother continued to report that the patient was still attempting to obtain matches and play with fire at home.

The fourth session was then extended to one hour and forty minutes. With ten minutes remaining in the session, the patient asked to stop, and readily engaged in a vigorous game of cops and robbers with the therapist.

The following week the patient's mother reported a rather dramatic change in the patient's over-all behavior — even in areas unrelated to fire.

Three additional satiation sessions were needed before the patient finally said, "I'd rather not light the matches," and during these sessions he repeatedly broke the rules (made smoke trails, lit two matches at once, etc.).

The mother is still returning for counseling, and after six months the fire symptoms have not returned.

><

DISCUSSION

As was demonstrated in the experiment by Ayllon (1963), the effectiveness of satiation as a therapeutic technique seems to be related to the aversive properties of oversatiation. Toward the end of the match-striking sessions, primarily in case number two, an obvious increase in variability of behavior occurred despite the "rules" set forth at the beginning of each session. In addition to the sheer boredom engendered by the match-striking rules, fatigue factors resulting from holding the arm in the air also contributed to the aversive nature of the situation. Clearly the repetitious nature of the response and the importance of the fatigue and boredom factors indicate that this technique has more than a casual similarity to the negative practice technique developed by Dunlap more than a quarter of a century ago. A careful review of the two case histories will indicate that the technique differs from that of negative practice in two primary ways: (1) in the negative practice technique the patient is desirous of ridding himself of the behavior he is asked to practice, whereas the two stimulus satiation patients were not particularly dissatisfied with their behavior, and (2) strong emphasis was placed on positive reinforcement, making the playroom a highly desirable place if and when the patient decided to stop lighting matches, and once then allowed to do so.

The difference in the speed of satiation between the two patients is somewhat more difficult to explain than the reasons the technique appears to work. It was clear that the first patient satiated much more rapidly than the second. Although these differences could have been due to personality differences between patients, it must be admitted that the stimulus situations were also quite different. Since the first patient had spent a considerable amount of time in "treatment" prior to his stimulus satiation sessions, he had been given the opportunity to get to know the therapist better than did the second youngster. Thus the first patient was allowed to habituate to the stimulus situation prior to training whereas the second was not allowed the same privilege.

A more important factor was probably the patient's individual perceptions of the situation. Both patients seemed to be highly reinforced by the playroom situation, after lighting matches started to become aversive. Because of the first child's prior experience with the playroom, he knew he was not required to light matches to have a "relationship" with the therapist. The second child, on the other hand, began lighting matches from the very start, and it would appear that his ambivalence in giving up the matches for the toys was partly fear that he could no longer attend the sessions if he ceased the abberant behavior. The patient was not unaware of the fact that his fire-setting behavior had brought him to therapy. Cessation of this behavior could, logically, terminate therapy. In addition, the therapist had obviously been a powerful reinforcer in lighting matches, since he had encouraged the patient to light one match after the other during each session. Nevertheless, the symptoms were definitely more persistent in the second than in the first patient, as the second patient was still displaying an interest in fire after three satiation sessions.

The individual differences that may have been of some importance were the second child's higher intelligence, higher energy level, difficulty the experimenter had in having him follow the match-lighting rules (he continually tried to switch from hand to hand, make smoke trails, light the matches under the table, etc.), and his longer list of accompanying symptoms. Of more importance, however, is the speed with which the stimulus satiation technique worked. The first child required three stimulus-satiation sessions to cause the symptoms to disappear at home, and the second required seven.

It is perhaps of passing interest to note that a number of other symptoms have also disappeared in the second patient incidental to the satiation sessions. This is in contrast to minimal changes in other behaviors seen following the treatment of the first patient. This would argue strongly against the common pronouncements of traditional therapists that behavior therapy techniques only treat one symptom at a time, and do not have any effect on the over-all personality. It is rather ironic that greater over-all change would be seen in the second patient than in the first child tested, since child # 1 had been receiving "traditional treatment" where child # 2 had not. In addition, child # 1's parents had been seen for an entire hour, while child # 2's mother had been seen for only five to ten minutes prior to each session.

In fairness to protagonists of traditional-insight psychotherapy, one cannot discount the importance of the therapist's relationship with both of these patients. While each patient was lighting the matches, the therapist was "right there," talking to the patient and relating to him. In addition, the parents of both patients received "help" in how to handle the problems outside the therapy situation. A question the traditionalist must still answer is: Would the dangerous fire-setting behavior have been eliminated so quickly utilizing a traditional approach, and does not one explain the change in behavior more easily by relating it to the stimulus conditions of the therapeutic situation?

I mentioned the technique under discussion to a dynamically oriented colleague. In the same vein as Ayllon — who reports that psychiatrically trained nurses usually have considerable difficulty accepting a behavior modification approach — my friend stated, "It's interesting, and I have several cases in treatment now that have continued to set fires despite half a year or more of therapy, but I'm not sure I could convince a mother that she should pay twenty-five dollars an hour while I sat with her son striking matches." Perhaps widespread use of certain behavior therapy techniques must await a change in the expectations of the general public as to what one should expect when one is in psychotherapy.

V

BEHAVIORAL APPROACHES TO SCHOOL AND MILD CONDUCT PROBLEMS

IN THE PAST, SCHOOL ADMINISTRATORS ASSUMED THAT THEY possessed neither the technical competence nor the social legitimacy to provide mental health services. Their traditional approach to behavior-problem children was to label them as "emotionally disturbed" and either exclude or refer them to other agencies such as child guidance clinics. In recent years it has increasingly been argued that schools, because of their critical and strategic social placement, must more readily assume responsibility for providing educational services for all children, including those with severe problem behavior. Accepting such responsibility, many school systems have moved not only to cooperate closely with traditional mental health agencies but also to develop their own pupil personnel services, with counselors, psychologists, psychometrists, and social workers.

Thus far most of the mental health work in schools has involved attempts to incorporate traditional psychodynamic, disease-entity concepts into the school structure, dealing with certain children as being "ill." Many writers, however, have criticized the mental illness model of behavior as being inapplicable to the school setting. They point out that educators now too readily ascribe children's otherwise unexplained learning disabilities and academic underachievement to "emotional disturbance." Such interpretation often led to public policies of exclusion or segregation of children, and a marked failure to deal directly with the realities of the problem behavior. They argue for a redefinition of concepts and tasks, embracing psycho-educational approaches based largely on psychological learning theory (including Graziano, 1969; Stiavelli and Shirley, 1968; Rhodes, 1967; Hewett, 1967; Harris, 1966; Reger, 1966; Quay et al., 1966; Trippe, 1963; Bower, 1962; Haring and Phillips, 1962; Bentzgen, 1962). These writers have offered alternative explanations which focus on the school environment itself rather than on internal psychopathology as the major agent of stress.

The extent of this conceptual shift from the disease-entity model to a learning model of maladaptive behavior is not clear. However, one major implication of such a change is of potentially great importance —as long as we accepted the illness model as valid, we continued to place primary responsibility on the quasi-medical agencies such as child guidance clinics. If the conceptual model shifts from *illness* to *behavior*, and from *treatment* to *teaching*, this obviously recasts the nature of our task with children, and argues for a corresponding change of responsibility and location of service away from the clinics and to the more relevant and real social settings of the schools where behavioral change rather than psychodynamic adjustment can be pursued. The schools themselves may then be able to deal with most of the behavior problems now relegated to clinics, and within the conceptual framework of the teaching task.

Part V focuses on maladaptive behaviors that are not part of the larger behavior patterns usually classed as "mental retardation" or "childhood psychoses." The articles deal with children who behave at least well enough to have been enrolled in some academic or school setting, whether public or private, with the expectations that they would achieve both academic and social progress. None of the children discussed here exhibited the massive and pervasive deficit and surplus behavior described earlier. In fact, the articles by Brison, Hart et al., and Esposito, bring our view increasingly within normal behavioral limits. In Esposito's brief note, for example, the behavior dealt with is completely within normal limits for children. Behavior modification concepts and techniques, then, are not limited to therapy with disturbed children, but are equally applicable as a framework for efficient teaching of "normal" children in "normal" settings.

Articles are presented in which problems commonly encountered by educators are approached from a behavioral point of view. In all but one paper (DeLeon and Mandell) direct intervention in the school setting is utilized to bring about behavior modification.

Brison addresses himself to school psychologists who are often the first mental health professionals to examine a child who exhibits behavior problems in school. School psychologists tend to utilize a psychopathology framework and often refer children to psychiatric clinics for psychotherapy. Brison argues that the school psychologist can achieve a great deal through behavioral analyses and manipulation of the significant contingencies in the school environment of the child.

Most of the studies presented thus far were based on the concepts of operant learning, while the study by Graziano and Kean and the study by Browning employed a respondent paradigm and, more specifically, the use of reciprocal inhibition. Davison utilized the reciprocal inhibition concept as a post hoc explanation of some of his results. The combined use of operant and respondent approaches is discussed in this section by Lazarus, Davison, and Polefka in their approach to modifying a school phobia. The authors suggest that neurotic avoidance behavior might be based on high anxiety, perpetuated by operant contingencies, or both. In the former situation classical counterconditioning techniques may be useful, whereas operant approaches appear most useful in the latter situation. In this case of school phobia, the authors' analysis led them to conclude that the child's refusal to attend school was due to both intense fear (respondent level) of the school situation and the secondary reinforcers, primarily adult attention, contingent upon his phobic behavior (operant level). They thus employed both counterconditioning and operant reinforcement contingencies to bring the phobic behavior under control. With regard to school phobias, Levine and Graziano (in press) noted in their review of the literature that school phobia appears to be readily modifiable through a variety of interventive methods, but that whatever the method almost all contemporary writers agree that some significant adult must firmly insist on the child's return to school.

De Leon and Mandell discuss the modification of a discrete and common maladaptive behavior in children — functional enuresis. They compared the results of conditioning procedures using an electronic alarm device, with a combination of child psychotherapy and parent counseling, and found the alarm device to be far more effective than psychotherapy plus counseling.

Patterson and Brodsky discuss their behavior modification program with a kindergarten boy whose behavior seriously disrupted the conduct of the class. The authors point out that while most reports of behavior modification approaches to children deal with single behavior problems, the children who are referred to clinics actually present multiple behavior problems. Thus Patterson and Brodsky attempted to deal with a larger and more complex segment of maladaptive behavior than do most studies.

Patterson, Jones, Whittier, and Wright describe their behavioral approaches to the control of a hyperactive, brain-injured child in a hospital school setting. Such hyperactivity in school situations is a common and disruptive occurrence, and the suggestions made by these authors seem to have relevance for any similar situations in school.

In the final two chapters in this section, we move into the nursery school. Hart, Allen, Buell, Harris, and Wolf describe two four-year-old boys who seem to be unassailably "normal" and free from "psychopathology." These children, however, despite their good all-around development, engaged in much operant crying which was, according to the authors' analysis, reinforced by the attention of parents and teachers. The authors then initiated extinction procedures, i.e., withholding the reinforcers for crying, and succeeded in bringing the excessive crying under control.

Esposito's paper is a brief and more informal note on the use of token reinforcement to develop group singing participation in four-year-old nursery school children. Here, as in the previous article, reinforcement procedures are applied not as therapy for disturbed behavior but as educational strategies to help the children. Certainly the use of token reinforcement as described by Esposito was carried out in as "warm," "natural," and "human" a situation as can be found, clearly indicating that objective approaches by staff are in no way incompatible with the expressed enjoyment of the children.

⊁ 27 ⊱

A Nontalking Child
in Kindergarten

David W. Brison

The case to be described in this article illustrates many of the points of difference between the behavioral school and more traditional therapies. In particular, the issue of the medical-disease model versus the learning theory model of psychopathology is clearly visible, especially as it relates to the problem of symptom substitution. This contrast is possible because the author did not approach the case from the viewpoint of the behavioral therapist although the final treatment plan can, in an admittedly *post hoc* manner, be analyzed in these terms. The basic aim of the paper is to demonstrate that an *a priori* consideration of learning theory would have been advantageous in this case and in many of the problems that are referred to the school psychologist.

⊱

CASE STUDY

Tom was first referred by his teacher in March of his kindergarten year. The presenting problem was that he had not talked in school either to the teacher or to his peers. Although a complete diagnostic appraisal was not completed before the end of the school year, it was decided at a case conference to have him repeat kindergarten if he still was not talking at the end of the year.

From *Journal of School Psychology*, 4:4 (1966), 65–69.

Concentrated attention was not focused on the case until March of Tom's second year in kindergarten, although contact had been maintained by the school psychologist and speech consultant with the teacher and nurse teacher at the school. At this time, Tom still had not talked. The psychological examination consisted of several individual sessions with Tom, observations in the classroom, and conferences with his teacher and both parents. The district speech consultant was also involved in all phases of the examination. The school nurse teacher had given him an audiometric examination and found some evidence of a hearing loss.

Several salient features of the case were immediately apparent. Tom did talk at home—his parents provided a tape recording of his voice and his speech was at an average or above average developmental level with no evidence of being affected by a hearing loss. He lived in a relatively isolated rural area, and his parents tended to provide their own entertainment and did not have excessive contact with other people. Tom's speech problem was not just school connected. His mother reported that he talked very little around his grandparents. There was one house nearby with young children and Tom talked to them but not in the presence of their mother. The parents were middle class, intelligent, and Tom's father was successful in his own business.

In individual sessions with the school psychologist, Tom showed highly restricted behavior. His drawings from session to session were almost identical. He was, of course, nonverbal and although he came willingly to the room, he appeared very apprehensive. On the Peabody Picture Vocabulary Test, he scored at the 5th percentile.

Tom had the same teacher in his second year in kindergarten and she was understandably upset with what she considered her failure to get him to talk. She attempted to structure situations so that he would have to talk to her or to others but to no avail. Tom had participated willingly, even eagerly, in nonverbal activities, but as the teacher's efforts to get him to talk increased he became less cooperative. Finally when he was placed in a speaking situation, marked emotional behavior was observed. His neck muscles tensed, eyes teared, and one time he fled to the back of the room. For the first time, his parents reported that he no longer wanted to go to school.

During the parent conferences, the parents described enough of Tom's behavior to convince the psychologist that Tom was capable of functioning at an average or above average intellectual level—at least he was at home. They told of his reaction to certain situations, compared his development with his older brother's, and also related how he repeated songs and instructions which he had heard at school. The parents were extremely worried about his repeating kindergarten without any apparent progress.

The school psychologist visited Tom's home one evening and was talking to his father when Tom ran in from outside and excitedly began to tell his father something. As soon as he noticed the psychologist, he refused to continue.

Next Tom was referred to a pediatrician for a medical examination. The pediatrician reported that Tom was psychogenically deaf and noted that there was a deep-seated emotional problem.

The parents were referred by the school psychologist to the child guidance clinic and the report from the clinic can be briefly summarized. They felt he was of average intelligence, emotionally disturbed, lacked security away from home because he was not given the usual responsibilities at home. They recommended psychotherapy which would involve both mother and child. The psychiatrist said that Tom probably would begin to talk with or without treatment. His speech was only one symptom of an emotional problem and treatment was imperative even if he did begin to talk. However, treatment would have been delayed until the following fall. Tom's parents were not impressed with the opportunities available at the clinic and were highly resistant to entering treatment.

By this time it was late in the school year, and finally a definite educational plan for Tom was devised. It was decided to move him into the first grade for the last few weeks of school. The teacher was instructed to make no reference to his speech and not to create any demands for him to talk. Tom had by now learned to discriminate any stimulus that would signal speech and would react emotionally with the symptoms mentioned before. The teacher also talked with the children in her class and instructed them not to mention the fact that he didn't talk. (This, incidentally, was successful.) In addition, the teacher attempted to reinforce Tom's nonverbal communication with both attention and approval.

At the start of the next school year, the teacher continued this course of action. However, she gradually began to stop reinforcing nonverbal behavior to the point where she would not attend to him when he tugged at her skirt or raised his hand to show her a picture. The teacher was extremely skillful at establishing herself as a reinforcer, dropping out reinforcement, and also removing cues for Tom to talk including those from other children in the room. It was also decided that when he did talk she would attend and smile but create no special "fuss."

Within four weeks after school started, Tom began to talk. The teacher first heard reports from other children that he was talking on the bus and in the playground. His first speech in the room was a sort of off-stage whisper which was followed shortly by direct communication with the teacher. No further problems were reported during the year and his achievement was one of the best in the class. Follow-up three years after indicates that Tom is not viewed by teachers or peers as a special problem.

✦

DISCUSSION

Bandura and Walters (1963), Eysenck (1961), and Ullmann and Krasner (1965) have commented on differences between the medical-disease model and learning model in respect to both formulation of etiology and designation of treatment alternatives. Those who apply the medical analogy to behavioral disorders view symptoms as a manifestation of an underlying cause. Although the cause can be thought of as neurologic disfunction, it is usually conceptualized as a conflict of underlying forces seeking, but not being able to find, direct expression. In the learning model, the behavioral disorder (symptom) is explained on the basis of prior learning, and the explanation of prior learning is extrapolated from formal learning theories.

In treatment, diametrically opposed courses of action are often pursued. Following the medical analogy, the symptom is not directly attacked because alleviation of the symptom, although possible, does not treat the underlying cause and other symptoms will appear (symptom substitution). In contrast, the behavioral therapist views the symptom as learned behavior which can be altered by the systematic application of appropriate procedures derived from learning theory. In practice this usually, but not always, results in careful manipulation of environmental contingencies.

In the case of Tom, both the psychiatrist and the pediatrician were consistent in their application of the medical model. Tom's nontalking, the symptom, was an indirect expression of an underlying cause and treatment of the symptom did not assume first priority. In fact, there was very little attention given to Tom's behavior when he was placed in a speaking situation. The emotional response and the characteristics of the stimulus that elicited the response were not carefully outlined.

The final educational plan illustrates a behavioral approach, although it should be emphasized that the plan was arrived at intuitively and did not represent preconceived, systematic application of learning theory principles. However, the symptom was the primary concern, at least one that the school had to deal with, and symptom substitution was probably thought of as the best of two evils.

In Skinnerian terms, Tom's emotional response to speaking situations can be viewed as a conditioned response. Requests to talk and subsequently the mere presence of other adults were conditioned stimuli for this emotional response. Treatment consisted of the presentation of the eliciting stimulus (teacher) without subsequent reinforcement. In other words, his response to the teacher was extinguished. This analysis follows a classical conditioning paradigm. How requests for speech in the presence of adults initially developed into a conditioned stimulus for the respondent response is not of central concern to the behavioral therapist.

Establishing speech could not solely depend on the teacher's immediate reinforcement because any reference she made to Tom's talking would serve only to elicit again his respondent response. The very act of talking was probably intrinsically reinforcing and of course produced stimuli which were reinforcing. The teacher's systematic withdrawal of reinforcement created an environmental contingency (i.e., in order to obtain her approval and attention, he had to respond differently).

It probably would have been possible to speed up the process considerably if other techniques had been applied. The parents were not involved in treatment other than to have them refrain from mentioning his failure to talk when he was transferred to the other class. Quite possibly they could have systematically desensitized his emotional response by getting him to talk in a progressive series of situations leading to speech in the classroom. For instance they could have had Tom talk when other adults were present but not attending (i.e., in a grocery store). Then he could have practiced talking to his parents at home when a familiar adult was there. This could have led to the point of speaking with his parents in the classroom when no adults were around.

Another interesting possibility might have been for Tom to actually hear recordings of his own voice in the school room, first when he was alone in the room and then with others. His father had recording equipment and would have certainly participated.

In summary, Tom was maintained in a situation for almost two complete years where he experienced a minimal amount of reinforcement in relation to the potential reinforcement present. His kindergarten teacher, who was very conscientious, thought of herself as a failure and experienced a great deal of frustration. Tom's parents, especially his mother, were continually upset for a period of one-and-a-half years. His failure to talk produced responses on the part of parents, teacher, and peers that only intensified his problems. In short, the consequences of not treating the symptom were dire. It is not possible to review the data on symptom substitution in this article, but Ullman and Krasner (1965) have concluded that there is little evidence to support the theory.

School psychologists can no longer afford to ignore behavioral approaches to the treatment of school problems. However, it would appear that acceptance of the behavioral viewpoint would violate the theoretical biases of many school psychologists. The contrast between opposing views on such issues as the medical model, symptom substitution, role of underlying dynamic factors, questions of values, and role of awareness in behavior should be clearly delineated. Many of the questions posed will be answered empirically and perhaps a reconciliation achieved on some points.

⊱28⊰

Classical and Operant Factors in the Treatment of a School Phobia

Arnold A. Lazarus, Gerald C. Davison, & David A. Polefka

Although the formal application of "learning theory" to clinical problems is widespread, the literature on this topic reflects a basic cleavage. Wolpe (1958) and Eysenck (1960) typify the use of the classical conditioning paradigm in the treatment of neurotic disorders, while Lindsley and Skinner (1954), King, Merrell, Lovinger, and Denny (1957), and Ferster (1961) exemplify the use of operant conditioning in the treatment of psychotic behavior. On the assumption that both "operants" and "respondents" enter into all therapeutic processes, the writers hypothesized that the deliberate and strategic use of both classical and operant conditioning procedures would have greater therapeutic effect than exclusive reliance on techniques derived from either procedure alone. The therapeutic utility of this rationale became obvious in the treatment of a severely disturbed (nonpsychotic) school-phobic child.

Strategy in "behavior therapy" consists essentially of introducing reinforcement contingencies that encourage the emergence of non-deviant response patterns. This may be achieved by pairing the reinforcer with a *stimulus* (as is the case in classical conditioning) and/or by making the reinforcer contingent upon a *response* (as is the case in operant conditioning). Apart from Patterson's (1965) successful application of predominantly operant techniques to a school-phobic

From *Journal of Abnormal Psychology*, 70:3 (June 1965), 225–229.

301

child, the treatment of children's phobias by conditioning methods has hitherto relied almost exclusively on the classical paradigm (Bentler, 1962; Jones, 1924; Lazarus, 1960; Lazarus and Abramovitz, 1962; Lazarus and Rachman, 1957; Wolpe, 1958). It could be argued, however, that some of the above-named investigators made inadvertent use of the operant rubric. In a case alluded to by Lazarus and Abramovitz (1962) for instance, a child with "widespread areas of disturbance" failed to benefit from counterconditioning therapy but required "broader therapeutic handling." The therapeutic mainstay in this instance actually amounted to persuading the parents to alter certain of their actions which were sustaining their child's deviant responses (i.e., an operant strategy). The reapplication of counterconditioning techniques then effected a rapid recovery. The present paper is an endeavor to illustrate how the deliberate (rather than inadvertent) use of these two theoretical models at crucial phases throughout treatment proved therapeutically expeditious.

➤

CASE STUDY

History of the Problem

When he was referred for therapy Paul, age nine, had been absent from school for 3 weeks. The summer vacation had ended 6 weeks previously, and on entering the fourth grade, Paul avoided the classroom situation. He was often found hiding in the cloakroom, and subsequently began spending less time at school each day. Thereafter, neither threats, bribes, not punishments could induce him to re-enter school.

Paul's history revealed a series of similar episodes. During his first day of kindergarten he succeeded in climbing over an extremely high wall and fled home. His first-grade teacher considered him to be "disturbed." Serious difficulties regarding school attendance were first exhibited when Paul entered the second grade of a parochial school. It was alleged that the second-grade teacher who, according to Paul, "looked like a witch," generally intimidated the children and was very free with physical punishment. (Vehement complaints from many parents finally led to the dismissal of this teacher.) Paul retrospectively informed his parents that he felt as though "the devil was in the classroom." At this stage he became progressively more reluctant to enter the school and finally refused entirely. A psychiatrist was consulted and is reported to have advised the parents to use coercion, whereupon Paul was literally dragged screaming to school by a truant officer. Paul was especially bitter about his experience with the psychiatrist. "All we did was talk and then the truant officer came." In the third grade Paul was transferred to the neighborhood public school where he spent a trouble-free year at the hands of an exceedingly kind teacher.

Family History

Paul was the fourth of eight children, the first boy in a devout, orthodox Roman Catholic family. His sisters were aged fourteen, thirteen, eleven, seven, and six years, respectively; his two brothers were eight and two and one-half years old. The father was a moody, anxiously ambitious electronics engineer who had insight into the fact that his subjective occupational insecurities intruded into the home. A harsh disciplinarian — "I run a tight ship" — he impulsively meted out punishment for any act which deviated even slightly from his perfectionistic standards. He found it significant that Paul, of all the children, was particularly sensitive to his moods, and described himself as being "especially close to Paul" while commenting that "he rarely tells me things." In his desire to protect his family from everyday hazards he was inclined to emphasize extreme consequences: "Don't touch that fluorescent bulb, son; there's poison in it and it will kill you!"

The mother, although openly affectionate and less rigid and demanding than her husband, took pains to respond toward her eight children in an unbiased fashion. She stressed, however, that "Paul touches my nerve center," and stated that they frequently quarreled in the father's absence. She had always found Paul "less cuddlesome" than his siblings. When he was two years old, she would lock him out of the house, "so as to develop his independence." It is significant to note that this occurred immediately following the birth of his first brother. In general, she was inclined to be inconsistent when administering rewards and punishment. Psychometric testing suggested that Paul was uncertain whether a given response would meet with criticism and rejection or kind attention from his mother. It was nevertheless evident that Paul was eager to receive a greater share of his mother's highly-rationed time.

The lad himself was somewhat small and frail-looking. Although reticent, essentially aloof and somewhat withdrawn, he was capable of unexpected vigor and self-assertion when he chose to participate in sporting activities. From the outset, the therapists noted his labile and expressive reactions to all stressful stimuli. The extent of his subjective discomfort was easily gauged by clearly discernible responses. As the magnitude of anxiety increased, there was a concomitant progression of overt signs — increased reticence, a postural stoop, a general constriction of movement, tear-filled eyes, mild trembling, pronounced blanching, culminating in sobbing and immobility. As will be shown below, these emotional indices were crucial in selecting appropriate therapeutic strategies.

A series of specific traumatic events commenced with his near-drowning when five years old. Toward the end of his third grade, he underwent a serious appendectomy with critical complications, which was followed by painful postoperative experiences in a doctor's consulting room. During one of these examinations, as Paul bitterly recounted, he had been left alone by his parents. Shortly after his recovery from surgery, he witnessed a drowning which upset him considerably. Following his entry into the fourth grade, the sudden death of a twelve-year-old girl, who had been a close friend of his elder sister, profoundly affected the entire family. It is also noteworthy that Paul's father experienced personal stress in his work situation during the child's turbulent second grade, as well as immediately preceding fourth grade. Finally, Paul seemed to have been intimidated by a warning from his eldest sister that fourth grade school work was particularly difficult.

Therapeutic Procedure

After the initial interview, it was evident that Paul's school phobia was the most disruptive response pattern of a generally bewildered and intimidated child. Although subsequent interviews revealed the plethora of familial tensions, situational crises, and specific traumatic events outlined above, the initial therapeutic objective was to reinstate normal school attendance. Nevertheless it was clearly apparent that the home situation in general, and more particularly, specific examples of parental mishandling would ultimately require therapeutic intervention.

The application of numerous techniques in the consulting room (e.g., systematic desensitization*) was abandoned because of the child's inarticulateness and acquiescent response tendency. It was obvious that his verbal reports were aimed at eliciting approval rather than describ-

* Systematic desensitization entails the presentation of carefully graded situations, which are subjectively noxious, to the imagination of a deeply relaxed patient until the most personally distressing events no longer evoke any anxiety (see Wolpe, 1961).

ing his true feelings. Desensitization *in vivo* was therefore employed as the principal therapeutic strategy.

The school was situated two and one-half blocks away from the home. The routine was for Paul to leave for school at 8:30 A.M. in order to arrive by 8:40. The first recess was from 10:00–10:30; lunch break from 12:00–1:00; and classes ended at 3:30 P.M. At the time when therapy was initiated, the boy was extremely surly and dejected in the mornings (as reported by the parents), refused breakfast, rarely dressed himself, and became noticeably more fearful toward 8:30. Parental attempts at reassurance, coaxing, or coercion elicited only sobbing and further withdrawal.

Accordingly, the boy was exposed to the following increasingly difficult steps along the main dimensions of his school phobia:

1. On a Sunday afternoon, accompanied by the therapists, he walked from his house to the school. The therapists were able to allay Paul's anxiety by means of distraction and humor, so that his initial exposure was relatively pleasant.

2. On the next 2 days at 8:30 A.M., accompanied by one of the therapists, he walked from his house into the schoolyard. Again, Paul's feelings of anxiety were reduced by means of coaxing, encouragement, relaxation, and the use of "emotive imagery" (i.e., the deliberate picturing of subjectively pleasant images such as Christmas and a visit to Disneyland, while relating them to the school situation; see Lazarus and Abramovitz, 1962). Approximately 15 minutes were spent roaming around the school grounds, after which Paul returned home.

3. After school was over for the day, the therapist was able to persuade the boy to enter the classroom and sit down at his desk. Part of the normal school routine was then playfully enacted.

4. On the following three mornings, the therapist accompanied the boy into the classroom with the other children. They chatted with the teacher, and left immediately after the opening exercises.

5. A week after beginning this program, Paul spent the entire morning in class. The therapist sat in the classroom and smiled approvingly at Paul whenever he interacted with his classmates or the teacher. After eating his lunch he participated in an active ball game, and returned to his house with the therapist at 12:30. (Since parent-teacher conferences were held during that entire week, afternoon classes were discontinued.)

6. Two days later when Paul and the therapist arrived at school, the boy lined up with the other children and allowed the therapist to wait for him inside the classroom. This was the first time that Paul had not insisted on having the therapist in constant view.

7. Thereafter, the therapist sat in the school library adjoining the classroom.

8. It was then agreed that the therapist would leave at 2:30 P.M. while Paul remained for the last hour of school.

9. On the following day, Paul remained alone at school from 1:45 P.M. until 2:45 P.M. (Earlier that day, the therapist had unsuccessfully attempted to leave the boy alone from 10 until noon.)

10. Instead of fetching the boy at his home, the therapist arranged to meet him at the school gate at 8:30 A.M. Paul also agreed to remain alone at school from 10:45 A.M. until noon provided that the therapist return to eat lunch with him. At 1:45 P.M. the therapist left again with the promise that if the boy remained until school ended (3:30 P.M.) he would visit Paul that evening and play the guitar for him.

11. Occasional setbacks made it necessary to instruct the lad's mother not to allow the boy into the house during school hours. In addition, the teacher was asked to provide special jobs for the boy so as to increase his active participation and make school more attractive.

12. The family doctor was asked to prescribe a mild tranquilizer for the boy to take on awakening so as to reduce his anticipatory anxieties.

13. After meeting the boy in the mornings, the therapist gradually left him alone at school for progressively longer periods of time. After 6 days of this procedure, the therapist was able to leave at 10 A.M.

14. The boy was assured that the therapist would be in the faculty room until 10 A.M., if needed. Thus, he came to school knowing the therapist was present, but not actually seeing him.

15. With Paul's consent the therapist arrived at school shortly *after* the boy entered the classroom at 8:40 A.M.

16. School attendance independent of the therapist's presence was achieved by means of specific rewards (a comic book, and variously colored tokens which would eventually procure a baseball glove) contingent upon his entering school and remaining there alone. He was at liberty to telephone the therapist in the morning if he wanted him at school, in which event he would forfeit his rewards for that day.

17. Since the therapist's presence seemed to have at least as much reward value as the comic books and tokens, it was necessary to enlist the mother's cooperation to effect the therapist's final withdrawal. The over-all diminution of the boy's anxieties, together with general gains which had accrued to his home situation, made it therapeutically feasible for the mother to emphasize the fact that school attendance was compulsory, and that social agencies beyond the control of both therapists and parents would enforce this requirement eventually.

18. Approximately 3 weeks later, Paul had accumulated enough

tokens to procure his baseball glove. He then agreed with his parents that rewards of this kind were no longer necessary.

>=<

THEORETICAL IMPLICATIONS

It should not be inferred that Paul's improvement followed a smooth monotonic progression. Numerous setbacks of varying degrees of severity occurred throughout the entire treatment program, which extended over four and one-half months. These episodes were differentially handled depending upon the therapist's assessment of the child's anxiety at that time, and his judgment of the degree to which the boy had mastered the preceding therapeutic steps.

It became apparent that the school phobia was comprised of two separate factors: (a) avoidance behavior motivated by intense fear of the school situation, and (b) avoidance behavior maintained by various secondary reinforcers, mainly attention from parents, siblings, and therapists. During the initial phases of therapy, the boy's high level of anxiety dictated the use of reciprocal inhibition methods (Wolpe, 1958). The therapists actively inhibited the boy's anxiety elicited by various aspects of the school setting (as in Step 2 above). The later stages of therapy were characterized by a decrease in Paul's over-all anxiety without a concomitant decrease in avoidance behavior. After Step 15 the boy appeared to be minimally anxious. An operant strategy which made various rewards contingent on school attendance was therefore selected.

A Proposed Model

Although the division between classical and operant procedures became clearly discernible toward the terminal phases of treatment, many situations arose which necessitated the deliberate choice of one or other paradigm. A model was developed for determining when each was likely to prove maximally effective. On several occasions for instance, Paul left the classroom, entered the library and told the therapist, "I'm scared." At this point the choice of strategy became crucial. In strict operant terms, active attempts to reduce anxiety by means of attention and reassurance would reinforce classroom-leaving behavior. On the other hand, the classical paradigm would predict that to withhold immediate attention and make it contingent upon returning to the classroom would augment the child's anxiety and thus reinforce avoidance behavior. The critical factor in determining the appropriate procedure was the degree of anxiety as judged by the therapist.

An inappropriate use of the operant model could prove anti-therapeutic. If the level of anxiety is very high, a premature re-exposure to the feared situation will probably lead to increased sensitivity. Moreover, if this heightened level of anxiety leads to another escape response, the resultant anxiety-reduction will strengthen the avoidance responses (classroom-leaving behavior in this instance). It was also reasoned that when highly anxious, the boy would be unable to attend to the teacher, interact with his peers, or make any other responses which ordinarily reduced his anxiety.

An inappropriate use of the classical model would also impede therapeutic progress. The very acts of inducing relaxation, employing "emotive imagery," and giving reassurance may provide positive reinforcement for dependent behavior. The afore-mentioned difficulties in "phasing out" may be attributed to this possible side effect of in vivo desensitization. The gains which accrue when high levels of anxiety are thus decreased, however, temporarily outweigh the disadvantages of increased dependency.

DISCUSSION

It may be argued that a disproportionate amount of time and effort was expended in attaining the principal therapeutic objective, viz., normal school attendance. Urgent cases, however, who are neurotically incapacitated and unamenable to interview techniques, would seem to require therapeutic intervention beyond the confines of the consulting room. It should be emphasized that school phobia in a child is almost as pressing and disruptive a problem as occupational fears in an adult.

Since therapy *in vivo* makes heavy demands on the therapist's time, the senior author decided to enlist the assistance of two graduate students in clinical psychology (the co-authors). During the first exposure to school (see Step 1) Paul rapidly developed an attachment to one of the cotherapists (G.C.D.). As the application of reciprocal inhibition methods is conceivably facilitated by the nonspecific anxiety-inhibiting effects of a "good relationship" (Lazarus, 1961), this therapist carried out the first eight steps. Thereafter, the choice of therapist was partly determined by the academic and clinical commitments of the respective authors. Significantly, very little disturbance was occasioned by the constant change of therapists. There was often a distinct advantage in being able to alternate therapists; it was found, following a setback, that it was helpful to change therapists in order to offset the negative effects of being associated with sensitizing experiences.

The adjunctive use of a tranquilizer seemed to be of limited therapeutic value. Initially, it appeared to reduce the boy's anticipatory anxieties, but the absence of negative effects whenever it was forgotten, suggests that a placebo would have been as effective.

The therapists kept in close communication with the parents, who were encouraged to telephone whenever situational crises arose. As soon as normal school attendance had been more or less reinstated (Step 14), the therapists held a "family conference." In the main, the implications of the father's harsh and restrictive tendencies, along with the mother's inconsistent and ambivalent attitudes, were made clear to them. A long list of specific "do's" and "dont's" was drawn up and discussed. Apart from minor points of disagreement, the parents responded in an intelligent and receptive manner and subsequently implemented many of the recommendations.

According to the mother's reports, Paul's behavior also improved in areas outside of the school situation. She referred to his marked decrease in moodiness, his increased willingness to participate in household chores, more congenial relationships with his peers, and general gains in self-sufficiency.

Ten months after the termination of therapy, a follow-up inquiry revealed that Paul had not only maintained his gains, but had made further progress.

29

A Comparison of Conditioning and Psychotherapy in the Treatment of Functional Enuresis

George DeLeon & Wallace Mandell

Many treatments of functional enuresis have been devised, all of which seem to have considerable effectiveness (Kanner, 1948). Yet no controlled study comparing treatments has been undertaken. In fact, only one study (Kahane, 1955) contained an untreated control group, and results from this investigation raised doubts as to the efficacy of the training device approach to treatment.

One of the difficulties in interpreting the findings of different studies is the lack of comparability in the dependent variables used to measure treatment effects. This study compares the outcomes of two therapeutic techniques, a limited form of psychotherapy-counseling and a training device approach based upon conditioning principles.

><

METHOD

Subjects. Ss consisted of 87 children, of both sexes, ages five and one-half to fourteen, referred with the diagnosis of functional enuresis

From *Journal of Clinical Psychology,* 22:3 (July 1966), 326–330.

This research was supported in part by Grant MH12083–01 from the National Institute of Mental Health, U.S. Department of Health, Education and Welfare, Public Health Service.

310

to a community mental health center by social agencies, family physicians, and pediatricians. Each *S* had a physical examination and was cleared for any organic involvement related to enuresis.

Procedure. In an initial phone contact with the clinic, the mother was informed by a clinic staff member that a doctor's referral would be needed and a nightly record of bedwetting was to be kept for which the mother was sent a special record-form facilitating record taking. She was instructed not to reveal to the child that records were being kept in order not to alter aspects of the family and home situation, since such alteration might have affected the child's basic wetting pattern. Throughout the entire study, the manner of record taking was as follows: The mother was instructed to look in on the child and record on the special form incidents of bedwetting once before she went to sleep, once during the night (around 3:00 A.M.) and once when the family awakened in the morning. In an effort to insure that the data were reliably kept, a visiting nurse made weekly telephone calls to the mother and reviewed any data-keeping problems.

Approximately two weeks after the initial telephone contact, the mother was seen in a clinic visit, the purpose of which was to obtain, with questionnaires and interview, information as to the child's personality, general symptomatology, school adjustment, developmental history, and the parent's view of the child's bedwetting problem. The child and father were seen in separate interviews approximately two weeks after that of the mother. The father's interview paralleled that of the mother's, while for the child interview, questionnaire and standard tests were applied to obtain data as to personality, intelligence, mood and his own view toward his bedwetting problem.

The above procedure was the same for all children in the study. However, upon receiving the doctor's referral note and prior to the child's initial interview, he was assigned to 1 of 3 groups, conditioning, psychotherapy-counseling, or the control group. The groups were similar in age and sex characteristics. Thus, for the conditioning and psychotherapy groups, the median age was eight years six months with the male-to-female ratio being 3:1. For the control group, the median age was nine years three months, the male-to-female ratio being 2:1. The procedure for the three groups was as follows:

The conditioning group. Approximately 3 weeks after the clinic visit, the visiting nurse delivered and installed the alarm device and sleeping pad in the home and instructed both parents and child in its use. For the first three days, the child slept on the unconnected pad to determine whether there was an apparatus effect on the child's bedwetting (pad alone phase). On the fourth day, the mother turned on the

TABLE 1.   Summary of Treatment Results for the 3 Groups

Item	Conditioning N	Conditioning %	Psychotherapy N	Psychotherapy %	Control N	Control %
Group size	56	100	13	100	18	100
Refused	3	5.4	1	7.7	0	00
Spontaneous remission	2	3.6	1	7.7	0	00
Completed treatment	51	91.1	11	84.6	18	100
Failures	7	13.7	9	81.8	16	88.9
Cured (reached criterion)	44	86.3	2	18.2	2	11.1
Days to cure	54.5		103.5		84	
Mean	54.5		103.5		84	
Median	37		103.5		84	
Range	11–371		100–107		53–115	
Relapsed	35	79.6*	2	100	1	50
Days to relapse						
Mean	88.7		1.5		1	
Median	42		1.5			
Range	1–343		1–2			

* The average follow-up period was 30 weeks (the range 4–88 weeks) with 75% of the children followed for at least 6 months.

apparatus and it remained operative until a failure or the success criterion was reached.

The training device consisted of a box containing a 6-volt DC battery, a house buzzer and an on-off light. Connected in series with the buzzer was an $18 \times 30''$ rubber sleeping pad embossed with a grid of $\frac{1}{2}''$ metal stripping. One drop of urine closed the circuit and produced a loud buzz which could only be turned off manually.

Psychotherapy-counseling group. Approximately 3 weeks following the initial clinic visit, psychotherapy treatment commenced. A session consisted of 40 minutes with the child and 20 minutes of counseling with the mother alone. Each S was seen for 12 sessions on a once a week basis. Psychotherapy-counseling was carried out by a psychiatrist, psychologist, or in two cases by a psychology intern. The form of the therapy was unspecified and remains as a variable to be investigated.

Control group. Following the initial clinic visit, these Ss received no treatment but nightly data were obtained for 90 days.

Criterion for Success. For the conditioning group, success involved seven successive nights of no wetting on the operative pad, 3 successive nights of no wetting while sleeping on the unconnected pad, and 3 successive nights of no wetting with both the pad and device out of the room. After this 13-day period, the apparatus was removed from the home. For the psychotherapy and control groups, success was defined as 13 successive nights of no wetting. A failure in the conditioning group was the case in which *S* was in treatment at least 90 days without reaching the success criterion and for whom treatment was terminated at some point after the 90-day period. Thus, some subjects remained in treatment as much as six or twelve months before reaching the success criterion. A failure in the psychotherapy group was any case which did not reach the cure criterion after 12 sessions of therapy (about 90 days), while for the control group a failure was any case that did not reach the cure criterion within 90 days.

Cured children in the study were seen in at least one post-treatment follow-up to determine personality and enuresis changes. Only the data on the enuresis changes are reported here.

✄

RESULTS

The measure of enuresis in the study was defined as follows: Enuresis Ratio* (ER) $= \dfrac{\text{\# wets}}{\text{\# nights recorded}}$. The basic findings are shown in Table 1 which contains the main items of data across which the 3 groups can be compared.

The item (N refused) refers to the case in which, following the initial interview, the child failed to remain at least 90 days in the study, e.g., cases in which treatment was never initiated by the parents, the child refused to accept the box, refused to sleep on the pad, cancelled sessions in psychotherapy, etc. The third item (spontaneous remission) refers to the fact that following the initial clinic interview with the child, the *S* stopped wetting through the criterion period of 13 days before any treatment was initiated. The fourth item (N completed treatment) is self-evident. The fifth item (N failures) refers to children who should be distinguished from those who refused treatment, in that failures are those who completed *at least* 90 days in a treatment without reaching the success criterion. The item (N cured) refers to the number of children who completed treatment and who reached the 13-day success criterion.

---

* This ratio is superior to a simple frequency count. Since it is an average based upon only recorded observations, it overcomes problems arising from individual differences in record taking and from nightly data which are missing.

Cures. Table 1 shows that the percentage cured is 86.3, 18.2, and 11.1 for the conditioning, psychotherapy, and control groups, respectively. The "cure" difference between the conditioning and the other 2 groups is obviously significant ($Chi^2 > 10.83$, $P < .002$, 2 tailed).

The difference between the conditioning and the other two groups with respect to the median number of days to cure is also apparent. Although for the conditioning group, there is a clear difference in the mean and median number of days to cure, suggesting a skewed distribution with respect to this variable, the criterion was reached between 11 and 66 days in 83 % of the "cured" cases.

Relapse. There is considerable difficulty involved in both the specification and interpretation of the relapse phenomenon. Thus, if relapse is viewed as the occurrence of at least a single wet following treatment, then Table 1 shows that for the conditioning group, 79.6% of the children cured with the device relapsed. While most of the relapses (91 %) occurred between 1 and 28 weeks following the criterion, the severity of wetting at the time of the reported relapse was grossly different from that during the basal period. Based upon the two consecutive weeks in which the largest number of wets occurred following attainment of the "cure" criterion, the mean ER for the relapsed Ss was .54 while the mean ER in the basal period for these S was 1.03. The difference between these means was significant ($P < .01$, 2 tailed).*

The central issue related to the relapse phenomenon, of course, is that of its definition. In this regard, there are no studies which report, for example, even what constitutes a "normal" relapse. Thus, for children who undergo "normal social" bladder training, it is not known what the rate of "accidents" is over some post-training follow-up period. In view of this difficulty it is hazardous to make judgments as to the meaning of the amount of the relapses which occurred for the conditioning group in the present study.

Reconditioning. Eleven of the children who relapsed have thus far been reconditioned and of these 3 failed and 8 were cured a second time in a median number of 22.5 days. The difference between the number of days to the first and second cure was significant ($P = .03$, 1 tailed).

It may be concluded then that of the two treatments, the most effective in modifying enuresis was the training device, with both the psychotherapy and the control subjects showing no impressive changes in their wetting frequency. Although with the device, the time to achieve the "cure" criterion was relatively short (approximately one and one-half

---

* Unless otherwise indicated, the significance of differences within groups across phases was tested with the Wilcoxon matched pairs signed ranks test, while for group differences the Mann-Whitney U test was employed. The mean values in the tables are shown only to indicate central tendency.

months) and the relapse rates high, retraining to criterion was accomplished rapidly.

Figure 1 shows the mean ER values for the basal phase, for the period between the child's initial clinic visit and initiation of treatment (post basal phase), and the 12 weeks of the treatment phase. Since Ss who had reached the cure criterion obtained an enuresis ratio of 0, this value was included in the computation of the weekly mean shown in the figure in an attempt to keep the N constant for each week in the treatment period.

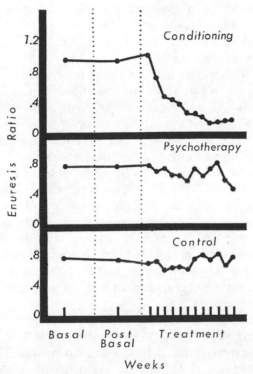

FIGURE 1. The enuresis ratio over 3 phases of the study. The values in the basal and post basal phases are data of several weeks combined while those plotted in the treatment phase are weekly means. Each mean is an average of subject ERs.

The 12-week curves for the psychotherapy and control groups are relatively unchanging while the curve for the conditioning groups falls rapidly within the first 3 or 4 weeks of treatment and, with time, approaches a low ER (0.1). This value did not reach 0 because, as has been noted, at the 12-week point some of the children had not reached the success criterion.

In the basal phase, the mean ER for the conditioning group (.94) was greater than that of the psychotherapy (.75), the control (.75), and the combined psychotherapy and control groups (.75). Only the difference between the conditioning and control groups was significant $(P = .02$, 2 tailed). While this difference reduced and was not significant in the post basal phase, the critical question involved in the basal phase difference asks whether a relationship existed between the outcome of treatment and the initial "severity" of the enuresis. In this regard, no significant correlation was found between the number of days to the success criterion and the magnitude of the ER in the cured children of the conditioning group (Spearman Rank correlation coefficient $r_s = .14$). Thus, though sampling error produced a somewhat different control group at the basal level, the effect of this error did not influence differential treatment outcome.

Not shown in Figure 1 is the fact that two significant changes in "severity" of enuresis occurred for the conditioning group in the post basal phase and in the pad alone phase. Firstly, there was a trend toward a decrease in the "severity" of enuresis following the initial clinic visit for most of the children in the conditioning group. Thus, of the Ss in this group who changed across the first two phases, 69% (29/42) showed a decrease in the ER from the basal to the post basal phases $(P = .04$, 2 tailed Sign Test). The trend suggests an "instructional" effect since the conditioning children were told in the initial interview that training with the device would begin within a few weeks. On the other hand, while the children in the control group were told that the device would be available to them at some unspecified future time, the psychotherapy children were given no such information and neither of these groups showed consistent basal to post basal changes in "severity" of enuresis.

Secondly, for the conditioning group there was a significant drop in the mean ER from basal (.94) to the pad alone phase (.69; $P = .04$, 2 tailed). It might be recalled that the latter phase consisted of the 3-night period during which the child slept on the pad with a nonoperative apparatus in the room. It is apparent then that the apparatus itself or in combination with instructions tended to reduce the severity of the enuresis.

DISCUSSION

An interesting feature of the conditioning curve is the rise in the ER seen in the first week of treatment. An hypothesis which asserts that the presence of the device initially effected an increase in the frequency of bedwetting is not consistent with the data which, in the pad alone phase, showed a decrease in wetting for the conditioning group. It is still possible that the introduction of the buzz itself could have altered the wetting pattern. However, it is more likely that the first week rise for the conditioning group was attributable to the device which reliably signaled the actual number of wetting occurrences.

Several points should be stressed with respect to the present data. For example, the form of the curve obtained with the device closely resembles familiar acquisition functions seen in the learning and conditioning literature. However, it cannot be unequivocally concluded that the obtained changes in the ER are simply conditioned effects since, among other things, no experimental control was employed to determine the specific effects of a *relationship* between the wetting response and the buzz stimulus. Such a control would consist of a group of enuretic children who received buzzes randomly and independently of a wetting response. Furthermore, aide from the possible instructional and general apparatus effects suggested in the present data, other factors cannot be ruled out. Thus, variables arising from, and mediated by, the increased parent-child interaction around the device could operate to modify the enuretic pattern.

Finally, firm conclusions concerning the efficacy of psychotherapy for functional enuresis cannot as yet be drawn from the present data. Such conclusions must await the exploration of other related parameters such as the form of the therapy, the number of therapeutic sessions, intersession time, and individual differences among therapists as to skill and experience.

✂

SUMMARY

This study compared a form of psychotherapy-counseling with a training device approach based upon conditioning principles, as treatments for functional nocturnal enuresis. The Ss were 87 male and female children ages $5\frac{1}{2}$ to 14 of whom 56 were assigned to conditioning, 13 to psychotherapy for 12 sessions, and 18 to an untreated control group which was followed for 90 days. The results showed that of the children who completed treatment, 44 of 51 (86.3%) were "cured" with the training device while 2 of 11 (18.2%) and 2 of 18 (11.1%) children were "cured" in the psychotherapy and control groups respectively. Although relapse rates were high in the conditioning group, the "severity" of enuresis in relapse was significantly lower than in the pre-treatment period and the retraining time was rapid relative to initial training.

30

Behavior Modification for a Child with Multiple Problem Behaviors

G. R. Patterson & G. Brodsky

Even now, in its infancy, the behavior modification movement has its full quota of prophets, critics and Don Quixotes (on both sides of the windmill). However, the present report is directed less to either crusaders or infidels, and more toward clinical psychologists who are in the process of deciding whether there may be something in behavior modification technology which is of practical value in changing the behavior of deviant children.

In considering this question, it seems to the present writers that there are at least three respects in which the behavior modification literature is deficient. The data which will be presented in this report are a modest attempt to rectify some of these deficiencies.

In general, the literature has been deficient in reports which present "*hard*" data, describing *successful* treatment of children who have *multiple* sets of problem behavior. All three deficiencies will have to be met before behavior modification technology can occupy a respectable position. These deficiencies are illustrated in sources such as the excellent review by Grossberg (1964) or the presentation of cases in the edited volume by Ullmann and Krasner (1965). In some of the studies the data collected were excellent, and describe dramatic changes, but the behavior studied represents only "mild" or single classes of deviance. Illustrations of such investigations are to be found in the classic study

From *Journal of Child Psychology and Psychiatry*, 7 (1966), 277–295, Pergamon Press. This project was financed by USPH grant MH 08009–03.

by Jones (1924a) on children's fears; Williams (1959) on tantrum behaviors; Harris et al. (1964) on crawling; and Jones' (1960) review of the literature on the treatment of enuresis. These studies perform the necessary function of establishing the *possibility* that principles from learning theories do have practical implications for the treatment of deviant children. The fact is, however, that most children referred to clinics have four or five problem behaviors. There have been attempts to deal with children displaying multiple problems or highly aversive behavior, but these attempts have been limited in several important respects. In some studies of this kind the investigators unfortunately have followed the clinical tradition and provided only general descriptions, by the therapist or parent, of behavior change. The reports by Lazarus and Abramovitz (1962) and Patterson (1965a) are examples of studies which do not provide adequate criterion data. Lacking these, it is not possible to evaluate the effectiveness of the treatment. In a movement that is less than ten years of age, it is perhaps to be expected that the earlier studies will show many defects. However, it is to be hoped that contemporary studies will not continue to make the same errors. It is of critical importance that we provide criterion data we can use to evaluate the effect of our efforts.

Another group of investigators provide an example of the second style of deficiency. This group has dealt with the behavior patterns of the extremely aversive child, and they have provided excellent data describing the effects of their treatment programs. However, these researchers have not as yet been *successful* in producing a remission of deviant behaviors in their subjects. This latter group of investigators have attempted to deal with "autistic" children; Ferster and DeMeyer (1961b), Wolf, Mees, and Risley (1964), Lovaas, Schaeffer, and Simons (1964), Bricker (1965), and Hingtgen, Sanders, and DeMeyer (1965). When compared to the results produced by traditional treatment programs, the efforts of the behavior modifiers are dramatic indeed. In spite of the fact that the data from these studies are of high quality and attest to significant changes in the behavior of these children, the primary patterns of deviant behavior persist for these subjects. If we hold to a rigorous definition of the term "successful" we cannot claim as an example the efforts of the behavior modifiers with autistic children.

The present report describes a set of conditioning programs for the treatment of a preschool boy who was referred for several behavior problems. The procedures are adaptations derived from the writings of Skinner (1953); in these procedures, both social and nonsocial reinforcers were used to shape the adaptive behaviors. The problem behaviors were "severe" in the sense that they were highly aversive to adults and to other children. In all respects he represented a typical case referred to child guidance clinics. In the study, an attempt was made to provide observation data showing the effect of the conditioning programs for each set of deviant behaviors. In an effort to maximize the generalization and persistence of treatment effects, most of the conditioning procedures were introduced in the schoolroom and the home. For the same reason, much of the effort was directed toward reprogramming the peer culture and the parents.

✄

METHODS

The Child

Karl was a five-year-old boy whose parents had been asked to remove him from kindergarten. From the parent's report, it seemed that Karl was characterized by a multitude of deviant behavior. For example, when separated from his mother, he became intensely aggressive, biting, kicking, throwing toys, screaming, and crying. The teacher's legs were a mass of black and blue marks; on several occasions he had tried to throttle her. The mother also reported sporadic enuresis. His speech pattern was immature, showing several minor articulation defects. There was a general negativism in his interaction with adults; for example, it was extremely difficult to get him to dress or feed himself. The mother thought he might be retarded, but his I.Q. tested at the end of the study was well within the normal range. The mother felt that the behavior pattern exhibited by Karl was so extreme and had persisted for such a period of time that it was extremely unlikely that he would change. As she said, Karl was very "strong headed." She was especially concerned about the behavior he exhibited when he was brought to school in the mornings. For example, on the previous week he had actually held on to her dress with his teeth in an effort to keep her at the school. At age two, Karl was hospitalized for a few days' diagnostic study for suspected leukemia. The results of the diagnostic studies were negative; however, following the hospitalization it was increasingly difficult to leave him with baby-sitters.

At the close of the first interview, the mother smiled ruefully and said that she did not think the program we outlined would help Karl. However, his behavior was so aversive to her that she agreed to participate in it.

His play interaction with other children was limited in frequency and rather primitive in quality. Much of the time he ignored the other children. When he did interact with them, there was an awkward and frequently aggressive quality to his behavior which led the teacher to be concerned about their safety. As a result, much of the time he was followed about the room by an adult.

When presenting a report of a single case in which multiple problems are evident, it is very difficult to provide an adequate means for specifying the conditions under which replication could occur. By keeping the description of the child somewhat vague, the present writers could always claim that unsuccessful replication attempts by other investigators were involved with subjects that were "really" not like the one described by the writer. For this reason some effort was made to provide a careful description of the child; a procedure for doing this has been outlined by Patterson (1964). Karl was observed during the occasion of his first visit to the clinic for the presence, or absence, of 149 behavioral items. These behavioral items, plus the report of the parent and teacher as to "symptoms," constituted the description of Karl.

The behavioral items and symptom list had been previously used with a sample of one hundred deviant boys to determine the factor structure which characterized this matrix. This analysis produced five oblique factors. The distribution of scores for each of the five factors had been transformed into deviation scores; and the distributions were normalized by the use of McCall's (1922) T score. The factor profile resulting from the combination of behavioral observation in Karl's first hour at the clinic, and the report by parents and teachers of his "symptoms," is shown in Figure 1.

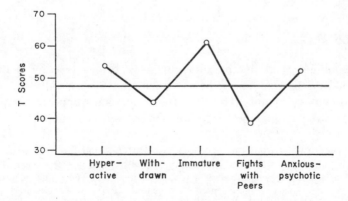

FIGURE 1. The profile of factor scores describing Karl.

To summarize the description, Karl would be characterized as high on the Immaturity factor, and moderately high on the Hyperactivity and Anxiety–Psychotic factors. This profile was very similar to the mean profile for a class of deviant children obtained by Patterson (1964).* The similarity of Karl's profile to that of the group indicated that he was a member of a class of patients that is often referred to clinics for treatment. As suggested earlier, these profile scores can serve as a basis of subject-comparison in attempts which might be made to replicate the present study.

The Parents

Karl's mother was an attractive woman, thirty years of age. She dressed appropriately and showed herself to be a reasonably well-organized housekeeper and mother. She had received an eleventh grade education. A cursory investigation of her background and behavior did not reveal any marked psychopathology; this was in keeping with her MMPI profile of —97.

Karl's father was a husky, assertive man, thirty-one years of age. He had received a tenth grade education. A semi-skilled laborer, he was away from home much of the time. It was our impression that there was no obvious psychopathology characterizing the father; this was also corroborated by his MMPI profile of 13′ 427 —09. Both the parents agreed in stating that the father had better control over Karl's behavior than did the mother. They believed that the improved control was due to Karl's fear of the physical punishment which the father used on occasion.

Formulation

A paradigm such as the one currently being used by behavior modifiers may generate statements which lead to successful outcomes of treatment programs. The fact that the data support statements about treatment outcomes does *not* necessarily lend support to other

---

* The mean factor scores for this group were: Hyperactive 53; Withdrawn 39.5; Immature 65.0; Fights with Peers 38.0; and Anxious-Psychotic 59.3. In the earlier study four out of a hundred deviant boys had profiles of this kind. This group of four boys were highly homogeneous as evidenced by Haggard's R (1958), coefficient of profile similarity, of 0.73. The intraclass correlation took into account variations in level, scatter, and ranking of profiles for the group.

statements, made from the same paradigm, which purport to "explain" the *antecedents* for the deviant behavior. These are two separate sets of statements, and each requires its own set of verification data. However, such tests will not be made until behavior modifiers explicate their "speculations" about probable antecedents for various classes of deviant behaviors. It is our intention to provide here a set of testable speculations about the antecedents for behaviors of the kind displayed by Karl.

After our initial observations in the school, we outlined the following formulation for the temper tantrum behaviors displayed at school.

Being left at school was a stimulus associated in the past with deprivation state.

This deprivation state, and cues associated with it, elicit an emotional state. This emotional state was labeled "separation anxiety."

The eliciting cues (*S*) and the anxiety state produce high amplitude behaviors which are reinforced in two ways. (1) These behaviors frequently terminate the presence of the aversive stimuli and (2) they are also maintained by positive social reinforcers.

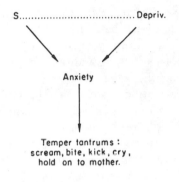

The key concept in this formulation was the use of a deprivation paradigm to explain the presence of anxiety in Karl. Such an approach is based upon the assumption that deprivation of social reinforcers creates an emotional state.* We assume that such deprivation must occur frequently in the lives of most children but that it is most likely to produce an intense emotional reaction in those children that we have labeled as "selective responders." Such a child has been conditioned to respond to social reinforcers dispensed by only a limited

---

* The existence of such a state, and the appropriateness of the label "anxiety" is attested to by a series of laboratory studies. A series of instrumental conditioning studies have shown that children who have been deprived of social contact for a time are more responsive to social reinforcers, Walters and Roy (1960), Walters and Karol (1960), Erickson (1962), Gewirtz and Baer (1958b). There are also data showing the relation between deprivation of social reinforcers and physiological measures of anxiety. Unpublished data from our own laboratories showed that social deprivation produced a significant increase in "anxiety" as measured by skin conductance. A group of fifteen first and second grade girls were isolated while they responded to the apparatus (without being reinforced). There was a significant increase in skin conductance from the first to the second half of the trial ($P = 0.03$ level).

number of social agents.* The main result of selective responding is that the absence of the mother (parents) signifies that social reinforcers are no longer forthcoming. Thus when left at school or with a baby-sitter, he is, in effect, placed in an immediate deprivation state. The stimuli associated with the onset of this deprivation constitute a set of eliciting stimuli for the emotional state which typically accompanies this kind of deprivation. This complex of eliciting stimuli. deprivation and accompanying emotional state are usually labeled as anxiety.†

It would seem to be the case that not all deprivations led to anxiety states for Karl. For example, he could play by himself in the yard for extensive periods of time. We assume that the stimuli associated with some deprivation states would be more aversive than others. For Karl, it seemed to be the case that he was most anxious in deprivation conditions that he could not terminate upon demand. For example, being left at school was a stimulus associated with long periods of social deprivation; in addition, he had no control over the length of time which he was to be deprived. His playing in the yard by himself was a deprivation state which he could terminate at any time by simply going into the house. In summary, it was postulated that there was a relationship between deprivation of social reinforcers and anxiety; a relation between selective responsiveness and anxiety; and a relation between control over the period of deprivation and level of anxiety.

Karl has learned to avoid the onset of this anxiety by throwing temper tantrums, kicking, biting, etc. This behavior was reinforced either when the mother remained at the kindergarten in an attempt to comfort her son; or when the teacher interacted with Karl and attempted to quiet him by holding him or reading to him, etc. Thus, Karl's behavior was being maintained both by the presentation of these positive rein-forcers and by the avoidance of the deprivation state. It is important

* Karl seemed to be a good example of the hypothesized relation between selective responding and deviant behavior outlined by Patterson and Fagot (1966). Their laboratory findings showed that some boys were responsive to social reinforcers dispensed by only one or two of the three major classes of social agents (mother, father, or peer). Such boys were more likely to be described as deviant when rated by teachers. In the present case we believe that Karl was responsive to social reinforcers dispensed by only a few people, e.g., his mother and his father. By and large, his behavior was not under the control of reinforcers dispensed by peers. Quite possibly this lack of control was due to the fact that Karl was raised in the country and had little opportunity to learn to be re-sponsive to peers.

† The data reported in the Patterson and Fagot publication offered some support for these speculations. Boys who were shown to be responsive to social reinforcers dispensed by mothers, fathers, and by peers were described by teachers as being the most anxiety-free. On the other hand, boys who were selectively responsive to only one or two of these agents were also rated as being more anxious.

in this respect to note that we assumed Karl to be responsive to the teacher. Observations of Karl suggested that this was so; it also seemed to be the case that the presence of other children in the room making demands upon the teacher created a situation in which Karl was being minimally deprived most of the time.

In planning a treatment program, it was assumed that the intense destructive behavior owed at least part of their amplitude to the presence of the emotion, anxiety. One of our behavior modification programs must then deal with anxiety. However, reducing the anxiety will *not* necessarily extinguish the destructive behaviors; it may, for example, only reduce their level of intensity. For this reason, a second major component of the treatment program involved the strengthening of socially adaptive behaviors which would compete with the occurrence of the behaviors associated with temper tantrums and other atavisms. Presumably relatively permanent elimination of deviant behaviors may best be achieved by programs that include the conditioning of socially adaptive behaviors which compete with their occurrence. This second point of focus involved the training of both the peer group and the parent to respond positively to socially adaptive behaviors displayed by Karl. In Karl's case, we suspected that the parents were using negative reinforcers to control his behavior and that there were few positive reinforcers dispensed by peers for socially adaptive behaviors. Most of the peer group seemed to find Karl's behavior quite aversive and avoided him as much as possible.

In addition to the temper tantrums, there was another class of deviant behavior which was of interest. The label used to characterize this second, broad class of responses was "negativism." Karl seemed to precede many of the dramatic temper displays, both at kindergarten and at the clinic, with a verbal warning. For example, he would state that he was going to kick the experimenter or the teacher. On many occasions he would refuse to comply with any requests with a flat "No." Frequently such behaviors would be reinforced by the behavior of the adult. When faced with such "warnings," the adults would withdraw their requests. Perhaps the mother learned that such "warnings" were stimuli preceding subsequent temper tantrums. Mother could avoid what was most certainly, for her, a negative reinforcer, by withdrawing her request of Karl. In this way, Karl was being reinforced in a variety of settings each day for a complex of behaviors which we have labeled as "negativistic."

It is clear that an effective treatment program will require several different conditioning procedures. It will be necessary to condition a new set of responses to the cues eliciting the anxiety reaction. It also will be necessary to extinguish the destructive behaviors and teach him some alternative mode of responding. We also must increase the frequency of the few socially adaptive behaviors he does demonstrate. The peers in turn must be reprogrammed to provide more social reinforcers for Karl, particularly for the occurrence of his socially adaptive behaviors. The latter set of procedures is pivotal, for it partially insures the persistence of any change in Karl's behavior produced by our intervention. Finally an effective way must be found of altering the set of contingencies provided by the parents for Karl's anxiety responses, his temper tantrums, his immature behaviors, and his negativistic behaviors.

Treatment Procedures

There were four conditioning programs used in the study. The procedures were as follows: (A) an extinction-counter conditioning program for the temper tantrum behaviors; (B) an extinction-counter conditioning program for the anxiety reactions elicited when being separated from mother; (C) a positive reinforcement program to increase the frequency of positive initiations between Karl and the peer group; and finally, (D) a program to change the schedule of reinforcements used by the parents to maintain negativistic and immature behaviors. As some of these programs were used simultaneously, confusion will be minimized by outlining the development of each of these procedures on a day-to-day basis.

October 5. Program A (temper tantrums). Karl was brought to the door of the mobile laboratory to obtain a laboratory measure of his responsiveness to social reinforcers. He looked frightened (his pupils were dilated), and refused to come. When carried into the laboratory, he kicked the experimenter, screamed, cried, and attempted to destroy the equipment. The experimenter brought him into one of the cubicles, closed the door and pinned Karl to the floor by the ankles. While Karl screamed, bit, and threw objects, *E* made every effort to prevent Karl from injuring him, and sat looking as bored as circumstances would permit. *E* looked at Karl and talked to him only when he was reasonably calm. Karl was told he could leave as soon as he quieted down. The episode lasted about 30 minutes.

Program D (retrain the parents). We had not planned beforehand to begin reprogramming the parent in this session. However, when Karl displayed his tantrum behaviors, the mother was brought to an adjoining room and observed the interaction through a one-way glass.

A second experimenter explained to her that we were introducing a "time-out" procedure for Karl. As long as the destructive behavior lasted, he would be pinned down and effectively removed from all of the usual sources of positive reinforcement. The mother was told that such adult behaviors as "the mother stays in the classroom," "the teacher hugs him," "the teacher looks frightened or reads him stories" were powerful reinforcers for temper tantrums. The behavior of the experimenter with Karl served as a model for behaviors which the mother was to imitate.

October 6. Program A (temper tantrums). The mother had to drag Karl to the clinic today. Once inside, he refused to accompany *E* to play room and was picked up (kicking, clawing, screaming and crying). In the play room he was pinned to the floor by his ankles and cried for 30 seconds. As soon as he stopped the tantrum behaviors, he was released.

Program B (anxiety). Patterson (1965a) described a technique in which dolls were used to represent situations in which a child would be separated from his mother. A similar procedure was used with Karl. After being presented with a situation in which the mother (doll) was separated from the body (doll), Karl was asked if "the doll" would be afraid. If he said "No," he was reinforced with an M & M chocolate candy. He was also reinforced whenever he described behaviors which would compete with the occurrence of fear or temper tantrums, i.e., "I would play." The dropping of his M & M in his cup was preceded by an auditory signal coming from his "Karl Box." The "Karl Box" contained an electric counter, light, and a rather loud bell. Any one, or all, of these could be activated by *E*.

During this first session (15 min.), Karl participated in a series of six doll sequences and received a total of thirty M & Ms.

Program D (retrain the parents). The mother and the second *E* observed Karl's play room behavior through an observation window. During the temper tantrum, the mother was shown the nonreinforcing (and nonpunitive) behavior of the *E* holding Karl. She, in turn, was encouraged to leave him quickly at school and thus reinforce the tantrum behaviors as little as possible. Mother was impressed with the fact that temper tantrums lasted only a few minutes today.

After the session in the play room, the two experimenters, Karl and the mother talked for 10 min. Mother was instructed to reinforce him on those occasions in which he did not act in a frightened way when being separated from her, when he was cooperative, and when he behaved in a grown-up fashion. She was instructed to bring in notes describing four occasions on which she had reinforced Karl for any of these following behaviors: for not being afraid, for being cooperative, for being "grown up." Karl listened to this interchange with some interest.

Program C (program to increase positive interaction between Karl and peers). The "Karl Box" was used during the recess period at kindergarten. Karl was told that the buzzer would sound each time that he "played with another kid without hurting him." If Karl were within range, *E* dispensed social reinforcers for appropriate initiations, i.e., "That is good, Karl." He was also informed that the candy which he earned would be divided among all of the children and distributed during snack time. He earned seventy M & Ms in a 10-minute period; during this time he displayed no aversive behaviors.

October 7. Program A (temper tantrums). The same tantrum behaviors were observed at the clinic. The same procedures were applied as described for the previous day. However, today the behavior terminated as soon as Karl was carried into the play room.

Program B (anxiety). The same doll play procedure was used as described for the previous day; the session lasted about 20 min. Karl earned thirty M & Ms and a plastic ship. (The latter we "traded" in for ten M & Ms.) All of the reinforcers were delivered immediately and accompanied by the sound of the bell in the "Karl Box."

Program D (retrain the parents). The mother observed Karl's behavior in the play room. She was told of the necessity for reinforcing appropriate behavior immediately. She was also reminded of the importance of *not* reinforcing maladaptive behaviors, such as non-cooperation, temper tantrums, or immature behaviors. The interactions of the experimenter and Karl were used to illustrate these points.

During the "group" interview which followed, the mother reported with pride that Karl was cooperative several times yesterday. Karl was very pleased with her remarks. She gave the following written examples of her efforts to reinforce him.

1. Karl put away his clothes for me and I told him that he was a good boy and hugged him.
2. Karl got a diaper for me and I told him how nice he was to help me take care of his baby brother.
3. Karl went to bed without any argument and didn't wet the bed and I told him how grown-up he was getting.
4. Karl picked up walnuts for me and I told him he was really gitting to be such a big boy and kissed him.

Program C (peer and Karl interaction). The other children had received their M & Ms from Karl's previous day's work and were curious when *E* again appeared with the box. They asked *E* what it was, and *E* told them that it was a "Karl Box." They asked, "What is a Karl Box"? *E* said, "It is a box that makes a noise, and gives candy whenever you talk to Karl." Immediately several children said "Hi Karl" to the box. *E* said, "No, you must say it to Karl, not to the box." The peers then received 150 reinforcers for initiating social contacts with Karl. He in turn was reinforced for responding appropriately and for initiating contacts of his own. The conditioning session lasted only about 10 min. The M & M bonanza was again distributed to all of the children.

October 8. Program A (temper tantrums). Karl began to whimper as soon as he saw the experimenter's reception room and ran and hid. He then kicked and clawed as he was picked up and began to cry loudly. He was told that he could earn M & Ms by walking up the stairs himself.

He was placed at the bottom of the stairs; but he refused to move. The experimenter commented that Karl was not screaming, kicking, or hurting people even though he was a little afraid. At this point the buzzer sounded on the "Karl Box." After a few seconds Karl was again asked to place his foot on the bottom step; but he refused. After a moment, the experimenter said, "Too bad, the next time the box went off you were going to earn one of these plastic boats. Guess I'll just have to keep the boat and carry you up the stairs again." There was a moment of silence at which point Karl said, "Suppose you touch my hand and see what happens." The experimenter touched Karl's hand. Karl immediately placed his feet on the stairs. The buzzer sounded and Karl was handed the plastic boat. At this point, he walked up the stairs and was reinforced by the bell for each step into the play room.

Program B (anxiety). Karl and experimenter sat in the doorway of the play room. The mother was instructed to say "Goodbye, Karl," and Karl in turn was told to say goodbye to the mother while she walked across the room. As Karl said "Goodbye," he was reinforced by the bell and by the *E* saying "Very good, Karl." Karl was asked if he was afraid. He said that he was. *E* said "But you did sit there. You didn't run after her, and you didn't scream or kick. That is very good." (Bell sounded.) This was repeated several times with the mother moving further away each time until she walked across the lawn as Karl waved goodbye from the second-story window.

Program D (retrain the parents). Mother reported that Karl was making good progress both in being able to tolerate her leaving him at school and also in his increasingly cooperative and mature behavior at home. Both the *E*s and the mother praised Karl, who was obviously very pleased. Mother brought her "homework" with examples of how she had reinforced Karl for these behaviors on the previous day.

1. Karl took his bath without any argument at all and I told him how proud I was of him and let him sit in my lap in the rocking chair for a while.
2. Karl went to bed and I told him how big he was for it and kissed him.
3. Karl got into the car to come to the University without arguing and I told him how nice he was.

We pointed out to the mother that she still found herself doing for Karl things which he could do for himself; e.g., tying his shoes, buttering his bread. We practiced breaking such a behavior down into small steps and providing reinforcement for *any kind of progress* rather than waiting for terminal behavior before reinforcing. We also set up a point system so that each time Karl cooperated in one of these new behaviors he received a point, which mother recorded as part of her homework. When he had earned ten points, Karl could select any one of the plastic toys from our display.

Program C (peer and Karl interaction). The school period was highly structured today. It was not possible to condition for peer interaction without disrupting the group. We left shortly; Karl was obviously disappointed, but remained in the group.

October 11. Programs A and B (temper tantrums and anxiety). Karl walked up to the play room to the accompaniment of the bell and much praise from his parents and both *E*'s. He said that now he only felt a little bit afraid when leaving his parents. We all agreed that he would no longer have to come to the clinic.

Program D (retrain the parents). The father, who had been absent from home during the past week, had returned. The procedures were reviewed for him in the clinic with mother and Karl present. Arrangements were made for the remainder of the work with parents to take place in the home.

Program C (peer and Karl interaction). Neither experimenter was able to go to the school today.

October 12. Program D (retrain the parents). One of the *E*s went to Karl's home along with an observer. Karl was extremely cooperative in following his parents' requests. *E* followed the mother around, offering suggestions on the best way to interact with Karl. When mother was slow in reinforcing him, *E* again explained the importance of the immediacy of reinforcement. In addition, the mother was again shown the principles of shaping successive approximations to a desired behavior. As an example, she asked Karl to comb his hair which he had not done before. She was then instructed to reinforce him for the *attempt* (which was actually a fairly good job). After several such successes it was explained to her that she was to reinforce Karl tomorrow only when he had done a better job. A similar procedure was begun in shaping the behaviors involved in tying his shoes.

Program C (peer and Karl interaction). The previous program was continued. M & Ms were made contingent upon Karl's initiating social contacts and peers initiating contacts to Karl.

October 13. Program D (retrain the parents). Karl was again observed at home. He showed no deviant behavior. Mother reported that she had reinforced Karl for improving in tying his shoes and for hair combing. *E* reviewed for mother the general principles underlying the approach with Karl and explained how she might adapt them to use in future situation, such at leaving Karl alone in the evenings with a baby-sitter. Mother reiterated that Karl was like a new boy and they were delighted with his progress.

Program C (peer and Karl interaction). Today there was no conditioning in the classroom.

October 14. Program B, C, and D. The mother came to the school and operated the "Karl Box." She was instructed to reinforce Karl for playing with other children, or any socially appropriate behaviors which resulted in his staying away from the immediate vicinity of his mother.

Mother, teacher, and Karl agreed that there was no reason for continuing the program as there were no further behaviors that anyone believed should be changed. It was arranged with the parents, and the teacher, to follow up the effects of the program by observing Karl in the school for several weeks following the study.

Procedures for Collecting Data

All of the observation data used in testing the effectiveness of the treatment programs were collected in the classroom setting. In the first introduction to this setting, two observers, seated in the classroom, dictated narrative accounts of Karl's behavior, and the reactions of the teachers and the peer group. These initial impressions provided a basis for constructing a checklist that was introduced during the second day's observation. Using the checklist, observers tabulated the occurrence of the following behaviors: (1) The frequency of positive initiations, i.e., talking to another child, smiling, by peers to Karl. (2) The frequency of his positive initiations to peers. (3) The occurrence of withdrawal or isolation from the group, e.g., sitting 3 or 4 feet away from the group and not attending to or participating in the group activities. (4) The occurrence of negativistic behaviors, e.g., when asked to join the group, play a game, come into the room, etc., his behavior indicated noncompliance. (5) Temper tantrums; when being left by parent behaviors occurred such as cry, scream, kick, bite, and hit.

The observations were made during periods ranging in length from 20 min. to 60 min. per day. The behaviors were tabulated by 14-sec. intervals. To reduce the variability somewhat, the observations were collected during the same 60-min. period each day (12.30 to 1.30). The data were collected each day during the time immediately prior to the conditioning procedures introduced in the classroom.*

During the study, the data were collected by three different observers, but chiefly by one. On several occasions she was accompanied by an untrained observer. On the first such occasion 300 separate events were recorded; but the two observers agreed only 61 per cent of the time. On the second occasion, 264 events were noted and the two observers agreed 84 per cent of the time. This suggests that with a minimum of training, comparatively unskilled observers can be used to collect these kinds of data.

➤

RESULTS

Each day the observers in the school provided an estimate of the duration of Karl's temper tantrum; this information was combined with the data from his behavior at the clinic to form a "total" score for the day. A tantrum was said to have stopped when Karl had ceased to cry, kick, or scream for at least half a minute. During the three weeks previous to the study, the teacher told us that Karl had averaged about 30 min. at the beginning of each school session. The data showing the effect of the program on temper tantrum behaviors are presented in Figure 2.

In many respects, both the data and the procedure are similar to

---

* It required 3 days of trial and error to construct the checklist; at this point we had intended to collect a week's baseline data for each of the deviant responses. However, on the third day of our being in the classroom, the teacher informed us that she would have to drop him from the class unless he improved. It seemed to us that her toleration of this behavior for 3 weeks had already been above and beyond the call of duty; consequently, we initiated our conditioning procedures. Being Good Samaritans, however, resulted in our obtaining only one day's baseline observation data.

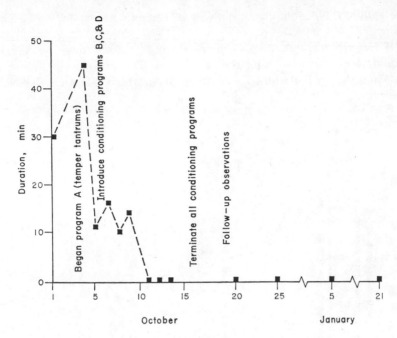

FIGURE 2. Duration of temper tantrums.

those described by Williams (1959) in which tantrum behaviors were controlled by the withdrawal of positive social reinforcees. As shown in Figure 2, there was a marked reduction in the duration of the temper tantrums by the second day of the program. After the initial, dramatic reduction in duration, they were being emitted at a reasonably steady rate for a period of about 4 days. During this "plateau," he displayed a total of about 10 min. of tantrums per day. Most of these were occurring in the classroom on the occasion of the mother's leaving him with the teacher. In this setting, both of the adults were providing him with a good deal of reinforcement for tantrums. However, by the sixth day of the program procedure, the adults no longer provided reinforcers for them and they terminated. They did not recur during the three-month follow-up.

The second set of data showed the change in frequency of occurrence of two classes of behaviors observed in the nursery school. The first category, "isolated," was defined by such behaviors as sitting several feet apart from the group.

Most of the time the children were engaged in a series of organized games, storytelling, and group singing. These provided an occasion in which the teacher frequently made suggestions or demands to each of the children. Noncompliance with such demands was coded as "negativism."

If either of the behaviors occurred during a 15-sec. time interval, it would receive one entry on the data sheet. The ordinate in Figure 3 indicates the per cent of the 15-sec. intervals in which they were observed to occur.

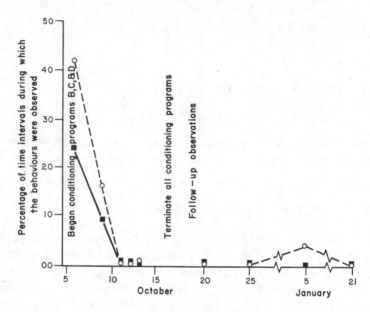

FIGURE 3.   Frequency of occurrence of negativistic (■) and isolated (O) behaviors.

The data showed that by the second day of conditioning there was a dramatic drop in the occurrence for both classes of deviant behavior. In both cases, the rate of occurrence dropped to almost zero and stayed there during the remainder of the three-month follow-up period.

In observing Karl, the baseline data showed that the other children tended to avoid him, probably as a result of the aversive quality of much of his behavior (pushing, elbowing, kicking, throttling, pinching). The prediction was that if Karl's aversive behaviors decreased in rate the peer group would increase the frequency of their social reinforcers. Data presented in the report by Patterson and Ebner (1965) showed that when the aversive behaviors were decreased for two hyperactive children in different classrooms, the change was accompanied by a marked increase in the amount of social reinforcers provided (by peers) for one of the subjects *but not for the other subject*. This would suggest that the effect of a reduction in aversive behaviors is somewhat a function of the social group in which it occurs. To the extent that these variables are not understood, the final outcome of our treatment program is determined in large part by chance factors. However, it should be possible to directly reprogram the schedule of reinforcement provided by the peer group, and the procedures innovated in the present study represented such an approach. If successful, the program should result in an increase in the frequency of social initiations by peers and a corresponding increase in their use of positive social reinforcers contingent upon Karl's behaviors. The data to be presented here represented only a partial test of the hypothesis because the data were collected only for the occurrence of social *initiations* by peers to Karl. It was predicted that the conditioning program would result in an increase in the frequency of initiations of positive social contacts made by the peer group to Karl and a corresponding increase in the frequency of positive initiations made by Karl to the peer group. The data for the frequency of social initiations consisted of such responses as talking, smiling, playing, and touching. These events were also recorded by 15-sec. intervals (Figure 4).

Early in the conditioning period, the frequency of occurrence of positive initiations by peers increased nine- or ten-fold. It should be kept in mind that these data were collected each day in the period immediately prior to the conditioning sessions; these data then reflect generalization, or transfer of conditioning effects.

There was a significant increase in frequency of social initiations by peers to Karl; there was also a significant increase in the frequency of positive social initiations by Karl to the peers. Both sets of initiations were at least doubled during conditioning. However, two months after the termination of the study it is clear that some of these earlier, more dramatic gains have been lost. The data from the end of the follow-up period show that the over-all gain was only two- or three-fold for both sets of behaviors.

Discussions with both parents and with the teacher during the follow-up period indicate that Karl is "a changed boy." The casual observer in the classroom would have no reason to select Karl as showing particularly deviant behavior. His behavior is characterized by less avoidance of social contacts and increased responsiveness to social reinforcers. Although still somewhat impulsive, Karl no longer

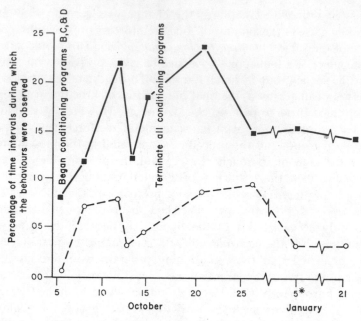

FIGURE 4.   Changes in the interaction between Karl (■) and his peers (O).

* Based upon only 20 min. of observation; the remainder of the period was too highly structured to permit social initiations.

displayed temper tantrums, nor did he isolate himself. During the baseline period. Karl would clutch a child by the arm and say such things to him as "I like you." He would then continue to hold the child's arm as he stared intently into the other child's face for a good 10 sec.* These primitive interactions no longer occurred. By any reasonable criteria, the changes in Karl constituted "successful treatment."

➤

DISCUSSION

In some respects, data of the kind presented in this report are becoming commonplace. They show that manipulation of reinforcement con-

* This latter set of behavior was of particular concern to the writers because of its similarities to atavistic behavior of this kind occasionally observed in schizophrenic children. Following the study, Karl was examined by an ophthalmologist who prescribed glasses. These "primitive" behaviors disappeared.

tingencies has a significant impact upon behavior; these findings in turn have practical implications for the treatment of children with deviant behavior problems. The first "rush" of data-collecting activity served both to reiterate our faith in the Law of Effect and also to definitely place the promissory note proffered by the behavior modifier in a place of prominence. However, at this point in the development of the field, we should be able to raise questions which are more sophisticated than those which characterized the earlier investigations. There is one set of questions which has been encountered repeatedly in attempts to carry out behavior modification studies in the laboratories here at Oregon. The general question concerns statements about the variables which determine the persistence and generality of treatment effects. In our first studies we were impressed by the fact that we were obtaining dramatic generalization of conditioning effects (Patterson, 1965a, 1965c). In one of these studies the control over hyperactive behaviors quickly generalized from the conditioning periods to occasions in which the child was not directly under the control of the apparatus. We assumed that the generalization occurred because of the similarity in stimulus components present during conditioning and those present during the remainder of the day. In fact, our procedures had been constructed in an effort to maximize just such transfer of effects. For example, in the series of studies using hyperactive children as subjects, the conditioning was carried out in the classroom setting on occasions when the subject was engaged in routine classroom activities (Patterson, 1965b). The observation data obtained in this series of studies showed that not only did the conditioning effects generalize, but they persisted over extended periods of time. The data presented by Patterson and Ebner (1965) showed that a drop in the rate of production of deviant behavior can produce an effect on the social environment. In *some* groups, when the subject becomes less deviant, the peers began to dispense more positive social reinforcers. Presumably, these reinforcers are contingent upon social behaviors which would compete with the occurrence of the deviant behaviors. However, as yet there are no data available which show that this latter hypothesis is indeed the case.

Our assumption is that the effect of the conditioning (or any successful treatment) produces a reprogramming of the social environment; the altered program of positive and negative reinforcers maintains the effect of the initial behavior modification. The fact that the peer group now responds by dispensing more social reinforcers also means that the effect would "generalize" to any social setting in which one would find members of this peer group. In effect the term "stimulus generalization" is an oversimplification. For this reason, in our own discussions about the process, we use the phrase "reprogramming the social environment" rather than "stimulus generalization."

There are several implications which follow from such a reformulation. For example, if the social environment does not increase the frequency of social reinforcers for socially adaptive behaviors, then any "improvement" occurring from a treatment program will be of short duration. *Or*, if the social environment continues to "pay off" for the deviant behavior at a very high rate, the likely outcome would be very little "improvement." An example of the latter would be the attempt to shape some socially adaptive behaviors in an institutional setting which is programmed to pay off heavily for deviant behaviors; e.g., institutions for delinquent adolescents have been shown to provide 70 per cent positive reinforcement for deviant behaviors (Patterson, 1963; Furness, 1964).

Taken together, the implications of these trends in the data are quite clear. The major focus of the behavior modifier should be upon the task of directly manipulating the reinforcement programs being provided by the social environment, rather than upon the behavior of the individual subject. In effect, we are accusing the behavior modifier of following too closely the medical model. In the medical model, the behavior modifier would remove the "tumor" (change the deviant behavior) and then terminate his treatment program. It is reasonable to believe that changing deviant behavior is simply not good enough; the goals for the behavior modifier must *also* be that of reprogramming the social environment in which the subject finds himself.

Attempts to reprogram the social environment are only just beginning. The program described by Birnbauer (1965) and by C. Hanf (personal communication) are extremely provocative. In these attempts, the parent and child are observed interacting under relatively controlled laboratory conditions. The parent is reinforced for appropriately reinforcing the child. In our own laboratories, we have recently completed the development of a programmed teaching manual for use by parents and teachers. The main program consisted of 120 frames which describe the concepts of social reinforcers, extinction, negative reinforcers, latency of reinforcement, and accidental reinforcement of deviant child behaviors. For each of the families which we are now investigating, the observation data in the home and the school are used to develop a branching program for use by other mothers who have children with similar problems. For example, based upon our experience with Karl, we now have a fifty-frame program on separation phobia and temper tantrum behaviors in children. These programs will be used in conjunction with our attempts to develop conditioning procedures to be used in retraining the parents *in the home*. This would mean devising new techniques to insure that the change in the program of social reinforcers is provided both by adults and by peers. For example, it may be necessary to change our thinking about confining deviant children to groups in which they are mutually reinforcing each other's deviant behaviors. It is also necessary for us to reconsider the traditional clinical models which present the 1 to 1 relationship as *the* basis for behavior change. Our speculations lead us to believe that rather than improving the technology for changing behavior on a 1 to 1 basis, procedures in the future may rather completely differ from techniques for directly changing the behavior of the child and focus instead upon a technology which will reprogram the social environment.

This is one further point which should be made in setting behavior modification procedures in proper perspective. We might take the changes observed in Karl's behavior as a case in point. Presumably, the conditioning procedures strengthened socially adaptive behaviors which competed with the occurrence of deviant behavior. However, we do *not* believe that the conditioning procedures *shaped new* classes of socially adaptive behaviors, nor do we believe that the classes of deviant behaviors have been *extinguished*. In the present context, the terms "shaping," "conditioning," or "extinction" refer only to the fact that rankings have been changed in the hierarchy of response probabilities. The term extinction does not imply that such behaviors as "negativism" have vanished. By the same token, such socially adaptive behaviors as "smiling at a peer" are not in any sense completely novel to the child's repertoire. "Conditioning" as it is used here implies only that a member of the class of responses such as "smiling at a peer" are more likely to occur. In a sense, we see the effect of most modification or treatment programs as consisting of the rearranging of social behaviors *within already existing hierarchies.*

In this perspective, the "therapists" main function is to *initiate* the first link in a chain reaction. Such a chain reaction could *not* occur unless the child had been previously conditioned for socially adaptive behaviors. Also, the major changes occur outside the conditioning trials as the social environment begins to respond differently to the child who is being treated. It is the social environment which supports (or sabotages) the changes produced in treatment. In some cases this change in the schedule of positive social reinforcements results in the increased visibility of a whole spectrum of social behaviors which had previously been at very low strength. This latter phenomenon is familiar to both behavior modifiers and to traditional therapists.

~ 31 ~

A Behavior Modification Technique for the Hyperactive Child

G. R. Patterson, R. Jones, J. Whittier, & M. A. Wright

This report describes a procedure for the conditioning of attending behavior in a brain injured hyperactive boy. The data from the experimental and control subject show that it is possible to condition these behaviors in a classroom setting and that the effects generalize from the conditioning period. Follow-up data show that these effects persist over at least a four-week period of time.

Taken together, the incidental findings from a large number of empirical studies would suggest that the activity level of the child is a critical variable in the socialization process. In the normal child, high activity levels are associated with a more frequent occurrence of a wide range of social behaviors, e.g., dependency and aggression, Sears et al. (1953), Hinsey, Patterson and Sonoda (1961); acceptance by peers, Tuddenham (1951). Data from the longitudinal study by Bayley and Schaefer (1953) showed that differences in activity level in infancy relate to a wide variety of adolescent behaviors such as friendliness, boldness, irritability, and distractibility. In this study, the correlations between activity level and these social behaviors were all positive. Factor analyses of the behaviors of normal children are consistent in showing an "activity" dimension (Walker, 1962; Baldwin, 1948).

From *Behavior Research and Therapy*, 2 (1965), 217–226,.Pergamon Press.

It is evident that *very* high rates of behavior are aversive to adults. Data collected by Patterson (1956) from four child clinics showed that "hyperactivity" was one of the most common problems for which children were referred to child clinics. Factor analysis of behaviors of "disturbed" children by Patterson (1964) and Dreger and Dreger (1962) showed "hyperactivity" as a factor dimension in both studies.

The antecedents for this behavior are poorly understood. Studies with animals are consistent in showing a relation between emotional and or deprivational states and activity levels (Campbell and Sheffield, 1953; Hill, 1958). There are also a series of studies with human subjects which strongly suggest constitutional factors (unspecified) as additional determinants.

The research of Irwin (1930) and Balint (1948) showed wide individual differences in activity level at birth. The data presented by Jones and Bayley (1950) and by Walker (1962) offer some support for a hypothesis as to constitutional differences in activity level in older children. A third, well-documented antecedent for variations in activity level was found in the relation between anoxic conditions at birth and later activity levels of the child (Parmellee, 1962; Graham, Ernhart, Thurston, and Craft, 1962).

Whatever the antecedents for this behavior, the matrix of empirical findings suggests an interesting hypothesis which has directed the attention of this research group to the problem of "controlling" so-called "hyperactive" behaviors. The general hypothesis is that there is a curvilinear relation holding between activity level of the child and the acquisition of socially acceptable behaviors. Up to moderately high levels of activity, the child's behavior will elicit an increasing number of reactions from peers and adults in the culture. Assuming that these reactions are, by and large, positive this should imply that the very active child will acquire social skills at a faster rate than the less active child. It is further assumed that *extremely high* rates of behavior are aversive to the social culture; hence, the reactions from the culture are more likely to be punitive. In this situation, the child operating at high activity levels may very well be punished *even* when he is displaying socially acceptable behaviors, e.g., "friendliness."

This higher ratio of punishment to reinforced behaviors for the hyperactive child should result in his developing social behaviors at a slower rate.

The *specific responses* emitted by the hyperactive child must be conditioned as a result of the social rewards and punishments provided by parents, teachers, and peers. This being the case, it should be possible to create a procedure for conditioning more appropriate behaviors in the hyperactive child. Patterson (1964) used a conditioning procedure to increase the frequency of attending behaviors in a hyperactive boy. This pilot study was carried out in a classroom setting using nonsocial reinforcers to shape these behaviors in a series of fifteen conditioning trials. James (1963) programmed the teacher's behavior so that social reinforcers were made contingent upon the occurrence of socially acceptable behavior in a group of hyperactive children. Over a twenty-month period, this arrangement seemed to produce dramatic changes in five of the children.

The present report describes a modified, and improved, technique for controlling the behavior of the hyperactive child. Observation data on the frequency of the occurrence of "nonattending" behaviors in the classroom constitute the data testing the effects of the conditioning procedure. These data were collected for both an experimental and a control subject. It was assumed that the classroom setting had been conditioning a variety of behaviors which competed with successful academic performance, e.g., such behaviors as looking out the window, walking about the room. In the conditioning procedure, immediate reinforcement was provided for brief intervals of responding in which *only* attending behaviors occurred. It was predicted that this procedure would result in a decrease in occurrence of nonattending behaviors during the conditioning sessions. Furthermore, it was predicted that these effects would generalize to occasions when the conditioning apparatus was not being used. Because the conditioning trials actually occurred in the classroom setting, it was expected that over a series of trials, many of the stimuli in the classroom would become conditioned to elicit attending rather than nonattending behaviors. Because of the complexity of the matrix of stimuli found in the classroom setting, the conditioning of attending behaviors may very well be "slower" than would be the case if the conditioning occurred in a more controlled laboratory setting. However, the classroom procedure should result in greater generalization of effects than would be obtained by conditioning in the more controlled laboratory setting.

The third hypothesis was that the effects would persist over a four-week extinction period. This "prediction" was based upon the subjective finding from the earlier study by Patterson (1964) in which parents and teachers reported effects which persisted over at least a six-month period. This apparent resistance to extinction seemed to be a function of a change in the reinforcement schedules provided by the peers and by the teacher. It was assumed that a similar situation would occur in the present case; a change in the child's aversive behavior should increase the ratio of positive reinforcement provided by peers and by the teacher. It is the change in the peer and teacher program of reinforcement which maintains the conditioning effects. Although the present report is concerned only with demonstrating the persistence of the conditioning effects, a study recently completed by Straughan (in preparation) shows that the peer group is in fact reprogrammed by a procedure similar to the one described in this report.

><

PROCEDURES

The Experimental Subject (ES)

Ten years of age, Raymond had been exposed to a series of foster and adoptive homes. Although the medical records described him as a full-term baby, he weighed only three and one-half pounds at birth. At the age of nine months his first adoptive parents returned him to the agency with the complaint that he never moved his left arm and leg. A craniotomy performed at that time revealed almost complete atrophy of the right cerebral hemisphere. Somewhat later in his development, the effects were manifested in the hemiplegic carriage and gait, increased tendon reflexes and positive Babinski. The movements of the tongue were also impaired, resulting in a moderate to severe articulation defect.

Until adopted at the age of five, Raymond had been placed in a total of nine different homes. His intellectual ability generally varied within the range of educable but retarded. At the age of six, he obtained an IQ of 59; more recently, he obtained an IQ of 65 on the verbal scale of the WISC and 86 on the performance scale.

Two years prior to the experiment he was admitted to the Children's Hospital School, a day care center for physically handicapped children. While in residence at the school he has been placed in a foster home (the same home in which the control subject resided). Immediately following his admission to the school, his teacher described him as having a short attention span, and as being aggressive to the younger children. All teacher evaluations which followed described him as being very hyperactive.

The Control Subject (CS)

Ricky was a ten-and-one-half-year-old boy who sustained a severe head injury at the age of six in an automobile accident. The head injury involved a skull fracture over the left parietal region and resulted in his being in a coma for five months. The skull fracture was lifted surgically and he was discharged from the hospital with the diagnosis of traumatic hemiplegia. The injury resulted in spastic functioning of the left arm and leg. Although he had good visual, tactile and auditory functioning, there was a marked impairment of motor functioning in lips, tongue, and perhaps the larynx. As a consequence there was no speech. On a variety of tests including the Peabody Picture Vocabulary and Raven Matrices given over a three-year period his scores ranged from the eighties to the low nineties.

Ricky's parents had arranged for him to stay in a foster home while in residence at the Children's Hospital School. Observations of his classroom behavior indicated that most of the time he displayed non-attending behaviors, e.g., walking about the room, staring off into space, almost continuous movement of arms or legs.

Observation

Both subjects were observed in the classroom setting over a period of two weeks in order to determine the specific characteristics of their nonattending behaviors. The general impression was that neither of them devoted much time to school work but were instead in almost constant motion. After several tryouts, a checklist was devised such that sixty ten-second observations in sequence could be taken on a given child, for a total of ten minutes per checklist. There were seven categories of nonattending behaviors which characterized these two subjects. Each of these categories had sixty observation cells following it.

A tape recording announced the beginning of each ten-second interval to the observer, who watched from behind a one-way screen. If a particular nonattending behavior occurred during a given ten-second period, a check mark was placed in the appropriate cell, and that behavior was ignored for the rest of that interval; if other nonattending behaviors occurred during that interval, check marks were placed in the appropriate cells, and they, too, were then ignored until the next ten-second interval began.

It was also recorded on the checklist whether the child being observed was (1) working alone, (2) in a classroom activity (e.g., story-telling, singing), or (3) receiving personal attention from an adult, during any given set of ten-second observation periods. Total scores for each of the categories of interfering behaviors, and a grand total, were recorded for each ten-minute period.

The behaviors observed in the final form of the checklist are described below:

1. Movements directed toward the body: e.g., wringing of hands, rubbing eyes, swinging arms, leaning forward in the chair, scratching, or stretching.

2. Movements in chair: e.g., shuffling of chair, sliding back and forth in chair, twisting of body in chair, or leaning clear out of chair so that buttocks no longer rested on it.

3. Distraction: e.g., looking over toward a noise, toward someone who has just entered the room (unless teacher also looks up), out of the window, or off into space.

4. Gross movements of legs and feet: e.g., pumping of leg, wiggling of feet, or crossing of legs, or other shift of their position.

5. Fiddling: Arm and hand movements directed toward objects: activities of the hand(s) that interfered with schoolwork or assigned activities, e.g., stroking the desk, fingering the box of color crayons.

6. Communicative or quasi-communicative activity interfering with schoolwork: e.g., talking to self, pointing, laughing, attempting to attract someone's attention, talking to someone without permission.

7. Walking or standing that was not encouraged or subsequently approved by the teacher.

Each child was observed for a minimum of ten minutes a day, four days a week. Four observers collected the data; each observer was responsible for one set of data per week. Three days of observations were made in the morning during a time when the children were working at independent projects at their desks. One of the observations was made during the afternoon in which the classroom setting tended to vary over a wide range of group activities.

After one week's practice in using the checklist, two pairs of observers were checked for agreement in data collecting. Total frequency of nonattending behaviors were summed for eight ten-minute intervals for each pair who had been observing the experimental subject. When using *total* frequency of occurrence of nonattending behaviors, the correlation between one pair of observers was .90 and the correlation between a second pair was .91.

The two subjects were seated close together in the class. The data presented in a later section of the paper show that the two subjects displayed about the same total frequency of nonattending behaviors at the beginning of the experiment. They did, however, differ somewhat in the kind of nonattending behaviors displayed. The control subject showed about three times the number of leg movements, about half the number of distraction responses and chair movements, and twice as much "walking" as did the experimental subject.

Conditioning

Baseline data were collected for both subjects during the period November 1 through November 19. The data were collected on eleven days during this interval.

Between November 20 and December 10, data were collected on nine days on the classroom behavior of both subjects. The experimental subject was taken out of the room for a brief period each day and adapted to the conditioning procedure and apparatus. The observation data were collected prior to the experimental subject's being taken from the classroom.

During this adaptation phase, ES was taken out of the classroom for approximately ten minutes each trial. He was told that the apparatus was being used in an effort to teach him to sit still so that he could study better. He was taken into a small room containing two chairs and a desk. After being seated at the table a pair of suspenders were snapped in place holding the small radio receiving unit on his back. After the earphone had been adjusted he was told to open his workbook and complete the homework assignment given him by the teacher. He was told that the buzz which he would hear indicated that he had earned an M & M candy. During the next few minutes E activated the microphone and dropped an M & M into a small cup in front of him for each ten-second period in which he did not display any of the nonattending behaviors. At the end of a trial, he was given his M & Ms and returned to the classroom.

A third phase lasted from December 11 through January 15. Data were collected for both subjects on eight days during this interval. Following the observation period on each of these days, ES was conditioned in the classroom for periods ranging from five to eighteen minutes.

On the first trial, the following announcement was made to the class:

> Raymond has some trouble with sitting still and this makes it hard for him to learn things. This little earphone which he is wearing will tell him when he is sitting still. When he sits still, he earns candy for himself and for the rest of you. When he is finished, we will take the earphone off and give him the candy that he has earned. He can pass it out to the rest of you at the end of the class period.

During the conditioning trial, E was in a one-day observation room (which contained a speaker) adjoining the classroom. Using a radio transmitter device, a signal was sent for each ten-second interval in which none of the nonattending behaviors occurred. This fixed interval schedule was maintained for the first four conditioning trials and M & Ms were used as rewards. The first conditioning trial lasted seven minutes, and the trials were increased by one to three minutes each day until twenty-minute trials were reached.

On the fifth and all preceding trials, a variable interval schedule was used, the units consisting of: 2, 5, 10, 15, 20, and 30 seconds. To counteract possible satiation, pennies were used on alternate days for reinforcing stimuli. After interviewing the teacher, plastic soldiers (a special preference of Raymond's) were also included in his "earnings." It was agreed that Raymond would keep all plastic soldiers for his own. The total number of reinforcers for a given trial ranged from fifteen to seventy.

Between January 17 and February 21 nine follow-up observations were made. These data constitute the extinction phase of the experiment.

><

RESULTS

The data in Figure 1 present the mean frequency per minute of the total for nonattending behaviors for both subjects in all three phases of the study. The points on the graph represent the mean number of responses per minute for each trial in which observations were made for *both* the experimental and control subjects in each of the four phases.

When examining these data, it is well to keep in mind that the observation data were *not* collected *during* the conditioning period but rather in the ten- or twenty-minute period immediately prior to each trial. In effect, each day's observation data for the experimental subject represented the cumulative effects of conditioning on preceding days. For the experimental subject, the data presented here are generalization data for the effects of conditioning.

In analyzing these data, the sign test was used to compare the total frequency scores obtained on the same days for the two subjects. The analysis shows that although the ES tended to show a higher frequency of nonattending behaviors during the baseline phase of the experiment, this difference was not significant. During the adaptation period, this trend is reversed; but again, the two subjects are not significantly

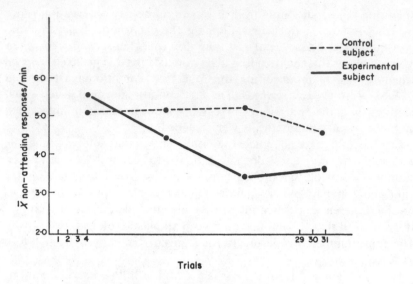

FIGURE 1.   Effect of behavior manipulation.

different from each other. During the conditioning phase, the experimental subject shows significantly fewer nonattending behaviors than does the control subject (P less than .06). This difference is maintained during the extinction phase (P less than .03).

These findings are in keeping with the main hypothesis that the procedure would significantly modify the behavior of the experimental subject. The data also support the prediction that the effects of the conditioning would generalize to occasions when the apparatus was not being used to control behavior. This latter finding is of particular importance when considering the practical implications of this procedure. The prediction that the effects would persist over a four-week period was also supported by the data.

The unexpected but interesting finding from the study is the fact that the control subject showed a drop of about 13 per cent in the occurrence of nonattending behaviors from the conditioning to the follow-up phase. Because of the limited number of observations involved for this single subject, it was not feasible to test for the significance of this decrease. However, in a study by Anderson (1964) using similar subjects and a design in which observations were made for a control subject in the *same classroom*, a similar decrease of 11 per cent was obtained. Furthermore, the drop also occurred during the period following the *termination* of the conditioning study. Although both sets of findings may be coincidental they suggest the possibility that other children in the classroom are affected by the procedure and the resulting change in the behavior of the experimental subject. In any case, these findings would suggest that in future studies, the control subjects should be observed in classrooms in which conditioning procedures are not introduced.

Because of the possibility that the different nonattending behaviors might be differentially affected, the frequency of occurrence for each of these responses was plotted separately for the ES. An inspection of these graphs showed that there were in fact differences in effects. The responses "fiddling" and "distraction" (the most frequent responses) were similarly affected in that both of them showed a small decrement during adaptation, a marked decrement during conditioning which continued to drop during the follow-up phase. However, "leg movements," "chair movements," and "arm movements" were similar in that all of them showed a marked drop during conditioning but a rapid increase during the extinction period. It is evident that these motor movements were only temporarily affected by the procedure. Inspection of the data relevant to the response "walking", indicates that it was not affected by the procedure. These findings suggest that the conditioning of attending behaviors has differential implications for the "fate" of the various nonattending responses with which they are in competition.

❯❮

DISCUSSION

These data offer strong support for the efficacy of behavior modification techniques for the control of the hyperactive child. The findings are in agreement with the earlier pilot study by Patterson (1964) and the more recent study by Anderson (1964).

Although the effects were significant in all three studies, there are some qualitative differences among the findings which would have implications for future studies of this type. In both the earlier pilot study and the Anderson (1964) study the effects seemed to be more "dramatic"; for these studies, the improvements in behavior were apparent to even the casual observer. These differences have led to the ad hoc assumption that the conditioning procedure initiated a chain of events which, although by-products, were probably of greater social significance than the decrease in nonattending behaviors.

The one variable which seems to account for the difference among studies is the greater involvement of the peer group in the Anderson study and the pilot study. In the pilot study, for example, there were loud cheers and clapping at the end of a trial and frequent social reinforcement by individuals in the classroom both during and following a trial. In these studies there seemed to be a change of status for ES within the peer group. Before the conditioning trials, both ESs had been tolerated or rejected. Following conditioning they were more accepted by the other children.

In the present study, however, the general atmosphere of the Hospital School is very much individual child oriented, e.g., occupational therapy, speech therapy, individual tutoring the class; it is our impression that this group of children is the least cohesive group we have observed to date and has an extremely high tolerance for deviant behavior. Perhaps it was this general lack of involvement by the peer group which accounts for the minimal change in the present instance. At this time, the functional importance of the reaction of the peer group or the teacher to decreases in high rate behaviors is an untested hypothesis. However, a recent study by Straughan (in preparation) shows that the peer group reactions do change and that they can be programmed to become contingent upon socially adaptive behaviors of the experimental subject. These findings would suggest that the development of techniques for reprogramming schedules of reward and punishment on the part of the parents and peer group could be of critical importance. Certainly, this type of programming deserves far more attention than it has received in behavior modification studies carried out thus far.

Our hypothesis at this point is that the importance of any change in behavior lies in the effect which it produces upon the reactions from the social culture. If, for example, a small decrement in rate of aversive behaviors is immediately followed by approval of the peer group or the teacher this should accelerate the acquisition of new behaviors. As these new behaviors are acquired, they should in turn lead to an even greater reaction from the peer culture. Under these conditions the change in behavior could be dramatic, even if the focus of observation is limited to the decrease in nonattending behaviors. The hypothesis would suggest, however, that the observation data should be expanded to include two vital types of information. On the one hand it would be imperative to collect data on the *kind of reactions* being elicited from the peer group and the *kind* of ES behaviors which elicit these reactions. Second, it should also include the occurrence of social behaviors which would be secondarily effected by an increase in positive reactions from the peer group, e.g., friendly behaviors, frequency of participation in group activities during recess. The assumption is that a change in status in the peer group implies peer reinforcement for socially acceptable behaviors of a wide variety. This should be reflected in a rapid increase in adaptive behaviors in addition to those which are specifically being conditioned by the experimenter.

This would suggest in turn (this hypothesis was offered by J. Straughan) that in the planning of behavior modification programs it would be important to arrange a hierarchy of child behaviors which lead to his being ignored or punished by the social culture. A change in the rate of such behavior — and "hyperactivity" might be such a response — would produce the greatest generalized effects in terms of a wide range of social responses. The question, of course, as to the nature of such a hierarchy is an empirical one, but it would seem of prime importance to collect these kinds of data as quickly as possible, the implication being that it is not necessary to devise a conditioning procedure to extinguish individually each of the variety of problem behaviors for which a child is referred to the clinic.

There seem to be enormous day-to-day fluctuations in the rate of occurrence of the nonattending behaviors. During the baseline period, for example, the experimental subject on one day showed an average of 9.4 nonattending responses per minute. This was a day on which a visiting teacher had taken over the class. Periods immediately preceding holidays also seemed associated with high rates of nonattending behaviors. Various daily activities within the classroom also seemed to have differential effects, e.g., data obtained during a group reading period showed the rate of nonattending behaviors to be only 3.3 responses per minute. It would be expected that to some extent these variations in situations would have a similar effect upon both the experimental and control subject; however, the data offer only limited support for this hypothesis. The correlation between total frequency of nonattending behaviors over the first six weeks for the ES and CS was only .25.

In spite of the extensive efforts made to collect data which accurately reflect the effects of the behavior modification technique used here, there is one respect in which adequate controls were lacking. This involves the potential lack of control over the behavior of the observer. Due to the fact that each observer also functioned as an experimenter in the conditioning trials, it is possible that a consistent bias is present in the data. This possibility would indicate the need for using observers who do not know which subject is the experimental and which is the control. This arrangement is being followed in studies now under way.

~32~

Effects of Social Reinforcement
on Operant Crying

**Betty M. Hart, K. Eileen Allen, Joan S. Buell, Florence R. Harris,
& Montrose M. Wolf**

The application of reinforcement principles as a preschool guidance technique under field conditions has recently come under study (Harris et al., 1964, Johnston et al., 1963). Other applications made under field conditions in hospital situations include Wolf's treatment of autism in a child (Wolf et al., 1964) and Ayllon's work with psychotic patients (Ayllon and Haughton, 1962). The present paper deals with the application of reinforcement principles to two cases of "operant crying."

Two classes of crying behavior seem readily discriminable on an "intuitive" basis by almost every teacher and parent: respondent crying and operant crying. Criteria for each class can be defined in terms of its dependent variables. Respondent crying occurs in response to a sudden unexpected and/or painful stimulus event. In general, preschool teachers assume crying to be respondent if the child has a hard or sudden fall; if he falls in an awkward position or is caught in equipment; if he is forced down and pummeled by a larger child; or if he has just faced a dire, unexpected event, such as a near accident. Teachers attend at once to respondent crying. Operant crying, on the other hand, is emitted and/or maintained depending upon its effects on the social environment. In general, the most clear-cut indication that a crying

From *Experimental Child Psychology,* 1:2 (July 1964), 145–153. Copyright © 1964 by Academic Press Inc.

episode is operant rather than respondent is that the child looks around momentarily and makes eye-contact with an adult before he begins to cry. An increase in the volume and intensity of the child's cry when an adult fails to attend immediately, together with the child's neither calling nor coming for help, provides other criteria for operant crying. Crying that is initially respondent may readily become operant.

Since by three years of age children vary widely in their patterns of response to pain-fear situations, any reasonably exact discrimination between respondent and operant crying of an individual child can be made only on the basis of close daily observation of his crying behavior.

This paper presents two studies of the systematic use of positive social reinforcement to help children showing a high rate of operant crying to acquire more effective behavior in mildly distressful situations. Although the studies were conducted at different times, procedures and recording methods were the same in each.

➤

METHOD

Subjects

Both subjects were enrolled in the Laboratory Preschool at the University of Washington. Both were in the same group, which included eight boys and eight girls of similar age (four to four and one-half), socioeconomic level (upper middle class), and intelligence (above average). All children attended school five mornings a week for approximately $2\frac{1}{2}$ hours.

Subject 1. The first subject, Bill, was four years and one month old when he entered school. He was a tall, healthy, handsome child with well-developed verbal, social, and motor skills. Outdoors he ran, climbed, and rode a tricycle with energy and agility; indoors, he made use of all the available materials, though he appeared to prefer construction materials such as blocks, or imaginative play in the housekeeping corner, to activities such as painting or working with clay. His verbalizations to both teachers and children were characterized by persuasive and accurate use of vocabulary, and frequently demonstrated unusually sophisticated conceptualizations. He and many of the other children who entered nursery school at the same time had been together in a group situation the previous year and were thus fairly well acquainted. His former teachers had described Bill as a child eagerly sought by other children as a playmate. His capability and desirability as a playmate were immediately evident at the beginning of the second year. He moved almost directly into play with two other boys, and with his many good ideas structured one play situation after another with them, situations which often lasted an entire morning. Bill was frequently observed arbitrating differences of opinion between his playmates, insisting on his own way of doing things, or defending his own rights and ideas; nearly always, he did so verbally rather than physically.

In the first few days of school, teachers noted that in spite of Bill's sophisticated techniques for dealing with children, he cried more often during the morning than any other child in school. If he stubbed his toe while running or bumped his elbow on a piece of furniture, he cried until a teacher went to him. If he fell down, or if he was frustrated or threatened with any kind of physical attack by another child, he screamed and cried; all play, his and his companions', stopped until Bill had had several minutes of comfort from a teacher. In view of his advanced verbal and social skills, teachers questioned whether his crying was due to actual injury or maintained by adult attention.

Subject 2. The second subject, Alan, lacked 2 weeks of being four years old when he entered the Preschool. He was enrolled in the same four-year-old group as Bill. Unlike Bill, however, Alan was new to the group and therefore had had no previous acquaintance with any of the children. He spent most of the first month of school exploring with vigor all the equipment, material, and social situations the school had to offer. He climbed, rode trikes, swung and dug, with skill and application. His use of creative materials was free and imaginative; his block-buildings were complex, intricately balanced structures. With children and adults he spoke confidently and assertively, often demanding that they listen to a lengthy story or fulfill his requests immediately. He defended himself both verbally and physically, holding on tenaciously to a possession or saying, "Don't!" over and over. Sometimes he forcibly appropriated an object from another child, calling names when the child resisted; but though he was the physical equal or superior of most of the others, he rarely attacked another child. He was attractive and vivacious as well as skillful. By the end of the first 6 weeks of school he was playing as an integral member of one or more groups of children every morning.

Though he did not cry quite as often as Bill, Alan cried equally as hard over much the same kinds of bumps and falls. Like Bill, he screamed and cried whenever another child succeeded in appropriating an object in his possession. He was observed to endure shoving and even hitting by a child smaller than he but to cry vociferously at a push by a child equal to him in size and strength. Though Alan's crying was noted from the beginning of school, the staff thought that Alan should fully adapt to the school situation and develop in play skills before any procedures were undertaken to deal directly with his crying behavior.

In dealing with both Alan and Bill, a distinction was made between respondent and operant crying. Teachers had observed that neither was unjustifiably aggressive; both could defend themselves, were physically strong and large relative to the group, and had better than average physical, verbal, and social skills. Neither had injured himself or been injured by another child in the group. Both were often observed to make momentary eye-contact with a teacher before beginning to cry, and the cries of both rapidly increased in volume until a teacher attended to them. Teachers agreed that both children would benefit if the frequency of crying episodes could be decreased and if more appropriate responses to mild pain and frustration could be developed.

Recording of Crying Episodes

In both cases the operant crying behavior was recorded by a teacher using a pocket counter. She depressed the level on the counter once for each crying episode. A crying episode was defined as a cry (a) loud enough to be heard at least 50 feet away and (b) of 5 seconds or more duration. At the end of the day the total number of crying episodes was recorded and plotted on a cumulative graph.

Procedures for Presenting and Withdrawing Reinforcers

For ten days before initiating reinforcement-extinction procedures, the number of Bill's operant crying episodes per morning was to be recorded in order to obtain a baseline record of the operant level of the behavior. This was done at the end of his first month of school. A baseline record of Alan's daily crying episodes was similarly planned several months later, after Alan had attended school for three months.

For each child, extinction of operant crying was to be instituted immediately after these data had been secured. Teachers were to ignore each child's operant cries, neither going to him, speaking to him, nor looking at him while he was crying, except for an initial glance in order to assess the situation. If he was in close proximity to a teacher when he began to cry, she was to turn her back or walk away to be busy with another child. However, every time that either child responded in a more appropriate manner after a fall, scrape, push, or dispossession, however minor, he was immediately to be given much teacher attention and approval.

In order to substantiate the hypothesis that the operant crying of these children was truly a function of adult reinforcement, it was judged necessary, if the extinction process was successful, to reinstate the behavior. At first teachers were to give attention to every approximation to a cry, such as whimpering and sulking; then, if and when the behavior was re-established in strength, they were to go to the child immediately every time he began to cry and give him solicitous attention for several minutes.

If and when operant crying had again reached a level similar to that of the baseline period, it was again to be extinguished. The procedures of the first extinction period were to be reinstituted, teachers ignoring all operant cries by turning away or focusing their attention elsewhere. At the same time, they were to reinforce the boys for all verbal responses emitted during mild pain or frustration. As the second extinction progressed, teachers were gradually to refine the criteria for reinforcement to "appropriate" verbal responses, and differentially reinforce more socially acceptable verbal behavior evoked by minor injuries and frustrations. Threats and name-calling were to be ignored, and attention given only for such verbalizations as "Stop that," "That hurts," "Ouch!" or explanation of prior possession.

➤

RESULTS

Subject 1. As can be seen in the baseline period for Bill (see Figure 1), at the beginning of the study he was crying 5–10 times every morning at school. Within 5 days after introduction of extinction procedures his operant crying decreased to between 0 and 2 episodes per day. When continuous adult attention was again given to all operant cries and approximations to cries, the baseline rate of crying episodes was soon re-established. Then, four days after reintroduction of extinction for operant crying, the behavior was practically eliminated.

Subject 2. Alan's rate of operant crying during the baseline period (see Figure 2) averaged about 5 episodes per morning. As with Bill, Alan's crying episodes decreased to 2 or fewer per day within five days after the introduction of extinction procedures. The behavior again reached a level nearly as high as baseline four days after reinforcement

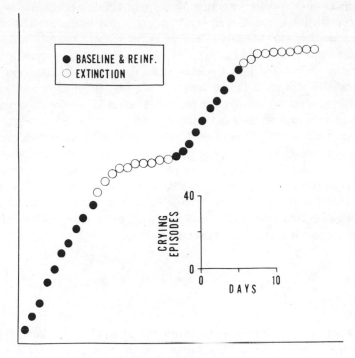

FIGURE 1. Cumulative record of daily operant crying episodes of Subject 1, Bill.

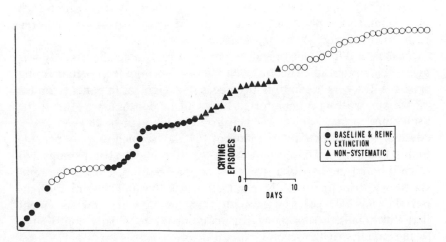

FIGURE 2. Cumulative record of daily operant crying episodes of Subject 2, Alan.

of operant crying was reinstituted, and maintained approximately this level for six days. On the eleventh day of reinstatement of operant crying, the behavior suddenly decreased to one or fewer episodes per day (day 28, Figure 2). After continuing reinforcement procedures for seven more days, teachers decided that, though their attention may have initially reinstated the behavior, other uncontrolled factors in the environment had apparently led to its cessation. Therefore, systematic reinforcement techniques were discontinued (after day 35 on Figure 2). However, very soon the behavior reappeared and gradually increased in frequency until on the 50th day it had reached a frequency almost double that of the baseline period. Extinction procedures were again introduced (on day 51, Figure 2). The rate of operant crying dropped much more gradually this time than had Bill's: there was a burst on the 56th day, and it was not until ten days later that operant crying episodes stabilized at one or fewer per day.

><

DISCUSSION

During the extinction periods for both Bill and Alan, teachers noticed no unexpected side-effects. They had anticipated that play would become more rewarding to both children once the frequent interruptions for crying episodes were eliminated. Each of the children, during the extinction periods, sustained a cooperative, sometimes directing, role in play. Each appeared to become more constructively absorbed in such play, often to the point of appearing oblivious to persons outside the realm of the imaginative play situation.

Subject 1. After Bill's operant crying was reinstated and his play was again being interrupted six or seven times a morning for operant crying episodes, teachers began to notice occasional signs of impatience on his part. Even as teachers comforted him and he continued to shriek, he sometimes turned away from their comfort, though he did not leave. Also, the extent of the interruption of his play seemed more noticeable than it had during the baseline period. At that time his companions had often ignored, or retreated from, his crying episodes. During the reinstatement period they usually remained near Bill, watching him throughout the episode. Teachers thought that the powerful reinforcement that Bill obtained from play with his companions greatly contributed to the rapidity of the second extinction process.

Subject 2. After Alan's operant crying had risen during the reinstatement period to a rate equal to that of the baseline period, the sudden disappearance of the behavior was completely unexpected. Teachers continued to reinforce all cries and approximations to cries for seven more days before deciding that some other factor in the environment had apparently decreased Alan's operant crying. Only after reinforcement procedures had been discontinued and the behavior had begun to reappear did teachers reflect on the possible significance of particular behaviors they had observed during the reinstatement period. At that time they had noticed that Alan often screwed up his face as though about to emit a loud cry when he was in close proximity to them. In accordance with the reinforcement procedures in effect, they immediately offered him comfort, and frequently he did not actually cry (only audible cries were counted in the data). One day, for example, Alan was climbing on an iron frame, a teacher watching him. As he climbed down from the frame he screwed up his face and clutched his ankle. The teacher approached at once, asked what had happened and comforted him. Alan explained that he had bumped his ankle, and then said, "I'm going to do that [climb the frame] again." As he descended the frame a second time, Alan bumped his leg and, looking at the teacher, emitted a low whimper. The teacher immediately comforted him, whereupon he again climbed the frame, and again bumped himself descending. On none of these occasions did Alan actually cry. It appeared, upon subsequent reflection, that Alan did not need to cry: he had apparently effectively "shaped up" a teacher to give him comfort and attention whenever he merely looked as if he were about to cry.

When systematic reinforcement procedures were discontinued and Alan's "looking as if he were about to cry" was no longer given immediate adult attention and comfort, full-scale operant crying reappeared and was apparently reinforced in the period that followed, on some sort of unsystematic intermittent schedule. The rate of operant crying increased irregularly; the decline in rate after several days of a rise in rate might possibly be correlated with (a) teachers' having inadvertently put the behavior on extinction for a time after it became aversive to them, and (b) such frequent interruptions in Alan's play that his playmates moved away from him and into other activities. These intervals of extinction, if such they were, were not, however, planned procedures.

After systematic extinction procedures were reinstated, Alan's operant crying behavior extinguished much more gradually than had Bill's. A possible cause was the preceding unsystematic intermittent schedule of reinforcement in Alan's case. In the literature (e.g., Ferster and Skinner, 1957) it has been well demonstrated that extinction after a continuous schedule of reinforcement is more rapid than after an intermittent schedule.

Though many of the findings concerning Alan's operant crying are still conjectural, the data from the studies seem to demonstrate that frequent crying may be largely a function of social reinforcement. The implications for parents and teachers in helping children to behave more appropriately appear evident.

Token Reinforcement to Increase Singing Participation in Nursery School Children

Fred G. Esposito

In a New England nursery school, teachers had noted the problem of waning, almost nonexistent participation by their children at group singing time. Of twenty-two nursery school children, only one participated in group singing. The teachers sought a method of improving choral singing, especially after hearing and accepting the psychologist's comments regarding the possible benefits which may accrue to youngsters in this multisensory, social, linguistic art form. The more obvious attempts at improvement, such as new songs, records, and improved piano accompaniment seemed to have had no effect.

Two groups of children were observed at singing time. The first group had twelve typical middle-class four-year-olds, but only one true singer. A "singer" was defined as a child who opens his mouth and emits tone-like sounds resembling words which serve as lyrics for the familiar melody rendered on the piano. Three boys in the first group and one boy and one girl in the second insisted on remaining both mute and at the most distant point from the piano. It was agreed that the groups would be treated one at a time, the untreated group serving informally as a control group.

Prior to singing time, the twelve children of the first group were introduced to two boxes — one containing varicolored plastic chips, the other containing Disney characters made of spongy rubber and approximately an inch or two in height. The children were advised that "singers" at music time would earn chips and at the end of singing time, the chips would be "cashed in" for a Disney character. The rate was set at four chips per character. Every one of the children showed four fingers when asked, "How many are four?" ("I am four years old, you know," was the familiar retort.)

The "Happy Birthday to You" song, familiar to all of these four-year-old was repeatedly sung (in honor of the fictionalized birthdate of the school's pet parakeet). The six children who sang heartily were immediately reinforced with chips. Two of the three boys sitting in the remote corner began gradually to move nearer to the piano. One of these boys began to sing and was reinforced for this desirable behavior. Three previously silent children opened their mouths to sing and they were reinforced. The child furthermost from the group emitted a boisterous sound and was reinforced, too. One child held his hands over his mouth but faint sounds came through from time to time nonetheless. Each child was reinforced for his successive approximation if full singing behavior was not exhibited.

At the conclusion of the first session, seven children had met the four-chip criteria for obtaining a Disney character. The others were allowed to retain their chips for future exchange. By the following week's end (five sessions), all children had earned at least one character, and some had acquired a half dozen or so. The escalation of criteria for various individuals rendered a numerical account of characters an unreliable indicator. By session five, all treatment group children participated in singing, honoring the fictionalized birthday of a pet.

In contrast, there appeared to be no change in singing behaviors of the control group. At this point the teachers could no longer be restrained and they were eager now to help the still largely-silent control group to sing and enjoy "music time." They utilized essentially the same procedures and, within seven sessions, all children in the second group were meeting the operational definition of singing. In time the reinforcements were "thinned out" through escalation of the criteria, and subsequent observations of music time indicated a continued high degree of participation. The singing behavior, reinforced during repetitions of the "Happy Birthday Song," was observed to generalize easily to the group singing of a great variety of nursery school songs.

VI

SOME IMPLICATIONS

OF BEHAVIOR

MODIFICATION CONCEPTS:

THE NEW THERAPISTS

ONE OF THE CRITICISMS OF TRADITIONAL PSYCHOTHERAPY IS that it seems usually to be applied in relatively isolated verbal sessions which have little relevance for the client's real life. While the psychotherapist talks, listens, and watches in fifty-minute segments, the child's behavior is, in reality, being shaped by contingencies far from the therapist's control, and under the direct control of parents and other persons who have most contact with the child. The therapist's endeavors thus may be quite irrelevant in the life of the child.

Traditionally, therapy with children has been thought to be dependent upon a relationship, variously defined, as a private form of communication between the child and the therapist. A tradition of mystique and sacred quality appears to have developed over the years, and parental involvement has been considered by many clinicians as an unwarranted and often supposedly destructive intrusion into the aura of trust and realm of confidentiality between client and therapist. It is not unusual to find a parent who has been given no detailed information about his child's treatment, even after many years of psychotherapy! In fact, therapists zealously guard the secrecy of their interaction with the child. This exclusiveness, common in the area of psychotherapy, has unfortunately also been incorporated into some other "helping professions" (Baron and Graziano, 1968).

This marked exclusion of parents from child treatment has been somewhat modified in recent years. Parents are now viewed by some professional workers as important contributors to the child's problems and are therefore in need of counseling to help resolve their own emotional reactions. This has led, it seems, to an automatic assumption that a "disturbed" child invariably has a "disturbed" parent and, accordingly, to treat the child effectively one must also effectively treat the parent. More attention has been paid to the parents as sources of information and as collateral clients-to-be-treated, and, very recently, some reports have been available on attempts to engage and utilize parents as active, positive, therapeutic agents.

Graziano (1963, 1967) found that parents of autistic and other psychotic children were readily trained not only as reliable observers but also as "parent-therapists" in individually tailored home programs. The parents were able to carry out structured programs of behavior modification based on detailed weekly training sessions with the psychologist, and to record and report on the progress of the children.

The conclusion that parents are important reinforcers for their children's behavior is also supported in research studies by Patterson et al. (1964), Wahler et al. (1965), and Allen and Harris (1966). Russo (1964), working with a very limited sample of only two cases, suggested that parents can carry out most of the conditioning necessary for behavior therapy with children. The author used two case studies to illustrate operant training procedures carried out by parents. Evans (1967) reported success with a novel approach of hiring and training the mother of a child in his residential program. The mother continues to work as a regular staff member, and reports a great deal of benefit from the training.

While there have been other reports based on small samples, the largest-scale research has been carried out by Walder et al. (1967), who reported success in the formal training of parents-as-therapists to condition improved behavior in their disturbed children.

The behavior therapist's emphasis on learning leads him to believe that in order effectively to modify the child's behavior, he must control the learning that occurs not only during therapy sessions but also during the vastly more powerful and larger periods which make up the child's "real life" situation. Thus the behavior therapist finds himself moving out of his office, into the child's home or school, and helping various important adults to become actively involved in the therapy attempts. This development, from passive office-listening to an active involvement with the child's real world requires training quite different from that of the traditional therapist.

For the therapist to "move out" into his client's real world is not a new idea — Witmer did this in his work with children in the early 1900s. What is new is that the behavior therapist now has some clearly defined, detailed, and objective ways of evaluating and modifying the child's behavior and environment. Add to these new, objective tools the fact that, like Witmer but in sharp contrast to the deliberately-maintained mysticism and never-shared "expertise" of the psycho-dynamic therapist, the behavior therapist believes that *it is important to share his knowledge and techniques* in order to teach others to bring about and maintain improved behavior in the child. There are undoubtedly many moral and ethical aspects to this sharing of responsibility by the professional, but, despite its complexity, we submit a rather simple position: the parents, by virtue of being parents, have assumed the major moral, ethical, and legal responsibility for their children; the parents have the greatest degree of contact with the child and greatest control over his immediate environment; the parents are typically both willing and fully capable of assuming and carrying out detailed and direct measures to help their children. Therefore, it is not the task of the therapist to assume the full burden of "treatment" and, in the process, allow the parent to relinquish his responsibility, but it is the therapist's task to help the parent directly to be more effective in carrying out a parent's moral, ethical, and legal obligation to care for his child.

In order to enter into a shared responsibility with parents, the therapist must be willing to give up some of the mystical dazzle of an aloof expertise. The responsibility and skills must be shared; the parents must be actively involved as co-therapists in a very literal way.

The final section of this book presents papers which discuss the professional training of the "new therapists" as well as some of the recent attempts to involve parents as active therapeutic agents in dealing with children.

The papers by Leonard Ullmann and Ernest Poser discuss implications of behavior therapy for the training of professional therapists. The remaining papers (Walder et al., Wahler et al., Allen and Harris, and Gardner) all deal with aspects of direct training with parents.

⌁34⌁

The Major Concepts Taught to Behavior Therapy Trainees

Leonard P. Ullmann

In discussing the training of behavior therapists, the first requirement is to define behavior therapy. This is not easy. The very composition of the present group of symposiasts illustrates that behavior therapy is not a single homogeneous doctrine. I think it is fair to say that Dr. Ayllon and I lean toward an operant and Skinnerian approach as much as Drs. Wolpe and Franks lean toward a Pavlovian and neo-Hullian model. Dr. Wolpe in his new book with Arnold Lazarus (1966) says some things about psychotics which I find inconsistent with work such as that by Lovaas et al. (1965, 1966) and by Graziano and Kean (1967) with autistic children and work with adult psychotics such as that by Ayllon and Azrin (1965) and Atthowe and Krasner (1968). Such differences, however, do not detract from behavior therapists. The point simply is that behavior therapy is not a pure school or pure social movement, and let us hope it never will be.

What binds behavior therapists together is that they seek to alter by *direct* rather than indirect methods *behavior* that the person himself or some significant other wishes to change. In this regard there are elements of behavior therapy in the writings of people as diverse as Albert Ellis, Hobart Mowrer, Alfred Adler, George Kelly, and Dale Carnegie. I know of no behavior therapist, even one as flexible as myself, who will accept as true everything every other behavior therapist suggests. But

Paper presented at the American Psychological Association, Washington, D.C., September 1, 1967.

the basic orientation is that the person's difficulty is his behavior in reaction to situations, and that this behavior is the result of previous and current reinforcing stimuli and is *not* symptomatic of some deeper, underlying discontinuity with normal functioning that must be dealt with prior to the emitted behavior.

One of the implications of the behavioral view is that there is no distinction between normal and abnormal other than as behavior is evaluated by criteria which change over time, over place, and over persons.

In operation, the social character of abnormal behavior is well recognized. Glasscote et al. (1966, p. 11) make the point as follows: "classification as a *psychiatric* emergency seems largely contingent on one's being conceived of as a *social* emergency." Jay Jackson (1964, p. 45) puts it this way: "It is unlikely that people are very often committed to state mental hospitals solely because they are unhappy or suffering; most often they are committed only when their behavior is such that they impose inconvenience, embarrassment, or suffering upon others. Thus, although the diagnostic categories employed may be psychiatric, the symptoms from which illness is inferred relate to social behavior." Once in the hospital a person is treated for a disease, and regardless of the change in his behavior it is this disease that justifies both his incarceration and his release.

This leads me to a general point and one I've long wished to make in public. McDougall (cited in Reisman, 1966, p. 148) once described Watson as follows: "Thus, by repudiating one-half of the methods of psychology and resolutely shutting his eyes to three-quarters of its problems, he laid down the program of Behaviorism and rallied to its standard all those who have a natural distaste for difficult problems and a preference for short, easy, and fictitious solutions."

An echo of this thundering indictment is a recent whimper: "The Skinnerian group...have no special theory of neurosis....Their approach rests heavily on *techniques* of operant conditioning, on the use of 'reinforcement' to control and shape behavior, and on the related notion that 'symptoms,' like all other 'behaviors,' are maintained by their effects" (Breger and McGaugh, 1965). Other than the bitchy quotation marks, the statement is accurate.

The issue is whether a theory is needed, even one full of words and scholarship, if it signifies nothing. Another way of saying this is that the Emperor has no clothes, that bedtime troubles do not arise from incubi and succubi, but good old-fashioned sex, and that symptom substitution is a thoroughly discredited hypothesis. Granted, if we deprived ourselves of the notion of mental illnesses we would loose a lot of articles on the differences between middle-aged hospitalized males called schizophrenics and college sophomores, both groups treated *exactly* the same because the work is *so* very scientific. But I have faith that there are sufficient reinforcers for publication that something else would soon fill the pages of our journals.

The Freudian has a view of symptom formation as the solution to an intrapsychic conflict and a basically pessimistic concept of man. The Rogerian view is of man as basically good, growing, and striving for self-actualization. Both these views have basic drives which are blocked and distorted; both see the therapist as a sort of passive midwife who helps without being responsible and who, with minor variations, always does the same thing. The ultimate of this formulation is the promulgation that the necessary and sufficient condition for therapeutic change is the establishment of a warm, nonevaluative relationship. All one has to do is be nice if one is a Rogerian, or expensive if a Freudian, and just wait around for a cure.

The behavioral alternative is to discard the concept of abnormality. Further, man is neither good nor bad; the assumption is made that he is alive, and he is what he learns to be. Therefore the behavior therapist is both active and responsible, and he is so in terms of individuals and not a process.

The first thing a behavior therapy trainee must learn, then, is a new view of people. This means that the target behavior is a normal, appropriate, reasonable outcome of past and continuing experience. This is a very therapeutic thing in and of itself. It leads the behavior therapist to address his client as a normal individual and one to be respected for the strengths he manifests in the majority of his activities. Such strengths are not defenses or reaction formations. The person's difficulties are not the outgrowth of his totally distorted psyche and are not the result of a compromise between intrapsychic conflicts. The person is a unique person and not a label or a diagnostic categorization. Specifically, we no longer deal with phobics who require a total overhaul, but with people who under limited and specifiable circumstances emit phobic behavior. We deal with responses to those circumstances, and we do not use peoples' occasional phobic responses to justify an excursion into their unconsciouses.

If people still want abstractions and formulations of abnormality, all human behavior, especially normal acts, become adequate models. For example, I think that anyone who can explain how a college girl comes to emit such biologically implausible behavior as maintaining her virginity, or who can explain how a decent college boy comes to drop jellied gas on civilians, has a perfect model for such utterly sick behaviors as sitting on a chair staring at a wall, failure of a New Yorker to assert himself, or that ultimate of vile behavior, drinking too much at an APA convention. Looking at behavior, truly there is nothing as far out as a square and nothing as bizarre as a rule-abiding, mid-twentieth-century American.

We want behavior therapy trainees to look at people and what they are doing. The key is the word *what*. In evaluating a situation, the behavior therapist must shift from the traditional *why* questions to *what* questions. He must ask: *What* is the person doing? Under *what* conditions are these behaviors emitted? *What* are the effects of these acts? *What* changes occur after they are emitted? *What* other behaviors might the person emit? He asks this last question in terms of *what* actions may have been extinguished, *what* situations are being avoided, and *what* acts may be encouraged or shaped up. He asks *what* reinforcers can be applied, *what* reinforcers can other interested people bring to bear in a response-contingent manner. He asks *what* needs to be done to have nurses, parents, teachers, or the patient himself follow through with the emission, reinforcement, and recognition of behavior change. Both the patient and his therapists must be able to spot the right time and place for emitting an act, they must be capable of emitting the act — that is, have it in their repertoires, and they must actually emit it. If these requirements are not met, the act will not be reinforced. All the insight and desire in the world will do no good if the person does not know when and how to emit the needed operants. Ambrose Bierce defines "abduction" as "a species of invitation without persuasion." Our task very often is to teach subjects — whether we call them patients, parents, teachers, or therapists — effective ways of persuading other members of the population. The behavior therapist does only a fraction of his job when he reduces the emission of a deviant response; he does his most important work when he teaches the person to emit the appropriate response to the situation.

Insight makes little difference if the person does not know how to act differently. If you have a Freudian or Rogerian model, trouble is a detour on the grand road of normal behavior; but if you are a behavior therapist you must take into account that the person may be raring to go and yet not have the act in his repertoire. I also think that insight probably follows rather than precedes changed behavior. To quote Franz Alexander (Alexander and French, 1946, p. 40): "Like the adage 'Nothing succeeds like success,' there is no more powerful therapeutic factor than the performance of activities which were formerly neurotically impaired or inhibited. No insight, no emotional discharge, no recollection can be as reassuring as accomplishment in the actual life situation in which the individual failed. Thus the ego regains that confidence which is the fundamental condition, the prerequisite, of mental health. Every success encourages new trials and decreases inferiority feelings, resentments, and their sequelae — fear, guilt, and resulting inhibitions. Successful attempts at productive work, love, self-assertion, or competition will change the vicious circle to a benign one; as they are repeated, they become habitual and thus eventually bring about a complete change in the personality."

We want the person to be different. We ask the *what* questions; these lead us to answers that are overt, measurable, and manipulatable behaviors. Asking the right questions is crucial in the training of a behavior therapist.

Asking the what questions may be contrasted with asking the why questions. The matter at a clinical level was put into a nutshell by Eric Berne (1964, p. 19) when he wrote: "Experience has shown that it is more useful and enlightening to investigate social transactions from the point of view of the advantages gained than to treat them as defensive operations." We are advocating the what, the advantages gained. If one asks why, the motivation or the defense, one enters an endless regress. Every behavior therapist has his own favorite hideous example. Mine is family therapy of schizophrenics (Bowen, 1960) in which parents are made to live on the wards with their "sick" children.

For brevity, however, here is the abstract of an article on "The truth as resistance to free association": "The truth is often a reaction formulation while lies represent the despised fecal product which the patient has consciously learned to abhor but unconsciously is still so attracted to that his tendency to lie cannot be permitted into consciousness. It might be conjectured that free association represents the polymorphous perverse activity of a child which at one time was all-pervasive and ego-syntonic." (Prager, 1967, p. 460). This quotation does not have the faults McDougall found in Watson; if anything it adds vastly to the problems, methods, and difficulties of psychology.

Having stripped himself of some of the myths and having learned to ask useful questions, the next locus for the behavior therapist is altering behavior. Since the behavior is considered the result of learning rather than some symptom, it may be changed directly. This implies that the behavior will be dealt with in a situation as close to the target as possible. As such, teachers, nurses, spouses, friends, parents, and fellow pupils may be programmed to provide conditions in which new and more desirable behaviors will be emitted and reinforced. Examples of the training of teachers in behavioral techniques have been provided by Zimmerman and Zimmerman (1962), Wolf et al. (1965), and O'Leary and Becker (1967); Ayllon and Michael (1959) have focused on the role of the nurse as a behavioral engineer; spouses play a crucial role in situations such as the treatment of impotence (Wolpe, 1958) and frigidity (Madsen and Ullmann, 1967); friends have been enlisted in the treatment of excessive drinking (Sulzer, 1965); parents have been trained to identify and differentially reinforce problem behavior in their children (Bijou, 1965, Wahler et al., 1965, Hawkins et al., 1966) and to extend therapeutic efforts to ameliorate difficulties such as stuttering (Rickard and Mundy, 1965); and fellow pupils have themselves been placed under such reinforcement contingencies that they will reinforce a fellow pupil's more adaptive behavior where previously it had provided a source of novelty in the midst of classroom boredom (Patterson, 1965). Finally, whether by chaining, self-reinforcement, emission of relaxation responses, or simply applying learning concepts such as extinction, the person himself may alter his own environment.

The wide range of people who are involved in behavior therapy has two implications. The first is that the psychologist's role as consultant shifts drastically from a focus on a particular case to the teaching of principles and programming of the environment. The second implication is that no invariant set of concepts is used. The focus in consultation is similar to the focus in treatment: to obtain changed behavior. The psychologist will therefore select and present his concepts in terms of what is serviceable for the person with whom he works rather than in terms of a "course" which must be completed.

The first point to be made is that when we talk of training behavior therapists, we talk of garden variety normal people and are not restricted to that deviant group known as clinical psychology graduate students. The same what questions asked in determining the course of action with the patient are asked in determining the course of action with parents, teachers, spouses, and nurses. Until the psychologist is clear as to his own program there is no reason to expect that other people will do what he considers desirable. Once the course of action has been decided upon, the specifics for training the therapists are no different from the specifics of training patients: both are normal people.

The literature on the cooperation and change of significant others is steadily growing. What would be said of them can be said of the therapist's major ally, the patient. Under what conditions will a person do what another suggests? In this regard, as Wolpe and Lazarus (1966, p. 28) point out, the establishment of a relationship is a necessary first step. The attitudes discussed earlier are a great step forward in achieving a relationship which indicates understanding and respect (without dependence) for the patient. The next step is that cues are given in the language and at the rate which the patient can use. If desensitization is to proceed the patient must know how to relax, how to visualize, and when and how to signal an increase in tension. If a person is to model, the model's actions must be as clear as the consequences of that activity. All the modeling in the world will do no good if the person does not attend or does not have the skill being modeled in his repertoire. The behavior therapist must make an analysis of *what* is most likely to be effective. This program is put to the test, and every behavioral technique for altering patients is appropriate for the training of behavior therapists. Selective response contingent reinforcement, records of changes, explicit statements of reinforcing contingencies, prompts and their fading, and so on, are used. The patient may keep records of his own behavior or provide himself with an aversive shock not only in the treatment session but as he moves throughout his daily life. To hearken back to the quotation from Alexander, the effective reinforcer for both patient and behavior therapist is new successful behavior. The behavior therapist uses every possible pedagogic device feasible to foster the new behavior, but once established and successful it is maintained because it works. There is little difficulty with termination or transference because of the therapist's attitude toward the patient, because the domain of discourse is real extra-therapy behavior, and because what is learned is not a relationship to the therapist but methods of dealing with people. These methods, when successful, not only are maintained, but are, like other behaviors that work, generalized.

The concepts taught to behavior therapists about themselves parallel most closely the role of teacher. The techniques and principles are those of social learning and behavior influence. I will not review them other than to say that simply handing out tokens does not mean a person has a token economy; and shocking a person contingent upon some behavior does not mean a person is a behavior therapist. To say this is equivalent to saying that anybody who runs rats is an experimenter. In both instances it is the design of the situation and not the implementation that is a crucial element.

The role is active. The behavior therapist assumes responsibility; he is not midwife to a process but involved in the specific behaviors attempted and the conditions under which the person lives. This is the exact opposite of Szasz's formulation of psychotherapy as a "game" divorced from reality. Treatment deals with real behavior and has its goal change in extra-therapy situations. The behavior therapist must be ready to accept this active responsible role. I find that parents, teachers, nursing personnel, spouses and friends, rather than being sick, as so much of the psychoanalytic literature pictures them, are actively interested in the patient. It is a source of gratification to find how quickly people not overly tainted by college courses or Ann Landers will delay their own gratifications in order to help another person. I think the reason for this favorable response to behavior therapy is that it makes sense because it is how normal people act toward each other.

There is one additional point for the professional behavior therapist: he must be prepared to make value judgments. Such judgments are inherent in the view that there is no behavior that is "sick" in and of itself. A whole range of decisions arise which did not exist when all deviant behavior was presumed to exist as a malfunctioning of the intrapsychic apparatus. In operation the therapist may decide on courses of action that would horrify the dean of students or the local minister. There are also times when the behavior therapist will arrange reinforcement contingencies in a manner that will lead to adjustment or conformity to such repressive forces as a child's parents or the orderly progress of classroom tuition. The point is that value problems cannot be forced aside by merely calling a behavior sick. The behavior therapist must look at the specific situation and work with an individual, not a disease label.

Techniques seem easy to apply and those who have little experience with behavior therapy think that one simply tells people what to do or simply gives shocks at one time and candy at another. Nothing could be further from the truth. By focusing on individual behavior, many concepts and many words have been found to be unnecessary and even malicious obstacles between the psychologist and his patient. But these concepts made life easier because they provided high-sounding words to bury problems. The behavior therapist in training others, whether they be patients or significant others, must constantly check what he himself is doing. It is very much the examined and the examining life.

While a lot of words drop out, behavior therapy is far from barren and mechanistic. Quite the contrary, for a person can no longer say he loves, empathizes, relates, or does other good things. Behavior therapy asks not what is the reason, but what is the action.

The behavior therapist must be taught new ways of looking at people. The people he works with are neither sick nor healthy, but simply behavior-emitting human beings. The same principles apply to training patients and therapists. The crucial element lies in the asking of questions likely to elicit explicit behavioral referents: that is, the asking of *what* questions rather than *why* questions. One result of this approach is that a great deal of theory about "sick" people becomes irrelevant other than in journals and on doctoral exams. A second result is that the behavior therapist assumes far greater responsibility than the typical midwife-to-a-process therapist. The behavior therapist is a real person dealing with other real people. And this, I think, is the theoretical, moral, and practical crux of training behavior therapists, whether those therapists are called psychologists, parents, or attendants. There is a pressure away from words and the labeling of motives and a movement toward the actual behaviors and operations. The result is demonstrably more effective in obtaining behavior change. Above all, the result is an active, responsible, and genuine engagement, not with abstractions, but with other people.

⪤ 35 ⪥

Training Behavior Therapists

Ernest G. Poser

Despite the recent spate of publications on behavior modification there is little in the literature to guide those responsible for the training of behavior therapists. One reason for this may well be that the majority of those now working in this field are essentially self-taught. Typically they acquired their new skills by extrapolation from concepts and techniques familiar to them from other settings, notably the psychological laboratory or the psychiatric clinic. In the early stages of any new professional enterprise such a state of affairs may be inevitable but to perpetuate it would be inconsistent with current manpower needs in the Mental Health professions.

Competent behavior therapists are now greatly in demand for hospital and research setting on both sides of the Atlantic yet there are few, if any, centers equipped to offer training in this speciality. To do so effectively requires facilities not always available in settings quite adequate to offer instruction in other treatment methods. It is the purpose of this paper to draw attention to the special needs of a Behavior Therapy Training Center and thereby to stimulate the development of appropriate teaching facilities for workers in this area of clinical practice.

From *Behavior Research and Therapy*, 5 (1967), 37–41, Pergamon Press.

➤

WHO IS ELIGIBLE?

Both Wolpe (1964) and Eysenck (1964) have forcefully pointed out that specialized training is required for the successful practice of behavior therapy. Marks and Gelder (1965), on the other hand, conclude from their findings on the outcome of Behavior Therapy that "the relevant skills are derived more from clinical experience in treating neurotic patients than from detailed knowledge of learning principles."

Such conflicting views may have arisen from failure to recognize that workers at different levels of training can be utilized in Behavior Therapy. For convenience they might be thought of as representing two levels of proficiency. The first would be adequate for those content to act as co-therapists while the second level of competence, for which advanced training in one of the mental health professions is prerequisite, would be required of those wishing to become behavior therapists.

It is proposed that the term "Behavior Therapist" be used only to denote a professionally trained person fully familiar with contemporary theories of psychopathology, the psychology of learning and the measurement of behavior change. On the basis of his clinical experience and specialized training in the behavior therapies, such an individual could take charge of a behavior therapy service and be responsible for the elaboration of treatment strategies for patients in his care.

The co-therapist, by contrast, does not require professional training in the mental health professions. Any mature individual who can master the basic principles and operations used in the behavior therapies can contribute at this level. Techniques of therapy such as relaxation training, the implementation of operant schedules, satiation methods and certain desensitization procedures can all be competently handled by personnel with little training other than that received on the job. In our experience nursing assistants, craft workers, and activity therapists have been particularly helpful as co-therapists in behavior modification. Undergraduate students have also been employed in this capacity (Davison, 1965).

It is one of the great advantages of the behavior therapies that other than professionally trained workers can be utilized in their implementation.

In practice we have found that any behavior therapist in full-time hospital employment can effectively supervise three to four co-therapists. This represents a sizeable extension of therapeutic services and makes for more economical use of highly skilled manpower always in short supply.

➤

IN WHAT SETTING ?

Behavior therapy is best taught in those centers where an active behavior therapy service already exists. This observation is not as self-evident as it may at first appear. It implies, among other things, that university departments of psychology are not, as a rule, well suited to offer such training unless they have access to a suitable service setting. To be suitable, such a service should be directed by a behavior therapist and deal with a wide variety of behavior deviations. At present the tendency is for behavior therapy services to specialize in this or that procedure to the exclusion of others. In a training center all methods should be taught and new ones constantly explored.

If these conditions are met the process of teaching behavior therapy differs little from that of other professional and research settings using the "apprenticeship" model of training. Essentially this consists of assigning the student to understudy an experienced behavior therapist. In the early stages this may be done by observing the senior therapists during the treatment process. Later the student may take on his own cases whose treatment is carried out in the presence of the instructor.

While the physical presence of students during a behavior therapy session is not considered undesirable (Geer, 1964; Geer and Katkin, 1966), a teaching unit should be equipped with a one-way screen and an intercommunication system so that students can observe treatment sessions.

It is likewise desirable that apparatus for the measurement of autonomic changes as well as timing and recording devices for operant conditioning be readily available. Equipment of this kind is indispensable for the monitoring of many behavior therapeutic procedures and should not be restricted to the research laboratory.

Ideally, behavior therapy should be taught in settings where other schools of therapy are also practiced. This is important because all methods of behavior modification, whether psychodynamic, client-centered, or behavioral are apt to develop cultish practices and esoteric terminologies. To guard against this it is useful to require students of behavior therapy to discuss their cases, at least occasionally, in the presence of senior staff not committed to behavior therapy. They should likewise be encouraged to participate in case presentations given by adherents of other schools of behavior modification. The aim of such a requirement is not to make students equally proficient in the techniques associated with other schools of therapy but to give them an appreciation of the similarities and differences involved.

Because methods of behavior therapy are rooted in experimental techniques largely derived from the psychological laboratory, trainees should have ready access to an academic department of psychology in which learning theory as an approach to behavior change is being actively investigated. Though desirable it is not necessary for the trainee to participate in such researches himself but he should have an opportunity to see at first hand how wide the gap still is between experimental findings and their clinical application.

CONTENT AND SEQUENCE OF TRAINING

As noted above, training in Behavior Therapy should be provided at two levels. Since aspirants to Level II will be supervising personnel at Level I, all trainees must necessarily master this level first. Level II candidates will, however, spend less time at the initial stage.

Level I. Training at the first level will be mainly along lines of an apprenticeship in which students first observe, and later assist, experienced therapists in their day-to-day routines. It will involve demonstration sessions by senior staff, supplemented by audio-visual aids. There are now a number of useful films on Behavior Therapy (Lindsley, 1966; Davison and Krasner, 1965), and tape recordings of various procedures. A phonographic recording of relaxation technique is commercially available (Troubadour, 1962). Programmed texts on the principles of conditioning can also be used to advantage (Holland and Skinner, 1961).

Once the trainee at Level I has become familiar with the above techniques of behavior modification he will quite naturally manifest curiosity about their purpose and rationale. At that point seminars and lectures might be introduced to cover relevant aspects of psychology.

The aim here would be to relate the principles of learning and conditioning to the modification and management of deviant behavior. Bookish theorizing should be avoided since it is likely to discourage the non-academic trainee and to accentuate unnecessarily the distinction between the two levels of training. As soon as the program of demonstrations and lectures is underway, it is advisable to have the trainee carry out the simpler procedures under supervision. In the early stages it is well for them to practice on fellow students or volunteers. As soon as the trainee demonstrates mastery of a technique, he should be assigned a suitable patient to treat by that method. If the "dry-run" is unduly prolonged students tend to become overawed by the theoretical complexities stressed in lectures and their readings. The resulting disenchantment may retard the effective use of practical skills involved in relaxation, desensitization, or operant conditioning.

The length of time required to complete the first level of training will depend not only on the attitude and previous experience of individual trainees, but also on the range of case material available to them. In an active behavior therapy teaching program, a period of 6 months should be adequate to produce competent personnel at Level I, provided that candidates have had some previous experience in the care of patients. Three or four months should suffice for those proceeding to advanced training at Level II.

Level II. Those eligible for the advanced program will have had formal training in one of the mental health professions, typically clinical psychology or psychiatry. To the extent that such training is at present rarely oriented toward interpretations of maladaptive behavior in learning theory terms prospective behavior therapists frequently have to unlearn some earlier notions incompatible with the behavioral approach. Learning to focus on overt rather than covert events and on performance rather than verbal behavior, are two cases in point. For those trained along psychoanalytic lines, the most difficult transition resides in the behaviorists single-minded concern for what maintains deviant behavior now, rather than what caused it originally. These theoretical difficulties have their counterparts in practice. Thus, in the management of patients, the traditional clinician's zeal for verbal expressions of empathic understanding and reassurance is often seen by the behavior therapist as verbal reinforcement of the very behavior he is trying to extinguish.

For these reasons training at Level II is ushered in by an intensive reading program in which the literature on verbal conditioning, the psychology of learning, personality theory, as well as the measurement of behavior change figures prominently. Next a short course of lectures is given in which fundamental concepts such as reinforcement, extinction, and generalization, etc., are reviewed in the context of psychological deficit in human behavior.

At this point the student is ready for a series of seminars in which the course content so far dealt with, at the experimental or theoretical level, is related to clinical case material. It is highly desirable that all participants in such a seminar themselves have at least one patient in behavior therapy. In that way, members of the group take turns in discussing the problems they have encountered and learn to benefit from each other's mistakes.

So much for the core program to be followed by all trainees wishing to acquire the skills necessary for the clinical application of behavior therapy. In some settings, however, specialized roles for behavior therapists are now emerging. In the main these have to do with the evaluation of patients before, during and after termination of treatment. This function is best performed by a psychologist with competence in statistics and biometric techniques. He should also be familiar with apparatus for recording and analyzing psychophysiological changes as these methods are being increasingly used in clinical assessment.

Instruments commonly used for psychodiagnosis such as projective techniques have so far contributed little to the quantification of symptomatic behavior change.

Another area of specialization now evolving is that of pharmacotherapy as an adjunct to behavior therapy. It is often the case that patients referred for Behavior Therapy have been treated by psychotropic drugs. Some of these, like chlorpromazine for instance, are known to inhibit classical conditioning and thereby to inhibit certain forms of learning. Hence other drugs may have to be substituted for these tranquilizers and increased use might be made of certain substances known to facilitate learning (Schachter and Latané, 1964). The development of pharmacological principles consistent with learning theory is clearly the task of appropriately qualified behavior therapists with medical training. It goes without saying that the ultimate responsibility for the physical welfare of all patients treated by behavior therapy rests with this class of personnel.

While every practitioner of behavior therapy might be expected to contribute to the advancement of knowledge in the area of behavior modification, there is a valid distinction to be made between such clinical research and the testing of theoretical hypotheses at the laboratory level. Training for the latter remains to be the province of the relevant university departments. It must be emphasized, however, that neither research training alone nor clinical experience alone can henceforth be regarded as sufficient preparation for those wishing to apply the techniques of classical and operant conditioning to the corrective management of maladaptive behavior.

~36~

Teaching Behavioral Principles
to Parents of Disturbed Children

Leopold O. Walder, Shlomo I. Cohen, Dennis E. Breiter,
Paul G. Daston, Irwin S. Hirsch, & J. Michael Leibowitz

The major purpose of our applied research is to develop various ways to train parents to be effective behavior therapists for their own disturbed children. We apply principles and techniques from the experimental psychology of learning. We assume the behavior of the child is a function of his environment and believe that the person who has the responsibility for the child's environment is the appropriate change agent. The parents are typically responsible for the child's environment; therefore, we attempt to give the parents technical information and consultation to help them do their job better.

Techniques we have utilized and continue to develop include having educational group meetings with parents, consulting with individual pairs of parents, and structuring a more controlled laboratory-like environment within the home. As part of our research program different families are exposed to all, one, or some combination of these educational techniques.

We typically deal with the parents of children who are labeled schizophrenic, autistic, brain damaged, or retarded. Currently nineteen families with behaviorally disturbed children are involved in three projects.

Paper presented at the Eastern Psychological Association, Boston, Massachusetts, April 6, 1967, as part of the symposium "Parents as Primary Change Agents for the Treatment of Children."

Project H (for Hirsch) studies 15 mothers. They are being given the *group education only* treatment, five mothers in one group and ten in another. An additional 15 mothers are on a waiting list to serve as replications.

Project B (for Breiter) studies one family. The parents are being given consultation in their home. In addition, each parent is the experimenter in one of two controlled learning environments in the home.

The third project studies three families. The three pairs of parents are being offered all three techniques. Together they attend a series of group educational meetings. Each of the three pairs of parents is offered a series of individual consultative interviews; these interviews are coordinated with the educational meetings. In each case the individual behavior consultant has advised the parents to structure within the home a laboratory-like learning environment for the child.

The rest of this paper is largely concerned with the three techniques as applied to this group of three families. One evening a week for 16 weeks the three pairs of parents come to the University Counseling Center. During all 16 weeks the six parents and two staff members meet for a one-hour group educational session. During the last 12 weeks, each pair of parents remains for an additional hour to meet with one or two staff members for a one-hour consultative session. We shall describe, in turn, these educational and consultative sessions.

The educational group is composed of the three pairs of parents, a group leader who is a member of our staff, and a second staff member who is a passive observer of group leader behaviors. The purposes of the group are to teach general principles of learning to the parents and to enable them to perform a functional analysis of behavior. Admission to the group is contingent upon the completion by each parent of a weekly written homework assignment. For example, the parents are to read short behavioral vignettes which describe specific behavior problems. Written answers to the questions which follow the vignettes are the parents' ticket of admission to the next week's group session. These answers provide data relevant to observing any changes in parent verbal sophistication in behavior control techniques during the 16 weeks of parent participation in the project. In efforts to define our educational techniques in the group we have observed and recorded such group leader behaviors as use of operant concepts, praising parents, etc. We have not observed the parents' behaviors in the group. However, tape recordings of all group sessions are available for observation of parent vocal behavior.

To achieve our group educational goals we have developed a four-step program. The first step is *to teach the parents how to observe behavior and record data accurately*. We have allotted four weeks to this phase. After a short introductory lecture on the importance of accurate observations and recording, the parents practice observing and recording. They observe, through a one-way mirror, short behavior interactions involving two people. Each weekly 5-minute observation period is followed by a 45-minute period devoted to reporting and discussing the observations. In addition to answering the questions following the behavioral vignettes, the parents are instructed to observe their child for some short period every day, and to submit a report at the following group meeting. Parents are also required to rank order the five most undesirable ongoing child behaviors to be weakened and the five most desirable behaviors to be instated. As the first four weeks continue, the parents refine these lists in clear behavioral terms. For example, a parent may initially list "negativism" as an undesirable behavior. By the fourth week, the behavior referred to may be more accurately described as "Johnny doesn't go to sleep when I tell him to."

We teach the parents to observe behavior and record data accurately so that the behavioral problem is precisely defined. Once this is accomplished a functional analysis of the problem is possible.

At week 5 we start the consultative interviews (to be described later) and the second step in the educational program. In this step we introduce contingencies into the observed behavioral interactions and *teach the parents to identify the contingencies*. A short lecture about the ABC's of behavior — Antecedent events, Behaviors, and Consequent events — introduces this phase of the program. Behavior-environment interactions are discussed and examples are given. A Greenspoonian situation is contrived in which one person says "uh-huh" or "yes" following each statement of self-reference made by a second person. In the discussion subsequent to this observation session, the operations of reinforcement and extinction as well as the terms themselves are clarified. Prepared written materials about these topics are given to the parents. Also, relevant studies from the professional literature together with questions on all the materials are distributed. Written answers to the questions comprise the homework assignment. Session 6 is used to demonstrate the immediacy of reinforcement. Written materials on shaping are distributed together with questions to be answered. Shaping is the tool required to deal with the child who is deficient in desirable behaviors.

Thus, the third step in the program is focused on *allowing parents to practice shaping*. We have allotted 8 weeks to this step. In session 7, the written educational materials and questions on shaping are discussed. Following this discussion the group leader demonstrates by shaping a behavior of one of the parents, while the other parents observe. In this session a shaping switch is used which operates a short tone designated as the reinforcer. Parents being shaped are instructed to earn as many tones as possible.

The next week a movie on "Reinforcement Therapy" is shown. Parents are asked to observe things in the film related to past discussions in the group sessions. For two sessions each parent is given the opportunity to shape some behavior of another parent by using the tone as feedback for a desired behavior. All sessions end with a discussion about what occurs during the shaping sessions.

For four sessions the parents are given the opportunity to shape two behaviors (bar pressing and rearing) in food-deprived rats and to study intermittent scheduling and its effects on extinction.

The last step in the group educational program is *to review the principles and procedures of behavior control and see how they have been applied by the parents.* In the final two sessions parents make case presentations of some of the procedures they instituted in their homes.

The second technique to be described here is consultation with individual pairs of parents. *Individual consultation* starts for these three families on the fifth week and overlaps with the remaining 12 weeks of the group educational series. After each of these 12 group meetings there is a 2-minute break. Each pair of parents enters one of three consultation rooms with their behavior consultant. Ideally the consultant has prepared an agenda for that meeting. What occurs is described in three ways. (1) Raters on the other side of one-way mirrors count occurrences of predetermined categories of consultant behaviors, (2) the consultant takes notes and dictates a report after the parents have left, and (3) the consultant records the session with an audio tape recorder. Copies of the agenda are given to the observers before the parents arrive and arc given to the parents at the start of the session.

The agenda first lists the assignments due from the previous consultative meeting. If the parents have not fulfilled the assignment, the session ends immediately after the assignments have been discussed and clarified. The parents are asked to return when the assignment is completed. If the parents have come with their homework, the complete agenda is followed: The homework may consist of a written progress report by the parents tallying the incidence of some behavior of the child and how the parent responded. In later interviews in the series the parents may be asked to prepare and bring in a plan describing changes in the way they will respond to one of the child's behaviors. At the end of the session the parents are given an assignment. Early in the series of interviews the consultant takes more responsibility for devising the assignment; progressively the parents are given more and more responsibility in planning subsequent procedures. An example may be useful. In order to get firsthand data on the mother-child interaction about which the parents complained the consultant rode in the car as the mother drove somewhere with two of her children. It became clear to the consultant that the mother responded to her children when their playing in the car interfered with her driving safely. She did not respond to them when they were not bothering her. In the next consultative interview the parents were told that they would have to specify the child behavior they wanted *more of* so we could help the parents build positive behaviors in the children. Completion of the assignment was of course their ticket of admission for future consultation.

This part of the method most resembles conventional psychotherapy or counseling. The two parents of the child meet weekly with a behavior consultant (and occasionally with a co-consultant); they talk for up to 45 minutes, helping the parents deal with their specific child by advising them in applying general principles of behavior control.

After the parents leave, the consultants meet as a group to receive feedback from the observers. In addition, consultants are praised if they are described as behaving within the specified limits of an operant framework. Some of the consultant behaviors which are praised are: teaching and advising parents, using operant concepts, selectively giving positive reinforcement for desired parental behaviors, working to reduce the parents' discomfort by helping them gain skills, shaping parental competence in behavior modification, and in general providing the parents with a model to imitate. In this way we not only describe our form of behavioral consultation but also attempt to control the behavior of the consultants.

The third technique to be described is the controlled learning environment. The use of operant techniques for the control of behavior requires that one have control of the environment in which the behavior is emitted. Investigators who have utilized behavior modification techniques in institutions have programmed the environment to respond selectively to specified response classes and have controlled the supply of reinforcers. The situation in the home is usually much different. Home environments maintain parent behaviors which are often incompatible with behaviors necessary for successful modification of child behaviors. One example is the frequent difficulty experienced in trying to get mothers to deprive their children. The home environment also supports child behaviors which compete with behaviors parents may wish to instate. When a parent is attempting to shape some behavior, the situation is usually one from which the child attempts to escape to some other area of the home where other behaviors are maintained. This escape behavior is usually reinforced. Unless some changes in the home environment are accomplished, attempts to modify behaviors will be only partially successful.

Our experience in establishing a controlled learning environment in the homes of the three families we have been discussing is still limited. We shall use as an example the family in Project B which is being given only individual consultation in their home. There the consultant helped the parents establish two controlled environments: one for about an hour each afternoon with the mother as experimenter, the other for about an hour each evening with the father as experimenter. In these settings the interactions between the child and a parent are recorded as the parent attempts to teach the child some skill. On the basis of these records, changes in the parents' response are suggested. Remarkable improvements in the child's behavior in those restricted learning environments have followed. In addition the parents are learning to treat her differently outside the session and gratifying changes in the child's behavior are becoming apparent.

Our plans with this technique include helping other families set up learning laboratories in their homes and introducing token economies. Such a controlled therapeutic environment in the home may be what is needed to more efficiently modify extreme behavior patterns.

To sum up, this is a research and development program. We are building new techniques, we are objectifying the techniques we have built, and we are evaluating these techniques. The evaluation of these techniques involves improving the quality of data and designing studies with adequate controls and comparisons. We have not had time in this paper to detail all our efforts. Our goal is to deliver to the clinical community efficient tools which are objective and which have demonstrated effectiveness.

~37~

Mothers as Behavior Therapists for their own Children

Robert G. Wahler, Gary H. Winkel, Robert F. Peterson,
& Delmont C. Morrison

Two reviews of the literature on behavior therapy (Bandura, 1961; Grossberg, 1964) reveal a large number of systematic attempts to apply principles of learning theory to psychotherapy. It would appear that many investigators, working within the conceptual frameworks of respondent and operant learning, have produced practical changes in the deviant behavior of both adults and children.

Typically, these investigators have implied that stimuli making up the adult's or child's natural environments are responsible for development and maintenance of the deviant behaviors involved. That is, through unfortunate contingencies between stimuli, or between stimuli and behavior, deviant behavior is produced and maintained. However, while most investigators have assumed that this is true, few have accepted the full implications of this position. Instead of changing "faulty" contingencies involving the natural environment, most research therapists have placed their subjects in artificial environments, designed to modify the deviant behavior through extinction, punishment, and/or reinforcement of responses which are incompatible with the deviant behavior. Although these techniques have produced some remarkable changes in the deviant behavior within the artificial environments — and in some cases within the natural environments — one wonders about the effect that the unmodified natural environments

From *Behavior Research and Therapy*, 3:2 (1965), 113–124, Pergamon Press.

would eventually have on the behavior changes; logically, it would be expected that the deviant behavior would again be strengthened, and behavior developed in the artificial environments would be weakened.

From the standpoint of methodology there is good reason for the behavior therapists' failure to deal with the natural environment. Since the efficacy of their techniques depends upon control of specific contingencies between stimuli, or between stimuli and behavior, they have typically chosen to work in settings that are highly contrived. However, the extent of this methodological problem is, in large part, correlated with the patient's age. Undoubtedly, the natural environment of the young child is far less complex than that of an adolescent or an adult, and it therefore should present fewer difficulties in systematic control. One might conclude that attempts to develop therapeutic techniques for the control of natural environments should initially utilize children as patient–subjects.

Most psychotherapists assume that a child's parents compose the most influential part of his natural environment. It is likely, from a learning theory viewpoint, that their behaviors serve a large variety of stimulus functions, controlling both the respondent and operant behaviors of their children. It then follows that if some of the child's behavior is considered to be deviant at a particular time in his early years, his parents are probably the source of eliciting stimuli and reinforcers which have produced, and are currently maintaining this behavior. A logical procedure for the modification of the child's deviant behavior would involve changing the parents' behavior. These changes would be aimed at training them both to eliminate the contingencies which currently support their child's deviant behavior, and to provide new contingencies to produce and maintain more normal behaviors which would compete with the deviant behavior.

Techniques of parent-child psychotherapy have been investigated by several researchers (Prince, 1961; Russo, 1964; Straughan, 1964). However, the procedures used in these studies did not permit assessment of variables which were maintaining the children's deviant behavior, nor did they permit analyses of those variables which were responsible for changing the deviant behavior. While the investigators concluded that changes in the children's deviant behavior were probably a function of changes in the parents' behavior, these conclusions could not be clearly supported. Thus, in the further study of parent–child therapeutic techniques it would be of value to utilize procedures which will provide information concerning those stimulus events provided by the parents which function to maintain deviant classes of the child's behavior. Once these controlling stimulus events are detected, it might prove feasible to modify the occurrence of these events in ways which will produce predictable and clinically significant changes in the child's behavior.

The present experiment was an attempt to modify the deviant behavior of three children by producing specific changes in the behavior of their mothers. The major purposes of the study were: (1) to experimentally analyze the mother–child interbehaviors in an effort to specify those variables (i.e., reinforcement contingencies) which may function to maintain the deviant behavior of the children; (2) to eliminate these variables in an effort to modify the children's deviant behavior. Therefore, the focus of the study was not on producing long-term changes in the children, but rather to discover how their deviant behavior is maintained and how appropriate changes may be brought about.

><

METHOD

Subjects and Apparatus

Subjects were three boys varying in age from four to six years and their respective mothers. While the children's behavior problems would probably be considered moderate by most clinical standards, all had exhibited behavior which was sufficiently deviant to motivate their parents to seek psychological help. More detailed information on the children and their mothers will be presented in a later section.

The apparatus was located in the Gatzert Child Development Clinic of the University of Washington. The equipment consisted of a playroom with two adjoining observation rooms which were equipped for visual and auditory monitoring of behavior in the playroom. Each observation room contained a panel with three microswitches which were connected to a Gerbrand six-channel event recorder; depression of the microswitches by observers activated selected channels of the event recorder. In addition, the playroom was equipped with a signal light which could be illuminated by the experimenter in one of the observation rooms.

General Procedure

Prior to the behavior therapy sessions, the parents of each child were seen in interviews aimed at obtaining descriptions of the behavior which created problems at home and/or at school. The interviewer also asked the parents to describe their typical reactions to these behavior patterns whenever they occurred.

All mother–child cases were seen separately for approximately twenty-minute sessions, held once or twice weekly in the playroom. The mother and her child were always the sole occupants of the playroom.

Classification of mother–child interbehavior. For the first two sessions, the mother was instructed, "Just play with —— as you might at home." These instructions were modified for one of the cases when a later analysis of the data revealed little or no evidence of what the parents had earlier described as deviant behavior. In this case the mother was given other instructions, based on her description of her typical behavior at home.

During these sessions, two observers, working in separate observation rooms, obtained complete written records of the child's and the mother's behavior. Analysis of these records began with a selection of the child's deviant behavior. This selection was based upon similarities between the recorded behavior and the behavior which the parents reported to create problems at home. A second classification of the child's behavior was made to establish a class of behavior which the experimenter regarded as incompatible with the deviant behavior. Later, strengthening of this class was used in eliminating the deviant behavior.

A second analysis of the written records involved a description of the mother's ways of reacting to her child's deviant behavior, and to his incompatible behavior. Essentially, this analysis provided a description of possible reinforcers provided by the mother for the two classes of the child's behavior.

Observer reliability and baseline measures of behavior. Following the classification sessions, instructions to the mother were the same; however, the observers now recorded only three classes of behavior — two for the child (deviant behavior and incompatible behavior) and one for the mother (her reactions to her child's behavior classes). This was done by depressing selected microswitches every five seconds for any of the previously classified deviant or incompatible behavior patterns which occurred during the five-second intervals. Another microswitch was reserved for any behavior of the mother's which occurred immediately after the child's two classes of behavior. Essentially, this system was a time-saving device which eliminated the laborious procedure of writing down behavior and then classifying it. Thus, once the child's deviant and incompatible behaviors, and the mother's reactions to them were defined and labeled by the experimenter, the observers' attention in further sessions was focused only on these behavior patterns.

The observational records obtained from the above sessions were also analyzed for observer reliability. For each behavior class an agreement or disagreement was tallied for every five-second interval. The percentage of agreements for observers was then computed for each behavior class, for each session. Observer agreement of 90 per cent or better was considered to be adequate; once this agreement was obtained on all behavior classes the baseline sessions were begun. Essentially, the baseline sessions provided a measure of the strength or rate of occurrence of the child's deviant or incompatible behavior, and a measure of how frequently the mother responded to them. These sessions were continued until both mother and child showed fairly stable behavioral rates.

Before the baseline sessions were begun, one of the observers was arbitrarily chosen to record the data, and the other observer served only as a reliability check. In all cases reliability checks showed observer agreement of 90 per cent or better.

Behavior modification procedures. Following the baseline sessions, E made systematic attempts to change the mother's reactions to her child's behavior. These attempts involved the use of instructions to the mother before and after the playroom sessions, plus signal light communications to her during the sessions. During initial sessions, E used the signal light as a cueing system, essentially to tell the mother when and how to behave in response to her child's behavior. As the mother improved in her ability to follow instructions, E eventually changed the function of the signal light from cueing system to reinforcement system. The mother was now required to discriminate and respond appropriately to her child's behavior without E's cueing. E used the signal light to provide immediate feedback to the mother concerning her correct and incorrect discriminations, thus teaching her appropriate discrimination responses.

Instructions and the coded significance of the signal light were determined from the baseline data and principles of operant learning theory. In general, the aim was to eliminate possible reinforcers provided by the mother for her child's deviant behavior, but to have her produce them following the child's incompatible behavior. It was thus hoped to train the mother to weaken her child's deviant behavior through a combination of extinction, and by reinforcement of behavior which would compete with the deviant behavior. To accomplish these goals, the mother was first shown the baseline data and given a complete explanation of it; she was also given numerous examples of her child's deviant behavior and his incompatible behavior. She was then told that in further sessions she must completely ignore her child's deviant behavior and respond in any approving way only to his incompatible behavior. The signal light was described to her as an aid which would help her to carry out the instructions. She was told to keep an eye on the light and to respond to her child *only* if it was illuminated; otherwise she was to sit in a chair, ostensibly reading a book and make no verbal or nonverbal contact with her child. *E*, of course, illuminated the light only following the child's incompatible behavior. In one case, where the child's deviant behavior proved to be usually resistant to extinction, the mother was trained in the use of a punishment technique as well as the differential reinforcement procedure.

When the observational data revealed that the mother was responding appropriately to the signal light, she was told that in later sessions she must make her own decisions to respond or not respond to her child. She was again told to keep an eye on the light, since it would now be illuminated following her correct decisions.

Experimental demonstration of mother's control. As later results will indicate, the behavior modification procedures appeared to be effective in producing expected changes in the behavior of the mothers and their children. However, there yet remained the task of demonstrating that modification of the child's behavior was solely a function of the mother's ways of reacting to him. In further sessions the mother was instructed to react to her child as she had done during the baseline sessions; that is, to again be responsive to the deviant behavior. If the mother's reactions to her child during the behavior modification sessions had been responsible for weakening his deviant behavior, one would expect that this procedure would strengthen the deviant behavior. Once this test for control had been made, the mother was instructed to again make her reinforcement contingent only upon the incompatible behavior, thus resuming her "therapeutic" ways of reacting to him.

⏣

RESULTS

Case 1

Danny was a six-year-old boy who was brought to the Child Development Clinic by his parents, because of his frequent attempts to force them to comply with his wishes. According to the parents, he virtually determined his own bedtime, foods he would eat, when the parents would play with him, and other household activities. In addition, he frequently attempted, with less success, to manipulate his teacher and peers. His parents reported they were simply "unable" to refuse his demands, and had rarely attempted to ignore or punish him. On the few occasions when they had refused him, they quickly relented when he began to shout or cry.

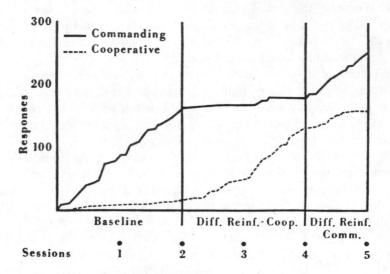

FIGURE 1.   Rate measures of Danny's commanding and cooperative behavior over baseline and therapy sessions.

During the classification and baseline sessions, Danny's mother reported that she was extremely uncomfortable, because of Danny's behavior and her knowledge that she was being observed. Figure 1 shows cumulative records of Danny's deviant and incompatible behaviors during all therapy sessions. His deviant behavior was labeled as "commanding behavior" during the classification sessions, and was defined as any verbal or nonverbal instructions to his mother (e.g., pushes his mother into a chair; "Now we'll play this"; "You go over there and I'll stay here"; "No, that's wrong. Do it this way."). The incompatible behavior, labeled as "cooperative behavior," was defined as nonimperative statements or actions or by questions. Note the marked difference in rate between the deviant and incompatible behaviors during the two baseline sessions. Figure 2 shows cumulative

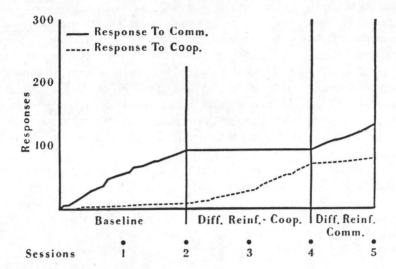

FIGURE 2. Rate measures of Mother's general responses to Danny's commanding and cooperative behavior over baseline and therapy sessions.

records of the mother's general reactions to Danny's two behavior classes during the therapy sessions. Her reactions usually consisted of following Danny's instructions and such verbal comments as "Okay, if that's what you think; am I doing it right now?"

Following the baseline sessions the mother was instructed to be responsive to Danny's cooperative behavior but to completely ignore his commanding behavior. Reference to Figure 2 indicates that she was successful in following these instructions. During the first two differential reinforcement sessions her rate of response to his commanding behavior dropped to zero, while her response to his cooperative behavior increased steadily in rate. (Use of the signal light as a cueing system was discontinued for the second differential reinforcement session.) Danny's behavior during the differential reinforcement sessions is shown in Figure 1. Note that his rate of commanding behavior dropped considerably compared to the baseline sessions, while his cooperative behavior increased sharply in rate. Interestingly enough, Danny's mother reported that she was much more comfortable with him during the last of these sessions.

The test of Mother's control was performed following the first two differential reinforcement sessions. This one session demonstration involved instructing the mother to behave as she had done during the baseline sessions. As the rate of response curves in Figures 1 and 2 indicate, change in the mother's behavior was again correlated with the expected change in Danny's behavior; his rate of commanding behavior increased compared to the previous two sessions, and his cooperative behavior declined in rate. Thus, the finding that Danny's commanding and cooperative behaviors could be weakened when his mother's reactions to these classes were eliminated, and strengthened when they were replaced, points with some certainty to the fact that her behavior changes were responsible for the changes in Danny's behavior.

Further sessions were planned to reinstate the contingencies of the first differential reinforcement sessions. Again the mother was instructed to reinforce only the cooperative behavior; unfortunately, administrative problems made it necessary to terminate this case before the sessions could be conducted.

Case 2

Johnny, age four, was brought to the Clinic by his parents because of what they termed "very dependent" behavior. In addition, they were concerned about a nursery-school teacher's report that he frequently hit or kicked his peers and teacher when they were inattentive to him. According to his mother, Johnny rarely showed this behavior at home, but instead tended to follow her around the house much of the day, asking questions and requesting her help for various tasks. She, in turn, tended to be very responsive to this behavior and also tended to interrupt him when he played alone or with his peers. When asked why she behaved in these ways, she reported that she was quite concerned about the possibility that he might break things in the house or get into trouble with his playmates; she felt much more comfortable when he was at her side or at least within sight.

Johnny's teachers felt that his aggressive behavior in nursery school was related to his "dependence on others for direction and support." They stated that if he was told what to do, or if a teacher watched him or played with him, the hitting and kicking was not likely to occur. However, it was also apparent from the teacher's report that, inadvertently, they may have been providing social reinforcement for his aggressive behavior.

Following an analysis of the classification session, two classes of Johnny's behavior were defined; the deviant class was labeled "dependent behavior," which included such behavior as questions and nonverbal requests for help (e.g., bringing a toy to her following a request for her to play with it or to show him how it works). Aggressive behavior, such as hitting or kicking did not occur. Behavior considered incompatible with the deviant class was labeled "independent behavior." This class included any behavior in which he played alone, with no verbal comment to his mother.

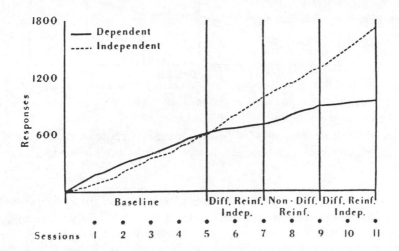

FIGURE 3. Rate measures of Johnny's dependent and independent behavior over baseline and therapy sessions.

Figure 3 shows cumulative records of Johnny's dependent and independent behaviors during all therapy sessions. Note that the response rates for his two behavior classes during the baseline sessions are roughly comparable. Figure 4 shows cumulative records of mother's general reactions to Johnny's two behavior classes during the therapy sessions. Her reactions to his dependent behavior usually involved answering his questions or granting his requests for help. Consistent with her self observations, Mother's reactions to Johnny's independent behavior almost always involved interrupting his play with imperative statements or nonverbal interference such as taking a toy away from him.

During the differential reinforcement sessions, Johnny's mother was instructed to ignore his dependency behavior and respond approvingly to his independent behavior. Reference to the differential reinforcement sessions shown in Figure 4 indicate that she was successful in following these instructions, even following elimination of the cueing system after the first session. As the rate of response curves show, her rate of

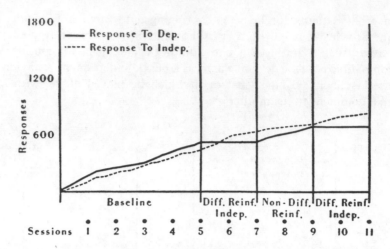

FIGURE 4.   Rate measures of Mother's general responses to Johnny's dependent and independent behavior over baseline and therapy sessions.

response to his independent behavior increased, and for his dependent behavior it dropped to zero. Correlated with his mother's behavior changes, Johnny's behavior changed in the expected ways. The rate of response curve for his dependent behavior, seen in Figure 3, dropped compared to the baseline sessions, while his independent behavior increased in rate.

Following the two differential reinforcement sessions, the test of mother's control was performed. She was now instructed to resume her baseline behavior, and as the data indicate, she was successful in following these instructions; her response rates shown in the non-differential reinforcement sessions in Figure 4, were roughly similar, and comparable to her baseline rates.

Again, correlated with these changes in Mother's behavior, Johnny's behavior changed in the expected ways. Reference to the nondifferential reinforcement sessions of Figure 3 shows that his response rates for the two behavior classes are comparable to his baseline rates.

The final two sessions involved reinstatement of Mother's differential reinforcement contingencies without use of the cueing system. The response rates shown in the last two sessions of Figures 3 and 4 indicate that this procedure was effective. Therefore, as was true in case number one, the finding that Johnny's deviant and incompatible behavior patterns could be weakened when his mother's reactions to these classes were eliminated, and strengthened when they were replaced, supports the contention that her behavior changes were responsible for the changes in Johnny's behavior.

Case 3

Eddie, age four, was brought to the Clinic because of what his parents referred to as "extreme stubbornness." According to the parents, this behavior occurred only in the presence of Eddie's mother. Essentially, this "stubbornness" involved ignoring her commands and requests or doing the opposite of what he was told or asked to do.

She reported that her reactions to this behavior usually involved pleas, threats, and spankings, none of which appeared to be effective. It also became clear that most of her interactions with him were restricted to his oppositional behavior; she rarely played games with him, read to him, or talked to him. She did however, attempt to respond approvingly to his infrequent cooperative behavior. When asked why she was so selective in her interactions with him, she reported that because of his opposition, she felt "frustrated with him" and "angry with him" most of the time. She was convinced that he opposed her because he "liked" to get her angry.

During the classification sessions it became necessary to modify the instructions to Eddie's mother. Initially she was told to "just play with Eddie as you would at home." However, as might have been expected, mother and child ignored each other. The instructions were then changed to require mother to ask Eddie to play with a different toy every sixty seconds. These instructions were in effect throughout all therapy sessions. Eddie's behavior was classified as either oppositional (not complying with mother's request) or cooperative (complying).

Figure 5 shows cumulative records of Eddie's oppositional and cooperative behaviors during all therapy sessions. Note that his rate of oppositional behavior during the baseline sessions is far greater than his rate of cooperative behavior. Figure 6 shows cumulative records of Mother's general reactions to Eddie's two behavior classes. Her reactions to his oppositional behavior almost always involved threats or repetition of her request. Following his few cooperative responses, she either ignored him or stated her approval in a low voice without smiling.

During the differential reinforcement sessions, Eddie's mother was instructed to ignore his oppositional behavior and respond enthusiastically and with a smile to his cooperative behavior. As the differential

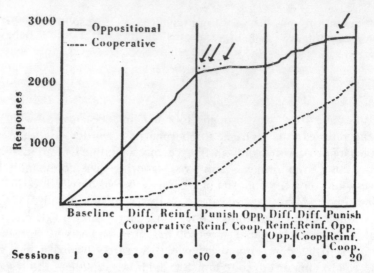

FIGURE 5.   Rate measures of Eddie's oppositional and cooperative behavior over baseline and therapy sessions.

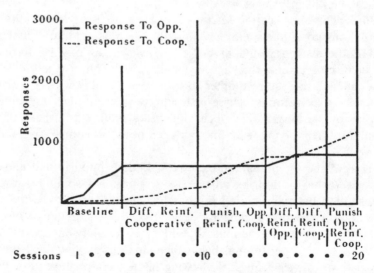

FIGURE 6.   Rate measures of Mother's general responses to Eddie's oppositional and cooperative behavior over baseline and therapy sessions.

reinforcement sessions shown in Figure 6 indicate, she was successful in following the instructions and use of the cueing system was discontinued after the second session. Reference to the same sessions in Figure 5 indicates that the expected changes in Eddie's behavior occurred gradually as the sessions progressed. However, note that the increase in his rate of cooperative behavior was not marked, and it declined during the fourth and fifth differential reinforcement sessions. Because of this problem, E decided to instruct Mother in the use of a punishment procedure which could be combined with the differential reinforcement technique. She was instructed to isolate Eddie in an empty room (adjacent to the playroom) immediately following any of his oppositional responses. She was also told to leave him alone in this room for five minutes, unless he exhibited other undesirable behavior such as temper tantrums; if this type of behavior occurred, he remained in the room until it terminated.

Eddie's behavior during the punishment-reinforcement sessions is shown in Figure 5. The arrows indicate those instances in which Mother was signaled via the cueing system, to initiate the punishment procedure. Note the marked change in Eddie's oppositional and co-operative behavior; his oppositional behavior declined sharply in rate while his rate of cooperative behavior increased markedly. As these records also indicate, modifications in Eddie's behavior were maintained during the last two punishment-reinforcement sessions by Mother's use of differential reinforcement alone. Interestingly enough, Eddie's mother reported, following one of these latter sessions, that she "actually enjoyed being with him."

The test of Mother's control of Eddie's behavior was complicated by the fact that she had used two procedures in the course of the therapy sessions. As a result, two questions had to be answered: (1) Was Mother responsible for the changes in Eddie's behavior? (2) Was one of her procedures more important than the other in producing these changes? To answer these questions, Mother was first instructed to respond only to Eddie's oppositional behavior. The differential-reinforcement-opposi-tional sessions of Figure 6 revealed that she was successful in following these instructions. Correlated with these changes in Mother's behavior, Eddie's oppositional behavior (Figure 5) increased in rate, while his cooperative behavior declined in rate. Thus, it seemed certain that Mother was responsible for the earlier changes in Eddie's behavior. To determine whether Mother's differential reinforcement or differential reinforcement *plus* punishment had produced these changes, she was instructed in one set of sessions to resume her differential reinforcement of Eddie's cooperative behavior; in another set of sessions she was instructed to differentially reinforce the cooperative behavior and punish the oppositional behavior. Mother's success in following these instruc-tions is shown in the last two sessions of Figure 6 and by the arrow in the last session of Figure 5. As Figure 5 also indicates, the expected changes in Eddie's behavior occurred only during the last set of sessions, thus demonstrating that Mother's combined use of differential rein- forcement and punishment was responsible for the modifications in Eddie's behavior.

➤

DISCUSSION

The data from two of the cases reported in this study indicate that a mother's social behavior may function as a powerful class of positive reinforcers for her child's deviant as well as his normal behavior. Experimental analysis of case number one revealed that Danny's mother was maintaining his commanding and cooperative behavior patterns through her reactions to these two response classes. A similar experimental analysis of case number two showed that Johnny's mother was maintaining his dependent and independent behavior through her reactions to these response classes. In both of these cases the response rates of the children's deviant and incompatible behavior patterns were weakened when their mothers' contingent behavior was eliminated, and strengthened when they were replaced. It would thus seem beyond a reasonable possibility of coincidence that the children's behavior classes were under the control of their respective mothers. However, this conclusion could not be supported by the data from case number three. It will be recalled that little rate change occurred in Eddie's oppositional and cooperative behavior following manipula- tion of the contingencies between these response classes and his mother's behavior; not until his mother utilized a punishment procedure did dramatic rate changes occur. Thus, little can be said concerning variables in Eddie's natural environment which were responsible for maintaining his deviant and incompatible behavior.

The data reported in this study are also of interest in terms of the modification of deviant child behavior. In all cases it proved possible to train the mothers in the effective use of behavior modification techniques based upon principles of operant learning theory. In two of the cases (Danny and Johnny) the techniques simply involved instructing the mothers to change the usual contingencies between their behavior and their children's deviant and incompatible behavior. Since it had been experimentally demonstrated with these cases that the mothers were providing social reinforcement for their children's deviant behavior, the next logical step would involve training the mothers to ignore these behavior patterns and to provide their reinforcers for behavior which was incompatible with the deviant behavior. As the data indicate, this differential reinforcement procedure was quite effective within the confines of the experimental setting.

Selection of the behavior modification technique used for the third case (Eddie) required more reliance on past research findings than on information gained from an analysis of mother-child interbehavior. Since *E* was unable after five sessions to determine the source of control of Eddie's deviant behavior, it was decided to stop the search for controlling stimulus events and concentrate on finding the most practical means of eliminating his deviant behavior. Past research (Wolf et al., 1964) has shown that social isolation may function as a highly effective punishment technique for deviant child behavior. As the data indicate, Eddie's mother made very effective use of this technique.

The design of this study did not permit assessment of the generality of the changes in the children's behavior. One would expect that since the mothers were responsible for the changes which were produced,' the question of generality would in part be a question of how well the mothers' "therapeutic" behaviors were maintained outside the experimental setting. That is, were their newly learned reactions to their children effective in obtaining reinforcement from the natural environment as well as from the experimental setting? Further research is planned to provide answers to this question.

⊰ 38 ⊱

Eliminating a Child's Scratching
by Training the Mother
in Reinforcement Procedures

K. Eileen Allen & Florence R. Harris

For the past three years the staff of the Laboratory Preschool has studied effects of adult attention on problem behaviors in normal children. Results have indicated that the behavior was controlled by its immediate consequence, the attention of adults. Those behaviors which were immediately followed by teacher attention tended to be maintained or to increase in rate; behaviors following which teacher attention was withheld or was immediately withdrawn tended to diminish rapidly or to drop out altogether. Some of the problem behaviors modified in accordance with the above adult social reinforcement contingencies included regressed crawling (Harris et al., 1964), socially isolate behavior (Allen et al., 1964), excessive crying and whining (Hart et al., 1964) and deficits in motor skills (Johnston et al., in press). Similar results have been reported in studies of modification of pathological behaviors through use of operant techniques (Ayllon and Haughton, 1962; Wolf, Risley, and Mees, 1964; Wolf et al., 1965).

The staff of the Developmental Psychology Laboratory receives many requests from parents for help with problem behaviors of their preschool children. A very limited number of these children can be

From *Behavior Research and Therapy*, 4 (1966), 79–84, Pergamon Press.

worked with directly by staff members. Parents, however, give several hours of attention to their children each day. The laboratory staff therefore decided to explore methods for teaching parents to modify their own attending behaviors in ways that might help them resolve their child's problem. Development of such a methodology could decrease the staff time required per child and thus increase the number of children and parents who might be helped.

The exploratory study reported here delineates the procedures used in helping a parent eliminate self-scratching behavior in her child through application of operant conditioning techniques. Although self-scratching might be considered a respondent behavior elicited by a preceding stimulus (skin irritation) rather than an operant behavior responsive largely to its immediate consequences, there is some evidence that dermatitis may be under operant control (Walton, 1960). Likewise, behaviors such as vomiting (Wolf et al., 1965) and crying (Hart et al., 1964) have been shown to be responsive to their social consequences. In the present study it was hypothesized that the self-scratching behavior of the child was a function of the mother's attending behaviors and the behavior could be reduced or eliminated to the extent that the mother could be helped to modify her own attending behaviors.

✂

CASE HISTORY

Fay, an alert, friendly, well-mannered child nearly five years old, was brought to the Developmental Psychology Laboratory by her mother. Consultation was sought because Fay, for almost a year, had been scratching herself until she bled. The scratching behavior had resulted in large sores and scabs on her forehead, nose, cheeks, chin, and one arm and leg. Neither pediatric nor psychiatric consultation had eliminated the scratching, although examinations had indicated that there was no basic medical problem. The last recommendation made to the mother was that Fay be fitted for expensive pneumatic arm splints in order to restrain her scratching activity. Though the mother was reluctant to do this, she saw little alternative if Fay were not to be permanently disfigured.

According to the mother, the parents had tried every disciplinary approach to stopping the scratching. The father spanked the child, sometimes severely, when she scratched. He berated the mother for her verbal but equally ineffectual techniques. The mother declared that she had come to dislike the child so intensely and to be so repelled by her appearance that she felt it might be better if Fay were placed outside the home to live. The marriage itself was threatened, according to the mother, due in large part to constant quarrels over disciplinary procedures.

At the time of initial contact, the mother was expecting another child in three months. This situation, together with what appeared to be the desperate state of both mother and daughter, prompted the staff to attempt an investigation of whether immediate help could be given through work with the mother. The duration of the study was necessarily limited.

><

PROCEDURES AND RESULTS

In the initial interview with the mother, the above information was secured. The mother was told that, although the investigators did not know whether or not they could help her resolve such a problem as scratching, they would be willing to try if she wished to cooperate in a program that would require her to follow specific procedures at home and to come weekly for a limited number of weeks with her daughter to the laboratory. When the mother expressed eagerness to cooperate, an appointment was made for her to bring Fay to the Laboratory Preschool the following week, after laboratory school hours.

Session One

The first session began with a fifteen-minute introductory period in the school playroom. While one investigator discussed tentative plans with the mother at one end of the large room, Fay became engrossed in the doll corner at the opposite end of the room. The other investigator attended and observed her. Following this brief introductory period, Fay and her mother were taken to a clinic play room equipped with a one-way viewing screen. The mother had been instructed to behave as normally as possible during a fifteen-minute observation period, which would be followed by a conference. The investigators then left the mother and child alone and went to the adjacent observation room. Two significant behavioral conditions were evident to the observers. One, Fay was a highly capable and competent little girl with a large repertoire of well-developed social, intellectual, and physical skills. Two, the mother spoke to the child only to criticize, direct, or explain why the child should behave in a different fashion.

At the close of the observation period, while Fay again played with an investigator in the school playroom, the mother was asked to keep a one-week record of the child's behavior as well as her own behaviors in response to the child. She was to note such things as how often Fay scratched, how often she engaged in other behaviors that mother disapproved of, how often she was spanked, isolated, scolded severely, how often she engaged in behaviors that the mother considered appropriate, and what these appropriate behaviors were.

Subsequent sessions followed the pattern of one investigator's working with the mother while the other attended Fay's play indoors and out. The results of the mother's work during each week were in this way observable by the investigators, and they could give weekly recognition and approval to any progress by the mother as it was evidenced in the child's appearance and the mother's behavior.

Session Two

When the mother returned the following week, her records, though kept inconsistently, yielded significant information. First, there were periods in the day when the child did not scratch herself. These periods usually coincided with the times Fay was engaging in some constructive play activity. Second, the mother was berating and punishing the child for a wide range of so-called misdeeds: sauciness, dawdling, poor table manners, playing with certain neighborhood children of whom the mother disapproved, and many minor misdemeanors. Third, even though the father punished Fay severely when she scratched herself to a bloody state, she and the father also had mutually enjoyable times together, both at home and on outings. By contrast, the mother, who was with the child a large portion of the day, never struck her, but verbally punished and criticized her continuously, perpetuating between herself and the child a constant state of friction. The mother stated again that she could hardly bear to look at Fay because of the angry state aroused by her daughter's unsightly appearance.

On the basis of the home observation records, two recommendations were made. One, the mother was not to attempt to change the father's behavior. It was pointed out that fathers differ from mothers in their methods of discipline. As long as the father and Fay had a good relationship in spite of the spankings, little would be accomplished by mother's direct attacks on father's disciplinary action. Mother agreed that this had already been demonstrated.

The second recommendation was that the mother discontinue her efforts to correct all of Fay's misbehaviors and concentrate her efforts first on eliminating the one behavior that troubled the mother most: the scratching behavior. A carefully structured program was suggested. First, all scratching was to be ignored, no matter how bloody the results. Mother said that they had already tried this procedure for a whole month and it had not worked. When asked for details, she said that she and the father had informed Fay that they were no longer going to discuss the scratching. During this period Fay came to them frequently to show them that she had not scratched herself for a whole morning or a whole afternoon. Mother cited her own response to Fay on these occasions: "I told you, we're not going to talk about it. We don't care whether you scratch or not. You're a big girl and it's up to you. I don't want to hear any more about it." It was pointed out to the mother that she had ignored or even punished the appropriate behavior of not scratching, thereby missing an opportunity to strengthen the desired behavior.

Ignoring the scratching, it was explained, meant giving absolutely no attention, positive or negative, to the child when she was actually scratching or had fresh evidence on her face and limbs of recent scratching. At all other times, Fay was to be given approval and attention for whatever commendable behavior was ongoing, such as play with dolls, helping set the table, looking at a book, and *not* scratching.

Although the previously cited studies in the laboratory preschool indicated that the approving attention of significant adults is a potent factor in shaping the behavior of young children, it seemed very difficult for this mother to attend to her child in a positive fashion. It was therefore decided to employ token reinforcement in addition to whatever social approval the mother could muster. For most young children gold stars are highly reinforcing, therefore, a system of token reinforcement was worked out as follows. Every 20 or 30 minutes, if Fay had not scratched during the interval, the mother was to go to Fay and approve her play in as warm a fashion as she was able, at the same time giving her a gold star to paste in a special little booklet. During the early days of the program every second or third gold star was to be accompanied by a primary reinforcer Fay liked, such as a cookie, a bit of candy, or a small glass of the child's favorite beverage. At midday and suppertime, if no scratching had occurred, the accumulated gold stars were to be counted, approved as an achievement, and reinforced by giving inexpensive trinkets which were pleasing to the child. The mother was to try this program for a week and report results at the weekly conference.

Session Three

In the third session, one week after the inception of reinforcement procedures, the mother reported that there had been some lessening of the scratching, but whatever progress had been made during the day seemed nullified at night, since Fay was still arriving at the breakfast table with evidences of freshly scratched sores. The mother was discouraged.

In consideration of time limitations on the total program, it seemed mandatory to find more powerful reinforcers at this point. A careful inquiry into the sorts of play things which were most pleasing to Fay revealed that she frequently asked for items for her Barbie doll. Fortunately these items were manufactured in endless variety. Too, the mother said she was willing and able to pay for whatever Fay might select. Therefore, it was planned that each afternoon of a scratch-free day the mother and Fay would go shopping for the next morning's reinforcer: a new Barbie doll item. Fay was to be allowed to choose what she wanted. Then the mother was to put the item out of reach but in plain view until the next morning. If there was no evidence of fresh scratching in the morning, Fay was to be given the item. The previous program of approving attention and gold stars, backed up by trinkets, was also to be continued. On the fifth day of this week, the mother spontaneously telephoned to report exuberantly that they had had four scratch-free days and nights.

Session Four

When mother and child came in for the fourth session, two weeks after beginning the reinforcement program, the mother pointed out that some of the sores had begun to heal. For the first time mother volunteered a description of newly-discovered desirable behaviors on Fay's part. The mother was given much social reinforcement by the investigator for her careful maintenance of the program. In addition, of course, she was already being highly reinforced by Fay's improved appearance and by Fay's evident efforts to please her.

The program continued for the next week with steady diminution of the sores.·

Near the end of this third week of reinforcement procedures, the mother telephoned one of the investigators to report with despair that the whole program had fallen apart. Fay had scratched herself during the night and drawn blood in several places. The father had flown into a frenzy in the morning and had spanked Fay until he left red marks. Both parents were ready to abandon the program as futile. The mother was asked to review the preceding day step by step. The reason for Fay's "backsliding" soon became evident.

When the mother and Fay had gone to the store to buy a Barbie accessory, the item Fay selected cost more money than the mother had with her. Five-year-olds, of course, have scant knowledge of the importance of various amounts of money. Fay insisted on the item she had chosen. Mother became irritated at what seemed to her highly unreasonable behavior and told Fay she would take what mother bought and like it. Fay did not like it and began to sulk. The mother bought the item anyway and put it on the customary shelf while Fay silently watched. That night Fay scratched open all of the nearly healed areas on her face. As the whole complex of interacting behaviors on the part of both mother and Fay were sorted out, the mother of her own accord volunteered the probable explanation for reinstatement of the nearly-extinguished scratching behavior. The mother was asked to take Fay the next day to buy the desired item and also to be sure to go adequately prepared on future buying expeditions.

Session Five

According to the mother's report in session five, a high point for her came shortly after the above episode, when the father said that he wanted her to help him refrain from whipping Fay when he was angry. He said that he had known all along that whippings had not been effective. Yet when nothing else worked, he whipped because he felt impelled to take some kind of action. The mother was advised to arrange with the father, in some calm moment, a cue she might give him when she saw him on the verge of losing control with Fay; for example, "Dear, will you please get a loaf of bread from the corner store?"

The next two weeks (fourth and fifth weeks of reinforcement procedures) went smoothly with no really low periods occurring. The parents could now, the mother reported, sit down together and discuss Fay without each accusing the other of employing faulty discipline. Fay's lesions continued to heal and to diminish in size.

Session Six

In the sixth session, when Fay's skin was practically clear of scabs, it seemed advisable to start a gradual reduction of extrinsic reinforcers.

First, the mother was instructed to omit one by one the mid-morning and mid-afternoon trinkets, at the same time maintaining a high level of social approval of all desirable behavior. Then the daily trips for Barbie doll accessories were to be made every other day; then bi-weekly, weekly, and finally only occasionally, when a whole page of stars would be exchanged for one item. The gold stars were retained largely because they seemed to be effective in reminding the mother to take overt notice of the many desirable behaviors that her little girl engaged in. Fay, too, was reported to be highly reinforced by filling the pages of her book with stars. However, the pleasure of her parents' approval of her many skills and her pretty appearance, coupled with the reduction of punishment by both mother and father, may have been sufficiently instrumental in maintaining Fay's nonscratching behavior.

Session Seven

At the end of six weeks of the mother's using reinforcement procedures, every sore was healed completely, although there remained vividly red scars, especially on the one cheek and chin. Session seven was the terminal session of the training program. Had circumstances permitted, the experimenters thought it would have been advisable to continue the sessions until the mother had completed her reduction of extrinsic reinforcement. Four months later, however, when Fay and her mother were seen at home in order to secure a post check on the guidance procedures, the scars had faded to a pale pink barely discernible without close scrutiny.

Results of the study suggest that a young child's problem behavior may be treated through helping the mother to modify her own behaviors, that is, through direct action guidance. Moreover, the behavior of self-scratching proved to be under the control of its immediate social consequences. Further investigation of direct action approaches seems to offer a promising extension of the treatment methods available to child guidance specialists.

Behavior Therapy Treatment Approach to a Psychogenic Seizure Case

James E. Gardner

In general, the behavior therapy model conceptualizes neurotic or maladaptive behavior as learned behavior, not as a manifestation of a mental illness. Treatment tends to focus on the "unlearning" or "relearning" of specific habit patterns and may take place in one or more of the following ways: (a) by the direct manipulation of environmental reinforcement contingencies (Ayllon and Haughton, 1962; Ayllon and Michael, 1959), (b) by direct counterconditioning and/or extinction procedures (Wolpe, 1958), or (c) by the provision of more appropriate social role models (Bandura, 1963).

With behavior therapy, as with traditional therapy, the type of treatment approach should be dictated by the type of problem. In this case, direct environmental manipulation of major social contingencies within the family was the treatment selected for a child manifesting seizure behavior of nonorganic origin.

From *Journal of Consulting Psychology*, 31:2 (1967), 209–212.

≻⪡

SUBJECT

The subject (*S*) was a light-complexioned, attractive, ten-year-old Negro female. She was the oldest of three children, attended a private school where she maintained average grades, and was considered well-liked by peers and teachers.

On the surface, as judged from background material initially taken by an attending physician and later elaborated by the therapist, the family history appeared unremarkable. The parents had never been separated or divorced, father was noted for steady employment and attention to his family, *S* had never manifested behavioral or other problems at school, disagreements between sibs at home seemed at about the "usual" level, and there was no history of prior seizure behavior on the part of any member of the family.

However, close analysis of the interactions between family members suggested some possible antecedents to *S*'s seizure behavior. For example, *S* had long been noted for her rivalry with her next younger sister and both children competed strongly for parental attention. Also, a "model" for psychosomatic behavior had been inadvertently provided by the mother some months prior to *S*'s manifestation of seizure behavior. At this time, the mother had experienced a headache of such intensity that she "rocked and banged" in pain and had to be taken to the hospital. Some further antecedents in the form of apparent inadvertent parental "shaping" of deviant behavior also seemed in evidence. This will be amplified below. However, it must be noted that this apparent shaping for deviate behavior on the part of the parents seemed well within the bounds of the type of situation that could relatively easily arise in a family (e.g., giving in to tantrum behavior, giving attention for somatic complaints, etc.).

According to the parents, *S* had for some weeks prior to her seizures manifested increasingly frequent somatic complaints. The parents could not recall whether the increase in somatic complaints closely followed the mother's illness or not. The *S* had also manifested several temper tantrums during the several weeks prior to the seizure episode, one of which, in the mother's words, "looked sort of like a convulsion."

The seizure episode which resulted in *S*'s hospitalization began mildly with complaints of a stomachache followed by a headache. These complaints were followed by rhythmical head rolling accompanied by hair pulling. The *S* was then taken to the hospital by her parents.

In the hospital, the results of all physical tests, including an electro-encephalograph study, were either negative or ambiguous. Psychological test results suggested a "hysteric-type" personality but no indications of severe emotional difficulty or neurological impairment. However, it was noted that S seemed to feel a high degree of sibling rivalry. It was also noted that a hysteric-type personality might be considered high in potential for some form of conversion reaction and/or somatic complaint.

✂

PROCEDURE

Psychological consultation was initiated with S's parents, prior to S's discharge from the hospital. The S received no counseling either during or after her hospitalization. In order to attempt to assess more clearly the effects of the parental counseling on S's seizure behavior, the usual seizure-inhibiting medications were withheld under medical supervision.

The parents were seen jointly in three weekly one-hour sessions. The first session was conducted prior to S's discharge from the hospital. When S returned home, a treatment plan devised in the first session was immediately put into effect by the parents.

In the counseling sessions, the emphasis was immediately placed on (a) analyzing the reinforcement contingencies within this particular family's structure and (b) devising means of altering some of these contingencies in an attempt to alter S's deviant behavior with a minimum of friction.

The parents seemed to readily grasp the behavioral principles involved. Whenever possible, they were encouraged to develop or elaborate aspects of the treatment plan. Whenever one or the other verbalized some plan which seemed fairly likely to be effective in this situation, further discussion was encouraged by the therapist. In this manner, an attempt was made to "shape" the parent's behavior toward more effective ways of dealing with S's deviant behavior. This procedure seemed to be more effective than direct suggestion, since the parents developed the notions themselves in the context of what was feasible in their home situation.

The relatively simple treatment plan was devised in the first session with the parents. The two later sessions were spent in elaborating or clarifying aspects of the initial basic treatment plan. The program consisted of the parents (a) being "deaf and dumb" whenever S manifested seizures or other highly deviant behavior such as tantrums, (b) rewarding S with their attention whenever S manifested appropriate behavior such as playing with sibs, helping mother, drawing, etc., while

(c) being alert for possible substitute behavior on *S*'s part, such as increased somatic complaints (which, if manifested, were to also be dealt with using the "deaf and dumb" method of nonreinforcement).

Follow-up telephone interviews were conducted approximately once every 2 weeks for 30 weeks. The frequency of *S*'s somatic complaints, tantrums, and seizures during this period was recorded from data furnished by the parents. The importance of this information was stressed to the parents, and it appeared that they attempted to comply with the requests for accurate observations. This method of estimating the frequency of the selected behaviors was obviously imprecise. However, laboratory controls were not possible under the circumstances. Also, ethical and practical considerations militated against delaying treatment for *S* until a more adequate baseline could be obtained, although the need for some estimate of the prehospitalization level of *S*'s seizure and related behaviors was realized. In order to approximate such a baseline, the parents were requested to estimate the frequency of *S*'s somatic complaints, tantrums, and seizures for the period 2 weeks prior to her hospitalization. The parents estimated *S*'s somatic complaints to be about 6 to 8 per week, and tantrums about 5 to 6 per week in frequency. Using this initial estimation, and the subsequent weekly follow-up parent reports, data was obtained which appeared adequate enough to reflect any major trends in the frequency of *S*'s deviant behaviors.

At the 26-week follow-up interval, the parents were instructed to reinstate attention for *S*'s deviant behaviors, including seizures if such should occur. This was done in order to attempt to demonstrate the functional relationship between *S*'s seizure behavior and parental attention, as well as to clarify the differential diagnosis between psychogenic and organic seizures.

➤

RESULTS

Within 2 weeks of *S*'s discharge from the hospital and the concomitant institution of the treatment plan as originated in the parent-counseling sessions (a) the frequency of *S*'s seizure behavior dropped to zero, (b) *S*'s tantrum behavior increased in frequency to about three per week (but did not rise to the estimated prehospitalization level of five to six per week), then dropped out altogether within the month, and (c) *S*'s somatic complaints gradually increased again to a frequency of about three per week, a level about half that of the pretreatment level as estimated by the parents.*

In the 26th week of follow-up, the parents were instructed to deliberately reinstate attention for S's somatic complaints as well as tantrums and seizures should such reappear. They were also instructed to return to the original "deaf and dumb" treatment for deviant behaviors once such behaviors had reappeared.

Within 24 hours of the deliberate reinstatement of parental attention for S's somatic complaints, this class of behavior showed a sharp increase to about one per hour. Then S manifested a seizure. As instructed, the parents then returned to the initial treatment plan of reinforcing appropriate behavior while ignoring deviant behavior. Subsequent to the parents' reinstatement of these contingencies, S manifested no more seizure behavior, two temper tantrums, and a rise in somatic complaints to a frequency of seven per week for the week following the deliberate reinstatement of the pretreatment contingencies. The somatic complaints then decreased gradually to about three per week, as before.

⤛

DISCUSSION

One of the principal consequences of the assumption that maladaptive behaviors are learned is that an individualized treatment plan must be developed. In the present case, in the absence of clear evidence regarding an organic basis for the seizures, S's seizure and other deviant behaviors were regarded as learned behaviors established and maintained by their consequences, in this case, the obtaining of parental attention.

A treatment plan involving the manipulation of reinforcement contingencies in S's home environment was formulated. This was accomplished by the parents who altered their responses to S's appropriate as well as inappropriate behavior. The parents were assisted in such modification by the aid of three counseling sessions.

Conceptually, the development of the seizure behavior in this case can be viewed as a function of differential reinforcement (shaping) for deviant behavior over a period of time. The parents, during the three counseling sessions, noted that they reacted with natural and appro-

---

* The author later informally checked the frequency of somatic complaints of children of various ages as reported by their parents. Data from five families showed the median number of somatic complaints per child to be a little over four per week. This evidence, though neither systematic nor from a large or random sample, suggests at the very least that S's three per week baseline of somatic complaints is probably not unduly high.

priate concern for any somatic complaints manifested by any of their children. However, the increasing frequency of such complaints from S, with no apparent physical basis, gradually tended to "desensitize" the parents to such complaints, and they began giving less attention to them. Shortly after the parents had virtually ceased reacting to S's somatic complaints, S manifested a head-banging, hair-pulling tantrum which succeeded in quickly eliciting much parental attention of a rather positive nature (i.e., concern, solicitousness). It appeared that there may have been several such adjustments and readjustments, with the cycle ultimately resulting in S's manifestation of seizure behavior.

On the other hand, an alternative viewpoint might be that the seizures were only incidentally, if at all, related to the reinforcing effects of parental attention, and that their cessation was simply a physiological remission. That such remission was not the case was shown in the follow-up phase 26 weeks after the initial counseling session with the parents. At this point, in order to demonstrate that S's seizure behavior was a function of parental attention as well as to more clearly establish the differential diagnosis between organic and functional aspects of the seizures, parental attention was again made contingent primarily upon deviant behavior.

Since no seizure activity was being manifested by S at that time, the parents were instructed to reinforce, with attention, S's somatic complaints. The need for this phase of the program in terms of clarifying the case, was explained to the parents, and they were in full agreement that it should be carried out.

Within 24 hours of the deliberate initiation of this parental reinforcement program, S manifested seizure behavior. The parents had been forewarned that S might again manifest seizure behavior under these conditions. As instructed, they then once more withdrew attention for all deviant behaviors while, as before, concomitantly giving much attention to S for more appropriate behaviors.

Conceptually, when the parents reinstated their concern regarding S's somatic complaints, this acted as a cue that the whole class of such behaviors (i.e., somatic complaints, tantrums, seizures, etc.) were now functional again with regard to the obtaining of parental attention. It is not suggested that the reappearance of such behaviors was volitional or necessarily even conscious on S's part. Rather, it is suggested that specific behaviors may be a function of specific stimulus circumstances, in this case largely external stimulus circumstances emanating from parental behavior.

The demonstration of the functional relationship between parental attention and S's seizure behavior was made possible by using S as her own control. For ethical and/or practical reasons this is not always feasible in a clinical setting. However, the baseline regarding the frequency of somatic complaints, tantrums, and seizures in this case seemed to reflect the effect of the treatment program. Because of this, a specific hypothesis relating the effect of parental attention on S's seizure behavior could be assessed.

Further follow-up interviews at the 28- and 30-week intervals revealed that S had manifested no further seizure behavior. A follow-up call to the mother one year after S's hospitalization revealed that S had manifested no seizure behavior in the interim. The mother also reported at this time that S seemed happy and well adjusted both at home and at school, that her grades were good, and that she seemed less competitive with her younger sister.

The primary implications of the above findings appear to be that (a) maladaptive or deviant behavior patterns may, in some cases, be a function of consequences of a socially reinforcing nature such as the control or manipulation of others, (b) it is possible to rearrange reinforcement contingencies even without complete environmental control, and (c) the systematic alteration of parental behavior can be a potent and efficient force in altering the maladaptive behavior of a child.

References

Adams, J. K. (1957). Laboratory studies of behavior without awareness. *Psychol. Bull.*, 54, 393–405.

Addison, R. M., and L. Homme (1966). The reinforcing event (RE) menu. *NSPI Journal,* 5 (1), 8–9.

Aichorn, A. (1935). *Wayward youth.* New York: The Viking Press.

Aiken, E. G. (1957). The effort variable in acquisition, extinction and spontaneous recovery of instrumental responses. *J. Exper. Psychol.,* 53, 47–51.

Alexander, F., and T. M. French (1946). *Psychoanalytic therapy.* New York: Ronald.

Allen, K. E., and F. R. Harris (1966). Elimination of a child's excessive scratching by training the mother in reinforcement procedures. *Behav. Res. Ther.,* 4, 79–84.

Allen, K. E., B. Hart, J. S. Buell, F. R. Harris, and M. M. Wolf (1964). Effects of social reinforcement on isolate behavior of a nursery school child. *Child Devel.,* 35, 511–518.

Anderson, D. (1964). Application of a behavior modification technique to the control of a hyperactive child. Unpublished Master's thesis, University of Oregon.

Anthony, J. (1958). An experimental approach to the psychopathology of childhood autism. *Brit. J. med. Psych.,* 31, 211–225.

Arbuckle, D. S., and L. A. Litwack (1960). A study of recidivism among juvenile delinquents. *Federal Probation,* 24, 44–46.

Armand, L. (1962). Machines, technology, and the life of the mind. In P. C. Obler and H. A. Estrin (Eds.). *The new scientist.* New York: Doubleday, 39–61.

Armstrong, S., and S. Rouslin (1963). *Group psychotherapy in nursing practice.* New York: Macmillan.

Astin, A. W. (1961). The functional autonomy of psychotherapy. *Amer. Psychologist,* 16, 75–78.

Atkinson, R. L. (1957). Paired-associate learning by schizophrenic and normal subjects under conditions of verbal reward and verbal punishment. Unpublished doctoral dissertation, Indiana University.

Atthowe, J. M., Jr., and L. Krasner (1968). A preliminary report on the application of contingent reinforcement procedures (token economy) on a "chronic" psychiatric ward. *J. abnorm. Psychol.*, 73, 37–43.

Ayllon, T. (1963). Intensive treatment of psychotic behavior by stimulus satiation and food reinforcement. *Behav. Res. Ther.*, 1, 53–61.

Ayllon, T., and N. Azrin (1964). Reinforcement and instructions with mental patients. *J. exper. Anal. Behav.*, 7, 327–331.

Ayllon, T., and N. Azrin (1965). The measurement and reinforcement of behavior of psychotics. *J. exper. Anal. Behav.*, 8, 357–384.

Ayllon, T., and E. Haughton (1962). Control of the behavior of schizophrenic patients by food. *J. exper. Anal. Behav.*, 5, 343–352.

Ayllon, T., and J. Michael (1959). The psychiatric nurse as a behavioral engineer. *J. exper. Anal. Behav.*, 2, 323–334.

Azrin, N. H., and W. C. Holz (1966). Punishment. In W. K. Honig (Ed.), *Operant behavior: Areas of research and application.* New York: Appleton-Century-Crofts.

Azrin, N. H., W. Holz, R. Ulrich, and L. Goldiamond (1961). The control of the content of conversation through reinforcement. *J. exper. Anal. Behav.*, 4, 25–30.

Azrin, N. H., and O. R. Lindsley (1956). The reinforcement of cooperation between children. *J. abnorm. soc. Psychol.*, 52, 100–102.

Bachrach, A. J. (Ed.), (1962). *Experimental foundations of clinical psychology.* New York: Basic Books.

Bachrach, A. J. (1964). Some applications of operant conditioning to behavior therapy. In J. Wolpe, A. Salter, and L. J. Reyna (Eds.), *The conditioning therapies: The challenge in psychotherapy.* New York: Holt, Rinehart and Winston.

Baer, D. M. (1961). Effect of withdrawal of positive reinforcement in an extinguishing response in young children. *Child Devel.*, 32, 67–74.

Baer, D. M. (1962a). A technique of social reinforcement for the study of child behavior: Behavior avoiding reinforcement withdrawal. *Child Devel.*, 33, 847–858.

Baer, D. M. (1962b). Laboratory control of thumbsucking by withdrawal and representation of reinforcement. *J. exper. Anal. Behav.*, 5, 525–528.

Baer, D. M., F. R. Harris, and M. M. Wolf (1963). Control of nursery school children's behavior by programming social reinforcement from their teachers. *Amer. Psychologist*, 18, 343 (Abstract).

Baer, D. M., R. F. Peterson, and J. A. Sherman (1967). The development of imitation by reinforcing behavioral similarity to a model. *J. exper. Anal. Behav.*, 10, 405–416.

Baer, D. M., and J. A. Sherman (1964). Reinforcement control of generalized imitation in young children. *J. exper. child Psychol.*, 1, 37–49.

Baer, D. M., and M. M. Wolf (1967). The entry into natural communities of reinforcement. Paper read at Amer. Psychol. Assoc. meeting, Washington, D.C.

Baldwin, A. L. (1948). Socialization and the parent-child relationship. *Child Devel.*, 19, 127–136.

Bales, R. F. (1950). *Interaction process analysis.* Cambridge, Mass.: Addison-Wesley.

Balint, M. (1948). Individual differences of behavior in early infancy: An objective method for recording. *J. genet. Psychol.*, 73, 57–79.

Ball, Thomas S. (1966). Behavior shaping of self-help skills in the severely retarded child. In J. Fisher and R. E. Harris (Eds.), *Reinforcement theory in psychological treatment: A symposium.* Research Monograph No. 8, 15–24.

Bandura, A. (1961). Psychotherapy as a learning process. *Psychol. Bull.*, 58, 143–159.

Bandura, A. (1962a). Social learning through imitation. In M. R. Jones (Ed.), *Nebraska symposium on motivation.* Lincoln: University of Nebraska Press.

Bandura, A. (1962b). Punishment revisited. *J. consult. Psychol.*, 26, 298–301.

Bandura, A. (1963). Behavior theory and identificatory learning. *Amer. J. Orthopsychiat.*, 33, 591–601.

Bandura, A. (1967). Behavioral psychotherapy. *Scient. Amer.*, 216, 78–86.

Bandura, A. (1969). *Principles of behavior modification.* New York: Holt.

Bandura, A., J. E. Grusec, and F. L. Menlove (1967). Vicarious extinction of avoidance behavior. *J. Pers. soc. Psychol.*, 5, 16–23.

Bandura, A., and C. J. Kupers (1964). Transmission of patterns of self-reinforcement through modeling. *J. abnorm. soc. Psychol.*, 69 (1), 1–9.

Bandura, A., D. Ross, and S. A. Ross (1963). Vicarious reinforcement and imitation. *J. abnorm. soc. Psychol.*, 66, 3–11.

Bandura, A., and R. H. Walters (1958). Dependency conflicts in aggressive delinquents. *J. soc. Issues*, 14, 52–65.

Bandura, A., and R. H. Walters (1963). *Social learning and personality development.* New York: Holt, Rinehart and Winston.

Barker, R. G., and H. F. Wright (1954). *Midwest and its children: The psychological ecology of an American town.* Evanston, Ill.: Row, Peterson.

Barnard, J. W., and R. Orlando (1967). *Behavior therapy bibliography.* George Peabody College.

Barrett, B. H. (1962). Reduction in rate of multiple tics by free-operant conditioning methods. *J. nerv. ment. Dis.*, 135, 187–195.

Barron, D. P., and Graziano, A. M. (1968). Parent participation in speech therapy. *Speech*, 3, 46–51.

Bayley, N., and E. S. Schaefer (1963). Maternal behavior, child behavior, and their intercorrelations from infancy through adolescence. *Monogr. soc. Res. child Devel.*, 28, No. 3.

Becker, W. C. (1960). The relationship of factors in parental ratings of self and each other to the behavior of kindergarten children as rated by mothers, fathers, and teachers. *J. consult. Psychol.*, 24, 507–527.

Becker, W. C., D. R. Peterson, Z. Zuria, D. J. Shoemaker, and L. A. Hellmer, (1961). Child behavior problems and parental attitudes. *Child Devel.*, 32, 151–162.

Beers, C. (1908). *A mind that found itself.* New York: Doubleday.

Bender, L. (1947). Childhood schizophrenia. *Amer. J. Orthopsychiat.*, 27, 68.

Bender, L., and W. H. Helme (1953). A qualitative test of theory and diagnostic indicators of childhood schizophrenia. *AMA Archives of Neurology and Psychiatry*, 70, 413–427.

Bensberg, G. J. (1965). *Teaching the mentally retarded.* Atlanta, Ga.: Southern Regional Education Board.

Bensberg, G. J., C. N. Colwell, and R. H. Cassel (1965). Teaching the profoundly retarded self-help activities by behavior shaping techniques. *Amer. J. ment. Def.*, 69, 674–679.

Bentler, P. M. (1962). An infant's phobia treated with reciprocal inhibition therapy. *J. child Psychol. Psychiat.*, 3, 185–189.

Bentzgen, F. A. (1962). Interdisciplinary research in educational programming for disturbed children. *Amer. J. Orthopsychiatry*, 32, 473–485.

Berdyaev, N. (1960). *The destiny of man.* New York: Harper.

Berg, I. A. (1952). Measures before and after therapy. *J. clin. Psychol.*, 8, 46–50.

Berg, I. A., and B. M. Bass (Eds.), (1961). *Conformity and deviation.* New York: Harper & Row.

Bergin, A. E. (1966). Some implications of psychotherapy research for therapeutic practice. *J. abnorm. Psychol.*, 71, 235–246.

Berne, E. (1964). *Games people play.* New York: Grove Press.

Bettelheim, B. (1950). *Love is not enough.* New York: The Free Press.

Bettelheim, B. (1952). Schizophrenic art: A case study. *Scient. Amer.*, 186 (4), 30–34.

Bettelheim, B. (1965). Early ego development in a mute, autistic child. Freud Lecture read at Philadelphia Association for Psychoanalysis, University of Pennsylvania.

Biderman, A. A., and H. Zimmer (Eds.), (1961). *The manipulation of human behavior.* New York: Wiley.

Bijou, S. W. (1955). A systematic approach to an experimental analysis of young children. *Child Devel.*, 26, 161–168.

Bijou, S. W. (1957). Methodology for an experimental analysis of child behavior. *Psychol. Rep.*, 3, 243–250.

Bijou, S. W. (1958). A child study laboratory on wheels. *Child Devel.*, 29, 425–427.

Bijou, S. W. (1965). Experimental studies of child behavior, normal and deviant. In L. Krasner and L. P. Ullmann (Eds.), *Research in behavior modification.* New York: Holt, Rinehart and Winston. Pp. 56–81.

Bijou, S. W., and D. M. Baer (1960). The laboratory experimental study of child behavior. In P. H. Mussen (Ed.), *Handbook of research methods in child development.* New York: Wiley.

Bijou, S. W., and D. M. Baer (1961). *Child Development: Vol. I: A systematic and empirical theory*. New York: Appleton-Century-Crofts.

Bijou, S. W., and D. M. Baer (1965). *Child Development. Vol. II: The universal stage of infancy*. New York: Appleton-Century-Crofts.

Birnbrauer, J. S., S. W. Bijou, M. M. Wolf, and J. D. Kidder (1965). Programmed instruction in the classroom. In L. P. Ullmann and L. Krasner (Eds.), *Case studies in behavior modification*. New York: Holt, Rinehart and Winston. Pp. 358–363.

Birnbrauer, J. S., M. M. Wolf, J. D. Kidder, and C. E. Tague (1965). Classroom behavior of retarded pupils with token reinforcement. *J. exper. child Psychol.*, 2, 219–235.

Blackwood, R. O. (1962). *The operant conditioning of social behaviors in severely retarded patients*. Unpublished doctoral dissertation, Ohio State University.

Blatt, B., and F. Kaplan (1967). *Christmas in purgatory: A photographic essay on mental retardation*. Boston: Allyn & Bacon.

Bloodstein, O. (1948). Study of the conditions under which stuttering is reduced or absent. Unpublished doctoral dissertation, University of Iowa.

Boardman, W. K. (1962). Rusty: A brief behavior disorder. *J. consult. Psychol.*, 26, 293–297.

Bockoven, J. S. (1963). *Moral treatment in American psychiatry*. New York: Springer.

Bower, E. M. (1962). Mental health in education. *Rev. ed. Res.*, 32, 441–454.

Bowen, M. (1960). A family concept of schizophrenia. In D. D. Jackson (Ed.), *The etiology of schizophrenia*. New York: Basic Books. Pp. 346–372.

Brackbill, Y. (1958). Extinction of the smiling response in infants as a function of reinforcement schedule. *Child Devel.*, 29, 115–124.

Brady, J., and D. L. Lind (1961). Experimental analysis of hysterical blindness. *Arch. gen. Psychiat.*, 4, 331–339.

Branch, C. H. (1963). Preparedness for progress. *Amer. Psychologist*, 18, 581–588.

Brawley, E., F. R. Harris, K. E. Allen, R. S. Fleming, and R. F. Peterson (1967). Behavior modification of an autistic child. Paper read at Midwestern Psychol. Assoc., Chicago.

Breger, L. and J. L. McGaugh (1965). Critique and reformulation of "learning theory" approaches to psychotherapy and neuroses. *Psychol. Bull.*, 63, 338–358.

Bricker, W. A. (1965). Learning approaches to differential diagnosis among mentally retarded children. Paper read at Southeastern Regional Meeting of the Amer. Assoc. on Mental Deficiency.

Brison, D. W. (1966). Case studies in school psychology. A non-talking child in kindergarten: An application of behavior therapy. *J. school Psychol.*, 65–69.

Brown, J. (1960). Prognosis from presenting symptoms of preschool children with atypical development. *Amer. J. Orthopsychiat.*, 30, 382–390.

Brown, P., and R. Elliott (1965). Control of aggression in a nursery school class. *J. exper. Child Psychol.*, 3, 102–107.

Browning, R. M. (1967). A same-subject design for simultaneous comparison of three reinforcement contingencies. *Behav. Res. Ther.*, 5, 237–243.

Buehler, R. E., G. R. Patterson, and J. M. Furniss (1966). The reinforcement of behavior in institutional settings. *Behav. Res. Ther.*, 4, 157–167.

Burchard, J. D. (1966). A residential program of behavior modification. Paper read at Amer. Psychol. Assoc., New York.

Burchard, J. D., and V. O. Tyler (1965). The modification of delinquent behavior through operant conditioning. *Behav. Res. Ther.*, 2, 245–250.

Burnham, W. H. (1924). *The normal mind.* New York: Appleton-Century-Crofts.

Cain, A. C. (1961). The presuperego turning inward of aggression. *Psychoanal. Quart.*, 30, 171–208.

Cairns, R. (1960). The influence of dependency-anxiety on the effectiveness of social reinforcers. Unpublished doctoral dissertation, Stanford University.

Campbell, B. A., and F. D. Sheffield (1953). Relation of random activity to food deprivation. *J. comp. Physiol. Psychol.*, 46, 320–322.

Cartwright, A. (1962). Memory errors in a morbidity survey. *Milbank Memorial Fund Quart.*, 16, 5–24.

Case, H. W. (1960). Therapeutic methods in stuttering and speech blocking. In H. J. Eysenck (Ed.), *Behavior therapy and the neuroses.* Oxford: Pergamon Press. Pp. 207–220.

Chapple, E. D., and G. Donald, Jr. (1946). A method for evaluating supervisory personnel. *Harv. Business Rev.*, 24, 197–214.

Church, R. M. (1963). The varied effects of punishment on behavior. *Psychol. Rev.*, 70, 369–402.

Cleckley, M. (1964). *The mask of sanity.* St. Louis: Mosby.

Cohen, H. L., J. A. Filipczak, and J. S. Bis (in press). CASE project: Contingencies applicable for special education. In R. E. Weber (Ed.), *Education and delinquency.* Washington, D.C.: Department of HEW.

Colby, K. M. (1964). Psychotherapeutic processes. *Ann. Rev. Psychol.*, 15, 347–370.

Coleman, J. C. (1963). *Abnormal psychology and modern life* (3rd ed.). Chicago: Scott, Foresman.

Commons, M. L., S. M. Paul, and G. A. Fargo (1966). Developing speech in an autistic boy using operant techniques to increase his rate of vocal-verbal responding. Paper read at Western Psychol. Assoc., Long Beach, Calif.

Cook, C., and H. E. Adams (1966). Modification of verbal behavior in speech-deficient children. *Behav. Res. Ther.*, 4, 265–271.

Coote, M. A. (1965). Apparatus for conditioning treatment of enuresis. *Behav. Res. Ther.*, 2, 233–238.

Cowan, P. A., and R. H. Walters (1963). Studies of reinforcement of aggression: I. Effects of scheduling. *Child Devel.*, 34, 543–551.

Cowden, R. C., and L. I. Ford (1962). Systematic desensitization with phobic schizophrenics. *Amer. J. Psychiat.*, 119, 241–245.

Dain, N. (1964). *Concepts of insanity in the United States*, 1789–1865. New Brunswick, N.J.: Rutgers University Press.

Das, J.,G. Sahu, and T. Panda (1965). The effect of ratio of reinforcement on performance in the selective learning by children. *British. J. Psychol.,* 56, 289–294.

Davidson, J. R., and E. Douglas (1950). Nocturnal enuresis: a special approach to treatment. *Brit. med. J.,* 1, 1345–1347.

Davison, G. C. (1964). A social learning therapy program with an autistic child. *Behav. Res. Ther.,* 2, 149–159.

Davison, G. C. (1965). The training of undergraduates as social reinforcers for autistic children. In L. P. Ullmann and L. Krasner (Eds.), *Case studies in behavior modification.* New York: Holt, Rinehart and Winston.

Davison, G. C., and L. Krasner (1964). Behavior therapy with an autistic child. 16 mm. sound film. U.S. Public Health Service Audiovisual Facility, Atlanta, Georgia, Cat. No. MIS–895.

Dayan, M. (1964). Toilet training retarded children in a state residential institution. *Ment. Retard.,* 2, 116–117.

DeLeon, G. and W. Mandell (1966). A comparison of conditioning and psychotherapy in the treatment of functional enuresis. *J. clin. Psychol.,* 22, 326–330.

DeMyer, M. K., and C. B. Ferster (1962). Teaching new social behavior to schizophrenic children. *J. Amer. Acad. child Psychiat.,* 1, 443–461.

Denny, M. R. (1966). A theoretical analysis and its application to training the mentally retarded. In N. R. Ellis (Ed.), *International review of research in mental retardation.* New York: Academic Press. Vol. 2, pp. 1–28.

Denny, M. R., and H. M. Adelman (1965). Elicitation theory: 1. An analysis of two typical learning situations. *Psychol. Rev.,* 87, 317–320.

Dinsmoor, J. A. (1966a). Operant conditioning. In J. B. Sidowski (Ed.), *Experimental method and instrumentation in psychology.* New York: McGraw-Hill.

Dinsmoor, J. A. (1966b). Comments on Wetzel's treatment of a case of compulsive stealing. *J. consult. Psychol.,* 30, 378–380.

Dittmann. L. (1959). *The mentally retarded child at home: A manual for parents.* Washington, D.C.: U.S. Children's Bureau, Department of HEW.

Dollard, J., L. W. Doob, N. E. Miller, O. H. Mowrer and R. R. Sears (1939). *Frustration and aggression.* New Haven: Yale University Press.

Dollard, J., and N. E. Miller (1950). *Personality and psychotherapy.* New York: McGraw-Hill.

Doubros, S. G. (1966). Behavior therapy with high-level, institutionalized, retarded adolescents. *Excep. Child.,* 33, 229–232.

Doubros, S. G., and G. J. Daniels (1966). An experimental approach to the reduction of overactive behavior. *Behav. Res. Ther.,* 4, 251–258.

Dreger, R., and G. E. Dreger (1962). Behavior classification project: Report No. 1. Jacksonville, Fla.: Jacksonville University.

Dubnoff, B. (1965). The habilitation and education of the autistic child in a therapeutic day school. *Amer. J. Orthopsychiat.,* 35, 385–386.

Dunlap, K. (1930). Repetition in the breaking of habits. *Scient. Monogr.*, 30, 66–70.

Edwards, A. L., and L. J. Cronbach (1952). Experimental design for research in psychotherapy. *J. clin. Psychol.*, 8, 51–59.

Eisenberg, L. (1956). The autistic child in adolescence. *Amer. J. Psychiat.*, 112, 607–612.

Eisenberg, L. (1957). The course of childhood schizophrenia. *AMA Archives Neurol. Psychiat.*, 78, 69–83.

Eisenberg, L., and L. Kanner (1956). Early infantile autism, 1943–1955. *Amer. J. Orthopsychiat.*, 26, 556–566.

Ellis, A. (1958). Rational psychotherapy. *J. gen. Psychol.*, 59, 35–49.

Ellis, N. R. (1963). Toilet training the severely defective patient: An S-R reinforcement analysis. *Amer. J. ment. Defic.*, 68, 98–103.

Ellis, N. R., C. E. Barret and M. W. Pryer (1960). Operant behavior in mental defectives. *J. exper. Anal. Behav.*, 3, 63–69.

Erickson, C. W. (1958). Unconscious processes. In M. R. Jones (Ed.), *Nebraska symposium on motivation.* Lincoln: University of Nebraska Press.

Erickson, M. T. (1962). Effects of social deprivation and satiation on verbal conditioning in children. *J. comp. Physiol. Psychol.*, 55, 953–957.

Ernest, E. (1960). Cited by H. G. Jones, Continuation of Yate's treatment of a ticquer. In H. J. Eysenck (Ed.), *Behavior therapy and the neuroses.* Oxford: Pergamon Press.

Evans, J. (1961). Rocking at night. *J. child Psychol. Psychiat.*, 2, 71–85.

Evans, R. L. (1967). An exploration of treatment systems in group living. Paper read at Regional Conf. on Residential Treatment, Wallingford, Conn.

Eysenck, H. J. (1952). The effects of psychotherapy: An evaluation. *J. consult. Psychol.*, 16, 319–324.

Eysenck, H. J. (1957). *The dynamics of anxiety and hysteria.* New York: Praeger.

Eysenck, H. J. (1960). *Behavior therapy and the neuroses.* Oxford: Pergamon Press.

Eysenck, H. J. (1961). The effects of psychotherapy. In H. J. Eysenck (Ed.), *Handbook of abnormal psychology.* New York: Basic Books. Pp. 697–725.

Eysenck, H. J. (1964a). *Crime and personality.* Boston: Houghton Mifflin.

Eysenck, H. J. (1964b). *Experiments in behavior therapy.* New York: Macmillan.

Eysenck, H. J. (1966). Behavior therapy: A new way of treating the neuroses. *Psychiat. Dig.*, 27 (5), 45–55.

Eysenck, H. J., and J. S. Rachman (1963). *The application of learning theory to child psychiatry.* New York: Pergamon Press.

Eysenck, H. J., and J. S. Rachman (1965). *The causes and cures of neuroses.* San Diego: Robert R. Knapp.

Feldman, R. B., and J. S. Werry (1966). An unsuccessful attempt to treat a ticqueur by massed practice. *Behav. Res. Ther.*, 4, 111–117.

Fenichel, O. (1941). *Problems of psychoanalytic technique* (D. Brunswick, Trans.). New York: Psychoanalytic Quarterly.

Ferster, C. B. (1958). Reinforcement and punishment in the control of human behavior by social agencies. *Psychiat. Res. Rept.*, 12, 101–118.

Ferster, C. B. (1961). Positive reinforcement and behavior deficits of autistic children. *Child Devel.*, 32, 437–456.

Ferster, C. B. (1965a). An operant reinforcement analysis of infantile autism. Unpublished ms., Institute for Behavioral Research, Silver Springs, Md.

Ferster, C. B. (1965b). Operant reinforcement in the natural milieu. Paper read at Council for Exceptional Children, Portland, Oregon.

Ferster, C. B. (1966). The repertoire of the autistic child in relation to principles of reinforcement. In L. A. Gottschalk and A. Auerback (Eds.), *Methods of research in psychotherapy*. New York: Appleton-Century-Crofts.

Ferster, C. B. (1967a). Arbitrary and natural reinforcement. *Psychol. Rec.*, 17, 341–347.

Ferster, C. B. (1967b). Perspectives in psychology: XXV. Transition from animal laboratory to clinic. *Psychol. Rec.*, 17, 147–150.

Ferster, C. B., and M. K. DeMyer (1961a). Increased performances of an autistic child with prochlorperizine administration. *J. exper. Anal. Behav.*, 4, 84.

Ferster, C. B., and M. K. DeMyer (1961b). The development of performances in autistic children in an automatically controlled environment. *J. chron. Dis.*, 13, 312–345.

Ferster, C. B., and M. K. DeMyer (1962). A method for the experimental analysis of the behavior of autistic children. *Amer. J. Orthopsychiat.*, 32, 89–98.

Ferster, C. B., J. Nurnberger, and E. Levitt (1962). The control of eating. *J. Mathematics*, 1, 87–109.

Ferster, C. B., and M. C. Perrott (1968). *Behavior principles*. New York: Appleton-Century-Crofts.

Ferster, C. B., and J. Simons (1966). An evaluation of behavior therapy with children. *Psychol. Rec.*, 16, 65–71.

Ferster, C. B., and B. F. Skinner (1957). *Schedules of reinforcement*. New York: Appleton-Century-Crofts.

Fishman, H. C. (1937). A study of the efficacy of negative practice as a corrective for stammering. *J. speech Disor.*, 2, 67–72.

Flanagan, B., I. Goldiamond, and N. Azrin (1958). Operant stuttering — the control of stuttering behaviour through response-contingent consequences. *J. exper. Anal. Behav.*, 1, 173–177.

Franks, C. M. (1964). *Conditioning techniques in clinical practice and research*. New York: Springer.

Franks, C. M. (1967). Implications of behavior therapy for the future of clinical psychology. Paper read at symposium, Training behavior therapists, A. M. Graziano, Chairman, Amer. Psychol. Assoc., Washington, D.C.

Franks, C. M. (Ed.) (1969). *Behavior therapy: Appraisal and status*. New York: McGraw-Hill.

Freedman, A. M., E. V. Ebin, and E. A. Wilson (1962). Autistic and schizophrenic children: An experiment in the use of d–Lysergic Acid Diethylamide

(LSD–25). *AMA Arch. gen. Psychiat.*, 6, 203–213.

French, T. M. (1933). Interrelations between psychoanalysis and the experimental work of Pavlov. *Amer. J. Psychiat.*, 89, 1165–1203.

Freud, A. (1954). Problems of infantile neuroses: A discussion. In *The psychoanalytic study of the child*, Vol. 9. New York: International Universities Press.

Freud, A. (1958). Adolescence. In *The psychoanalytic study of the child*, Vol. 13. New York: International Universities Press. Pp. 255–277.

Fuller, P. R. (1949). Operant conditioning of a vegetative human organism. *Amer. J. Psychol.*, 62, 587–590.

Furness, J. M. (1964). Peer reinforcement of behavior in an institution for delinquent girls. Unpublished Master's thesis, Oregon State University.

Gardner, J. E. (1967). Behavior therapy treatment approaches to a psychogenic seizure case. *J. consult. Psychol.*, 31: 2, 209–212.

Garvey, W. P., and J. R. Hegrenes (1966). Desensitization techniques in the treatment of school phobia. *Amer. J. Orthopsychiat.*, 36, 147–152.

Geer, J. H. (1964). Phobia treated by reciprocal inhibition. *J. abnorm. soc. Psychol.*, 69, 642–645.

Geer, J. H., and E. S. Katkin (1966). Treatment of insomnia using a variant of systematic desensitization: A case report. *J. abnorm. soc. Psychol.*, 71, 161–164.

Gelber, H., and B. Meyer (1965). Behavior therapy and encopresis: Complexities involved in treatment. *Behav. Res. Ther.*, 2, 227–231.

Gelfand, D. M., S. Gelfand, and W. R. Dobson (1967). Unprogrammed reinforcement of patients' behavior in a mental hospital. *Behav. Res. Ther.*, 5, 201–207.

Gelfand, D. M., and D. P. Hartmann (1968). Behavior therapy with children: A review and evaluation of research methodology. *Psychol. Bull.*, 69, 3, 204–215.

Gewirtz, J. L., and D. M. Baer (1958a). The effect of brief social deprivation on behaviors for a social reinforcer. *J. abnorm. soc. Psychol.*, 56, 49–56.

Gewirtz, J. L., and D. M. Baer (1958b). Deprivation and satiation of social reinforcers as drive conditions. *J. abnorm. soc. Psychol.*, 57, 165–172.

Girardeau, F., and J. Spradlin (1964). Token rewards in a cottage program. *Ment. Retard.*, 2, 275–279.

Gittleman, M. (1965). Behavior rehearsal as a technique in child treatment. *J. child Psychol. Psychiat.*, 6, 251–255.

Glasscote, R. M., E. Cumming, D. W. Hammersley, L. D. Ozarin, and L. H. Smith (1966). *The psychiatric emergency*. Washington, D.C.: Joint Information Service.

Goldfarb, W. (1945). Psychological privation in infancy. *Amer. J. Orthopsychiat.*, 15, 247–255.

Goldfarb, W. (1965). Saul Albert Memorial Lecture, Corrective socialization: A rationale for the treatment of schizophrenic children. *Canad. Psychiat. Assoc. J.*, 10, 481–496.

Goldfarb, W., P. Braunstein, and I. Lorge (1956). A study of speech patterns in a group of schizophrenic children. *Amer. J. Orthopsychiat.*, 26, 544–555.

Goldfarb, W., and R. C. Pollack (1964). The childhood schizophrenic's response to schooling in a residential treatment centre. Proceedings of American Psycho-Pathological Association, P. H. Hoch and J. Zubin (Eds.), 221–226.

Goldiamond, I. (1962). The maintenance of ongoing fluent verbal behavior and stuttering. *J. Math.*, 1, 57–95.

Goldiamond, I. (1965a). Self-control procedures in personal behavior problems. *Psychol. Rep.*, 17, 851–868.

Goldiamond, I. (1965b). Stuttering and fluency as manipulatable operant response classes. In L. Krasner and L. P. Ullmann (Eds.), *Research in behavior modification.* New York: Holt, Rinehart and Winston.

Goldstein, A. P., K. Heller, and L. B. Sechrest (1966). *Psychotherapy and the psychology of behavior change.* New York: Wiley.

Goodman, C. (1964). Implementing Public Law 182. *Nurs. Outl.*, 12, 1.

Graham, F., C. Ernhart, C. Thurston, and M. Craft (1962). Organic development three years after prenatal anoxia and other potentially damaging newborn experiences. *Psychol. Monogr.*, 76, 53.

Gray, J. S. (1932). A biological view of behavior modification. *J. educ. Psychol.*, 23, 611–620.

Gray, P. G. (1955). The memory factor in social surveys. *J. Amer. statist. Assoc.*, 50, 344.

Graziano, A. M. (1963). A description of a behavioral day-care and treatment program for psychotic children. Report to the Connecticut State Department of Mental Health, Division of Children's Services.

Graziano, A. M. (Chairman), (1967a). Training behavior therapists. Symposium, Amer. Psychol. Assoc., Washington, D.C.

Graziano, A. M. (1967b). Programmed psychotherapy: A behavioral approach to emotionally disturbed children. Paper read at Eastern Psychol. Assoc., Boston.

Graziano, A. M. (1968). Clinical innovation and the mental health power structure. Paper read at Eastern Psychol. Assoc., Washington, D.C.

Graziano, A. M. (1969a). An historical note on J. Stanley Gray's "A biological view of behavior modification." *J. hist. soc. Sciences.* (In press).

Graziano, A. M. (1969b). Mental health, psychotherapy and the new therapists. *J. psychiat. Nurs.*, 7, 69–73.

Graziano, A. M. (1969c). The reluctant client: Counterpoint to a "pop" theme. Paper read at Amer. Publ. Health Assoc., Philadelphia.

Graziano, A. M., and S. G. Graziano (1968). *Myth, magic and psychiatry.* Unpublished manuscript.

Graziano, A. M., and J. E. Kean (1967). Programmed relaxation and reciprocal inhibition with psychotic children. In *Proceedings,* 75th Annual Convention, Amer. Psychol. Assoc. Washington, D.C. Pp. 253–254.

Greenacre, P. (1954). Problems of infantile neurosis: A discussion. In *The psychoanalytic study of the child*, Vol. IX. New York: International Universities Press.

Greenspoon, J. (1962). Verbal conditioning and clinical psychology. In A. J.

Bachrach (Ed.), *Experimental foundations of clinical psychology*. New York: Basic Books.

Grossberg, J. M. (1964). Behavior therapy: A review. *Psychol. Bull.*, 62, 73–88.

Guthrie, E. R. (1935). *The psychology of learning*. New York: Harper.

Haberman, J. V. (1917). Probing the mind, normal and abnormal. First report. Feeling, association and the psychoreflex. *Med. Rec.*, 92, 927–933.

Haggard, E. A. (1958). *Intraclass correlations and the analysis of variance*. New York: Dryden.

Hallsten, E. A., Jr. (1965). Adolescent anorexia nervosa treated by desensitization. *Behav. Res. Ther.*, 3, 87–91.

Hamilton, J., L. Stephens, and P. Allen (1967). Controlling aggressive and destructive behavior in severely retarded institutionalized residents. *Amer. J. ment. Defic.*, 71, 852–856.

Haring, N. G., and E. L. Phillips (1962). *Educating emotionally disturbed children*. New York: McGraw-Hill.

Harris, F. R., M. K. Johnston, C. S. Kelley, and M. M. Wolf (1964). Effects of positive social reinforcement on regressed crawling of a nursery school child. *J. educ. Psychol.*, 55, 35–41.

Harris, F. R., M. M. Wolf, and D. M. Baer (1964). Effects of adult social reinforcement on child behavior. *Young Child.*, 20, 8–17.

Hart, B. M., K. E. Allen, J. S. Buell, F. R. Harris, and M. M. Wolf (1964). Effects of social reinforcement on operant crying. *J. exper. child Psychol.*, 1, 145–153.

Hartmann, H., E. Kris, and R. M. Lowenstein (1949). Notes on the theory of aggression. In *The psychoanalytic study of the child*. Vol. IV. New York: International Universities Press.

Hathaway, S. R. (1948). Some considerations relative to nondirective counseling as therapy. *J. clin. Psychol.*, 4, 226–231.

Hawkins, R. P., R. F. Peterson, E. Schweid, and S. W. Bijou (1966). Behavior therapy in the home: Amelioration of problem parent–child relations with the parent in a therapeutic role. *J. exper. child Psychol.*, 4, 99–107.

Hayes, C. (1951). *The ape in our house*. New York: Harper.

Heathers, G. L. (1940). The avoidance of repetition of maze reaction on the rat as a function of the time interval between trials. *J. Psychol.*, 10, 359–380.

Hebb, D. O. (1949). *The organization of behavior*. New York: Wiley.

Hebb, D. O. (1955). Drives and the C.N.S. (conceptual nervous system). *Psychol. Rev.*, 62, 243–254.

Hefferline, R. F. (1962). Learning theory and clinical psychology — an eventual symbiosis? In A. J. Bachrach (Ed.), *Experimental foundations of clinical psychology*. New York: Basic Books. Pp. 97–138.

Hersch, C. (1968). The discontent explosion in mental health. *Amer. Psychologist*, 23, 497–506.

Hewett, F. M. (1964). Teaching reading to an autistic boy through operant conditioning. *The Reading Teacher*, 17, 613–618.

Hewett, F. M. (1965). Teaching speech to an autistic child through operant conditioning. *Amer. J. Orthopsychiat.*, 35, 927–936.

Hewett, F. M. (1967). Educational engineering with emotionally disturbed children. *Excep. Child.*, 33, 459–467.

Hill, W. F. (1958). The effect of long confinement on voluntary wheel running on rats. *J. comp. Physiol. Psychol.*, 51, 770–773.

Hington, J. N., B. Sanders, and M. K. DeMyer (1965). Shaping cooperative responses in early childhood schizophrenia. In L. P. Ullmann and L. Krasner (Eds.), *Case studies in behavior modification.* New York: Holt, Rinehart and Winston.

Hington, J. N., and Trost, F. C. Jr. (1964). Shaping cooperative responses in early childhood schizophrenics: II. Reinforcement of mutual physical contact and vocal responses. Paper read at Amer. Psychol. Assoc., Los Angeles.

Hinsey, C., R. Patterson, and B. Sonoda (1961). Validation of a technique for conditioning aggression in children. Paper read at Western Psychol. Assoc.

Hobbs, N. (1962). Sources of gain in psychotherapy. *Amer. Psychologist*, 17, 741–747.

Holland, J. G., and B. F. Skinner (1961). *The analysis of behavior: A program for self instruction.* New York: McGraw-Hill.

Hollingshead, A. B., and F. C. Redlich (1958). *Social class and mental illness: A community study.* New York: Wiley.

Holzberg, J. D. (1963). The companion program: Implementing the manpower recommendations of the Joint Commission on Mental Illness and Health. *Amer. Psychologist*, 18 (4), 224–226.

Homme, L. (1966). Contingency management. Newsletter, Section on Clinical Child Psychology, Division of Clinical Psychology, Amer. Psychol. Assoc., 5, No. 4.

Homme, L. (1967). A behavior technology exists—here and now. Paper read at Acrospace Education Foundation, Washington, D.C.

Homme, L., P. C. DeBaca, J. V. Devine, R. Steinhorst, and E. J. Rickert (1963). Use of the Premack principle in controlling the behavior of nursery school children. *J. exper. Anal. Behav.*, 6, 544.

Homme. L., and D. J. Klaus (1967). *Laboratory studies in the analysis of behavior* (3rd ed.). Albuquerque: Westinghouse Learning Corporation.

Honig, W. K. (Ed.) (1966). *Operant behavior: Areas of research and application.* New York: Appleton-Century-Crofts.

Hughes, J. et al. (1965). Mirror room projects for childhood psychotics. Presented at the Regional Assoc. of Mental Deficiency, Tacoma.

Hundziak, M., R. A. Maurer, and L. S. Watson, Jr. (1965). Operant conditioning and toilet training of severely mentally retarded boys. *Amer. J. ment. Defic.*, 70, 120–124.

Hunter, W. S. (1928). *Human behavior.* Chicago: University of Chicago Press.

Irwin, O. C. (1930). The amount and nature of activity of new-born infants during the first ten days of life. *Genet. Psychol. Monogr.*, 8, 1–92.

Isaacs, W., J. Thomas, and I. Goldiamond (1960). Application of operant conditioning to reinstate verbal behavior in psychotics. *J. Speech Hearing Dis.*, 25, 8–12.

Jackson, J. (1964). Toward the cooperative study of mental hospitals: Characteristics of the treatment environment. In A. F. Wessen (Ed.), *The psychiatric hospital as a social system*. Springfield, Ill.: Charles C Thomas.

Jacobsen, E. (1938). *Progressive relaxation*. Chicago: University of Chicago Press.

James, C. E. (1963). *Operant conditioning in the management and behavior of hyperactive children: Five case studies*. Unpublished manuscript, Orange State College, Cited in G. R. Patterson, R. Jones, J. Whittier, and M. A. Wright (1965). A behavior modification technique for the hyperactive child, *Behav. Res. Ther.*, 2, 217–226.

James, W. H., and J. B. Rotter (1958). Partial and 100 per cent reinforcement under chance and skill conditions. *J. exper. Psychol.*, 55, 397–403.

Jersild, A. T., and F. B. Holmes (1935). Methods of overcoming children's fears. *J. Psychol.*, 1, 75–104.

Johns, J. H. and H. C. Quay (1962). The effect of social reward on verbal conditioning in psychopathic and neurotic military offenders. *J. consult. Psychol.*, 26, 217–220.

Johnson, B. G., A. Williams, and J. L. Landrum (1965). The use of the superheterodyne as a means of behavior control. *Amer. J. ment. Defic.*, 70, 148.

Johnston, M. S., C. S. Kelley, J. S. Buell, F. R. Harris, and M. M. Wolf (1963). *Effects of positive social reinforcement on isolate behavior of a nursery school child*. Unpublished manuscript.

Johnston, M. K., C. S. Kelley, F. R. Harris, and M. M. Wolf (1966). An application of reinforcement principles to development of motor skills of a young child. *Child Devel.*, 37, 379–387.

Joint Commission on Mental Illness and Health (1963). *Action for Mental Health: Final Report*. New York: Basic Books.

Jones, E. L. (1955). Exploration of experimental extinction and spontaneous recovery in stuttering. In W. Johnson (Ed.), *Stuttering in children and adults*. Minneapolis: University of Minnesota Press. Pp. 226–231.

Jones, H. G. (1960). The behavioural treatment of enuresis nocturna. In H. J. Eysenck (Ed.), *Behaviour therapy and the neuroses*. Oxford: Pergamon Press.

Jones, M. C. (1924a). A laboratory study of fear: The case of Peter. *Pedag. Semin.*, 31, 308–315.

Jones, M. C. (1924b). The elimination of children's fears. *J. exper. Psychol.*, 7, 382–390.

Jones, M. C., and N. Bayley (1950). Physical maturing among boys as related to behavior. *J. educ. Psychol.*, 41, 129–148.

Kadlub, K. (1956). The effects of two types of reinforcement on the performance of psychopathic and normal criminals. Unpublished doctoral dissertation, University of Illinois.

Kahane, M. (1955). An experimental investigation of a conditioning treatment and a preliminary study of the psychoanalytic theory of the etiology of nocturnal enuresis. *Amer. Psychologist,* 10, 369–370.

Kanfer, F. H. (1961). Comments on learning in psychotherapy. *Psychol. Rep.,* Monogr. Suppl. No. 6, 9, 681–699.

Kanfer, F. H., and J. Phillips (1965). Behavior therapy: A panacea for all ills or a passing fancy? Mimeographed paper, Portland, Oregon: University of Oregon Medical School.

Kanner, L. (1943). Autistic disturbances of affective contact. *Nerv. Child,* 2, 217–250.

Kanner, L. (1948). *Child psychiatry* (2nd ed.). Springfield, Ill.: Charles C Thomas.

Kanner, L. (1949). Problems of nosology and psychodynamics of early infantile autism. *Amer. J. Orthopsychiat.,* 19:3, 416–426.

Kanner, L. (1954a). To what extent is early infantile autism determined by constitutional inadequacies? *Proc. Assoc. Res. nerv. ment. Dis.,* 33, 378–385.

Kanner, L. (1954b). General concept of schizophrenia at different ages. *Proc. Assoc. Res. nerv. ment. Dis.,* 34, 451–453.

Kanner, L., and L. Eisenberg (1955). Notes on the follow–up studies of autistic children. In P. H. Hoch and J. Zubin (Eds.), *Psychopathology of childhood.* New York: Grune & Stratton.

Kanner, L., and L. I. Lesser (1958). Early infantile autism. *Pediat. Clin. N. Amer.,* 5, 711–730.

Kantorovich, N. (1929). An attempt at associative-reflex therapy in alcoholism. *Nov. Refl. Fiziol. Nerv. Sist.,* 3, 436–447. (Psychol. Abstr., 1930, 4, 493.)

Keehn, J. D. (1965). Brief case report: Reinforcement therapy of incontinence. *Behav. Res. Ther.,* 2, 239.

Keller, F. S., and W. N. Schoenfeld (1950). *The principles of psychology.* New York: Appleton-Century-Crofts.

Kendall, M. G. (1948). *Rank correlation methods.* London: Griffin.

Kennedy, T. (1964). Treatment of chronic schizophrenia by behavior therapy — case reports., *Behav. Res. Ther.,* 2, 1–6.

Kerr, N., L. Meyerson, and J. A. Michael (1965). A procedure for shaping vocalization in a mute child. In L. P. Ullmann and L. Krasner (Eds.), *Case studies in behavior modification.* New York: Holt, Rinehart and Winston.

Kiesler, D. J. (1966). Some myths of psychotherapy research and the search for a paradigm. *Psychol. Bull.,* 65, 110–136.

Kimbrell, D. L., R. E. Luckey, P. F. Barbuto, and J. G. Love (1967). Operation dry pants: an intensive habit training program for severely and profoundly retarded. *Ment. Retard.,* 6, 32–36.

King, G. F., and S. G. Armitage (1957). An operant interpersonal therapeutic approach to schizophrenics of extreme pathology. *Amer. Psychologist,* 13, 358. Abstract.

King, G. F., S. G. Armitage, and J. R. Tilton (1960). A therapeutic approach to schizophrenics of extreme pathology. *J. abnorm. soc. Psychol.,* 61, 276–286.

King, G. F., D. Merrill, E. Lovinger, and M. Denny (1957). Operant motor behavior in acute schizophrenics. *J. Pers.*, 25, 317–326.

King, P. D. (1964). Considerations of psychotherapy with a schizophrenic child. *Amer. Acad. child Psychiat.*, 3, 638–649.

Knapp, R. H., and J. D. Holzberg (1964). Characteristics of college students volunteering for service to mental patients. *J. consult. Psychol.*, 28 (1), 82–85.

Konorski, J., and S. Miller (1937). On two types of conditioned reflex. *J. gen. Psychol.*, 16, 264–272.

Krasner, L. (1958). Studies of the conditioning of verbal behavior. *Psychol. Bull.*, 55, 148–170.

Krasner, L. (1962). The therapist as a social reinforcement machine. In H. H. Strupp and L. Luborsky (Eds.), *Research in psychotherapy*, Vol. II, Washington, D.C.: Amer. Psychol. Assoc.

Krasner, L., and L. P. Ullmann (1965). *Research in behavior modification.* New York: Holt, Rinehart and Winston.

Lang, P., and A. Lazovick (1960). Systematic desensitization psychotherapy: Experimental analogue. Mimeographed manual of procedure. Madison, Wisc.: University of Wisconsin.

Lang, P. and A. Lazovick (1963). Experimental desensitization of a phobia. *J. abnorm. soc. Psychol.*, 66, 519–525.

Lang, P., A. Lazovick, and D. J. Reynolds (1965). Desensitization, suggestibility, and pseudotherapy. *J. abnorm. soc. Psychol.*, 70, 395–402.

Lazarus, A. A. (1959). The elimination of children's phobias by deconditioning. *Med. Proc. So. Africa*, 5, 261–265.

Lazarus, A. A. (1960). The elimination of children's phobias by deconditioning. In H. J. Eysenck (Ed.), *Behaviour therapy and the neuroses.* Oxford: Pergamon.

Lazarus, A. A. (1961). Group therapy of phobic disorders by systematic desensitization. *J. abnorm. soc. Psychol.*, 63, 505–510.

Lazarus, A., and A. Abramovitz (1962). The use of "emotive images" in the treatment of children's phobias. *J. ment. Sci.*, 108, 191–195.

Lazarus, A., G. C. Davison, and B. A. Polefka (1965). Classical and operant factors in the treatment of school phobias. *J. abnorm. Psychol.*, 70, 225–229.

Lazarus, A., and S. Rachman (1957). The use of systematic desensitization in psychotherapy. *S. African med. J.*, 31, 934–937.

Lefcourt, H. M., K. E. Barnes, L. D. Parke, and F. S. Schwartz (1966). Anticipated social censure and aggression-conflict as mediators or responses to aggression-induction. *J. soc. Psychol.*, 70, 251–263.

Lehman, M. (1963). *This high man: The life of Robert H. Goddard.* New York: Farrar, Straus.

Leitenberg, H. (1965). Is time-out from positive reinforcement an aversive event? A review of the experimental evidence. *Psychol. Bull.*, 64, 428–441.

Levine, G. R., and J. T. Simons (1962). Response to praise by emotionally disturbed boys. *Psychol. Rep.*, 11, 10.

Levine, M., and A. M. Graziano (1969). Mental health intervention in elementary schools. In S. Golan and C. Eisdorfer (Eds.), *Handbook of community psychology and mental health*. New York: Appleton-Century-Crofts. (In press.)

Levitt, E. E. (1957). Results of psychotherapy with children: an evaluation. *J. consult. Psychol.*, 11, 189–196.

Levy, D. M. (1943). *Maternal overprotection*. New York: Columbia University Press.

Lindsley, O. R. (1956). Operant conditioning methods applied to research in chronic schizophrenia. *Psychiat. Res. Rep.*, 5, 118–139.

Lindsley, O. R. (1960a). Characteristics of the behavior of chronic psychotics as revealed by free-operant conditioning methods. *Dis. Nerv. Syst.*, 21, 66–78.

Lindsley, O. R. (1960b). Man as he behaves. 16 mm. film available from University of Kansas Medical Center, Kansas City.

Lindsley, O. R. (1963). Free operant conditioning and psychotherapy. *Current psychiatric therapies*. New York: Grune & Stratton.

Lindsley, O. R. (1966). An experiment with parents handling behavior at home. *Johnstone Bull.*, 9. 27–36.

Lindsley, O. R., and B. F. Skinner (1954). A method for the experimental analysis of the behavior of psychotic patients. *Amer. Psychologist*, 9, 419–420.

Lord, R. D., F. C. Bellrose, and W. W. Cochran (1962). Radiotelemetry of the respiration of a flying duck. *Science*, 137, 39–40.

Lovaas, O. I. (1965). Teaching intellectual skills to schizophrenic children. Unpublished manuscript.

Lovaas, O. I., J. P. Berberich, B. F. Perloff, and B. Schaeffer (1966). Acquisition of imitative speech by schizophrenic children. *Science*, 151, 705–707.

Lovaas, O. I., G. Freitag, V. J. Gold, and I. C. Kassorla (1965). Experimental studies in childhood schizophrenia: Analysis of self-destructive behavior. *J. exp. child Psychol.*, 2, 67–84.

Lovaas, O. I., G. Freitag, M. I. Kinder, D. B. Rubenstein, B. Schaeffer, and J. B. Simons (1964). Experimental studies in childhood schizophrenia: Developing social behavior using electric shock. Paper read at Amer. Psychol. Assoc., Los Angeles.

Lovaas, O. I., G. Freitag, M. I. Kinder, B. Rubenstein, and J. B. Simons (1966). Establishment of social reinforcers in two schizophrenic children on the basis of food. *J. exper. child Psychol.*, 4, 109–125.

Lovaas, O. I., B. Schaeffer, and J. B. Simons (1965). Building social behavior in autistic children by use of electric shock. *J. exper. Res. Pers.*, 1, 99–109.

Lovaas, O. I., and J. B. Simons (1965). A reinforcement theory approach to childhood schizophrenia: An overview of the treatment program. Paper read at Amer. Psychol. Assoc., Chicago.

Lovibond, S. H. (1961). Conditioning and enuresis. Unpublished doctoral dissertation, University of Adelaide.

Lovibond, S. H. (1963a). The mechanism of conditioning treatment of enuresis. *Behav. Res. Ther.*, 1, 17–21.

Lovibond, S. H. (1963b). Intermittent reinforcement in behavior therapy. *Behav. Res. Ther.*, 1, 127–132.

Lovibond, S. H. (1964). *Conditioning and enuresis*. Oxford: Pergamon Press.

Luckey, R. E., C. M. Watson, and J. K. Musick (1968). Aversive conditioning as a means of inhibiting vomiting and rumination. *Amer. J. ment. Defic.*, 73 (1), 139–142.

Luria, A. R. (1961). *The role of speech in the regulation of normal and abnormal behavior*. New York: Liveright.

Lykken, D. T. (1957). A study of anxiety in the sociopathic personality. *J. abnorm. soc. Psychol.*, 55, 6–10.

MacKay, R.S. (1961). Radio telemetering from within the body. *Science*, 134, 1196–1202.

Madsen, C. H., Jr. (1965). Positive reinforcement in the toilet training of a normal child: A case report. In L. P. Ullmann and L. Krasner (Eds.), *Case studies in behavior modification*. New York: Holt, Rinehart and Winston.

Madsen, C. H., Jr. and L. P. Ullmann (1967). Innovations in the desensitization of frigidity. *Behav. Res. Ther.*, 5, 67–68.

Mahler, M. (1952). On child psychosis and schizophrenia. In *The psychoanalytic study of the child*, 7, 286–305.

Mahler, M. (1965). On early infantile psychosis: The symbiotic and autistic syndromes. *J. Amer. Acad. child Psychiat.*, 4, 554–568.

Malleson, N. (1959). Panic and phobia. A possible method of treatment. *Lancet*, 1, 225–227.

Marshall, G. R. (1966). Toilet training of an autistic eight-year-old through conditioning therapy. A case report. *Behav. Res. Ther.*, 4, 242–245.

Max, L. W. (1935). Breaking up a homosexual fixation by the conditioned reaction technique: a case study. *Psychol. Bull.*, 32, 734. (Abstract.)

McCall, W. A. (1922). *How to measure in education*. New York: Macmillan.

McCord, J. and W. McCord (1961). Cultural stereotypes and the validity of interviews in child development. *Child Devel.*, 32, 171–185.

McCord, W., J. McCord, and I. K. Zola (1959). *Origins of crime*. New York: Columbia University Press.

McCorkle, L. W., A. Elias, and F. L. Bixby (1958). *The Highfields story*. New York: Holt.

Mednick, S. A. (1958). A learning theory approach to research in schizophrenia. *Psychol. Bull.*, 55, 316–327.

Mednick, S. A., and C. Wild (1961). Stimulus generalization in brain damaged children. *J. Consult. Psychol.*, 25, 525–527.

Meese, B. G. (1961). An experimental program for juvenile delinquent boys. Unpublished doctoral dissertation, University of Maryland.

Metz, J. R. (1965). Conditioning generalized imitation in autistic children. *J. exp. Child Psychol.*, 2, 389–399.

Michael, J., and L. Myerson (1966). A behavior approach to human control. In R. Ulrich, T. Stachnik, and J. Mabry (Eds.), *Control of human behavior*.

Glenview, Ill.: Scott, Foresman.

Miller, D. R., and G. E. Swanson (1960). *Inner conflict and defense*. New York: Holt, Rinehart and Winston.

Miller, N. E., and J. Dollard (1941). *Social learning and imitation*. New Haven: Yale University Press.

Morgan, J. B., and F. J. Witmer (1939). The treatment of enuresis by the conditioned reaction technique. *J. Genet. Psychol.*, 55, 59–65.

Mowrer, O. H. (1950). *Learning theory and personality dynamics*. New York: Ronald.

Mowrer, O. H. (1956). Two-factor learning theory reconsidered, with special reference to secondary reinforcement and the concept of habit. *Psychol. Rev.*, 63, 114–128.

Mowrer, O. H. (1965). Learning theory and behavior therapy. In B. Wolman (Ed.), *Handbook of clinical psychology*. New York: McGraw-Hill.

Mowrer, O. H. (1968). A resume of basic principles of learning. In H. H. Gregory (Ed.), *Learning theory and stuttering therapy*. Evanston, Ill.: Northwestern University Press.

Mowrer, O. H., and W. M. Mowrer (1938). Enuresis — a method for its study and treatment. *Amer. J. Orthopsychiat.*, 8, 436–459.

Neal, D. H. (1963). Behavior therapy and encopresis in children. *Behav. Res. Ther.*, 1, 139–150.

O'Leary, K. D., and W. C. Becker (1967). Behavior modification of an adjustment class: A token reinforcement program. *Except. Child.*, 33, 637–642.

Orlando, R. and S. Bijou (1960). Single and multiple schedules of reinforcement in developmentally retarded children. *J. exper. Anal. Behav.*, 3, 339–348.

Orne, M. T. (1962). On the social psychology of the psychological experiment with particular reference to demand characteristics and their implications. *Amer. Psychologist*, 17, 776–783.

Osgood, C. E. (1953). *Method and theory in experimental psychology*. New York: Oxford University Press.

Parmellee, A. (1962). European neurological studies of the newborn. *Child Devel.*, 33, 169–180.

Pascal, C. R. (1959). *Behavioral change in the clinic: A systematic approach*. New York: Grune and Stratton.

Patterson, G. R. (1955). A tentative approach to the classification of children's behavior problems. Unpublished doctoral dissertation, University of Minnesota.

Patterson, G. R. (1959). A preliminary report: fathers as reinforcing agents. Paper read at Western Psychological Assn. Meeting.

Patterson, G. R. (1963). State institutions as teaching machines for delinquent behavior. Mimeographed paper. Child Study Center, University of Oregon.

Patterson, G. R. (1964). An empirical approach to the classification of disturbed children. *J. Clin. Psychol.*, 20, 326–337.

Patterson, G. R. (1965a). A learning theory approach to the treatment of the school phobic child. In L. P. Ullmann and L. Krasner (Eds.). *Case studies in behavior modification*. New York: Holt, Rinehart and Winston.

Patterson, G. R. (1965b). An application of conditioning techniques to the control of a hyperactive child. In L. P. Ullmann and L. Krasner (Eds.), *Case studies in behavior modification*. New York: Holt, Rinehart and Winston.

Patterson, G. R. (1965c). The modification of hyperactive behavior in children. Paper read at Society for Research in Child Development, Minneapolis, Minn.

Patterson, G. R., and D. Anderson (1964). Peers as social reinforcers. *Child Devel.*, 35, 951–960.

Patterson, G. R., and G. A. Brodsky (1966). A behavior modification program for a child with multiple problem behaviors. *J. child Psychol. Psychiat.*, 7, 277–296.

Patterson, G. R., and M. Ebner (1965). Applications of learning principles to the treatment of deviant children. Paper read at the Amer. Psychol. Assn., Chicago.

Patterson, G. R., and B. Fagot (1966). Children's responsiveness to multiple agents in a social reinforcement task. Mimeographed paper. Child Study Center, University of Oregon.

Patterson, G. R., and W. C. Hinsey (1964). Investigation of some assumptions and characteristics of a procedure for instrumental conditioning in children. *J. exp. Child Psychol.*, 1, 111–122.

Patterson, G. R., R. Jones, J. Whittier, and M. A. Wright (1965). A behavior modification technique for the hyperactive child. *Behav. Res. Ther.*, 2, 217–226.

Patterson, G. R., R. A. Littman, and W. C. Hinsey (1964). Parental effectiveness as reinforcers in the laboratory and its relation to child-rearing practices and child adjustment in the classroom. *J. Pers.*, 32, 180–199.

Patterson, G. R., and M. Ludwig (1961). A preliminary report: Parents as reinforcing agents. Paper read at Oregon Psychological Assn.

Paul, G. L. (1966). *Insight versus desensitization in psychotherapy*. Stanford, Calif.: Stanford University Press.

Peters, H. N. (1953). Multiple choice learning in the chronic schizophrenic. *J. clin. Psychol.*, 9, 328–333.

Peterson, D. R., and P. A. London (1965). A role for cognition in the behavioral treatment of a child's eliminative disturbance. In L. P. Ullmann and L. Krasner (Eds.), *Case studies in behavior modification*. New York: Holt, Rinehart and Winston.

Peterson, R. F., and L. R. Peterson (1967). Mark and his blanket: A study of self-destructive behavior in a retarded boy. Unpublished manuscript. Chicago: Illinois State Department of Mental Health.

Phares, E. J. (1957). Expectancy changes in skill and chance situations. *J. abnorm. soc. Psychol.*, 54, 339–342.

Phares, E. J. (1962). Perceptual threshold decrements as a function of skill and chance expectancies. *J. Psychol.*, 53, 339–407.

Phillips, E. L. (1957). Contribution to a learning theory account of childhood autism. *J. Psychol.*, 43, 117–124.

Phillips, E. L. (1960). Parent–child psychotherapy: A follow-up study comparing two techniques. *J. Psychol.*, 49, 195–202.

Polsky, H. W. (1962). *Cottage six*. New York: Russell Sage Foundation.

Poser, E. G. (1967). Training behavior therapists. *Behav. Res. Ther.*, 5, 37–41.

Powers, E., and H. Witmer (1951). An experiment in the prevention of delinquency. New York: Columbia University Press.

Prager, D. (1967). Abstract of an article by R. Stern, The truth as resistance to free association. *Psychol. Abstr.*, 41, No. 4740, 460.

Premack, D. (1959). Toward empirical behavior laws: I. Positive reinforcement. *Psychol. Rev.*, 66, 219–233.

Prince, G. S. (1961). A clinical approach to parent–child interaction. *J. child Psychol. Psychiat.*, 2, 169–184.

Pubols, B. H. (1960). Incentive magnitude, learning and performance in animals. *Psychol. Bull.*, 57, 89–115.

Pumroy, D. K., and S. S. Pumroy (1965). Reinforcement in toilet training. *Psychol. Rep.*, 16, 467–471.

Quay, H. C., and W. A. Hunt (1965). Psychotherapy, psychopathy, neuroticism and verbal conditioning: A replication and extension. *J. Consult. Psychol.*, 29, 283.

Rachman, S. (1962). Learning theory and child psychology: therapeutic possibilities. *J. child Psychol. Psychiat.*, 3, 149–163.

Raymond, M. S. (1956). A case of fetishism treated by aversion therapy. *Brit. med. J.*, 2, 854–857.

Redl, F., and D. Wineman (1957). *The aggressive child*. New York: The Free Press.

Reed, G. F. (1963). Elective mutism in children: a re-appraisal. *J. child Psychol. Psychiat.*, 4, 99–107.

Reger, R. (1966). The questionable role of specialists in special education programs. *J. Special Educ.*, 1, 53–59.

Reisman, J. M. (1966). *The development of clinical psychology*. New York: Appleton-Century-Crofts.

Reyna, L. J. (1964). Conditioning therapies, learning theory and research. In J. Wolpe, A. Salter, and L. J. Reyna (Eds.), *The conditioning therapies*. New York: Holt, Rinehart and Winston.

Reynolds, G. S. (1961). Behavioral contrast. *J. exp. anal. Behav.*, 4, 57–71.

Rheingold, H., J. Gewirtz, and H. Ross (1959). Social conditioning of vocalization in the infant. *J. comp. Physiol. Psychol.*, 52, 68–73.

Rhodes, W. C. (1967). The disturbing child: A problem of ecological management. *Excep. Child.*, 28, 333–338.

Rice, H. K., and M. W. McDaniel (1966). Operant behavior in vegetative patients. *Psychol. Rec.*, 16, 279–281.

Rickard, H. C., and M. B. Mundy (1965). Direct manipulation of stuttering behavior: An experimental-clinical approach. In L. P. Ullmann and L. Krasner (Eds.), *Case studies in behavior modification*. New York: Holt, Rinehart and Winston.

Riley, D. A., and A. M. Shapiro (1952). Alteration behavior as a function of effortfulness of task and distribution of trials. *J. comp. Physiol. Psychol.*, 46, 108–114.

Rimland, B. (1964). *Infantile autism: The syndrome and its implications for a neural theory of behavior*. New York: Appleton-Century-Crofts.

Rioch, M. J., C. Elkes, and A. Flint (1965). Pilot project in training mental health counselors. Publication No. 1254, U.S. Public Health Service.

Rioch, M. J., C. Elkes, A. Flint, B. Udansky, R. G. Newman, and E. Silber (1963). National Institute of Mental Health pilot study in training mental health counselors. *Amer. J. Orthopsychiat.*, 33, 678–689.

Risley, T. (1966). The establishment of verbal behavior in deviant children. Unpublished doctoral dissertation, University of Washington.

Risley, T., and Wolf, M. M. (1964). Experimental manipulation of autistic behaviors and generalization into the home. Paper read at Amer. Psychol. Assn.

Robinson, H. B., and N. M. Robinson (1965). *The mentally retarded child: A psychological approach*. New York: McGraw-Hill.

Roff, M. (1949). A factorial study of the Fels parent behavior scales. *Child Devel.*, 20, 29–45.

Rogers, C. R. (1951). *Client-centered therapy*. Boston: Houghton Mifflin.

Roos, P. (1965). Development of an intensive habit-training unit at Austin State School. *Ment. Retard.*, 3, 12–15.

Rosenblith, W. A. (1961). On some social consequences of scientific and technological change. *Daedalus*, 90, 498–513.

Rosenthal, R. (1963). On the social psychology of the psychological experiment. *Amer. Scientist*, 51, 268–283.

Rosenthal, R. (1964). Experimenter outcome orientation and the results of the psychological experiment. *Psychol. Bull.*, 61, 405–412.

Rosenthal, R., and K. L. Fode (1962). Three experiments in experimenter bias. Department of Social Relations, Harvard University, mimeographed paper.

Ross, A. O. (1964). Learning theory and therapy with children. *Psychother. Theory Res. Pract.*, 1, 102–107.

Rostand, J. (1959). *Can man be modified?* New York: Basic Books.

Rotter, J. B., S. Liverant, and D. P. Crowne (1961). The growth and extinction of expectancies in chance-controlled and skilled tasks. *J. Psychol.*, 52, 161–177.

Russo, S. (1964). Adaptations in behavioral therapy with children. *Behav. Res. Ther.*, 2, 43–47.

Salter, A. (1949). *Conditioned reflex therapy: The direct approach to the reconstruction of personality*. New York: Capricorn.

Salter, A. (1964). The theory and practice of conditioned reflex therapy. In J. Wolpe, A. Salter, and L. Reyna (Eds.), *The conditioning therapies*. New

York: Holt, Rinehart and Winston.

Salzinger, K., and S. Portnoy (1964). Verbal conditioning in interviews: Application to chronic schizophrenics. *J. Psychiat. Res.,* 2, 1–9.

Salzinger, K., R. S. Feldman, J. E. Cowan, and S. Salzinger (1965). Operant conditioning of verbal behavior of two young speech-deficient boys. In L. Krasner and L. P. Ullmann (Eds.), *Research in behavior modification.* New York: Holt, Rinehart and Winston.

Sandler, J. (1964). Masochism: An empirical analysis. *Psychol. Bull.,* 62, 197–204.

Sargent, H. D. (1960). Methodological problems of follow-up studies in psychotherapy research. *Amer. J. Orthopsychiat.,* 30, 495–506.

Saslow, G. (1954). Psychotherapy. *Ann. Rev. Psychol.,* 5, 311–336.

Scanlon, J. B., D. T. Leberfeld, and R. Freibrun (1963). Language training in the treatment of an autistic child functioning on a retarded level. *Ment. Retard.,* 1, 305–310.

Schacter, S., and B. Latane (1964). Crime, cognition and the autonomic nervous system. In D. Levine (Ed.), *Nebraska symposium on motivation.* Lincoln, Nebr.: University of Nebraska Press.

Schurmans, M. J. (1965). Five functions of the group therapist. *Amer. J. Nurs.,* January, 108–111.

Schwitzgebel, R. (1964). *Street-corner research: An experimental approach to the juvenile delinquent.* Cambridge, Mass.: Harvard University Press.

Schwitzebel, R. (1967). Short-term operant conditioning of adolescent offenders on socially relevant variables. *J. abnorm. Psychol.,* 72, 134–142.

Schwitzgebel, R., and D. A. Kolb (1964). Inducing behavior change in adolescent delinquents. *Behav. Res. Ther.,* 1, 297–304.

Sears, R. R. (1936). Functional abnormalities of memory with special reference to amnesia. *Psychol. Bull.,* 33, 229–274.

Sears, R. R., E. Maccoby, and H. Levin (1957). *Patterns of child rearing.* New York: Harper & Row.

Sears, R. R., J. W. Whiting, V. Nowles, and P. Sears (1953). Some child rearing antecedents of aggression and dependency in young children. *Genet. Psychol. Monogr.,* 47, 135–236.

Shannon, L. W. (1961). The problem of competence to help. *Federal Probation,* 25, 32–39.

Sheehan, J. G. (1950). The modification of stuttering through non-reinforcement. *J. abnorm. soc. Psychol.,* 46, 51–63.

Sheehan, J. G., and R. B. Voas (1957). Stuttering as conflict: I. Comparison of therapy techniques involving approach and avoidance. *J. Spch. Hring. Disor.,* 22, 714–723.

Sherman, J. A. (1965). Use of reinforcement and imitation to reinstate verbal behavior in mute psychotics. *J. abnorm. soc. Psychol.,* 70, 155–164.

Shoben, E. J. (1949). Psychotherapy as a problem in learning theory. *Psychol. Bull.,* 46, 366–392.

Shpuntoff, W. (1959). Personal communication, quoted in Hefferline, R. F. (1962).

Learning theory and clinical psychology—an eventual symbiosis? In A.J. Bachrach (Ed.), *Experimental foundations of clinical psychology*. New York: Basic Books, pp. 97–138.

Sidman, M. (1960). *Tactics of scientific research*. New York: Basic Books.

Sidman, M. (1962). Operant techniques. In A. J. Bachrach (Ed.), *Experimental foundations of clinical psychology*. New York: Basic Books.

Siegel, S. (1956). *Nonparametric statistics for the behavioral sciences*. New York: McGraw-Hill.

Silver, A. A. (1963). Progress in therapy with children. In L. E. Alt and B. F. Riess (Eds.), *Progress in clinical psychology*, Vol. V. New York: Grune and Stratton.

Skinner, B. F. (1938). *The behavior of organisms*. New York: Appleton-Century-Crofts.

Skinner, B. F. (1948). *Walden Two*. New York: Macmillan.

Skinner, B. F. (1953). *Science and human behavior*. New York: Macmillan.

Skinner, B. F. (1954a). A new method for the experimental analysis of the behavior of psychotic patients. *J. Nerv. Ment. Dis.*, 120, 403–406.

Skinner, B. F. (1954b). The science of learning and the art of teaching. *Harv. Ed. Rev.*, 24, No. 2, 86–97.

Skinner, B. F. (1956). What is psychotic behavior? In *Theory and Treatment of psychosis: Some new aspects*. St. Louis: Washington University.

Skinner, B. F. (1957). *Verbal behavior*. New York: Appleton-Century-Crofts.

Skinner, B. F. (1958). Teaching machines. *Science*, 128, 3330, 969–977.

Skinner, B. F. (1965). Why teachers fail. *Sat. Rev.*, October 16, p. 80.

Slack, C. (1960). Experimenter-subject psychotherapy. *Mental Hygiene*, 44, 238–256.

Sloane, H. W. Jr., M. K. Johnston, and S. W. Bijou (1966). Successive modification of aggressive behavior and aggressive fantasy play by management of contingencies. Unpublished manuscript, University of Utah.

Smith, M., and N. Hobbs (1966). *The community and the community mental health center*. Washington, D.C.: Amer. Psychol. Assn.

Solomon, R. L. (1964). Punishment. *Amer. Psychol.*, 19, 239–253.

Southerland, E., and D. Cressey (1960). *Principles of criminology*. Philadelphia: Lippincott.

Speers, R. W., and C. Lansing (1964). Group psychotherapy with preschool psychotic children and collateral group therapy of their parents. *Amer. J. Orthopsychiat.*, 34, 659–666.

Sperry, ·C. J. Jr., C. P. Gadsden, C. Rodriguez, and L. M. N. Bach (1961). Miniature subcutaneous frequency-modulated transmitter for brain potentials. *Science*, 134, 1423–1424.

Spielberger, D. C., I. H. Bernstein, and R. G. Ratcliff (1966). Information and incentive value of the reinforcing stimulus in verbal conditioning. *J. exper. Psychol.*, 71, 26–31.

Spradlin, J. E. (1962). Effects of reinforcement schedules on extinction in severely mentally retarded children. *Amer. J. ment. Defic.*, 66, 634–640.

Staats, A. W. (1964). *Human learning*. New York: Holt, Rinehart and Winston.

Staats, A. W., and C. K. Staats (1963). *Complex human behavior*. New York: Holt, Rinehart and Winston.

Stevens, H. A. (1964). Overview. In H. Stevens and R. Heber (Eds.), *Mental Retardation*. Chicago: University of Chicago Press, pp. 1–15.

Stevenson, H. W. (1961). Social reinforcement with children as a function of CA, sex of E and sex of S. *J. abnorm. soc. Psychol.*, 63, 147–154.

Stevenson, H., R. Hickman, and R. M. Knights (1963). Parents and strangers as reinforcing agents for children's performance. *J. abnorm. soc. Psychol.*, 63, 147–154.

Stiavelli, R. E., and D. T. Shirley (1968). The citizenship council: A technique for managing behavior disorders in the educationally handicapped class. *J. school Psychol.*, 6, 147–156.

Straughan, J. H. (1964). Treatment with child and mother in the play room. *Behav. Res. Ther.*, 2, 37–41.

Straughan, J. H., W. K. Potter, and S. H. Hamilton (1965). The behavioral treatment of an elective mute. *J. child Psychol. Psychiat.*, 6, 125–130.

Strauss, A. A., and L. Lehtenin (1950). *Psychopathology and education of the brain-injured child*. New York: Grune and Stratton.

Sulzer, E. S. (1965). Behavior modification in adult psychiatric patients. In L. P. Ullmann and L. Krasner (Eds.), *Case studies in behavior modification*. New York: Holt, Rinehart and Winston.

Talbot, M. (1957). Panic in school phobia. *Amer. J. Orthopsychiat.*, 27, 286–295.

Tate, B. G., and G. S. Baroff (1966). Aversive control of self-injurious behavior in a psychotic boy. *Behav. Res. Ther.*, 4, 281–287.

Terrace, H. S. (1963a). Discrimination learning with and without "errors." *J. exp. anal. Behav.*, 6, 1–27.

Terrace, H. S. (1963b). Errorless transfer of a discrimination across two continua. *J. exp. anal. Behav.*, 6, 223–232.

Terrace, H. S. (1966). Stimulus control. In W. K. Konig (Ed.), *Operant behavior: Areas of research and application*. New York: Appleton-Century-Crofts, pp. 271–344.

Teuber, H., and D. Powers (1951). The effects of treatment of delinquents. *Research Publications of the Association of Nervous Mental Disorders*, 31, 139–147.

Thirman, J. (1949). Conditioned reflex treatment of alcoholism. *New England J. Med.*, 241, 368–370, 406–410.

Thompson, C. N., and B. Bielinski (1953). Improvement in psychosis following conditioned treatment in alcoholism. *J. Nerv. Ment. Dis.*, 117, 537–543.

Thorndike, E. L. (1914). *Educational psychology*, Vol. I, New York: Columbia University Press.

Timmons, E., C. Noblin, H. Adams, and J. Butler (1965). Operant conditioning with schizophrenics comparing verbal reinforcers versus psychoanalytic interpretations: Differential extinction effects. *J. pers. soc. Psychol.*, 1, 373–377.

Tolman, E. C. (1938a). The determiners of behavior at a choicepoint. *Psychol. Rev.*, 45, 1–41.

Tolman, E. C. (1938b). The law of effect: A round table discussion. *Psychol. Rev.*, 45, 200–203.

Trippe, M. (1963). Conceptual problems in research in educational provisions for disturbed children. *Ex. child.*, 29, 400–406.

Troubadour Records, Learn to relax (1962). Phonograph record. Johannesburg: Audio-Ethical Publications.

Tuddenham, R. D. (1951). Studies in reputation: I. Sex and grade difference in school children's evaluation of their peers. II. The diagnosis of social maladjustment. *Psychol. Monogr.*, 66 (1), 58.

Tyler, V. O. (1965). Exploring the use of operant techniques in the rehabilitation of delinquent boys. Paper read at Amer. Psychol. Assn., Chicago.

Ullmann, L. P. (1967a). *Institution and outcome: A comparative study of psychiatric hospitals*. New York: Pergamon Press.

Ullmann, L. P. (1967b). The major concepts taught to behavior therapy trainees. Paper read at a symposium, A. M. Graziano, chairman, Training behavior therapists, Amer. Psychol. Assn., Washington, D.C.

Ullmann, L. P., and L. Krasner (Eds.) (1965). *Case studies in behavior modification*. New York: Holt, Rinehart and Winston.

Ullmann, L. P., and L. Krasner (1969). *A psychological approach to abnormal behavior*. Englewood Cliffs, N.J.: Prentice-Hall.

Ulrich, R., T. Stachnick, and J. Mabry (Eds.) (1966). *Control of human behavior*. Glenview, Ill.: Scott, Foresman.

Van Wagenen, R. K., and E. E. Murdock (1966). A transistorized signal-package for toilet training of infants. *J. exp. child Psychol.*, 3, 312–314.

Voegtlen, W. L. (1940). The treatment of alcoholism by establishing a conditioned reflex. *Amer. J. Med. Sci.*, 119, 802–810.

Von Hipple, A. (1959). *Principles of modern materials research*. Tech. Report No. 136, Laboratory for Insulation Research, Massachusetts Institute of Technology.

Wahler, R. G., G. H. Winkle, R. E. Peterson, and D. C. Morrison (1965). Mothers as behavior therapists for their own children. *Behav. Res. Ther.*, 3 (2), 113–124.

Walder, L. O., S. I. Cohen, D. E. Breiter, P. Daston, I. S. Hirsch, and J. M. Leibowitz (1967). Teaching behavioral principles to parents of disturbed children. Paper read at East. Psychol. Assn., Boston.

Walker, R. (1962). Body build and behavior in young children. *Monogr. Soc. Res. Child Devel.*, 27 (3), 94 p.

Wallace, J. A. (1949). The treatment of alcoholics by the conditioned reflex method. *J. Tenn. Med. Assn.*, 42, 125–128.

Walters, R. H. (1966). Implications of laboratory studies of aggression for the control and regulation of violence. *The Annals*, 364, 60–72.

Walters, R. II., and L. Demkow (1963). Timing of punishment as a determinant of response inhibition. *Child Devel.*, 34, 207–214.

Walters, R. H., and P. Karol (1960). Social deprivation and verbal behavior. *J. Pers.*, 28, 89–107.

Walters, R. H., M. Leat, and L. Mezei (1963). Inhibition and disinhibition of responses through empathic learning. *Canad. J. Psychol.*, 17, 235–243.

Walters, J. C., D. Pearce, and L. Dahms (1957). Affectional and aggressive behavior of preschool children. *Child Devel.*, 28, 15–26.

Walters, R. H., and E. Roy (1960). Anxiety, social isolation and reinforcer effectiveness. *J. Pers.*, 28, 358–367.

Walton, D. (1960). The application of learning theory to the treatment of a case of neurodermatitis. In H. J. Eysenck (Ed.), *Behavior therapy and the neuroses*. Oxford: Pergamon Press, pp. 272–274.

Walton, D. (1961). Experimental psychology and the treatment of a tiquer. *J. child Psychol. Psychiat.*, 2, 148–155.

Walton, D., and M. D. Mather (1963). The relevance of generalization techniques to the treatment of stammering and phobic symptoms. *Behav. Res. Ther.*, 1, 121–125.

Watson, J. B. (1924). *Psychology from the standpoint of a behaviorist*. Philadelphia: Lippincott.

Watson, J. B. (1930). *Behaviorism*. Chicago: University of Chicago Press.

Weiland, H., and R. Rudnick (1961). Considerations of the development and treatment of autistic children. In *The Psychoanalytic Study of the Child*. New York: International Universities Press, Vol. XVI, pp. 549–563.

Weiner, H. (1962). Some effects of response cost upon human operant behavior. *J. exp. anal. Behav.*, 5, 201–208.

Weiss, A. P. (1929). *Theoretical basis of human behavior*. R. G. Adams.

Weitzman, B. (1967). Behavior therapy and psychotherapy. *Psychol. Rev.*, 74, 300–317.

Welsh, R. S. (1968). The use of stimulus satiation in the elimination of juvenile fire-setting behavior. Paper read at East. Psychol. Assn., Washington, D.C.

Werry, J. S. (1966). The conditioning treatment of enuresis. *Amer. J. Psychiat.*, 123, 226–229.

Werry, J. S., and J. Cohrssen (1965). Enuresis: An etiologic and therapeutic study. *J. Pediatr.*, 67, 423–431.

Werry, J. S., and J. P. Wollersheim (1967). Behavior therapy with children: A broad overview. *Amer. Acad. child Psychiat. J.*, 6, 346–370.

Wetzel, R. (1966). Use of behavioral techniques in a case of compulsive stealing. *J. consult. Psychol.*, 30, 367–374.

Wetzel, R., J. Baker, M. Roney, and M. Martin (1966). Outpatient treatment of autistic behavior. *Behav. Res. Ther.*, 4, 169–177.

White, J. G. (1959). The use of learning theory in the psychological treatment of children. *J. Clin. Psychol.*, 15, 227–229.

White, J. C. Jr., and D. J. Daylor (1967). Noxious conditioning as a treatment for rumination. *Ment. Retard.*, 5, 30–33.

Whitney, L. R., and K. E. Barnard (1966). Implications of operant learning theory for nursing care of the retarded child. *Ment. Retard.* 4 (3), 26–29.

Wickes, I. G. (1958). Treatment of persistent enuresis with the electric buzzer. *Arch. Dis. Child.*, 33, 160–164.

Williams, C. D. (1959). The elimination of tantrum behavior by extinction procedures. *J. abnorm. soc. Psychol.*, 59, 269.

Williams, R. I. (1959). Verbal conditioning in psychotherapy. Abstract. *Amer. Psychol.*, 14, 388.

Williams, D. B., and P. Teitelbaum (1956). Control of drinking behavior by means of an operant conditioning technique. *Science*, 124, 1294–1296.

Wolf, M. (1965). Reinforcement procedures and the modification of deviant child behavior. Paper read at Council on Exceptional Children, Portland, Oregon.

Wolf, M., J. S. Birnbrauer, R. Williams, and J. Lawler (1965). A note on apparent extinction of the vomiting behavior of a retarded child. In L. P. Ullmann and L. Krasner (Eds.), *Case studies in behavior modification*. New York: Holt, Rinehart and Winston.

Wolf, M., H. Mees, and T. Risley (1964). Application of operant conditioning procedures to the behavior problems of an autistic child. *Behav. Res. Ther.*, 1, 305–312.

Wolpe, J. (1954). Reciprocal inhibition as the main basis of psychotherapeutic effects. *AMA Arch. Neurol. Psychiat.*, 72, 205–226.

Wolpe, J. (1958). *Psychotherapy by reciprocal inhibition*. Stanford, Calif.: Stanford University Press.

Wolpe, J. (1961). The systematic desensitization treatment of neuroses. *J. Nerv. Ment. Dis.*, 132, 189–203.

Wolpe, J. (1964). Behavior therapy in complex neurotic states. *Brit. J. Psychiat.*, 110, 28–34.

Wolpe, J. (1964). The resolution of neurotic suffering by behavioristic methods: An evaluation. *Amer. J. Psychother.*, 18 (1), Supplement 1, 23–32.

Wolpe, J., and A. Lazarus (1966). *Behavior therapy techniques*. Oxford: Pergamon Press.

Wolpe, J., A. Salter, and L. J. Reyna (1965). *The conditioning therapies: The challenge in psychotherapy*. New York: Holt, Rinehart and Winston.

Yates, A. J. (1958). The application of learning theory to the treatment of tics. *J. abnorm. soc. Psychol.*, 56, 175–182.

Zeilberger, J., S. E. Sampen, and H. N. Sloane, Jr. (1966). Modification of child problem behavior in the home with the mother as therapist. Unpublished manuscript, City College of New York.

Zimmerman, E. H., and J. Zimmerman (1962). The alteration of behavior in a special classroom situation. *J. exp. anal. Behav.*, 5, 59–60.

Name Index

447

Subject Index